Introduction to Fixed Income Analytics

Frank J. Fabozzi, Ph.D., CFA

Steven V. Mann, Ph.D.

Published by Frank J. Fabozzi Associates

FJF

*To my wife Donna and my children,
Francesco, Patricia, and Karly*

SVM

To my parents, Patricia and Robert Mann

Acknowledgments

The authors wish to thank Joe Camp of Fleet Mortgage for his assistance. The following graduate students at the University of South Carolina assisted in proofreading the book: Yvette Farrugia, Apurva Parikh, Uday J. Shah, and Vlodimir Zdorovtsov.

© 2001 By Frank J. Fabozzi Associates
New Hope, Pennsylvania

ISBN: 1-883249-94-5

Printed in the United States of America

Table of Contents

1. Time Value of Money   1

2. Yield Curve Analysis: Spot Rates and Forward Rates   27

3. Day Count Conventions and Accrued Interest   53

4. Valuation of Option-Free Bonds   65

5. Yield Measures   91

6. Valuation of Bonds with Embedded Options   117

7. Cash Flow for Mortgage-Backed Securities and Amortizing Asset-Backed Securities   141

8. Valuation of Mortgage-Backed and Asset-Backed Securities   179

9. Analysis of Floating-Rate Securities   203

10. Total Return   227

11. Measuring Interest Rate Risk   249

12. Analysis of Interest Rate Swaps   297

13. Estimating Yield Volatility   327

Index   337

About the Authors

Frank J. Fabozzi is editor of the *Journal of Portfolio Management* and an Adjunct Professor of Finance at Yale University's School of Management. He is a Chartered Financial Analyst and Certified Public Accountant. Dr. Fabozzi is on the board of directors of the Guardian Life family of funds and the BlackRock complex of funds. He earned a doctorate in economics from the City University of New York in 1972 and in 1994 received an honorary doctorate of Humane Letters from Nova Southeastern University. Dr. Fabozzi is a Fellow of the International Center for Finance at Yale University.

Steven V. Mann is an Associate Professor of Finance at the Darla Moore School of Business, University of South Carolina. He earned a doctorate in finance from the University of Nebraska in 1987. His research interests are in the area of investments, particularly fixed-income securities and derivatives. He has published over 35 articles in finance journals and books. Dr. Mann is an accomplished teacher, winning 16 awards for excellence in teaching. He is a consultant to investment/commercial banks and has conducted more than 60 training programs for financial institutions throughout the United States.

Chapter 1

Time Value of Money

A security is a package of cash flows. The cash flows are delivered across time with varying degrees of uncertainty. To value a security, we must determine how much this package of cash flows is worth today. This process employs a fundamental finance principle — the *time value of money*. Simply stated, one dollar today is worth more than one dollar to be received in the future. The reason is that the money has a time value. One dollar today can be invested, start earning interest immediately, and grow to a larger amount in the future. Conversely, one dollar to be received one year from today is worth less than one dollar delivered today. This is true because an individual can invest an amount of money less than one dollar today and at some interest rate it will grow to one dollar in a year's time.

The purpose of this chapter is to introduce the fundamental principles of future value (i.e., compounding cash flows) and present value (i.e., discounting cash flows). These principles will be employed in every chapter in the remainder of the book. To be sure, no matter how complicated the security's cash flows become (e.g., bonds with embedded options, interest rate swaps, etc.), determining how much they are worth today involves taking present values. In addition, we will introduce the concept of yield which is a measure of potential return and explain how to compute the yield on any investment.

FUTURE VALUE OF A SINGLE CASH FLOW

Suppose an individual invests $100 at 5% compounded annually for three years. We will call the $100 invested the *original principal* and denote it as P. In this example, the annual interest rate is 5% and is the compensation the investor receives for giving up the use of his/her money for one year's time. Intuitively, the interest rate is a bribe offered to induce an individual to postpone their consumption of one dollar until some time in the future. If interest is compounded annually, this means that interest is paid for use of the money only once per year.

We will denote the interest rate as i and it will be in decimal form. In addition, N is the number of years the individual gives up use of his/her funds and FV_N is the future value or what the original principal will grow to after N years. In our example,

$$P = \$100$$
$$i = 0.05$$
$$N = 3 \text{ years}$$

So the question at hand is how much \$100 will be worth at the end of three years if it earns interest at 5% compounded annually?

To answer this question, let's first determine what the \$100 will grow to after one year if it earns 5% interest annually. This amount is determined with the following expression

$$FV_1 = P(1 + i)$$

Using the numbers in our example

$$FV_1 = \$100(1.05) = \$105$$

In words, if an individual invests \$100 that earns 5% compounded annually, at the end of one year the amount invested will grow to \$105 (i.e., the original principal of \$100 plus \$5 interest).

To find out how much the \$100 will be worth at the end of two years, we repeat the process one more time

$$FV_2 = FV_1(1 + i)$$

From the expression above, we know that

$$FV_1 = P(1 + i)$$

Substituting this in the expression and then simplifying, we obtain

$$FV_2 = P(1 + i)(1 + i)$$
$$= P(1 + i)^2$$

Using the numbers in our example, we find that

$$FV_2 = \$100(1.05)^2 = \$110.25$$

Note that during the second year, we earn \$5.25 in interest rather than \$5 because we are earning interest on our interest from the first year. This example illustrates an important point about how securities' returns work; returns reproduce multiplicatively rather than additively.

To find out how much the original principal will be worth at the end of three years, we repeat the process one last time

$$FV_3 = FV_2(1 + i)$$

Like before, we have already determined FV_2, so making this substitution and simplifying gives us

$$FV_3 = P(1 + i)^2(1 + i)$$
$$FV_3 = P(1 + i)^3$$

Using the numbers in our example, we find that

$$FV_3 = \$100(1.05)^3 = \$115.7625$$

The future value of $100 invested for three years earning 5% interest compounded annually is $115.7625.

The general formula for the future value of a single cash flow N years in the future given an interest rate i is

$$FV_N = P(1 + i)^N \tag{1}$$

From this expression, it is easy to see that for a given original principal P the future value will depend on the interest rate (i) and the number of years (N) that the cash flow is allowed to grow at that rate. For example, suppose we take the same $100 and invest it at 5% interest for ten years rather than five years, what is the future value? Using the expression presented above, we find that the future value is

$$FV_N = \$100(1.05)^{10} = \$162.8894$$

Now let us leave everything unchanged except the interest rate. What is the future value of $100 invested for ten years at 6%? The future value is now

$$FV_N = \$100(1.06)^{10} = \$179.0848$$

As we will see in due course, the longer the investment, the more dramatic the impact of even relatively small changes in interest rates on future values.

PRESENT VALUE OF A SINGLE CASH FLOW

The present value of a single cash flow asks the opposite question. Namely, how much is a single cash flow to be received in the future worth today given a particular interest rate? Suppose the interest rate is 10%, how much is $161.05 to be received five years hence worth today? This question can be easily visualized on the time line presented below:

Alternatively, given the interest rate is 10%, how much would one have to invest today to have $161.05 in five years? The process is called "discounting" because as long as interest rates are positive, the amount invested (the present value) will be less than $161.05 (the future value) because of the time value of money.[1]

Since finding present values or discounting asks the opposite question from the future value, the mathematics should be opposite as well. We know the expression for the future value for a single cash flow is given by the expression:

$$FV_N = P(1 + i)^N$$

Let us plug in the information from the question above

$$\$161.05 = P(1.10)^5$$

In order to answer the question of how much we would have to invest today at 10% to have $161.05 in five years, we must solve for P

$$P = \frac{\$161.05}{(1.10)^{10}} = \$100$$

So, the present value of $161.05 delivered five years hence at 10% is $100.

It is easy to see that the mathematics conform to our intuition. When we calculate a future value, we ask how much will the dollars invested today be worth in the future given a particular interest rate. So, the mathematics of future value involve multiplication by a value greater than one (i.e., making things bigger). Correspondingly, when we find present values, we ask how much a future amount of dollars is worth today given a particular interest rate. Thus, the mathematics of present value involve division by a value greater than one (i.e., making things smaller).

The general formula for the present value (PV) of a single cash flow N years in the future given an interest rate i is

$$PV = \frac{FV_N}{(1 + i)^N} \tag{2}$$

Note that we have replaced P with PV. In addition, PV does not have a subscript because we assume it is the value at time 0 (i.e., today).

It is instructive to write the expression for the present value of a single cash flow as follows

$$PV = FV_N \left[\frac{1}{(1 + i)^N} \right]$$

The term in brackets is equal to the present value of one dollar to be received N years hence given interest rate i and is often called a *discount factor*. The present value of a single cash flow is the product of the cash flow to be received (FV_N)

---

[1] The interest rates used to determine present values are often called "discount rates."

and the discount factor. Essentially, the discount factor is today's value of one dollar that is expected to be delivered at some time in the future given a particular interest rate. An analogy will illustrate the point.

Suppose a U.S. investor receives cash payments of $200,000, ¥500,000, and £600,000. How much does the investor receive? We cannot simply add up the cash flows since the three cash flows are denominated in different currencies. In order to determine how much the investor receives, we would convert the three cash flows into a common currency (say, U.S. dollars) using currency exchange rates. Similarly, we cannot value cash flows to be received at different dates in the future merely by taking their sum. The expected cash flows are delivered at different times and are denominated in different "currencies" (Year 1 dollars, Year 2 dollars, etc.). We use discount factors just like exchange rates to convert cash flows to be received across time into a "common currency" called the present value (i.e., Year 0 dollars).

To illustrate this, we return to the last example — what is the present value of $161.05 to be received five years from today given that the interest rate is 10%? The present value can be written as

$$PV = \$161.05\left[\frac{1}{(1.10)^5}\right]$$

$$= \$161.05(0.6209) = \$100$$

One dollar to be received in five years is worth $0.6209 today given the interest rate is 10%. We expect to receive $161.05 Year 5 dollars each worth 0.6209 dollars today. The present value is $100 which is the quantity ($161.05) multiplied by the price per unit ($0.6209).

As can be easily seen from the present value expression, the discount factor depends on two things. First, holding the interest rate constant, the longer the time until the cash flow is to be received, the lower the discount factor. To illustrate this, suppose we have $100 to be received ten years from now and the interest rate is 10%. What is the present value?

$$PV = \$100\left[\frac{1}{(1.10)^{10}}\right]$$

$$= \$100(0.3855) = \$38.55$$

Now suppose the cash flow is to be received 20 years hence instead, all else the same. What is the present value?

$$PV = \$100\left[\frac{1}{(1.10)^{20}}\right]$$

$$= \$100(0.1486) = \$14.86$$

The discount factor falls 0.3855 to 0.1486. This is simply the time value of money at work. The present value is lower the farther into the future the cash flow will be received.

Why this occurs is apparent from looking at the present value equation. The numerator remains the same and is being divided by a larger number in the denominator as one plus the discount rate is being raised to ever higher powers. This is an important property of the present value: for a given interest rate, the farther into the future a cash flow is received, the lower its present value. Simply put, as cash flows move away from the present, they are worth less to us today. Intuitively, we can invest an even smaller amount now ($14.86) today and it will have more time to grow (20 years versus 10 years) to be equal in size to the payment to be received, $100.

The second factor driving the discount factor is the level of the interest rate. Specifically, holding the time to receipt constant, the discount factor is inversely related to the interest rate. Suppose, once again, we have $100 to be received ten years from now at 10%. From our previous calculations, we know that the present value is $38.55. Now suppose everything is the same except that the interest rate is 12%. What is the present value when the interest rate increases?

$$PV = \$100\left[\frac{1}{(1.12)^{10}}\right]$$
$$= \$100(0.3220) = \$32.20$$

As the interest rate rises from 10% to 12%, the present value of $100 to be received ten years from today falls from $38.55 to $32.20. The reasoning is equally straightforward. If the amount invested compounds at a faster rate (12% versus 10%), we can invest a smaller amount now ($32.20 versus $38.55) and still have $100 after ten years.

The relationship between the present value of a single cash flow ($100 to be received ten years hence) and the level of the interest rate is presented in Exhibit 1. For now, there are two things to note about present value/interest rate relationship depicted in the exhibit. First, the relationship is downward sloping. This is simply the inverse relationship between present values and interest rates at work. Second, the relationship is a curve rather than a straight line. In fact, the shape of the curve in Exhibit 1 is referred to as convex. By convex, it simply means the curve is "bowed in" relative to the origin.

This second observation raises two questions about the convex or curved shape of the present value/interest rate relationship. First, why is it curved? Second, what is the significance of the curvature? The answer to the first question is mathematical. The answer lies in the denominator of the present value formula. Since we are raising one plus the discount rate to powers greater than one, it should not be surprising that the relationship between the present value and the interest rate is not linear. The answer to the second question requires an entire chapter. Specifically, as we will see in Chapter 11, this convexity or bowed shape has implications for the price volatility of a bond when interest rates change. What is important to understand at this point is that the relationship is not linear.

Exhibit 1: PV/Interest Rate Relationship

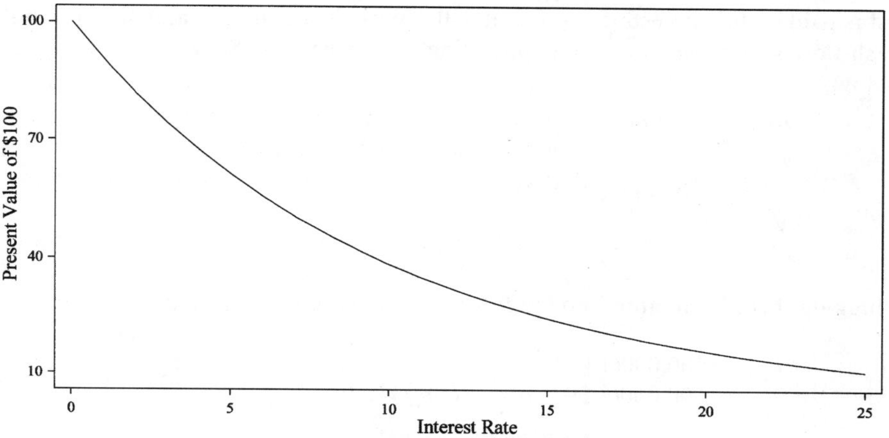

Present value of $100 to be received in 10 years compounded semiannually

---

COMPOUNDING/DISCOUNTING WHEN INTEREST IS PAID MORE THAN ANNUALLY

An investment may pay interest more frequently than once per year (e.g., semiannually, quarterly, monthly, weekly). If an investment pays interest compounded semiannually, then interest is added to the principal twice a year. To account for this, the future value and present value computations presented above require two simple modifications. First, the annual interest rate is adjusted by dividing by the number of times that interest is paid per year. The adjusted interest rate is called a *periodic interest rate*. Second, the number of years, N, is replaced with the number of periods, n, which is found by multiplying the number of years by the number of times that interest is paid per year.

Future Value of a Single Cash Flow with More Frequent Compounding

The future value of a single cash flow when interest is paid m times per year is as follows:

$$FV_n = P(1 + i)^n \tag{3}$$

where

i = annual interest rate divided by m
n = number of interest payments ($= N \times m$)

To illustrate, suppose that a portfolio manager invests $500,000 in an investment that promises to pay an annual interest rate of 6.8% for 5 years. Interest is paid on this investment semiannually. What is the future value of this single cash flow given semiannual compounding? The answer is $698,514.45 as shown below:

$$PV = \$500,000$$
$$m = 2$$
$$i = 0.034\ (= 0.068/2)$$
$$N = 5$$
$$n = 10\ (5 \times 2)$$

Plugging this information into the future value expression gives us:

$$FV_{10} = \$500,000(1.034)^{10}$$
$$= \$500,000(1.397029) = \$698,514.50$$

This future value is larger than if interest were compounded annually. With annual compounding, the future value would be $694,746.34. The higher future value when interest is paid semiannually reflects the fact that the interest is being added to principal more frequently which in turn earns interest sooner.

Lastly, suppose instead that interest is compounded quarterly rather than semiannually. What is the future value of $500,000 at 6.8% compounded quarterly for 5 years? The future value is larger still, $700,469, for the same reasoning as shown below:

$$PV = \$500,000$$
$$m = 4$$
$$i = 0.017\ (= 0.068/4)$$
$$N = 5$$
$$n = 20\ (5 \times 4)$$

Plugging this information into the future value expression gives us:

$$FV_{20} = \$500,000(1.017)^{20}$$
$$= \$500,000(1.400938) = \$700,469$$

Present Value of a Single Cash Flow Using Periodic Interest Rates

We must also adjust our present value expression to account for more frequent compounding. The same two adjustments are required. First, like before, we must convert the annual interest rate into a periodic interest rate. Second, we need to convert the number of years until the cash flow is to be received into the appropriate number of periods that matches the compounding frequency.

The present value of a single cash flow when interest is paid m times per year is written as follows:

$$PV = \frac{FV_n}{(1 + i)^n} \tag{4}$$

where

i = annual interest rate divided by m
n = number of interest payments ($= N \times m$)

To illustrate this operation, suppose an investor expects to receive $100,000, 10 years from today and the relevant interest rate is 8% compounded semiannually. What is the present value of this cash flow? The answer is $45,638.69 as shown below:

FV_{10} = $100,000
m = 2
i = 0.04 ($= 0.08/2$)
N = 10
n = 20 (10×2)

Plugging this information into the present value expression gives us:

$$PV = \frac{\$100,000}{(1.04)^{20}} = \$45,638.69$$

This present value is smaller than if interest were compounded annually. With annual compounding, the present value would be $46,319.35. The lower value when interest is paid semiannually means that for a given annual interest rate we can invest a smaller amount today and still have $100,000 in ten years with more frequent compounding.

Moving to quarterly compounding, all else equal, should result in an even smaller present value. What is the present value of $100,000 to be received 10 years from today at 8% compounded quarterly? The present value is smaller still, $45,289.04, as shown below:

FV_{40} = $100,000
m = 4
i = 0.02 ($= 0.08/4$)
N = 10
n = 40 (10×4)

Plugging this information into the present value expression given by equation (4) gives

$$PV = \frac{\$100,000}{(1.02)^{40}} = \$45,289.04$$

FUTURE AND PRESENT VALUES OF AN ORDINARY ANNUITY

Most securities promise to deliver more than one cash flow. As such, most of the time when we make future/present value calculations, we will be working with multiple cash flows. The simplest package of cash flows is called an *annuity*. An annuity is a series of payments of fixed amounts for a specified number of periods. We will first consider an ordinary annuity. The adjective "ordinary" tells us that the annuity payments come at the end of the period and the first payment is one period from now.

Future Value of an Ordinary Annuity

Suppose an investor expects to receive $100 at the end of each of the next three years and the relevant interest rate is 5% compounded annually. This annuity can be visualized on the time line presented below:

What is the future value of this annuity at the end of year 3? Of course, one way to determine this amount is to find the future value of each payment as of the end of year 3 and simply add them up. The first $100 payment will earn 5% interest for two years while the second $100 payment will earn 5% for one year. The third $100 payment is already at the end of the year (i.e., denominated in year 3 dollars) so no adjustment is necessary. Mathematically, the summation of the future values of these three cash flows can be written as:

$$\$100(1.05)^2 = \$100(1.1025) \quad = \quad \$110.25$$
$$\$100(1.05)^1 = \$100(1.0500) \quad = \quad \$105.00$$
$$\$100(1.05)^0 = \$100(1.0000) \quad = \quad \underline{\$100.00}$$
$$\text{Total future value} \qquad\qquad\qquad \$315.25$$

So, if the investor receives $100 at the end of each of the next three years and can reinvest the cash flows at 5% compounded annually, then at the end of three years the investment will have grown to $315.25.

The procedure for computing the future value of an annuity presented above is perfectly correct. However, there is a formula that can be used to speed up this computation. Let us return to the example above and rewrite the future value of the annuity as follows:

$$\$100(1.05)^2 + \$100(1.05)^1 + \$100(1.05)^0 = \$315.25$$

This expression can be rewritten as follows by factoring out the $100 annuity payment:

$$\$100[(1.05)^2 + (1.05)^1 + (1.05)^0]$$

Since $[(1.05)^2 + (1.05)^1 + (1.05)^0] = 3.1525,$

$$\$100\ [3.1525] = \$315.25$$

The term in brackets is the *future value of an ordinary annuity of $1 per year.* Multiplying the future value of an ordinary annuity of $1 by the annuity payment produces the future value of an ordinary annuity.

The general formula for the future value of an ordinary annuity of $1 per year is given by

$$FV_N = A\left[\frac{(1+i)^N - 1}{i}\right] \tag{5}$$

where

A = amount of the annuity ($)
i = annual interest rate (in decimal form)

Let us rework the previous example with the general formula where

A = $100
i = 0.05
N = 3

therefore,

$$FV_N = \$100\left[\frac{(1.05)^3 - 1}{0.05}\right]$$
$$= \$100(3.1525) = \$315.25$$

This value agrees with our earlier calculation.

Future Value of an Ordinary Annuity when Payments Occur More Than Once per Year

The future value of an ordinary annuity can be easily generalized to handle situations in which payments are made more than one time per year. For example, instead of assuming an investor receives and then reinvests $100 per year for 3 years, starting 1 year from now, suppose that the investor receives $50 every 6 months for 3 years, starting 6 months from now.

The general formula for the future value of an ordinary annuity when payments occur m times per year is

$$FV_N = A\left[\frac{(1+i)^n - 1}{i}\right] \tag{6}$$

where

A = amount of the annuity ($)

i = periodic interest rate which is the annual interest rate divided by m (in decimal form)

n = $N \times m$

The value in brackets is the future value of an ordinary annuity of $1 per period.

Let us return to the example above and assume an annuity of $50 for 6 semiannual periods. The number line would appear as follows:

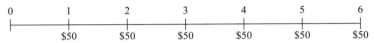

Note the numbers across the top of the time line represent semiannual periods rather than years. The future value of 6 semiannual payments of $50 to be received plus the interest earned by investing the payments at 5% compounded semiannually is found as follows:

A = $50
m = 2
i = 0.025 (0.05/2)
N = 3
n = 6 (3 × 2)

therefore,

$$FV_6 = \$50 \left[\frac{(1.025)^6 - 1}{0.025} \right]$$

$$= \$50(6.387737) = \$319.39$$

Although the total of the cash payments received by the investor over 3 years is $300 in both examples, the future value is higher ($319.39) when the cash flows are $50 every six months for 6 periods rather than $100 a year for 3 years ($315.25). This is true because of the more frequent reinvestment of the payments received by the investor.

Present Value of an Annuity

The coupon payments of a fixed-rate bond are an ordinary annuity. Accordingly, in order to value a bond, we must be able to find the present value of an annuity. In this section, we turn our attention to this operation. Suppose we have an ordinary annuity of $300 for 3 years. These cash flows are pictured on the time line below:

Suppose that the relevant interest rate is 12% compounded annually. What is the present value of this annuity? Of course, we can take the present value of each cash flow individually and then sum them up. The present value is $720.57. To see this, we employ the present value of a single cash flow as follows:

$$PV = \frac{\$300}{(1.12)^1} = \$267.87$$

$$PV = \frac{\$300}{(1.12)^2} = \$239.16$$

$$PV = \frac{\$300}{(1.12)^3} = \$213.54$$

Total $\overline{\$720.57}$

We can rewrite the summation of these present values horizontally as shown below:

$$\frac{\$300}{(1.12)^1} + \frac{\$300}{(1.12)^2} + \frac{\$300}{(1.12)^3} = \$720.57$$

This expression can be rewritten by factoring out the $300 annuity payment as follows:

$$\$300\left[\frac{1}{(1.12)^1} + \frac{1}{(1.12)^2} + \frac{1}{(1.12)^3}\right]$$

$$\$300[0.8929 + 0.7972 + 0.7118]$$

Since the sum of the three terms in brackets is 2.4018, we can write

$$\$300(2.4018) = \$720.57$$

The term in brackets is the present value of an ordinary annuity of $1 for 3 years at 12%.

Once again, there is a general formula for the present value of an ordinary annuity of $1 for N years that can used to greatly simplify taking present values. The general formula is given below:

$$PV = A\left[\frac{1 - \dfrac{1}{(1 + i)^N}}{i}\right] \tag{7}$$

where

A = amount of the annuity ($)
i = annual interest rate (in decimal form)
N = length of the annuity in years

Let us rework the previous example with the general formula where

A = $300
i = 0.12

$$N = 3$$

therefore,

$$PV = \$300\left[\frac{1 - \dfrac{1}{(1.12)^3}}{0.12}\right]$$

$$= \$300(2.4018) = \$720.57$$

This value agrees with our earlier calculation.

Present Value of an Ordinary Annuity when Payments Occur More Than Once per Year

The present value of an ordinary annuity can be generalized to deal with cash payments that occur more frequently than one time per year. For example, instead of assuming an investor receives $300 per year for 3 years, starting 1 year from now, suppose instead that the investor receives $150 every 6 months for 3 years, starting 6 months from now.

The general formula for the present value of an ordinary annuity when payments occur m times per year is

$$PV = A\left[\frac{1 - \dfrac{1}{(1 + i)^n}}{i}\right] \tag{8}$$

where

A = amount of the annuity ($)
i = periodic interest rate which is the annual interest rate divided by m (in decimal form)
n = $N \times m$

The value in brackets is the *present value of an ordinary annuity of $1 per period.*

Let us return to the example above and assume an annuity of $150 for 6 semiannual periods. The time line would appear as follows:

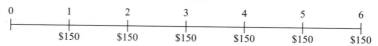

Note once again that the numbers across the top of the time line represent semiannual periods rather than years. The present value of 6 semiannual payments of $150 to be received plus the interest earned by investing the payments at 12% compounded semiannually is found as follows:

A = $300
m = 3
i = 0.06 (0.12/2)

$$N = 3$$
$$n = 6 \, (3 \times 2)$$

therefore,

$$PV = \$150 \left[\frac{1 - \dfrac{1}{(1.06)^6}}{0.06} \right]$$

$$= \$150(4.9173) = \$737.60$$

Although the total cash payments received by the investor over 3 years are $900 in both examples, the present value is higher ($737.60) when the cash flows are $150 every six months for 6 periods rather than $300 a year for 3 years ($720.57). This result makes sense because half the cash flows are six months closer when they are received semiannually so their present value should be higher.

Present Value of a Perpetual Annuity

We now consider the special case of an annuity that lasts forever, which is called a *perpetual annuity*. The cash flow of some securities can be thought of as perpetual annuities (e.g., preferred stock). So, how do we take the present value of a stream of cash flows expected to last forever? The computation is surprisingly straightforward and is given by the expression:

$$PV = \frac{A}{i} \qquad (9)$$

where

$$A = \text{perpetual annuity payment}$$
$$i = \text{interest rate (in decimal form)}$$

The reason equation (9) is so simple can be found in equation (8) which is the general formula for the present value of an ordinary annuity of $1 per period. As the number of periods n gets very large, the numerator of the term in brackets in equation (8) collapses to 1 because the term $1/(1 + i)^n$ approaches zero producing equation (9) which is the present value of the perpetual annuity formula.

Let's use equation (9) to find the present value of a perpetual annuity. Suppose a financial instrument promises to pay $350 per year in perpetuity. The investor requires an annual interest rate of 7% from this investment. What is the present value of this package of cash flows?

The present value of the $350 perpetual annuity is equal to $5,000, as shown below:

$$A = \$350$$
$$i = 0.07$$

$$PV = \frac{\$350}{0.07} = \$5,000$$

Present Value of a Package of Cash Flows with Unequal Interest Rates

To this point in our discussion, we have used the same interest rate to compute present values regardless of when the cash flows were to be delivered in the future. This will not generally be the case in practice. As we will see in Chapter 2, the interest rates used to compute present values will depend on, among other things, the shape of the Treasury yield curve. Each cash flow will be discounted back to the present using a unique interest rate. Accordingly, the present value of a package of cash flows is the sum of the present values of each individual cash flow that comprises the package where each present value is computed using a unique interest rate.

As an illustration of this process, consider a 4-year 9% coupon bond with a $1,000 maturity value. Assume, for simplicity, the bond delivers coupon interest payments annually. The bond's cash flows and required interest rates are shown below:

Years from Now	Annual Cash Payments (in dollars)	Required Interest Rate (%)
1	$90	6.07
2	90	6.17
3	90	6.70
4	1,090	6.88

The present value of each cash flow is determined using the appropriate interest rate as shown below:

Years From Now	Annual Cash Payments (in dollars)	Required Interest Rate (%)	Discount Factor	Present Value of Payment (in dollars)
1	$90	6.07	0.942774	$84.84966
2	90	6.17	0.887149	79.84341
3	90	6.70	0.823203	74.08827
4	1,090	6.88	0.766327	835.29643
			Total Present Value	$1,074.07777

The present value of the cash flows is $1,074.07777.

Since the process of discounting cash flows with multiple interest rates is so important to our work in later chapters, let's work through another example. We will demonstrate how to find the present value of the fixed-rate payments in an interest rate swap. As explained in Chapter 12, in an interest rate swap, two counterparties agree to exchange periodic interest payments. The dollar amount of the interest payments exchanged is based on some notional principal. The dollar amount each counterparty pays to the other is the agreed-upon periodic interest rate multiplied by the notional principal.

To illustrate an interest rate swap, suppose that for the next five years party A agrees to pay party B 10% per year, while party B agrees to pay party A 6-month LIBOR (the reference rate). Party A is a fixed-rate payer/floating-rate receiver, while party B is a floating-rate payer/fixed-rate receiver. Assume the notional principal is $50 million, and that payments are exchanged every six months for the next five years. This means that every six months, party A (the fixed-rate payer/floating-rate receiver) will pay party B $2.5 million (10% × $50 million × 0.5). The amount that party B (floating-rate payer/fixed-rate receiver) will be 6-month LIBOR × $50 million × 0.5. For example, if 6-month LIBOR is 7%, party B will pay party A $1.75 (7% × $50 million × 0.5). Note that we multiply by 0.5 because one-half year's interest is being paid.[2]

Let's compute the present value of the fixed-rate payments made by party A. As we will see in Chapter 2, every cash flow should be discounted using its own interest rate. These interest rates are determined using Eurodollar CD futures contracts as described in Chapter 12. For now, we will take the interest rates as given. The interest rate swap's fixed-rate payments and required semiannual interest rates are shown below:

Periods from Now	Semiannual fixed-rate payments (in millions of dollars)	Required Semiannual Interest Rate (%)
1	$2.5	3.00
2	2.5	3.15
3	2.5	3.20
4	2.5	3.30
5	2.5	3.38
6	2.5	3.42
7	2.5	3.45
8	2.5	3.50
9	2.5	3.53
10	2.5	3.54

The present value of this interest rate swap's fixed-rate payments using the appropriate semiannual interest rates is shown below:[3]

Periods from Now	Semiannual Cash Flows (in millions of dollars)	Required Semiannual Interest Rate (%)	Discount Factor	Present Value of Payment (in millions of dollars)
1	$2.5	3.00	0.970874	2.427184
2	2.5	3.15	0.939856	2.349641
3	2.5	3.20	0.909831	2.274578
4	2.5	3.30	0.878211	2.195527
5	2.5	3.38	0.846871	2.117178
6	2.5	3.42	0.817284	2.043209
7	2.5	3.45	0.788654	1.971635
8	2.5	3.50	0.759412	1.898529
9	2.5	3.53	0.731820	1.829549
10	2.5	3.54	0.706185	1.765462
		Total Present Value		20.87249

[2] We will see in Chapter 12 that the payments must be adjusted by the number of days in the payment period.
[3] The discount factor is:

$$\frac{1}{(1 + \text{required semiannual rate})^{\text{periods from now}}}$$

The present value of the fixed-rate payments in this interest rate swap is $20.87249 million.

YIELD (INTERNAL RATE OF RETURN)

Yield is a measure of potential return from an investment over a stated time horizon. We will discuss several yield measures for both fixed-rate and floating-rate securities (e.g., yield-to-maturity, yield-to-call, discounted margin, etc.) in later chapters. In this section, we will explain how to compute the yield on any investment.

Computing the Yield on Any Investment

The yield on any investment is computed by determining the interest rate or discount rate that will make the present value of an investment's cash flow equal to its price. Mathematically, the yield, y, on any investment is the interest rate that will make the following relationship hold:

$$P = \frac{C_1}{(1+y)^1} + \frac{C_2}{(1+y)^2} + \frac{C_3}{(1+y)^3} + \dots + \frac{C_N}{(1+y)^N} \tag{10}$$

where

P = market price
C_t = cash flow in year t
N = number of years

The individual terms summed to produce the price are the present values of the cash flow. The yield calculated from the expression above is also termed the *internal rate of return.*

There is no closed-form expression for determining an investment's yield given its price (except for investments with only one cash flow). The yield is, therefore, found by an iterative process. The objective is to find the interest rate that will make the present value of the cash flows equal to the price. The procedure is as follows:

1. Select an interest rate.

2. Compute the present value of each cash flow by using the interest rate selected in Step 1.

3. Total the present value of the cash flows found in Step 2.

4. Compare the total present value found in Step 3 with the price of the investment. Then, if the present value of the cash flows found in Step 3

is equal to the price of the investment, the interest rate selected in Step 1 is the yield. If the total present value of the cash flows found in Step 3 is more than the price of the investment, the interest rate selected is not the yield. Go back to Step 1 and use a higher interest rate. If the total present value of the cash flows found in Step 3 is less than the price of the investment, the interest rate used is not the yield. Go back to Step 1 and use a lower interest rate.

We will illustrate how these steps are implemented.

Suppose a financial instrument offers the following annual payments for the next 5 years as displayed in Exhibit 2.

Suppose that the price of this financial instrument is $1,084.25. What is the yield or internal rate of return offered by this financial instrument?

To compute the yield, we must compute the total present value of these cash flows using different interest rates until we find the one that makes the present value of the cash flows equal to $1,084.25 (the price). Suppose 5% is selected, the calculation is presented in Exhibit 3.

The present value using a 5% interest rate exceeds the price of $1,084.25, so a higher interest rate must be tried. If a 7% interest rate is utilized, the present value is $1,041.00 as seen in Exhibit 4.

At 7%, the total present value of the cash flows is less than the price of $1,084.25. Accordingly, the present value must be computed with a lower interest rate. The present value at 6% is presented in Exhibit 5.

The present value of the cash flows at 6% is equal to the price of the financial instrument when a 6% interest rate is used. Therefore, the yield is 6%.

Exhibit 2: Cash Flows from a Financial Instrument

Years from Now	Annual Cash Payments (in dollars)
1	$80
2	80
3	80
4	80
5	1,080

Exhibit 3: Present Value at 5%

Years from Now	Annual Cash Payments (in dollars)	Present Value of Cash Flow at 5%
1	$80	$76.1905
2	80	72.5624
3	80	69.1070
4	80	65.8162
5	1,080	846.2083
Total Present Value		1,129.88

Exhibit 4: Present Value at 7%

Years from Now	Annual Cash Payments (in dollars)	Present Value of Cash Flow at 7%
1	$80	$74.7664
2	80	69.8751
3	80	65.3038
4	80	61.0316
5	1,080	770.0251
Total Present Value		$1,041.00

Exhibit 5: Present Value at 6%

Years from Now	Annual Cash Payments (in dollars)	Present Value of Cash Flow at 6%
1	$80	$75.4717
2	80	71.1997
3	80	67.1695
4	80	63.3675
5	1,080	807.0388
Total Present Value		$1,041.00

Although the formula for the yield is based on annual cash flows, the formula can be easily generalized to any number of periodic payments delivered during a year. The generalized formula for computing the yield is

$$P = \frac{C_1}{(1+y)^1} + \frac{C_2}{(1+y)^2} + \frac{C_3}{(1+y)^3} + ... + \frac{C_n}{(1+y)^n} \tag{11}$$

where

C_t = cash flow in period t
n = number of periods

It is important to bear in mind that the yield computed using equation (11) is now the yield for the period. If the cash flows are delivered semiannually, the yield is a semiannual yield. If the cash flows are delivered quarterly, the yield is a quarterly yield, and so forth. The annual rate is determined by multiplying the yield for the period by the number of periods per year (m).

As an illustration, suppose an investor is considering the purchase of a financial instrument that promises to deliver the following *semiannual* cash flows:

- 8 payments of $35 every 6 months for 4 years
- $1,000 eight semiannual periods from now

Suppose the price of this financial instrument is $934.04. What yield is this financial instrument offering? The yield is calculated via the iterative procedure explained before and the results are summarized in Exhibit 6.

Exhibit 6: Yield Calculation with Semiannual Cash Flows

Annual Interest Rate (%)	Semiannual Interest Rate (%)	Total Present Value ($)
6	3.0	1,035.10
7	3.5	1,000.00
8	4.0	966.34
9	4.5	934.04

When a semiannual rate interest rate of 4.5% is used to compute the total present value of the cash flows, the total present value is equal to the price of $934.04. Therefore, the semiannual yield is 4.5%. Doubling this yield gives an annual yield of 9%.

Yield Calculation When There is Only One Cash Flow

If a security delivers a single cash flow, it is possible to determine the yield analytically rather than using the iterative procedure. For example, suppose that a financial instrument can be purchased for $4,139.25 and delivers a single cash flow of $5,000 in 3 years. So, if the price is $4,139.25 and the future value is $5,000, at what yield must the money grow over the next 3 years? In other words, what value of y will satisfy the following relationship:

$$\$4,139.25(1 + y)^3 = \$5,000$$

We can solve this expression for y by first dividing both sides by $4,139.25:

$$(1 + y)^3 = \frac{\$5,000}{\$4,139.25} = 1.20795$$

Next, we take the third root of both sides which is the same as raising both sides to ($\frac{1}{3}$) power:

$$(1 + y) = (1.20795)^{\frac{1}{3}} = 1.065$$

Finally, we subtract 1 from both sides:

$$y = 1.065 - 1 = 0.065$$

The yield on this investment is therefore 6.5%

Of course, once the process is well understood, the following formula that greatly simplifies the yield calculation can be used:

$$y = (\text{future value per dollar invested})^{1/n} - 1 \tag{12}$$

where

n = number of periods until the cash flow will be received

$$\text{future value per dollar invested} = \frac{\text{cash flow from investment}}{\text{price}}$$

As an illustration, suppose that a security can be purchased for $71,298.62 today and promises to pay $100,000 five years hence. What is the yield? The answer is 7% and the calculation is detailed below:

$$\text{future value per dollar invested} = \frac{\$100,000}{\$71,298.63} = 1.40255$$

$$y = (1.40255)^{\frac{1}{5}} - 1$$
$$= 1.07 - 1 = 0.07 \text{ or } 7\%$$

Annualizing Yields

Up to this point in our discussion, we have converted periodic interest rates (semiannual, quarterly, monthly, etc.) into annual interest rates by simply multiplying the periodic rate by the frequency of payments per year. For example, we converted a semiannual rate into an annual rate by multiplying it by 2. Similarly, we converted an annual rate into a semiannual rate by dividing it by 2.

This simple rule for annualizing interest rates is not correct due to the mathematics of compound interest. A simple example will illustrate the problem. Suppose that $1,000 is invested for 1 year at 10% compounded annually. At the end of the year, the interest earned will be $100. Now suppose that same $1,000 is invested at 10% compounded semiannually or 5% every six months. The interest earned during the year is determined by calculating the future value of $100 one year hence at 10% compounded semiannually:

$$\$1,000(1.05)^2 = \$1,000(1.1025)$$
$$= \$1,102.50$$

Interest is $102.50 on a $1,000 investment and the yield is 10.25% ($102.50/$1,000). The 10.25% is called the *effective annual yield.*

The general expression for calculating the effective annual yield for a given periodic interest rate is given by:

$$\text{effective annual yield} = (1 + \text{periodic interest rate})^m - 1 \tag{13}$$

where

m = frequency of payments

Using the numbers from the previous example, the periodic (semiannual) yield is 5% and the frequency of payments is twice per year. Therefore,

$$\text{effective annual yield} = (1.05)^2 - 1$$
$$= 1.1025 - 1 = 0.1025 \text{ or } 10.25\%$$

If interest is paid quarterly, then the periodic interest rate is 2.5% and the frequency of payments per year is 4. The effective annual yield is 10.38% as compute below:

$$\text{effective annual yield} = (1.025)^4 - 1$$
$$= (1.1028) - 1 = 0.1038 \text{ or } 10.38\%$$

We can reverse the process and compute the periodic interest rate that will produce a given annual interest rate. For example, suppose we need to know what semiannual interest rate would produce an effective annual yield of 8%. The following formula is employed:

$$\text{period interest rate} = (1 + \text{effective annual yield})^{1/m} - 1 \tag{14}$$

Using this expression, we find that the semiannual interest rate required to produce an effective annual yield of 8% is 3.9231%:

$$\text{Periodic interest rate} = (1.08)^{1/2} - 1$$
$$= 1.039231 - 1 = 0.039231 \text{ or } 3.9231\%$$

APPENDIX

COMPOUNDING AND DISCOUNTING IN CONTINUOUS TIME

Most valuation models of derivative instruments (futures/forwards, options, swaps, caps, floors) utilize continuous compounding and discounting. Thus, in this section, we develop these important ideas. As we will see, although the mathematics are somewhat more involved, the basic principles we have learned to this point are exactly the same.

Normally, when computing present and future values, we assume that interest is added to the principal once each period, where the period may be one year, a month, a day, etc. Consider an extreme example: the future value of $100 one year hence, given a 100% interest rate and annual compounding is $200. This amount represents the present value ($100) plus the interest earned over the year ($100) which is added to the principal at the end of the year.

If the other factors remain unchanged, increasing the frequency with which interest is added to the principal (e.g., semiannually, quarterly, monthly, etc.) increases the future value. The future value of $100 one year hence, given a 100% rate and semiannual compounding is $225. Two steps are required to arrive at this amount. At the end of the first six months, the original $100 grows to $150 which represents the original principal ($100) plus the interest earned ($50) over the first six months at a periodic rate of 50%. The periodic rate is simply the annual rate (100%) divided by 2, which is the number of times that interest is paid per year. During the second six months, although the account is still earning interest at a periodic rate of 50%, the principal is now $150. Accordingly, an additional $75 interest is added at the end of the period, bringing the total to $225. We earn $25 more in interest in the second six months (as opposed to the first six months) because our interest is also earning interest at a periodic rate of 50%.

So it goes with compound interest. The sooner interest is added to the principal, the sooner interest is earned on a larger balance at the same periodic rate. Therefore, it is not surprising that as annual periods are divided into even smaller increments of time (e.g., quarterly, monthly, daily, etc.), the future value of our $100 at the end of one year continues to grow.

Exhibit A1 depicts what happens to the future value of $100 one year hence given a 100% interest rate as we increase the number of times per year interest is added to the principal. The vertical axis measures the future value at year end; the horizontal axis measures the frequency of compounding per year. The "1" on the horizontal axis is annual compounding, the "2" semiannual compounding, and so forth to "8760" which represents compounding interest every hour.

The rate of increase in the future value is decreasing as we move from annual compounding ($200) to weekly compounding ($269.26) to hourly compounding ($271.81). As it turns out, no matter how frequently the interest is added to our account (every minute, every second, ...), the future value of $100 one year hence at 100% interest can be no more than $271.83. The amount $271.83 is the future value of $100 at 100% if interest is added to our balance continuously; interest is added to our account at literally each instant of time rather than once per period. The future value of $271.83 is the highest possible, given an interest rate of 100%. A future value computed when interest is compounded continuously represents a natural upper bound, similar to the speed of light.

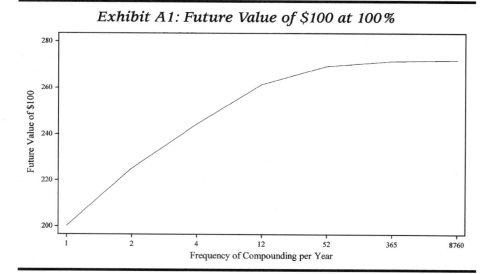

Exhibit A1: Future Value of $100 at 100%

This exercise usually engenders two questions. First, why is there an upper bound? Second, why is the upper bound $271.83? We will consider each in turn.

Let's answer the first question by appealing to an analogy. Suppose you are going to fill a bathtub with water. You turn the faucet a quarter turn to the left and water begins to pour into the bathtub. This is analogous to how interest is added to the principal when interest is compounded continuously — the water tumbles out in a continuous stream. Suppose you are going to fill the bathtub for four minutes. Even though the water is coming out of the faucet in a continuous stream, the amount of water in the bathtub will only reach a certain level. The only way we can get more water in the bathtub in a given amount of time is to increase the water pressure. Similarly, if we invest $100 for 1 year, the only way we can achieve a higher future value than $271.83 is to increase the interest rate above 100%.[4]

The answer to the second question requires a brief mathematical interlude. The future value of $1 when interest is compounded more than once per year is given by $(1 + i/m)^m$ where i is the annual interest rate and m is the frequency of compounding. When i is 100% and as m goes to infinity (i.e., continuous compounding), the future value of $1 converges to 2.71828... This number, which is denoted by the letter e in honor of the famous Swiss mathematician Euler, is one of the most important numbers in mathematics. Among its many attributes, e is the base of natural logarithms (i.e., the natural logarithm of e is one).[5]

To this point, we have learned why the future value of $1 one year hence given a particular interest rate has a limit. Moreover, when the interest rate is 100% and compounded continuously on a principal of $1, the limit is $2.71828 or $$e.$[6] Now let's take up the general case and allow the interest rate to take on values other than 100%.

Let's define some terms. As before, let i be the annual interest rate. Let t denote the date to which we are computing the present value and T denote the terminal date of the investment. Accordingly, $(T–t)$ represents the number of periods for which one is investing a particular amount. Finally, let FV and PV denote the future value and present value, respectively. To compute a future value in continuous time, we need to evaluate the following expression:

$$FV = PV\, e^{i(T-t)} \tag{A.1}$$

From our discussion above, $e^{i(T-t)}$ represents the future value of $1 at interest rate i for $(T–t)$ years. Consider a simple example. Suppose one invests $1 continuously compounded at 10% for one year. What is the future value? In this case, $T = 1$, $t = 0$, and $i = 0.10$. Inserting these numbers into the expression we get

---

[4] Compounding interest continuously is an example of the more general process of exponential growth which can apply to a number of phenomena (e.g., population growth).

[5] The exponential function is transcendental so our value for e (2.71828) is only an approximation. In fact, e has an infinite number of decimal places that do not repeat.

[6] When the interest rate is 100% and compounded hourly on an original principal of $1, the future value is $2.71813 while continuous compounding gives the same number out to 3 decimal places.

$$FV = 1e^{0.10(1-0)}$$
$$= \$1.1052$$

From this example, it is apparent that a cash flow invested for one year at 10% compounded continuously, and one invested at 10.52% compounded annually will produce the same future value. In other words, the effective annual rate (or annual percentage rate) of 10% compounded continuously is 10.52%.

One brief aside is worth mentioning at this point. The preceding example takes a continuously compounded rate and tells us the equivalent simple interest rate. It is also quite easy to reverse the process. That is, given a simple rate, what is the equivalent continuously compounded rate? Since we use the exponential function to move from continuously compounded to simple interest rates, we use its inverse function (i.e., natural logarithmic function) to move in the other direction. Suppose we have a simple rate of 10.52%, what continuously compounded rate will give the same effective interest rate? To compute this, take the natural logarithm of one plus the simple interest rate, $\ln(1.1052) = 0.10$.

The only issue remaining is how to discount cash flows when interest is paid continuously. To do this, we must evaluate the following expression:

$$PV = FV e^{i(t-T)} \tag{A.2}$$

The quantity $(t-T)$ is a negative number and represents the number of years we are discounting the cash flow back in time. Let's rework the previous example: what is the present value of $1.1052 to be received 1 year from today given continuous discounting at 10%? Just like before, $t = 0$, $T = 1$, and $i = 0.10$. Insert these numbers into the equation (A.2)

$$PV = 1.1052\ e^{0.10(0-1)} = 1$$

Two final points should be noted. First, the quantity $e^{-0.10}$ is equal to 0.9048 and represents the present value of $1 discounted back one year given the continuously compounded interest rate of 10%. Second, discounting (or compounding) for more than one period is accomplished merely by increasing T.

Chapter 2

Yield Curve Analysis: Spot Rates and Forward Rates

A bond's yield is a measure of its potential return given certain assumptions about how the future will unfold. The yield curve is the graphical depiction of the relationship between the yield to maturity and term to maturity for bonds that are alike in every other respect except term to maturity. When market participants refer to the "yield curve," they usually mean the U.S. Treasury yield curve. A key function of the Treasury yield curve is to serve as a benchmark for pricing bonds and to determine yields in all other sectors of the debt market (e.g., corporate debt, mortgages, bank loans, etc.) This is also true in bond markets around the world where government securities often serve as benchmark securities for pricing other instruments. The purpose of this chapter is to develop the fundamental tools of yield curve analysis. We will discuss *par rates*, *spot rates*, and *forward rates* — how they are computed, how they are related to each other, and how they are utilized by market participants.

A BOND IS A PACKAGE OF ZERO-COUPON INSTRUMENTS

The traditional approach to valuation is to discount every cash flow of a fixed income security using the same interest or discount rate. The fundamental flaw of this approach is that it views each security as the same package of cash flows. For example, consider a 5-year U.S. Treasury note with a 6% coupon rate. The cash flows per $100 of par value would be 9 payments of $3 every six months and $103 ten 6-month periods from now. The traditional practice would discount every cash flow using the same discount rate regardless of when the cash flows are delivered in time and the shape of the yield curve. Finance theory tells us that any security should be thought of as a package or portfolio of zero-coupon bonds.[1]

The proper way to view the 5-year 6% coupon Treasury note is as a package of zero-coupon instruments whose maturity value is the amount of the cash flow and whose maturity date coincides with the date the cash flow is to be received. Thus, the 5-year 6% coupon Treasury issue should be viewed as a package of 10 zero-coupon instruments that mature every six months for the next five years. This approach to valuation does not allow a market participant to realize an arbi-

---

[1] Moreover, as explained in later chapters a complex security is a package of zero-coupon bonds with at least one option attached.

trage profit by breaking apart or "stripping" a bond and selling the individual cash flows (i.e., stripped securities) at a higher aggregate value than it would cost to purchase the security in the market. Simply put, arbitrage profits are possible when the sum of the parts is worth more than the whole or vice versa. We will describe the process of stripping Treasuries shortly. Because this approach to valuation precludes arbitrage profits, we refer to it as the *arbitrage-free valuation approach*.

By viewing any security as a package of zero-coupon bonds, a consistent valuation framework can be developed. We do this in Chapter 4. Viewing a security as a package of zero-coupon bonds means that two bonds with the same maturity and different coupon rates are viewed as different packages of zero-coupon bonds and valued accordingly. Moreover, two cash flows that have identical risk delivered at the same time will be valued using the same discount rate even though they are attached to two different bonds.

To implement the arbitrage-free approach it is necessary to determine the theoretical rate that the U.S. Treasury would have to pay on a zero-coupon Treasury security for each maturity. We say "theoretical" because other than U.S. Treasury bills, the Treasury does not issue zero-coupon bonds. Zero-coupon Treasuries are, however, created by dealer firms. The name given to the zero-coupon Treasury rate is the *Treasury spot rate*. Our next task is to explain how the Treasury spot rate can be calculated.

THEORETICAL SPOT RATES

The theoretical spot rates for Treasury securities represent the appropriate set of interest or discount rates that should be used to value default-free cash flows. A default-free theoretical spot rate can be constructed from the observed Treasury yield curve or *par curve*. We will begin our quest of how to estimate spot rates with the par curve.

Par Rates

The raw material for all yield curve analysis is the set of yields on the most recently issued (i.e., on-the-run) Treasury securities. The U.S. Treasury routinely issues seven securities — the 3-month, 6-month and 1-year bills, the 2-, 5-, and 10-year notes, and the 30-year bond.[2] These on-the-run Treasury issues are default risk-free and trade in one of the most liquid and efficient secondary markets in the world. Because of these characteristics, Treasury yields serve as a reference benchmark for risk-free rates which are used extensively for pricing other securities.

Exhibit 1 presents the PX1 Governments screen from Bloomberg. Data for the most recently issued bills and when-issued bills appears in the upper left-hand corner. Similarly, data for the most recently issued and when-issued notes and bonds appear in the lower left-hand corner and continues in the upper right-

---

[2] The Treasury also issues Treasury inflation-protected securities (TIPS).

hand corner. The first and second columns indicate the security and its maturity date. In the third column, there is an arrow indicating an up or down tick for the last trade. The fourth column indicates the current bid/ask rates for the bills and the current bid/ask prices for the notes/bonds. A bond equivalent yield using the ask yield/price is contained in column (5). For bills, the last column contains the change in bank discount yields based on the previous day's closing rates as of the time posted. For notes/bonds, the last column contains the change in change in price in "ticks" (i.e., $32nd$ of a point) based on the previous day's closing prices as of the time posted. The plus sign "+" following the number of ticks indicates that a $64th$ (½ of a $32nd$) is added to the number of ticks.

In practice, however, the observed yields for the on-the-run Treasury coupon issues are not usually used directly. Instead, the coupon rate is adjusted so that the price of the issue would be the par value.[3] Accordingly, the par yield curve is the adjusted on-the-run Treasury yield curve where coupon issues are at par value and the coupon rate is therefore equal to the yield to maturity. The exception is for the 6-month and 1-year issues that are Treasury bills; the bond-equivalent yields for these two issues are already spot rates.

Exhibit 1: Bloomberg PX1 Screen

```
<HELP> for explanation, <MENU> for similar functions.      P060 Govt   PX1
Hit PAGE FWD for off-the-run Bills, Notes, and Bonds.
14:33              CURRENTS/WHEN  ISSUED        Bloomberg
        TREASURY BILLS                                        GENERIC
1)3Mo   8/03/00 ↓   5.79/78   5.96  +.05  17) 5¼   2/29   ↓ 85-04 /06   6.38 - 16+
2)WIB   8/10/00 ↓   5.88/86   6.05  +.05  18) 6⅛   8/29   ↓ 97-06+/08+  6.33 - 16+
3)6Mo  11/02/00 ↓   6.02/ 1   6.28  +.07  19) 6¼   5/30 30yr↓100-25 /26  6.19 - 16
4)WIB  11/09/00 ↓   6.08/ 6   6.36  +.09
5)1Yr   3/01/01 ↓   5.92/91   6.22  +.07  20)TII  5 YR    ↓ 99-17 /19   3.82 - 07+
        NOTES/BONDS                       21)TII 10 YR    ↓101-13 /15   4.06 - 16+
6) 6½   2/02  ↓ 99-11+/13+  6.84 - 04     22)TII 30 YR    ↓ 99-00 /02   3.93 - 30+
7) 6½   3/02  ↓ 99-11 /13   6.83 - 04
8) 6⅜   4/02 2yr↓ 99-05+/06  6.82 - 04            OTHER MARKETS
                                          23)US Long(CBT) 14:33 ↓  93-20   - 06
9) 5¼   5/04  ↑ 94-22+/24+  6.76 - 08+     24)10Y Fut(CBT) 14:33 ↓  95-09   - 09
10) 6   8/04  ↓ 97-05 /07   6.76 - 10      25)5Yr Fut(CBT) 14:25 ↑  96-29   - 06+
11) 5⅞ 11/04 5yr↓ 96-18 /18+ 6.77 - 10+    26)EURO$ (IMM)  14:28 ↓  92.765  -.050
12) WI  5 YR    ↑    6.74/72  99.08 +7.50   27)Fed Funds    14:16 ↓   5.9375  -.1250
                                          28)S&P 500 Ind  14:33 ↓ 1433.65 +24.08
13) 5½   5/09  ↓ 92-14 /16   6.62 - 16     29)NASDAQ Comp  14:33 ↑ 3810.03 +89.79
14) 6    8/09  ↓ 95-27+/29+  6.59 - 16+    30)DowJones Ind 14:33 ↑ 10575.99 +163.50
15) 6½   2/10 10yr↓ 99-29 /30 6.51 - 19     31)Gold (CMX)   14:32 ↑  280.40   -.80
16) WI 10 YR    ↑    6.52/51  99.90 +8.00   32)Crude Oil    14:33 ↓   27.08   +.10
Copyright 2000 BLOOMBERG L.P.  Frankfurt:69-920410  Hong Kong:2-977-6000  London:171-330-7500  New York:212-318-2000
Princeton:609-279-3000    Singapore:226-3000    Sydney:2-9777-8686    Tokyo:3-3201-8900    Sao Paulo:11-3048-4500
                                                                    I457-293-1 05-May-00 14:33:40
```

Source: Bloomberg

---

[3] The reason for this adjustment is that the observed price and yield may reflect cheap repo financing available from an issue if it is "on special."

Exhibit 2: Bloomberg Par Curve

<HELP> for explanation, <MENU> for similar functions.   P060 Govt   **C4**

13:21   **CURRENT MARKET** (BLOOMBERG GENERIC)

		CURRENT SECURITIES (*)			WHEN ISSUED SECURITIES (W)		
3 Mo	8/ 3/00	5.79	5.78	5.96	8/10/00	5.91	5.89
6 Mo	11/ 2/00	6.02	6.01	6.28	11/ 9/00	6.08	6.06
1 Yr	3/ 1/01	5.93	5.92	6.24			
2 Yr	6³⁄₈ 4/02	99-05+	99-06	6.82			
5 Yr	5⁷⁄₈ 11/04	96-18	96-18+	6.77	6¹⁄₂ 5/05	6.74	6.72
10Yr	6¹⁄₂ 2/10	99-29	99-30	6.51	6¹⁄₂ 2/10	6.52	6.51
30Yr	6¹⁄₄ 5/30	100-27	100-28	6.18			

Copyright 2000 BLOOMBERG L.P.   Frankfurt:69-920410   Hong Kong:2-977-6000   London:171-330-7500   New York:212-318-2000
Princeton:609-279-3000   Singapore:226-3000   Sydney:2-9777-8686   Tokyo:3-3201-8900   Sao Paulo:11-3048-4500
                                                                                 1457-293-1 05-May-00 13:21:57

Bloomberg

Source: Bloomberg

Deriving a par curve from a set of six points starting with the yield on the 6-month bill and ending the yield on the 30-year bond is not a trivial matter. The end result is a curve that tells us "if the Treasury were to issue a security today with a maturity equal to say 12 years, what coupon rate would the security have to pay in order to sell at par?" Exhibit 2 presents a Bloomberg screen of the par curve (linearly interpolated) using the yields for the seven on-the-run Treasuries (function C4 <Govt>) for May 5, 2000. The fifth column contains the yields on a bond equivalent basis used to construct the curve.

Some analysts contend that estimating the par curve with only the yields of the on-the-run Treasuries uses too little information that is available from the market. In particular, one must estimate the back-end of the yield curve with only two securities i.e., the 10-year note and the 30-year bond. Some analysts prefer to use the on-the-run Treasuries and selected off-the-run Treasuries. For example, Bloomberg allows the user to estimate a Treasury par curve using on-the-run Treasuries plus selected off-the-run issues grouped by their coupon levels. Currently, the groups are (1) coupons less than 6%; (2) coupons between 6% and 6.625%; (3) coupons between 6.75% and 10.875%, and (4) coupons greater than 10.875%. Exhibit 3 presents a plot from Bloomberg of the Treasury par curves estimated using these four different ways for May 5, 2000. Exhibit 4 presents the actual yields used to construct these four curves. Note that while these yields are typically within a few basis points of each other, some differ by more than 30 basis points.

Exhibit 3: Treasury Par Curves Using Off-the-Run Treasuries

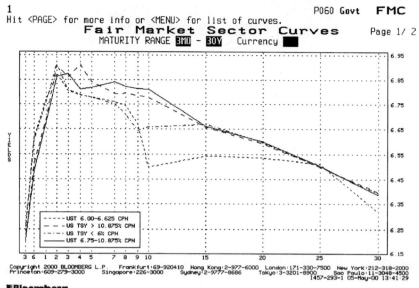

Source: Bloomberg

Exhibit 4: Four Treasury Par Curves

Curve	B1 +	B2 +	B3 +	BB +		
Title	UST 6.75-10.875% CPN	US TSY < 6% CPN	US TSY > 10.875% CPN	UST 6.00-6.625 CPN		
3MO	6.21	6.26	6.20	6.24		
6MO	6.49	6.61	6.51	6.62		
1YR	6.68	6.76	6.69	6.77		
2YR	6.86	6.90	6.90	6.87		
3YR	6.87	6.81	6.86	6.81		
4YR	6.81	6.79	6.91	6.79		
5YR	6.82	6.78	6.84	6.78		
7YR	6.84	6.75	6.80	6.76		
8YR	6.82	6.71	6.80	6.75		
9YR	6.81	6.65	6.79	6.67		
10YR	6.81	6.66	6.78	6.50		
15YR	6.67	6.67	6.66	6.55		
20YR	6.60	6.60	6.59	6.54		
25YR	6.51	6.50	6.50	6.51		
30YR	6.39	6.39	6.40	6.32		

+ indicates curve floats intraday with benchmark curve

Source: Bloomberg

Exhibit 5: Hypothetical Treasury Par Yield Curve

Period	Years	Annual Yield to Maturity (BEY) (%)[*]	Price	Spot Rate (BEY) (%)[*]
1	0.5	3.00	—	3.0000
2	1.0	3.30	—	3.3000
3	1.5	3.50	100.00	3.5053
4	2.0	3.90	100.00	3.9164
5	2.5	4.40	100.00	4.4376
6	3.0	4.70	100.00	4.7520
7	3.5	4.90	100.00	4.9622
8	4.0	5.00	100.00	5.0650
9	4.5	5.10	100.00	5.1701
10	5.0	5.20	100.00	5.2772
11	5.5	5.30	100.00	5.3864
12	6.0	5.40	100.00	5.4976
13	6.5	5.50	100.00	5.6108
14	7.0	5.55	100.00	5.6643
15	7.5	5.60	100.00	5.7193
16	8.0	5.65	100.00	5.7755
17	8.5	5.70	100.00	5.8331
18	9.0	5.80	100.00	5.9584
19	9.5	5.90	100.00	6.0863
20	10.0	6.00	100.00	6.2169

* The yield to maturity and the spot rate are annual rates. They are reported as bond-equivalent yields. To obtain the semiannual yield or rate, one half the annual yield or annual rate is used.

In summary, a par rate is the average discount rate of many cash flows (those of a par bond) over many periods. This begs the question "the average of what?" As we will see, par rates are complicated averages of the implied spot rates. Thus, in order to uncover the spot rates, we must find a method to "break apart" the par rates. There are several approaches that are used in practice. The approach that we describe below for creating a theoretical spot rate curve is called *bootstrapping.*

Bootstrapping the Spot Curve

Bootstrapping begins with the par curve. To illustrate bootstrapping, we will use the Treasury par curve shown in Exhibit 5. The par yield curve shown extends only out to 10 years. Our objective is to show how the values in the last column of the exhibit (labeled "Spot Rate") are obtained. Throughout the analysis and illustrations to come, it is important to remember the basic principle is that the value of the Treasury coupon security should be equal to the value of the package of zero-coupon Treasury securities that duplicates the coupon bond's cash flows.

The key to this process is the existence of the Treasury strips market. ("STRIPS" is the most common type of strips product and is an acronym for *se*parately *t*raded, *r*egistered *i*nterest and *p*rincipal *se*curities.) A government securities dealer has the ability to take apart the cash flows of a Treasury coupon security (i.e., strip the security) and create zero-coupon securities. These zero-coupon securities, which are called *Treasury strips*, can be sold to investors. (The Treasury strips created from the coupon payments are called *coupon strips*; the Treasury strip created from the principal payment is called the *principal strip*.) At what interest rate or yield can these Treasury strips be sold to investors? The answer is they can be sold at the Treasury spot rates. If the market price of a Treasury security is less than its value after discounting with spot rates (i.e., the sum of the parts is worth more than the whole), than a dealer can buy the Treasury security, strip it, and sell off the Treasury strips so as to generate greater proceeds than the cost of purchasing the Treasury security. The resulting profit is an arbitrage profit.

We now ask what happens when a Treasury issue's market price is greater than its value when discounted using spot rates? In this case, the sum of the parts is worth less than the whole. Obviously, a dealer will refrain from stripping the Treasury issue since the proceeds generated from doing so will be less than the cost of purchasing the issue. When such situations occur, the dealer will follow a procedure called *reconstitution*.[4] Basically, the dealer can purchase a package of Treasury strips so as to create a synthetic Treasury coupon security that is cheaper than the same maturity and same coupon Treasury issue. This difference represents an arbitrage profit.

In summary, the process of stripping and reconstitution assures that the price of a Treasury issue will not depart materially from its arbitrage-free value. This is simply a fundamental market principle at work. Namely, prices adjust until there are no opportunities to make arbitrage profits. In other countries, as more and more governments permit the stripping and reconstitution of their issues, the value of non-U.S. government issues has also moved toward their arbitrage-free value. Strips of German and French government bonds have been available for several years while U.K. gilt strips began trading on December 1997 followed by Spanish and Italian government strips in 1998. Exhibits 6 through 9 presents four Bloomberg screens (function IYC1) that depict the strips curves on May 9, 2000 for the following countries: United States, Germany, Spain, and the United Kingdom.

Before we proceed to our illustration of bootstrapping, a very sensible question must be addressed. Specifically, if Treasury strips are in effect zero-coupon Treasury securities, why not use strip rates (i.e., the rates on Treasury strips) as our spot rates? In other words, why must we estimate theoretical spot rates via bootstrapping using yields from Treasury bills, notes, and bonds when we already have strip rates conveniently available? There are three major reasons. First, although Treasury strips are actively traded, they are not as liquid as on-the-run

---

[4] To analyze the profit/loss potential of these transactions, see, for example, Bloomberg's Strip/Reconstruction Analysis function (SPRC <Govt>).

Treasury bills, notes, and bonds. As a result, Treasury strips have some liquidity risk for which investors will demand some compensation in the form of higher yields. Second, the tax treatment of strips is different from that of Treasury coupon securities. Specifically, the accrued interest on strips is taxed even though no cash is received by the investor. Thus they are negative cash flow securities to taxable entities, and, as a result, their yield reflects this tax disadvantage. Finally, there are maturity sectors where non-U.S. investors find it advantageous to trade off yield for tax advantages associated with a strip. Specifically, certain non-U.S. tax authorities allow their citizens to treat the difference between the maturity value and the purchase price as a capital gain and tax this gain at a favorable tax rate. Some will grant this favorable treatment only when the strip is created from the principal rather than the coupon. For this reason, those who use Treasury strips to represent theoretical spot rates restrict the issues included to coupon strips.

Exhibit 10 is a Bloomberg screen (function STR4 <Govt>) that displays the U.S. Treasury strips curve versus the implied spot curve derived from the Treasury par curve in the top graph from May 5, 2000. Yields are on the vertical axis and maturity is on the horizontal axis. The bottom graph plots the spread between the Treasury strip rates (vertical axis) against the maturity (horizontal axis).

Exhibit 6: U.S. Treasury Strips Curve

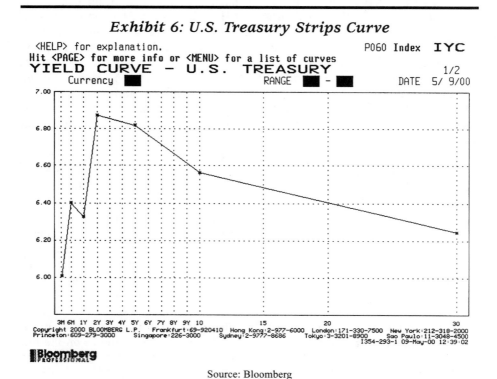

Source: Bloomberg

Exhibit 7: German Strips Curve

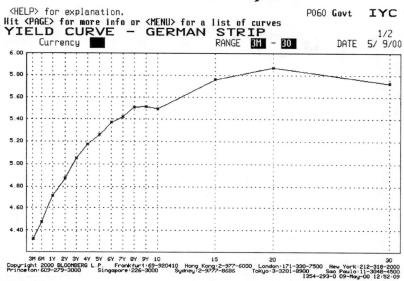

Source: Bloomberg

Exhibit 8: Spanish Strips Curve

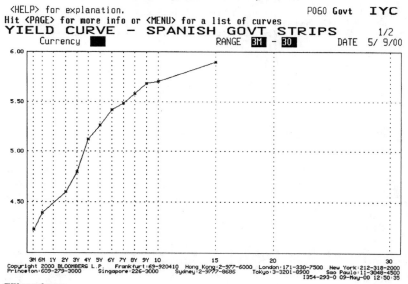

Source: Bloomberg

Exhibit 9: U.K. Strips Curve

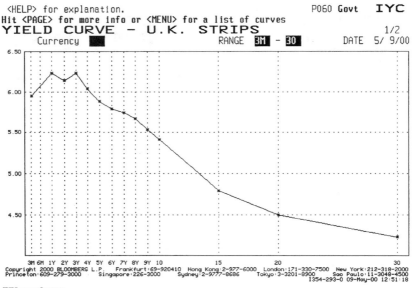

Source: Bloomberg

Exhibit 10: Strips Curve versus Implied Spot Curve

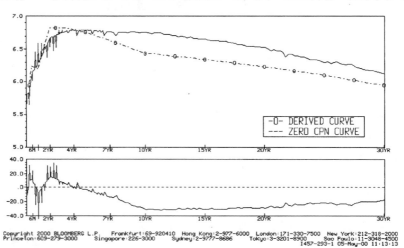

Source: Bloomberg

Consider the 6-month and 1-year Treasury securities in Exhibit 5. These two securities are Treasury bills and they are issued as zero-coupon instruments. Therefore, the annualized bond-equivalent yield (not the bank discount yield) of 3.00% for the 6-month Treasury security is equal to the 6-month spot rate. Similarly, for the 1-year Treasury security, the cited yield of 3.30% is the 1-year spot rate. Given these two spot rates, we can compute the spot rate for a theoretical 1.5-year zero-coupon Treasury. The value of a theoretical 1.5-year Treasury should equal the present value of the three cash flows from the 1.5-year coupon Treasury, where the yield used for discounting is the spot rate corresponding to the time of receipt of the cash flow. Since all the coupon bonds are selling at par, as explained in the previous section, the yield to maturity for each bond is the coupon rate. Using $100 as par, the cash flows for the 1.5-year coupon Treasury are:

$$
\begin{array}{llll}
0.5 \text{ year} & 0.035 \times \$100 \times 0.5 & = \$ & 1.75 \\
1.0 \text{ year} & 0.035 \times \$100 \times 0.5 & = \$ & 1.75 \\
1.5 \text{ years} & 0.035 \times \$100 \times 0.5 + 100 & = \$ & 101.75
\end{array}
$$

The present value of the cash flows is then:

$$
\frac{1.75}{(1+z_1)^1} + \frac{1.75}{(1+z_2)^2} + \frac{101.75}{(1+z_3)^3}
$$

where

$$
\begin{aligned}
z_1 &= \text{one-half the annualized 6-month theoretical spot rate} \\
z_2 &= \text{one-half the 1-year theoretical spot rate} \\
z_3 &= \text{one-half the 1.5-year theoretical spot rate}
\end{aligned}
$$

Since the 6-month spot rate is 3% and the 1-year spot rate is 3.30%, we know that:

$$
z_1 = 0.0150 \text{ and } z_2 = 0.0165
$$

We can compute the present value of the 1.5-year coupon Treasury security as:

$$
\frac{1.75}{(1+z_1)^1} + \frac{1.75}{(1+z_2)^2} + \frac{101.75}{(1+z_3)^3} = \frac{1.75}{(1.015)^1} + \frac{1.75}{(1.0165)^2} + \frac{101.75}{(1+z_3)^3}
$$

Since the price of the 1.5-year coupon Treasury security is equal to its par value (see Exhibit 5), the following relationship must hold:[5]

$$
\frac{1.75}{(1.015)^1} + \frac{1.75}{(1.0165)^2} + \frac{101.75}{(1+z_3)^3} = 100
$$

---

[5] If we had not been working with a par yield curve, the equation would have been set to the market price for the 1.5-year issue rather than par value.

Note we are treating the 1.5 year par bond as if it were a portfolio of three zero-coupon bonds. Moreover, each cash flow has its own discount rate that depends on when the cash flow is delivered in the future and the shape of the yield curve. This is in sharp contrast to the traditional valuation approach that forces each cash flow to have the same discount rate.

We can solve for the theoretical 1.5-year spot rate as follows:

$$1.7241 + 1.6936 + \frac{101.75}{(1+z_3)^3} = 100$$

$$\frac{101.75}{(1+z_3)^3} = 96.5822$$

$$(1+z_3)^3 = \frac{101.75}{96.5822}$$

$$(1+z_3)^3 = 1.05351$$

$$z_3 = 0.017527 = 1.7527\%$$

Doubling this yield we obtain the bond-equivalent yield of 3.5053%, which is the theoretical 1.5-year spot rate. This is the rate that the market would apply to a 1.5-year zero-coupon Treasury security if, in fact, such a security existed. In other words, all Treasury cash flows to be received 1.5 years from now should be valued (i.e., discounted) at 3.5053%.

Given the theoretical 1.5-year spot rate, we can obtain the theoretical 2-year spot rate. The cash flows for the 2-year coupon Treasury in Exhibit 5 are:

0.5 year	$0.039 \times \$100 \times 0.5$	= \$ 1.95
1.0 year	$0.039 \times \$100 \times 0.5$	= \$ 1.95
1.5 years	$0.039 \times \$100 \times 0.5$	= \$ 1.95
2.0 years	$0.039 \times \$100 \times 0.5 + 100$	= \$101.95

The present value of the cash flows is then:

$$\frac{1.95}{(1+z_1)^1} + \frac{1.95}{(1+z_2)^2} + \frac{1.95}{(1+z_3)^3} + \frac{101.95}{(1+z_4)^4}$$

where z_4 = one-half of the 2-year theoretical spot rate.

Since the 6-month spot rate, 1-year spot rate, and 1.5-year spot rate are 3.00%, 3.30%, and 3.5053%, respectively, then:

$$z_1 = 0.0150 \quad z_2 = 0.0165 \quad z_3 = 0.017527$$

Therefore, the present value of the 2-year coupon Treasury security is:

$$\frac{1.95}{(1.0150)^1} + \frac{1.95}{(1.0165)^2} + \frac{1.95}{(1.017527)^3} + \frac{101.95}{(1 + z_4)^4}$$

Since the price of the 2-year coupon Treasury security is equal to par, the following relationship must hold:

$$\frac{1.95}{(1.0150)^1} + \frac{1.95}{(1.0165)^2} + \frac{1.95}{(1.017527)^3} + \frac{101.95}{(1 + z_4)^4} = 100$$

We can solve for the theoretical 2-year spot rate as follows:

$$\frac{101.95}{(1 + z_4)^4} = 94.3407$$

$$(1 + z_4)^4 = \frac{101.95}{94.3407}$$

$$z_4 = 0.019582 = 1.9582\%$$

Doubling this yield, we obtain the theoretical 2-year spot rate bond-equivalent yield of 3.9164%.

One can follow this approach sequentially to derive the theoretical 2.5-year spot rate from the calculated values of z_1, z_2, z_3, and z_4 (the 6-month-, 1-year-, 1.5-year-, and 2-year rates), and the price and coupon of the 2.5-year bond in Exhibit 5. Further, one could derive theoretical spot rates for the remaining 15 half-yearly rates. The spot rates thus obtained are shown in the last column of Exhibit 5. They represent the term structure of default-free spot rate for maturities up to 10 years at the particular time to which the bond price quotations refer.

Let us summarize to this point. We started with the par curve which is constructed using the adjusted yields from the on-the-run Treasuries. A par rate is the average discount rate of many cash flows over many periods. Specifically, par rates are complicated averages of spot rates. The spot rates are uncovered from par rates via bootstrapping. A spot rate is the average discount rate of a single cash flow over many periods. It appears that spot rates are also averages. As we will see shortly, spot rates are averages of one or more forward rates.

Exhibit 11 plots the par and spot curves using the data presented in Exhibit 5. If the par curve is upward sloping (monotonically), the spot curve will be above the par curve at every point except for the shortest interest rate (e.g., 6-month rate in our illustration) and the difference between the curves will increase as maturity increases. The reason is simple. Par rates are complicated averages of spot rates and averaging dampens volatility. Thus, the par curve will always be the flatter of the two curves. The exception to this is when the yield curve is perfectly flat and the two curves are identical. If the par curve is inverted, the ordering of the two curves is reversed with the par curve being the flatter of the two plotting above the spot curve.

Exhibit 11: Spot Curve versus Par Curve

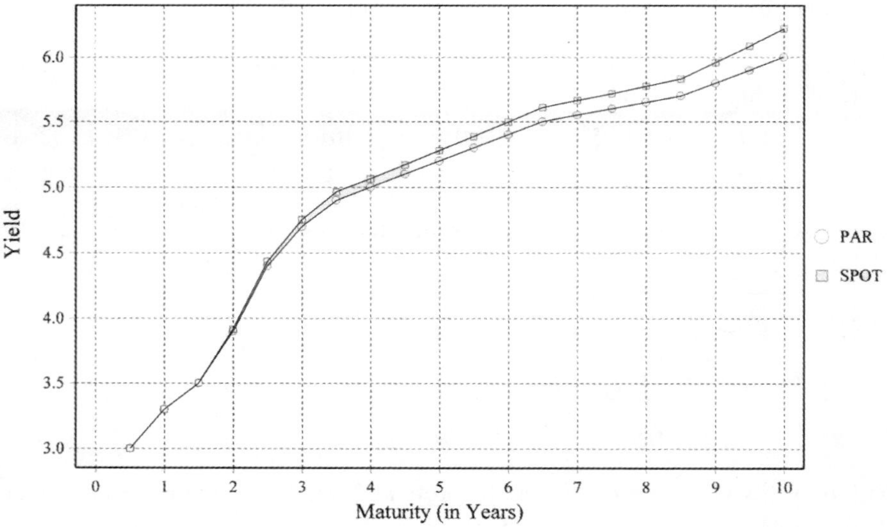

Source: Bloomberg

FORWARD RATES

We have just described how a default-free theoretical spot rate curve can be extrapolated from the Treasury yield curve. Additional information useful to market participants can be extrapolated from the default-free theoretical spot rate curve: forward rates. A forward rate is the fundamental unit of yield curve analysis. Forward rates are the building blocks of interest rates just as atoms are building blocks of solid matter in physics. A forward rate is the discount rate of a single cash flow over a single period. Under certain assumptions, these rates can be viewed as the market's consensus of future interest rates.[6]

Examples of forward rates that can be calculated from the default-free theoretical spot rate curve are the:

- 6-month forward rate six months from now
- 6-month forward rate three years from now
- 1-year forward rate one year from now
- 3-year forward rate two years from now
- 5-year forward rates three years from now

---

[6] See, Antti Illmanen, "Market's Rate Expectations and Forward Rates," Part 2, *Understanding the Yield Curve* (New York: Salomon Brothers, 1995).

Since the forward rates are implicitly extrapolated from the default-free theoretical spot rate curve, these rates are sometimes referred to as *implicit forward rates*. Recall, spot rates are averages of implied forward rates so it should not be surprising that we "break apart" spot rates to uncover forward rates. We begin by showing how to compute the 6-month forward rates. Then we explain how to compute any forward rate between any two periods in the future.

Deriving 6-Month Forward Rates

To illustrate the process of extrapolating 6-month forward rates, we will use the yield curve and the corresponding spot rate curve from Exhibit 5. We will use a very simple no arbitrage principle as we did earlier in this chapter when deriving the spot rates. Namely, the "law of one price" says that if two goods are perfect substitutes they must sell for the same price. Specifically, if two investments produce the same expected cash flows and have the same risk, they should have the same value.

Suppose an investor has a 1-year anticipated investment horizon. In general, an investor has three basic ways to satisfy this maturity preference. First, an investor can purchase a security having a maturity that matches the investment horizon. For example, an investor can buy a 1-year zero coupon bond and hold it to maturity. We will call this a "buy and hold" strategy. Second, an investor can invest in a series of short-term securities (e.g., buy a 6-month zero-coupon bond today, hold it to maturity, and reinvest the proceeds into another 6-month zero-coupon bond six months from now.) We will call this a "rollover" strategy. Finally, an investor can invest in a security with a maturity greater than the anticipated holding period and sell it at the appropriate time (e.g., buy a 2-year zero coupon bond and selling it after one year). If the yield curve is upward-sloping, this strategy is called "riding the yield curve."

For simplicity, let's consider an investor who has a 1-year investment horizon and is faced with the following two alternatives (we will return to the riding the yield curve strategy shortly):

- buy a 1-year Treasury bill (buy-and-hold strategy), or
- buy a 6-month Treasury bill, and when it matures in six months buy another 6-month Treasury bill (rollover strategy).

The investor will be indifferent between the two alternatives if they produce the same expected return over the 1-year investment horizon. The investor knows the spot rates that are available on the 6-month Treasury bill and the 1-year Treasury bill. However, she does not know what yield will be available on a 6-month Treasury bill that will be purchased six months from now (i.e., the second leg of the rollover strategy). That is, she does not know the 6-month forward rate six months from now. Given the spot rates for the 6-month Treasury bill and the 1-year Treasury bill, the forward rate on a 6-month Treasury bill is the rate that equalizes the expected dollar return between the two alternatives.

Exhibit 12: Graphical Depiction of the Six-Month Forward Rate Six Months from Now

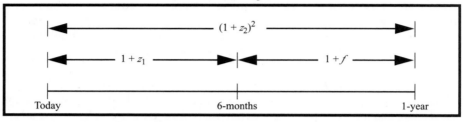

To see how that rate can be determined, suppose that an investor purchased a 6-month Treasury bill for \$$X$. At the end of six months, the value of this investment would be:

$$X(1 + z_1)$$

where z_1 is one-half the bond-equivalent yield (BEY) of the theoretical 6-month spot rate. Intuitively, this product tells us how much money the investor will have available to reinvest in the second 6-month bill, six months from now.

Let f represent one-half the forward rate (expressed as a BEY) on a 6-month Treasury bill available six months from now. If the investor were to roll-over her investment by purchasing that bill at that time, then the future dollars available at the end of one year from the \$$X$ investment would be:

$$X(1 + z_1)(1 + f)$$

Note we cannot calculate this expression because we do not know f as of yet.

Now consider the buy-and-hold strategy. Namely, buying the 1-year Treasury bill and maturing it. If we let z_2 represent one-half the BEY of the theoretical 1-year spot rate, then the future dollars available at the end of one year from the \$$X$ investment would be:

$$X(1 + z_2)^2$$

The reason that the squared term appears is that the amount invested is being compounded for two periods at one-half the 1-year spot rate due to semiannual compounding.

The two choices are depicted in Exhibit 12. Now we are prepared to analyze the investor's choices and what this tells us about forward rates. The investor will be indifferent between the two alternatives confronting her if she makes the same dollar investment (\$$X$) and expects to receive the same future dollars from both alternatives at the end of one year. That is, the investor will be indifferent if:

$$X(1 + z_1)(1 + f) = X(1 + z_2)^2$$

Dividing both sides by X (the initial investment) leaves the following:

$$(1 + z_1)(1 + f) = (1 + z_2)^2$$

We can interpret the left-side of this expression as the expected holding-period return of the rollover strategy. Likewise, the right-hand side is the expected holding-period return of the buy-and-hold strategy. Given z_1 and z_2 are known, what does f have to be six months hence for these two strategies to have the same holding-period returns? In simple words, f is the value that makes the right side equal the left side. Note this result is courtesy of the no-arbitrage condition. Solving for f, we get:

$$f = \frac{(1 + z_2)^2}{(1 + z_1)} - 1$$

Doubling f gives the BEY for the 6-month forward rate six months from now.

We can illustrate the use of this formula with the theoretical spot rates shown in Exhibit 5. From that exhibit, we know that:

6-month bill spot rate = 0.030, therefore $z_1 = 0.0150$
1-year bill spot rate = 0.033, therefore $z_2 = 0.0165$

Substituting into the formula, we have:

$$f = \frac{(1.0165)^2}{(1.0150)} - 1 = 0.0180 = 1.8\%$$

Therefore, the 6-month forward rate six months from now is 3.6% (1.8% × 2) BEY.

Let's confirm our results. If X is invested in the 6-month Treasury bill at 1.5% and the proceeds then reinvested for six months at the 6-month forward rate of 1.8%, the total proceeds from this alternative would be:

$$X(1.015)(1.018) = 1.03327\ X$$

Investment of X in the 1-year Treasury bill at one-half the 1-year rate, 1.65%, would produce the following proceeds at the end of one year:

$$X(1.0165)^2 = 1.03327\ X$$

Both alternatives deliver the same payoff if the 6-month Treasury bill yield six months from now is 1.8% (3.6% on a BEY). This means that, if an investor is guaranteed a 1.8% yield (3.6% BEY) on a 6-month Treasury bill six months from now, she will be indifferent between the two alternatives.

It is quite helpful to think of forward rates as break-even rates. In our example, the yield curve is upward-sloping. As a result, an investor picks up additional yield by investing in the 1-year bill rather than the 6-month bill. The 6-month forward rate tells us how much the 6-month spot rate must rise six months from now so that an investor buying the 6-month bill and intending to rollover the proceeds into another 6-month bill will earn the same 1-year holding-period return. Obviously, the 6-month spot needs to rise over the next six months to offset the 1-year bill's yield advantage. As we have seen, if the 6-month spot rate is 3.6% six months from now, an investor will be indifferent between the two strategies. Simply put, forward rates tell us how much the spot curve needs to change over the next period so that all Treasury securities earn the same holding-period return.

Forward rates can also be interpreted as equating the holding period return of buying and holding a 6-month bill and the holding period return of buying a 1-year bill and selling it after six months. As noted, the latter strategy is known as "riding the yield curve." In our example, since the yield curve is upward sloping and *if it does not change* over the next six months, the 1-year bill will earn a higher return because of the increase in price due to the decrease in yield relative to the forecast at which it is priced. Accordingly, investors will earn an additional return. The forward rate tells us how much the 6-month spot rate must rise over the next six months to offset this additional return.

For example, suppose an investor purchases a 1-year bill with a maturity value of $100 currently yielding 3.3% on a bond-equivalent basis. The 1-year bill's price would be $96.7799. Further, suppose the investor sells the bill after six months. If the 6-month spot rate rises to 3.6%, the 1-year bill (which now has six months until maturity) is priced at $98.2318. If this occurs, the investor's holding-period return is 1.5% (3% BEY). Note that this is same return the investor would have obtained by buying and holding the 6-month bill. Thus, buying and holding the 6-month bill and riding the yield curve for six months with the 1-year bill will have the same holding period return over the next six months. In summary, if changes in spot rates implied by the forward rates are subsequently realized, all three strategies (i.e., buy and hold, rollover, and riding the yield curve) will earn the same holding-period return.

The same line of reasoning can be used to obtain the 6-month forward rate beginning at any time period in the future. For example, the following can be determined:

- the 6-month forward rate three years from now
- the 6-month forward rate five years from now

The notation that we use to indicate 6-month forward rates is $_1f_m$ where the subscript 1 indicates a 1-period (six months in our illustration) rate and the subscript m indicates the period beginning m periods from now. When m is equal to zero, this means the current rate. Thus, the first 6-month forward rate is simply the current 6-month spot rate. That is, $_1f_0 = z_1$.

The general formula for determining a 6-month forward rate is:

$$_1f_m = \frac{(1 + z_{m+1})^{m+1}}{(1 + z_m)^m} - 1$$

This expression tells us if the $m + 1$-period and m-period spot rates are known, the 1-period forward rate between periods m and $m+1$ is computed by dividing $m+1$-period zero-coupon bond's holding-period return by the m-period zero-coupon bond's holding-period return.

For example, suppose that the 6-month forward rate four years (eight 6-month periods) from now is sought. In terms of our notation, m is 8 and we seek $_1f_8$. The formula is then:

$$_1f_8 = \frac{(1 + z_9)^9}{(1 + z_8)^8} - 1$$

From Exhibit 5, since the 4-year spot rate is 5.065% and the 4.5-year spot rate is 5.1701%, z_8 is 2.5325% and z_9 is 2.58505%. Then,

$$_1f_8 = \frac{(1.0258505)^9}{(1.025325)^8} - 1 = 3.0064\%$$

Doubling this rate gives a 6-month forward rate four years from now of 6.01%

Exhibit 13 shows all of the 6-month forward rates for the Treasury yield curve and corresponding spot rate curve shown in Exhibit 5. The forward rates reported in Exhibit 13 are the annualized rates on a bond-equivalent basis. The set of these forward rates is called the *short-term forward-rate curve*.

Relationship between Spot Rates and Short-Term Forward Rates

Suppose an investor invests $\$X$ in a 3-year zero-coupon Treasury security. The total proceeds three years (six periods) from now would be:

$$X(1 + z_6)^6$$

Alternatively, the investor could buy a 6-month Treasury bill and reinvest the proceeds every six months for three years. The future dollars or dollar return will depend on the 6-month forward rates. Suppose that the investor can actually reinvest the proceeds maturing every six months at the calculated 6-month forward rates shown in Exhibit 13. At the end of three years, an investment of $\$X$ would generate the following proceeds:

$$X(1 + z_1)(1 + {_1f_1})(1 + {_1f_2})(1 + {_1f_3})(1 + {_1f_4})(1 + {_1f_5})$$

Since the two investments must generate the same proceeds at the end of three years, the two previous equations are set equal to one another:

$$X(1 + z_6)^6 = X(1 + z_1)(1 + {_1f_1})(1 + {_1f_2})(1 + {_1f_3})(1 + {_1f_4})(1 + {_1f_5})$$

Exhibit 13: Six-Month Forward Rates: The Short-Term Forward Rate Curve (Annualized Rates on a Bond-Equivalent Basis)

Notation	Forward Rate
$_1f_0$	3.00
$_1f_1$	3.60
$_1f_2$	3.92
$_1f_3$	5.15
$_1f_4$	6.54
$_1f_5$	6.33
$_1f_6$	6.23
$_1f_7$	5.79
$_1f_8$	6.01
$_1f_9$	6.24
$_1f_{10}$	6.48
$_1f_{11}$	6.72
$_1f_{12}$	6.97
$_1f_{13}$	6.36
$_1f_{14}$	6.49
$_1f_{15}$	6.62
$_1f_{16}$	6.76
$_1f_{17}$	8.10
$_1f_{18}$	8.40
$_1f_{19}$	8.72

Solving for the 3-year (6-period) spot rate, we have:

$$z_6 = [(1 + z_1)(1 + {_1f_1})(1 + {_1f_2})(1 + {_1f_3})(1 + {_1f_4})(1 + {_1f_5})]^{1/6} - 1$$

This equation tells us that the 3-year spot rate depends on the current 6-month spot rate and the five 6-month forward rates. Earlier we described a spot rate as the average discount rate of a single cash flow over many periods. We can see now that long-term spot rates are averages of the current single period spot rate and the implied forward rates. In fact, the right-hand side of this equation is a *geometric* average of the current 6-month spot rate and the five 6-month forward rates.

Let's use the values in Exhibits 5 and 13 to confirm this result. Since the 6-month spot rate in Exhibit 5 is 3%, z_1 is 1.5% and therefore

$$z_6 = [(1.015)(1.018)(1.0196)(1.02577)(1.0327)(1.03165)]^{1/6} - 1$$
$$= 0.023761 = 2.3761\%$$

Doubling this rate gives 4.7522%. This agrees with the 3-year spot rate shown in Exhibit 5.

In general, the relationship between a T-period spot rate, the current 6-month spot rate, and the 6-month forward rates is as follows:

$$z_T = [(1 + z_1)(1 + {}_1f_1)(1 + {}_1f_2) \dots (1 + {}_1f_{T(1)})]^{1/T} - 1$$

Therefore, discounting at the forward rates will give the same present value as discounting at the spot rates. For example, suppose we have a single default-free cash flow to be delivered three years from today. There are two equivalent ways to discount this cash flow back to time zero. First, discount the cash flow back six periods at one-half the 3-year spot rate. Second, discount the cash flow back one period at a time using the appropriate forward rate each period. So, it does not matter whether one discounts cash flows by spot rates or forward rates, the value is the same.

The same principle applies with equal force for coupon-paying bonds. As an illustration of the equivalence of discounting with spot rates and forward rates, suppose a 2-year bond carries a 5% coupon and pays cash flows semiannually. Suppose further the relevant spot rate and forward rate curves used for pricing this bond are presented in Exhibits 5 and 13, respectively. Discounting each of the cash flows using one-half the appropriate spot rates gives us a bond price of $102.1051 (per $100 of par value) as shown below:

$$\frac{2.50}{(1.015)^1} + \frac{2.50}{(1.0165)^2} + \frac{2.50}{(1.0175265)^3} + \frac{102.50}{(1.019582)^4} = 102.1051$$

We will now discount the same cash flows back to the present using the forward rates. Recall, a forward rate is the discount rate of a single cash flow over a single period. Accordingly, if a cash flow is to be delivered two periods in the future, we will discount the cash flow back to the present using two different discount rates. If a cash flow is to be delivered three periods in the future, we will discount the cash flow back to the present using three different discount rates and so forth. Using one-half the first four forward rates in Exhibit 13 to discount the bond's cash flows, we obtain a bond price of $102.1058 (per $100 of par value) as shown below:

$$\frac{2.50}{(1.015)} + \frac{2.50}{(1.015)(1.018)} + \frac{2.50}{(1.015)(1.018)(1.0196)}$$

$$+ \frac{102.50}{(1.015)(1.018)(1.0196)(1.02575)} = 102.1058$$

The two present values (i.e., bond prices) are the same (i.e., within rounding error).

Computing Any Forward Rate

Using spot rates, we can compute any forward rate. Using the same arbitrage arguments as used above to derive the 6-month forward rates, any forward rate can be obtained.

There are two elements to the forward rate. The first is when in the future the rate begins or simply "how far forward?" The second is the length of time for the rate. For example, the 2-year forward rate three years from now means a rate three years from now for a length of two years. The notation used for a forward rate, f, will have two subscripts — one before f and one after f as shown below:

$$_t f_m$$

The subscript before f is t and is the length of time that the rate applies. The subscript after f is m and is when the forward rate begins. That is,

the length of time of the forward rate f when the forward rate begins

Remember our time periods are still 6-month periods. Given the above notation, here is what the following mean:

Notation	Interpretation for the forward rate
$_1 f_{12}$	6-month (1-period) forward rate beginning 6 years (12 periods) from now
$_2 f_8$	1-year (2-period) forward rate beginning 4 years (8 periods) from now
$_6 f_4$	3-year (6-period) forward rate beginning 2 years (4 periods) from now
$_8 f_{10}$	4-year (8-period) forward rate beginning 5 years (10 periods) from now

To see how the formula for the forward rate is derived, consider the following two alternatives for an investor who wants to invest for $m + t$ periods:

- buy a zero-coupon Treasury bond that matures in $m + t$ periods (buy-and-hold strategy), or
- buy a zero-coupon Treasury bond that matures in m periods and invest the proceeds at the maturity date in a zero-coupon Treasury bond that matures in t periods (rollover strategy).

As before, the investor will be indifferent between the two alternatives if they produce the same return over the $m + t$ investment horizon.

For $100 invested in the buy-and-hold alternative, the proceeds for this investment at the horizon date assuming that the semiannual rate is z_{m+t} are

$$\$100(1 + z_{m+t})^{m+t}$$

For the rollover alternative, the proceeds for this investment at the end of m periods assuming that the semiannual rate is z_m are

$$\$100(1 + z_m)^m$$

When the proceeds are received in m periods, they are reinvested at the forward rate, $_t f_m$, producing a value for the investment at the end of $m + t$ periods of

$$\$100(1 + z_m)^m (1 + {}_t f_m)^t$$

Once again, we appeal to the no-arbitrage condition. Namely, for the investor to be indifferent to the two alternatives, the following relationship must hold:

$$\$100(1 + z_{m+t})^{m+t} = \$100(1 + z_m)^m (1 + {}_t f_m)^t$$

Solving for $_tf_m$ we get:

$$_tf_m = \left[\frac{(1 + z_{m+t})^{m+t}}{(1 + z_m)^m}\right]^{1/t} - 1$$

The numerator is the holding-period return of the $m+t$-period buy-and-hold strategy, while the denominator is the holding-period return of the first leg (m periods) of the rollover strategy. Notice that if t is equal to 1, the formula reduces to the 1-period (6-month) forward rate.

To illustrate for the spot rates shown in Exhibit 5, suppose that an investor wants to know the 2-year forward rate three years from now. In terms of the notation, t is equal to 4 and m is equal to 6. Substituting the values for t and m into the equation for the forward rate we have:

$$_4f_6 = \left[\frac{(1 + z_{10})^{10}}{(1 + z_6)^6}\right]^{1/4} - 1$$

This means that the following two spot rates are needed: z_6 (the 3-year spot rate) and z_{10} (the 5-year spot rate). From Exhibit 5, we know

z_6 (the 3-year spot rate) = 4.752%/2 = 0.02376
z_{10} (the 5-year spot rate) = 5.2772%/2 = 0.026386

then

$$_4f_6 = \left[\frac{(1 + z_{10})^{10}}{(1 + z_6)^6}\right]^{1/4} - 1$$

Therefore, $_4f_6$ is equal to 3.0338% and doubling this rate gives 6.0675%, the forward rate on a bond-equivalent basis.

We can verify this result. Investing $100 for 10 periods at the spot rate of 2.6386% (5.2772% divided by 2) will produce the following value:

$$\$100 (1.026386)^{10} = \$129.7499$$

By investing $100 for six periods at 2.376% (4.7520% divided by 2) and reinvesting the proceeds for four periods at the forward rate of 3.030338% we get the same value

$$\$100(1.02376)^6(1.030338)^4 = \$129.75012 \text{ (difference due to rounding)}$$

As long as we have the appropriate spot rates, we can calculate the forward rate for any time in the future for any investment horizon. As an illustration, Exhibit 14 presents a Bloomberg screen that displays implied forward rates generated from the on-the-run Treasury par curve (function C18 <Govt>) on May 5, 2000. The first row of the matrix contains the current Treasury par curve and the columns indicate the number of years to maturity. The second row indicates the 1-year rate one year from now, the 2-year rate one year from now, and so forth. The graph below the matrix displays the current yield curve (i.e., par curve) and the forward rate curve at a pre-selected number of years in the future (e.g., five years forward).

Forward Rates as the Market's Expectation of Future Rates

Two questions about forward rates must be addressed before we close our discussion of yield curve analysis. First, are implied forward rates the market's expectation of future spot rates? Second, how well do implied forward rates do at predicting future interest rates? We will answer each question in turn.

According to the *pure expectations theory of interest rates*, forward rates exclusively represent expected future spot rates. Thus, the entire yield curve at a given time reflects the market's expectations of the family of future short-term rates. Under this view, an upward-sloping yield curve indicates that the market expects short-term rates to rise throughout the relevant future. Similarly, a flat yield curve reflects an expectation that future short-term rates will be mostly constant, while a downward-sloping yield curve must reflect an expectation that future short-term rates will decline. Of course, there are factors that influence the yield curve other than the market's expectations of future interest rates.

Exhibit 14: Forward Curve

<HELP> for explanation, <MENU> for similar functions.   P060 Govt   **C18**
Enter all values and hit <GO>.
13:15   **COUPON IMPLIED FORWARD RATES: USA**

YRS TO MATURITY

F	1	2	3	4 ^	5	7 ^	10	20^	30	
O										
R NOW	**6.25**	**6.84**	**6.82**	**6.79**	**6.77**	**6.67**	**6.52**	**6.35**	**6.19**	
W										
A 1	7.43	7.10	6.98	6.90	6.82	6.67	6.52	6.34		
R										YIELDS
D 2	6.77	6.75	6.73	6.66	6.60	6.49	6.41	6.27		ARE
										2/YR
Y 3	6.73	6.71	6.63	6.56	6.50	6.39	6.36	6.23		COMPOUND
R										
S **5**	6.46	6.41	6.36	6.31	6.26	6.28	6.27	6.15		

^:interpolated
YIELD CURVES

0-TODAYS

*- 5 YRS FWD

IYC CURVE #**25**

Copyright 2000 BLOOMBERG L.P.   Frankfurt:69-920410   Hong Kong:2-977-6000   London:171-330-7500   New York:212-318-2000
Princeton:609-279-3000   Singapore:226-3000   Sydney:2-9777-8686   Tokyo:3-3201-8900   Sao Paulo:11-3048-4500
1457-293-1 05-May-00 13:15:28

Bloomberg
PROFESSIONAL

Source: Bloomberg

The statement that forward rates reflect the market's consensus of future interest rates is strictly true only if investors do not demand an additional risk premium for holding bonds with longer maturities and if investors' preference for positive convexity does not influence the yield curve's shape. Antti Illmanen states in series of articles called *Understanding the Yield Curve*, "Whenever the spot rate curve is upward sloping, the forwards imply rising rates. That is, rising rates are needed to offset long-term bonds' yield advantage. However, it does not necessarily follow that the market expects rising rates."[7] In certain circumstances, risk premiums and the convexity bias can exert considerable influence on yields.

In response to the second question, several empirical studies suggest that forward rates do a poor job in predicting future spot rates.[8] For example, Michele Kreisler and Richard Worley present evidence that suggests there is little or no relationship between the yield curve's slope and subsequent interest rate movements.[9] In other words, increases in rates are as likely to follow positively-sloped yield curves as flat or inverted yield curves.

Exhibit 15 is a Bloomberg screen (function C15 <Govt>) that displays in the top panel two on-the-run Treasury yield curves. The dashed curve is from January 3, 2000 while the solid curve is from May 5, 2000. The January 3 yield curve has the normal positively-sloped shape which according to pure expectations theory portends rising rates in the foreseeable future. Approximately four months later, short-term were indeed higher thanks to two hikes in the target federal funds rate by the Federal Open Market Committee on February 2 and March 21. However, longer-term rates (10-year and 30-year) are lower due in part to the reduced supply of longer-term securities as a result of the Treasury buyback program and U.S. government surpluses.

Why then should fixed-income practitioners care about implied forward rates? As we have noted, forward rates should be interpreted as break-even levels for future spot rates. By definition, if forward rates are subsequently realized, all government bonds (regardless of maturity) will earn the same 1-period return. Given this property, forward rates serve as benchmarks to which we compare our subjective expectations of future interest rates. It is not enough to say "interest rates will rise over the next six months." This is an empty statement — rise relative to what? The "to what" is the implied forward rate. If the yield curve is upward-sloping and one believes spot rates will rise more than suggested by the implied forward rates, then a rollover strategy dominates a buy-and-hold. Conversely, if one believes spot rates will rise by less than the implied forward rates suggest, then the reverse is true.

---

[7] Antti Illmanen, "Market's Rate Expectations and Forward Rate," *Understanding the Yield Curve: Part II* (New York: Salomon Brothers, 1995).

[8] See, for example, John Y. Campbell, Andrew W. Lo and Craig MacKinlay, *The Econometrics of Financial Markets* (Princeton, NJ: Princeton University Press, 1997).

[9] Michele A. Kreisler and Richard B. Worley, "Value Measures for Managing Interest-Rate Risk," Chapter 3 in Frank J. Fabozzi (ed.), *Managing Fixed-Income Portfolios* (New Hope, PA: Frank J. Fabozzi Associates, 1997)

Exhibit 15: Treasury Yield Curves on 1/3/00 and 5/5/00

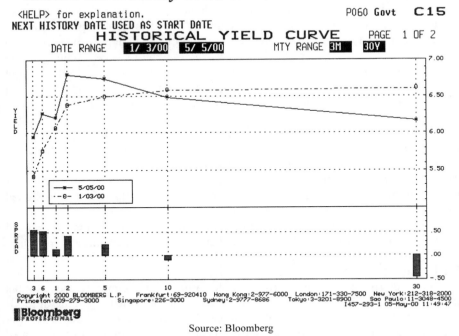

Source: Bloomberg

As noted earlier in the chapter, forward rates can also be interpreted as equating the holding period return of buying and holding a 6-month bill and the holding period return of buying a 1-year bill and selling it after six months (i.e., "riding the yield curve"). If the yield curve is upward-sloping and one believes spot rates will rise more than suggested by the implied forward rates, then a buy-and-hold strategy dominates a riding the yield curve strategy. Conversely, if one believes spot rates will rise by less than the implied forward rates suggest, then the reverse is true.

Chapter 3

Day Count Conventions and Accrued Interest

When we computed present values in previous chapters, we assumed that the next cash flow was one full period away (i.e., the exponent on the first discount factor was one). When we value a coupon-paying bonds that deliver cash flows semiannually in the next chapter, we will see that the next coupon payment is one full period away on only two days a year — the coupon payment dates. This is true for the traditional coupon bond because the compounding frequency and payment frequency are the same (i.e., semiannual). On all other dates, the next cash flow is less than one full period away.

Two complications arise when we try to value a bond between coupon payment dates. The first complication is the procedure used in the bond market for calculating the number of days between two dates (e.g., the number of days between the settlement date and the next coupon payment). These procedures are called *day count conventions*. Second, when the settlement date falls between coupon payment dates, a bond will have *accrued interest*. Simply put, accrued interest is that portion of the bond's next coupon payment that the buyer owes the seller on the settlement date when a bond changes hands between coupon payment dates. These two complications are the subject of this chapter.

DAY COUNT CONVENTIONS

The *day count basis* specifies the convention used to determine the number days in a month and in a year. According to the *Securities Industry Association Standard Securities Calculation Methods*, the notation used to identify the day count basis is:[1]

(number of days in a month)/(number of days in a year)

Although there are numerous day count conventions used in the fixed-income markets around the world, there are three basic types.[2] All day count conventions used worldwide are variations of these three types.

---

[1] See, Jan Mayle, *Standard Securities Calculation Methods, Volume 2* (New York; Securities Industry Association, 1994)

[2] Bloomberg identifies 24 different day count conventions. For a more detailed discussion see Dragomir Krigin, *Global Fixed Income Calculations* (New Hope, PA: Frank J. Fabozzi Associates, 2001).

The first type specifies that each month has the actual number of calendar days in that month and each year has the actual numbers of calendar days in that year or in a coupon period. This day count convention is referred to as "Actual/Actual." The second type specifies that each month has the actual number of calendar days in that month but restricts the number of days in each year to a certain number of days regardless of the actual number of days in that year. For example, if a year is assumed to have 360 days, this day count convention is referred to as "Actual/360." The third type restricts both the number of days in a month and in a year to a certain number of days regardless of the actual number of days in that month/year. For example, if each month is assumed to have 30 days and a year 360 days, this day count convention is referred to as "30/360." Below we will define and illustrate the three types of day count conventions.

Actual/Actual

Treasury notes, bonds, and STRIPS use an Actual/Actual (in period) day count convention. When calculating the number of days between two dates, the Actual/Actual day count convention uses the actual number of calendar days as the name implies. Let's illustrate the Actual/Actual day count convention with a 5.75% coupon, 10-year U.S. Treasury note with a maturity date of August 15, 2010. The Bloomberg Security Display (DES) screen for this security is presented in Exhibit 1. In the "Security Information" box on the left-hand side of the screen we see that the day count is specified as "ACT/ACT." From the "Issuance Info" box on the right-hand side of the screen, we see that interest starts accruing on August 15, 2000 (the issuance date) and the first coupon date is February 15, 2001. Suppose this bond is traded with a settlement date of September 14, 2000. How many days are there between August 15, 2000 and September 14, 2000 using the Actual/Actual day count convention?

To answer this question, we simply count the actual number of days between these two dates.[3] To do this, we utilize Bloomberg's DCX (Days Between Dates) function presented in Exhibit 2. The function tells us there are 30 actual days between August 15, 2000 and September 14, 2000 (17 days in August and 13 days in September). Note that the settlement date (September 14) is *not* counted. In the same manner, we can also determine the actual number of calendars days in the full coupon period. A full 6-month coupon period can only have 181, 182, 183, or 184 calendar days. For example, the actual number of days between August 15, 2000 and February 15, 2001 is 184.

---

[3] This is particularly easy to accomplish using software that can convert a Gregorian date (MM/DD/YY) into a Julian date (the number of days since some base date).

Exhibit 1: Bloomberg Security Display for a 10-Year Treasury Note

DES   DG36 Govt   **DES**

SECURITY DISPLAY
US TREASURY N/B   T 5 ³₄ 08/15/10   100-5   /100-6   (5.73 /72) BGN   @17:00

SECURITY INFORMATION	
CPN FREQ	2
CPN TYPE	FIXED
MTY/REFUND TYP	NORMAL
CALC TYP (	1)STREET CONVENTION
DAY COUNT(	1)ACT/ACT
MARKET ISS	US GOVT
COUNTRY/CURR	USA/ DOL
SECURITY TYPE	USN
AMT ISSUED	12360(MM)
AMT OUTSTAND	12360(MM)
MIN PIECE	1000

ISSUER INFO	
NAME	US TREASURY N/B
TYPE	US GOVT NATIONAL

IDENTIFICATION #'s	
CUSIP	9128276J6
MLNUM	H2614
SEDOL 1	2619329
WERTPAP	543457
ISIN	US9128276J61
AUSTRIAN	543457

REDEMPTION INFO	
MATURITY DT	8/15/10
NEXT CALL DT	
WORKOUT DT	8/15/10
RISK FACTOR	7.50

ISSUANCE INFO	
ISSUE DATE	8/15/00
INT ACCRUES	8/15/00
1ST CPN DT	2/15/01
PRC @ ISSUE	99.326

PRICE FORMAT	
32-nds	100-6
Decimal	100.18750000
Repurch Pgm	

TENDERS ACCEPTED: $10003MM.

Bloomberg
PROFESSIONAL

Source: Bloomberg

Exhibit 2: Bloomberg DCX (Days Between Dates) Function

<HELP> for explanation.   DG36 Govt   **DCX**

Tue 8/15/2000
(228:138)

A U G 0 0						
SU	MO	TU	WE	TH	FR	SA
		1	2	3	4	-
-	7	8	9	10	11	-
-	14	15	16	17	18	-
-	21	22	23	24	25	-
-	28	29	30	31		

S E P 0 0						
SU	MO	TU	WE	TH	FR	SA
					1	-
-	*	5	6	7	8	-
-	11	12	13	14	15	-
-	18	19	20	21	22	-
-	25	26	27	28	29	-

9/14/2000 Thu
(258:108)

30 actual days   (30 NoLeap Days)
29 30/360 SIA calendar day counting (29 ISMA)
21 business days for US United States

SEP 4 LABOR DAY

Bloomberg
PROFESSIONAL

Source: Bloomberg

Exhibit 3: Bloomberg Security Display for a 52-Week Treasury Bill

```
DES                                                    DG36 Govt   DES
Enter 10 <GO> To View News On This Security
                        SECURITY DISPLAY
TREASURY BILL      B 08/30/01      5.78   / 5.77   ( 6.12 /11) BGN  @17:00
```

```
                          ┌─ ISSUER INFO ──────────┐ ┌─ REDEMPTION INFO ──────┐
┌─ SECURITY INFORMATION ─┐│NAME   TREASURY BILL     ││MATURITY DT      8/30/01 │
│                        ││TYPE   US GOVT NATIONAL  ││                         │
│ CPN TYPE        NONE    │└─────────────────────────┘│                         │
│ MTY/REFUND TYP  NORMAL  │┌─ IDENTIFICATION #'s ───┐ │RISK FACTOR      0.88    │
│ CALC TYP ( 5)DISCOUNT   ││CUSIP     912795HL8      │└─────────────────────────┘
│ DAY COUNT( 2)ACT/360    ││MLNUM     H25P4          │┌─ ISSUANCE INFO ────────┐
│ MARKET ISS     US GOVT  ││SEDOL 1   2623706        ││ISSUE DATE       8/31/00 │
│ COUNTRY/CURR   USA/ DOL ││ISIN      US912795HL86   │└─────────────────────────┘
│ SECURITY TYPE  USD      │└─────────────────────────┘                          
│ AMT ISSUED     13036(MM)│                           │DISC @ ISSUE     5.85    │
│ AMT OUTSTAND   13036(MM)│                           └─────────────────────────┘
│ MIN PIECE      1000     │
└────────────────────────┘
┌─────────────────────────────────────────────────────────────────────────────┐
│TENDERS ACCEPTED: $13032MM.                                                    │
│                                                                               │
└─────────────────────────────────────────────────────────────────────────────┘
Copyright 2000 BLOOMBERG L.P.  Frankfurt:69-920410  Hong Kong:2-977-6000  London:207-330-7500  New York:212-318-2000
Princeton:609-279-3000     Singapore:226-3000    Sydney:2-9777-8686   Tokyo:3-3201-8900    Sao Paulo:11-3048-4500
                                                                         I464-169-1 13-Sep-00 17:08:38
```

Bloomberg PROFESSIONAL

Source: Bloomberg

Actual/360

Actual/360 is an example of the second type of day count convention. Specifically, Actual/360 posits that each month has the same number of days as indicated by the calendar. However, each year is assumed to have 360 days regardless of the actual number of days in a year. Actual/360 is the day count convention used in the U.S. money market. Let's illustrate the Actual/360 day count with a 52-week U.S. Treasury bill which matures on August 30, 2001. The Bloomberg Security Display (DES) screen for this security is presented in Exhibit 3. From the "Security Information" box on the left-hand side of the screen, we see that the day count is specified as "ACT/360." Suppose this Treasury bill is purchased with a settlement date on September 14, 2000 at a price of 94.3902778. How many days does this bill have until maturity using the Actual/360 day count convention?

Once again, the question is easily answered using Bloomberg's DCX (Days Between Dates) function and specifying the two dates of interest. This screen is presented in Exhibit 4. We see that with a settlement date of September 14, 2000 there are 350 calendar days until maturity on August 30, 2001. This can be confirmed by examining the Bloomberg's YA (Yield Analysis) screen in Exhibit 5. We see that with a settlement date of September 14, 2000 this Treasury bill has 350 days to maturity. This information is located just above the "Price" box in the center of the screen.

Exhibit 4: Bloomberg DCX (Days Between Dates) Function

```
<HELP> for explanation.                                    DG36 Govt   DCX

Thu  9/14/2000        S E P   0 0              A U G   0 1          8/30/2001  Thu
     (258:108)    SU MO TU WE TH FR SA      SU MO TU WE TH FR SA       (242:123)
                                1  -                      1  2  3  -
                  -  *  5  6  7  8  -       -  6  7  8  9 10  -
                  - 11 12 13 [14]15  -      - 13 14 15 16 17  -
                  - 18 19 20 21 22  -       - 20 21 22 23 24  -
                  - 25 26 27 28 29  -       - 27 28 29 [30]31


                     350  actual days    (  350 NoLeap Days)
                     346  30/360 SIA calendar day counting (   346 ISMA)
                     240  business days for US United States

        SEP  4  LABOR DAY
```

Copyright 2000 BLOOMBERG L.P.   Frankfurt:69-920410 Hong Kong:2-977-6000 London:207-330-7500 New York:212-318-2000
Princeton:609-279-3000   Singapore:226-3000   Sydney:2-9777-8686   Tokyo:3-3201-8900   Sao Paulo:11-3048-4500
                                                                        I464-169-1 13-Sep-00 17:11:25

Bloomberg
PROFESSIONAL

Source: Bloomberg

Exhibit 5: Bloomberg Yield Analysis Screen for a 52-Week Treasury Bill

```
YA                                                         DG36 Govt   YA
Enter all values and hit <GO>.
           DISCOUNT/YIELD ANALYSIS      CUSIP    912795HL8
TREASURY BILL    B 08/30/01     5.78  / 5.77   ( 6.12 /11) BGN  @17:00
  DISCOUNT  5.77000  SETTLEMENT DATE  9/14/2000
  MATURITY    8/30/2001  350 DAYS TO MATURITY   ISSUE: 8/31/2000
  PRICE          94.3902778    CASHFLOW ANALYSIS
  YIELD                    TAXED      FOR  1000M FACE AMOUNT
  CALCULATIONS            28.00%    PRINCIPAL[RND(Y/N)N]   943902.78
  U.S. TREASURY CONVENTION   6.109  4.416    REDEMPTION        1000000.00
  U.S. GOVT BOND EQUIVALENT  6.097  4.406    PROFIT              56097.22
  SIMPLE INTEREST (ACT/360)  6.113  4.401    REPO RATE            6.480
  MEDIUM TERM CD  (ACT/360)  6.025  4.355    OVERNIGHT REPO EQUIV 6.113
  U.S. TREASURY with LEAP YR 6.125  4.428    COST OF CARRY (PTS) -0.367
                                             NET P&L             -9.62
  SENSITIVITY ANALYSIS
  DURATION(YEARS)              0.959    FURTHER ANALYSIS
  ADJ/MOD DURATION             0.932    1 <GO> COST OF CARRY ANALYSIS
  RISK                         0.879    2 <GO> DISCOUNT EQUIVALENT TABLE
  CONVEXITY                    0.000    3 <GO> DISCOUNT/YIELD TABLE

         A  0.01   CHANGE IN
    DISCOUNT/ PRICE/ YIELD  D
  RESULTS IN A -0.00972 CHANGE IN PRICE
         AND A  0.01106 CHANGE IN YIELD
```

Copyright 2000 BLOOMBERG L.P.   Frankfurt:69-920410 Hong Kong:2-977-6000 London:207-330-7500 New York:212-318-2000
Princeton:609-279-3000   Singapore:226-3000   Sydney:2-9777-8686   Tokyo:3-3201-8900   Sao Paulo:11-3048-4500
                                                                        I464-169-1 13-Sep-00 17:09:23

Bloomberg
PROFESSIONAL

Source: Bloomberg

When computing the number of days between two dates, Actual/360 and Actual/Actual will give the same answer. What then is the importance of the 360-day year in the Actual/360 day count? The difference is apparent when we want to compare, say, the yield on 52-week Treasury bill with a coupon Treasury which has one year remaining to maturity. U.S. Treasury bills, like many money market instruments, are discount instruments. As such, their yields are quoted on a bank discount basis which determine the bill's price (which we explain in detail in Chapter 5). The quoted yield on a bank discount basis for a Treasury bill is not directly comparable to the yield on a coupon Treasury using an Actual/Actual day count for two reasons. First, the Treasury bill's yield is based on a face-value investment rather than on the price. Second, the Treasury bill yield is annualized according to a 360-day year while a coupon Treasury's yield is annualized using the actual number of days in a calendar year (365 or 366). These factors make it difficult to compare Treasury bill yields with yields on Treasury notes and bonds. We demonstrate how these yields can be adjusted to make them comparable in Chapter 5.

Another variant of this second day count type is the "Actual/365." Actual/365 specifies that each month has the same number of days as indicated by the calendar and each year is assumed to have 365 days regardless of the actual number of days in a year. Actual/365 does not consider the extra day in a leap year. This day count convention is used to compute accrued interest for Canadian government bonds.

30/360

The 30/360 day count is the most prominent example of the third type of day count convention which restricts both the number of days in a month and in a year to a certain number of days regardless of the actual number of days in that month/year. With the 30/360 day count all months are assumed to have 30 days and all years are assumed to have 360 days. The number of days between two dates using a 30/360 day will usually differ from the actual number of days between the two dates.

To determine the number of days between two dates, we will adopt the following notation:

$Y1$ = year of the earlier date
$M1$ = month of the earlier date
$D1$ = day of the earlier date
$Y2$ = year of the later date
$M2$ = month of the later date
$D2$ = day of the later date

Since the 30/360 day count assumes that all months have 30 days, some adjustments must be made for months having 31 days and February which has 28 days (29 days in a leap year). The following adjustments accomplish this task:[4]

---

[4] See, Mayle, *Standard Securities Calculation Methods, Volume 2.*

Exhibit 6: Bloomberg Security Description Screen for a Fannie Mae Bond

```
DES                                              DG36 Corp   DES
SECURITY  DESCRIPTION              Page 1/ 1      ▆▆▆▆▆
FANNIE MAE        FNMA 7 ¼ 05/30    104-26+/104-30+   (6.87/6.86) BGN  MATRIX
┌──────────────────────────┬────────────────────┐  1) Additional Sec Info
│ ISSUER INFORMATION       │ IDENTIFIERS        │  2) Identifiers
│ Name FANNIE MAE          │ Common   011131018 │  3) Ratings
│ Type Sovereign Agency    │ ISIN  US31359MFP32 │  4) Fees/Restrictions
│ Market of Issue GLOBAL   │ CUSIP    31359MFP3 │  5) Sec. Specific News
├──────────────────────────┼────────────────────┤  6) Involved Parties
│ SECURITY INFORMATION     │ RATINGS            │  7) Custom Notes
│ Country US    Currency USD│ Moody's     Aaa   │  8) ALLQ
│ Collateral Type BONDS    │ S&P         NA     │  9) Pricing Sources
│ Calc Typ(  1)STREET CONVENTION│ Composite  AAA│ 10) Prospectus Request
│ ▉Maturity▉ ▉5/15/2030▉ Series │ ISSUE SIZE   │ 11) Related Securities
│ NORMAL                   │ Amt Issued         │ 12) Issuer Web Page
│ ▉Coupon▉ ▉7 ¼▉    FIXED  │ USD  4,500,000 (M) │
│ S/A      ▉30/360▉        │ Amt Outstanding    │
│ Announcement Dt  5/ 3/00 │ USD  4,500,000 (M) │
│ Int. Accrual Dt  5/ 5/00 │ Min Piece/Increment│
│ 1st Settle Date  5/ 5/00 │   1,000.00/ 1,000.00│
│ 1st Coupon Date 11/15/00 │ Par Amount 1,000.00│
│ Iss Pr  98.7080          ├────────────────────┤
│ SPR @ ISS  125.5 vs T 6 ¼ 05/30 │ GS,LEH,SSB  │ 65) Old DES
│ HAVE PROSPECTUS          │ BOOK RUNNER/EXCHANGE│ 66) Send as Attachment
BENCHMARK BONDS. UNSEC'D. LONG 1ST CPN. BOOK-ENTRY. ADD'L $2.5 BLN ISS'D 8/2/00.
@ 103.476 FOR SETTLE ON 8/4/00. ORIG SPREAD: 132.5BP OVER T 6.25 5/15/30.
Copyright 2000 BLOOMBERG L.P.   Frankfurt:69-920410  Hong Kong:2-977-6000  London:207-330-7500  New York:212-318-2000
Princeton:609-279-3000   Singapore:226-3000   Sydney:2-9777-8686   Tokyo:3-3201-8900   Sao Paulo:11-3048-4500
                                                          I464-169-1 13-Sep-00 17:13:18
█Bloomberg
PROFESSIONAL
```

Source: Bloomberg

1. If the bond follows the End-of-Month rule[5] and $D2$ is the last day of February (the 28th in a non-leap year and the 29th in a leap year) and $D1$ is the last day of February, change $D2$ to 30.
2. If the bond follows the End-of-Month rule and $D1$ is the last day of February, change $D1$ to 30.
3. If $D2$ is 31 and $D1$ is 30 or 31, change $D2$ to 30.
4. If $D1$ is 31, change $D1$ to 30.

Once these adjustments are made, the formula for calculating the number of days between two dates is as follows:

$$\text{Number of days} = [(Y2 - Y1) \times 360] + [(M2 - M1) \times 30] + (D2 - D1)$$

To illustrate the 30/360 day count convention, let's use a 7.25% coupon bond which matures on May 15, 2030, issued by Fannie Mae. The Bloomberg Security Description (DES) screen for this bond is presented in Exhibit 6. We see

---

[5] This is the standard convention for bonds in the U.S. and it states that if a bond's maturity date falls on the last day of the month so do the bond's coupon payments.

that in the "Security Information" box that the bond has a 30/360 day count. Suppose the bond is purchased with a settlement date of September 14, 2000. We see from the lower left-hand corner of the screen that the first coupon date is November 15, 2000 and the first interest accrual date is May 5, 2000. How many days have elapsed in the first coupon period from May 5, 2000 until the settlement date of September 14, 2000 using the 30/360 day count convention?

Referring back to the 30/360 day count rule, we see that adjustments 1 through 4 do not apply in this example so no adjustments to $D1$ and $D2$ are required. Accordingly, in this example,

$$Y1 = 2000$$
$$M1 = 5$$
$$D1 = 5$$
$$Y2 = 2000$$
$$M2 = 9$$
$$D2 = 14$$

Inserting these numbers into the formula, we find that the number of days between these two dates is 129, which is calculated as follows:

$$\text{Number of days} = [(2000 - 2000) \times 360] + [(9 - 5) \times 30] + (14 - 5)$$
$$= 0 + 120 + 9 = 129$$

To check this, let's employ Bloomberg's DCX (Days Between Dates) function presented in Exhibit 7. The function tells us there are 129 days between May 5, 2000 and September 14, 2000 using a 30/360 day count. Note that the actual number of days between these two dates is 132.

Exhibit 7: Bloomberg DCX (Days Between Dates) Function

<HELP> for explanation.   DG36 Corp DCX

```
Fri  5/ 5/2000        M A Y  0 0                  S E P  0 0          9/14/2000 Thu
     (126·240)   SU MO TU WE TH FR SA        SU MO TU WE TH FR SA       (258·108)
                  1  2  3  4 [5] -                         1  -
                 - 8  9 10 11 12  -         - * 5  6  7  8  -
                 - 15 16 17 18 19  -        - 11 12 13 [14] 15  -
                 - 22 23 24 25 26  -        - 18 19 20 21 22  -
                 - * 30 31                  - 25 26 27 28 29  -

                        132  actual days   (  132 NoLeap Days)
                        129  30/360 SIA calendar day counting (   129 ISMA)
                         91  business days for US United States

         MAY 29  MEMORIAL DAY              SEP  4  LABOR DAY
```

Copyright 2000 BLOOMBERG L.P.   Frankfurt:69-920410 Hong Kong:2-977-6000 London:207-330-7500 New York:212-318-2000
Princeton:609-279-3000   Singapore:226-3000   Sydney:2-9777-8686   Tokyo:3-3201-8900   Sao Paulo:11-3048-4500
                                                                  I464-169-1 13-Sep-00 17:15:29

Bloomberg
PROFESSIONAL

Source: Bloomberg

It is tempting to conclude from this example that the 30/360 day count will always result in a fewer number of days between dates than the Actual/Actual day count. This makes sense because we are eliminating 31-day months. However, this is not the case. To see this, we will consider some additional examples.

Differences Between 30/360 and Actual/Actual

The number of days between dates using a 30/360 day count can be larger than the actual number of days, especially when the time period includes February. To see this, we ask how many days are there between January 31, 2000 and March 1, 2000 using both the 30/360 and the Actual/Actual day counts? Applying the 30/360 adjustments 1 through 4, we note that $D1$ is 31 so we must change it to 30 (adjustment 4) which gives us the following inputs:

$$Y1 = 2000$$
$$M1 = 1$$
$$D1 = 30$$
$$Y2 = 2000$$
$$M2 = 3$$
$$D2 = 1$$

Inserting these numbers into the 30/360 formula, we find that the number of days between these two dates is 31, which is calculated as follows:

$$\text{Number of days} = [(2000 - 2000) \times 360] + [(3 - 1) \times 30] + (1 - 30)$$
$$= 0 + 60 + (-29) = 31$$

Let's check our calculation using Bloomberg's DCX (Days Between Dates) function presented in Exhibit 8. The function tells us there are 31 days between January 31, 2000 and March 1, 2000 using a 30/360 day count. Note that the actual number of days between these two dates is 30.[6]

Let's work another example using the 30/360 day count, asking how many days are between August 31, 2000 and September 14, 2000 using the 30/360 and Actual/Actual day counts? Once again, we must check adjustments 1 through 4 for the 30/360 day count. We see that since $D1$ equals 31, it must be changed to 30 (adjustment 4), giving us the following inputs:

$$Y1 = 2000$$
$$M1 = 8$$
$$D1 = 30$$
$$Y2 = 2000$$
$$M2 = 9$$
$$D2 = 14$$

---

[6] Recall, there are 29 days in February because 2000 is a leap year.

Exhibit 8: Bloomberg DCX (Days Between Dates) Function

```
<HELP> for explanation.                        DG36 Govt   DCX

Mon  1/31/2000        J A N   0 0              M A R   0 0        3/ 1/2000 Wed
       (31:335)      SU MO TU WE TH FR SA     SU MO TU WE TH FR SA    (61:305)
                                         -                 1  2  3  -
                     -  3  4  5  6  7  -     -  6  7  8  9 10  -
                     - 10 11 12 13 14  -     - 13 14 15 16 17  -
                     -  *  18 19 20 21  -    - 20 21 22 23 24  -
                     - 24 25 26 27 28  -     - 27 28 29 30 31
                     - 31

                          30 actual days  (    29 NoLeap Days)
                          31 30/360 SIA calendar day counting (    31 ISMA)
                          21 business days for US United States

            JAN  1  NEW YEAR'S DAY
            JAN 17  MARTIN L. KING DAY

Copyright 2000 BLOOMBERG L.P.   Frankfurt:69-920410  Hong Kong:2-977-6000  London:207-330-7500  New York:212-318-2000
Princeton:609-279-3000    Singapore:226-3000    Sydney:2-9777-8686    Tokyo:3-3201-8900    Sao Paulo:11-3048-4500
                                                                      I464-169-0 12-Jun-00 17:43:46
Bloomberg
PROFESSIONAL
```

Source: Bloomberg

Exhibit 9: Bloomberg DCX (Days Between Dates) Function

```
<HELP> for explanation.                        DG36 Govt   DCX

Thu  8/31/2000        A U G   0 0              S E P   0 0        9/14/2000 Thu
       (244:122)     SU MO TU WE TH FR SA     SU MO TU WE TH FR SA    (258:108)
                             1  2  3  4  -                     1  -
                     -  7  8  9 10 11  -     -  *  5  6  7  8  -
                     - 14 15 16 17 18  -     - 11 12 13 14 15  -
                     - 21 22 23 24 25  -     - 18 19 20 21 22  -
                     - 28 29 30 31          - 25 26 27 28 29  -

                          14 actual days  (    14 NoLeap Days)
                          14 30/360 SIA calendar day counting (    14 ISMA)
                           9 business days for US United States

                         SEP  4  LABOR DAY

Copyright 2000 BLOOMBERG L.P.   Frankfurt:69-920410  Hong Kong:2-977-6000  London:207-330-7500  New York:212-318-2000
Princeton:609-279-3000    Singapore:226-3000    Sydney:2-9777-8686    Tokyo:3-3201-8900    Sao Paulo:11-3048-4500
                                                                      I464-169-1 13-Sep-00 17:10:18
Bloomberg
PROFESSIONAL
```

Source: Bloomberg

Inserting these numbers into the 30/360 formula, we find that the number of days between these two dates is 14 which is calculated as follows:

$$\text{Number of days} = [(2000 - 2000) \times 360] + [(9 - 8) \times 30] + (14 - 30)$$
$$= 0 + 30 + (-16) = 14$$

We once again check our calculation using Bloomberg's DCX (Days Between Dates) function presented in Exhibit 9. The function tells us there are 14 days between August 31, 2000 and September 14, 2000 using a 30/360 day count.

This coincides with the actual number of days between these two dates. Some additional examples of the difference between dates for Actual/Actual and 30/360 day counts are presented in Exhibit 10.

COMPUTING THE ACCRUED INTEREST

When a bond is sold between coupon payment dates, a bond will have accrued interest. Accrued interest is the amount of interest earned by the bond's seller since the last coupon payment date. The buyer pays accrued interest and the seller receives accrued interest. The calculation of accrued interest will differ across bonds due to day count conventions.

To compute accrued interest, the first step is to determine the number of days in the accrued interest period (i.e., the number of days between the last coupon payment date and the settlement date) using the appropriate day count convention. For ease of exposition, we will assume in the following example that the bond uses the actual/actual calendar. We will also assume there are only two bondholders in a given coupon period — the buyer and the seller.

The percentage of the next semiannual coupon that the seller has earned as accrued interest is found as follows:

$$\frac{\text{days in the accrued interest period}}{\text{days in the coupon period}}$$

Note that this ratio simply represents the fraction of the coupon period that has elapsed as of the settlement date. Given this value, the amount of accrued interest (AI) is equal to:

$$\text{AI} = \text{semiannual coupon payment} \left(\frac{\text{days in the accrued interest period}}{\text{days in the coupon period}} \right)$$

This expression tells us simply that coupon interest accrues linearly over the period.

Exhibit 10: Additional Examples of the Number of Days Between Dates Using Actual/Actual and 30/360 Day Counts

First Date	Second Date	Actual/Actual	30/360
December 31, 1999	December 31, 2000	366	360
September 14, 2000	November 15, 2000	62	61
July 1, 2000	August 1, 2000	31	30
February 28, 1999	February 29, 2000	366	360
January 2, 2000	February 29, 2000	58	57

As an illustration, we return to an earlier example with the 5.75% coupon Treasury note from Exhibit 1. There are 184 days in the coupon period (i.e., the actual number of days between August 15, 2000 and February 15, 2001) and there are 30 days in the accrued interest period (see Exhibit 2). Therefore, the percentage of the next coupon payment that is accrued interest is:

$$\frac{30}{184} = 0.1630 = 16.30\%$$

Accordingly, using a 5.75% Treasury note with a settlement date of September 14, 2000, the portion of the next coupon payment that is accrued interest is:

$2.875 \times (0.1630) = \$0.468625$ (per $100 of par value)

This amount represents the amount of interest that the Treasury note buyer pays the seller on the settlement date when the bond is purchased.

If we compute a bond's accrued interest using a different day count convention (e.g., 30/360), the only part of the calculation that changes is the fraction of the coupon period that has elapsed as of the settlement date. To see this, let's compute the accrued interest for the 7.25% coupon Fannie Mae bond in Exhibit 6. Recall, the day count convention is 30/360 since it is a corporate bond. Suppose, once again, the bond is purchased with a settlement date of September 14, 2000 and the first interest accrual date is May 5, 2000. What is the accrued interest?

To compute the accrued interest, we need to know the number of days in the accrued interest period and the number of days in the coupon period using the appropriate day count. From Exhibit 7, we see there are 129 days between May 5, 2000 and September 14, 2000 using a 30/360 day count. Moreover, there are 180 days (360/2) in a full coupon period using a 30/360 day count because each year is assumed to have 360 days. The percentage of the next coupon payment that is accrued interest is:

$$\frac{129}{180} = 0.7167 = 71.67\%$$

As a result, using a 7.25% coupon Fannie Mae corporate bond with a settlement date of September 14, 2000, the portion of the next coupon payment that is accrued interest is:

$3.625 \times (0.7167) = \$2.5980$ (per $100 of par value)

This amount represents the amount of interest that the Fannie Mae bond buyer pays the seller on the settlement date when the bond is purchased.

Chapter 4

Valuation of Option-Free Bonds

V aluation is the process of determining the fair value of a financial asset. Once this process is complete, we can compare a financial asset's fair value to its market price to determine whether it is overvalued (i.e., rich) or undervalued (i.e., cheap). After this comparison, we can then take the appropriate position (short or long) in order to benefit from any differences. In well-functioning markets, however, fair values and market prices should be reasonably close.

In this chapter, we will explain the general principles of fixed-income security valuation. We will confine the discussion in this chapter to the valuation of option-free bonds. Models for valuing bonds with embedded options will be described in Chapters 6 and 8.

GENERAL PRINCIPLES OF VALUATION

The fundamental principle of valuation is that the value of any financial asset is equal to the present value of its expected future cash flows. This principle holds for any financial asset from zero-coupon bonds to interest rate swaps. Thus, the valuation of a financial asset involves the following three steps:

Step 1: Estimate the expected future cash flows.
Step 2: Determine the appropriate interest rate or interest rates that should be used to discount the cash flows.
Step 3: Calculate the present value of the expected future cash flows found in Step 1 by the appropriate interest rate or interest rates determined in Step 2.

Estimating Cash Flows

Cash flow is simply the cash that is expected to be received in the future from owning a financial asset. For a fixed-income security, it does not matter whether the cash flow is interest income or repayment of principal. A security's *cash flows* represent the sum of each period's expected cash flow. Even if we disregard default, the cash flows for only a few fixed-income securities are simple to forecast accurately. Noncallable U.S. Treasury securities possess this feature since they have known cash flows.[1] For Treasury coupon securities, the cash flows consist of the coupon interest payments every six months up to and including the maturity date and the principal repayment at the maturity date.

Many fixed-income securities have features that make estimating their cash flows problematic. These features may include one or more of the following:

1. the issuer or the investor has the option to change the contractual due date of the repayment of the principal, or
2. the coupon and/or principal payment is reset periodically based on a formula that depends on one or more market variables (e.g., interest rates, inflation rates, exchange rates, etc.), or
3. the investor has the choice to convert or exchange the security into common stock or some other financial asset.

Callable bonds, putable bonds, mortgage-backed securities, and asset-backed securities are examples of (1). Floating-rate securities and Treasury Inflation Protected Securities (TIPs) are examples of (2). Convertible bonds and exchangeable bonds are examples of (3).

For securities that fall into the first category, a key factor determining whether the owner of the option (either the issuer of the security or the investor) will exercise the option to alter the security's cash flows is the level of interest rates in the future relative to the security's coupon rate. In order to estimate the cash flows for these types of securities, we must determine how the size and timing of their expected cash flows will change in the future. For example, when estimating the future cash flows of a callable bond, we must account for the fact that when interest rates change the expected cash flows change. As we will see in Chapter 6, this introduces an additional layer of complexity to the valuation process. For bonds with embedded options, estimating cash flows is accomplished by introducing a parameter that reflects the expected volatility of interest rates.

Determining the Appropriate Interest Rate or Rates

Once we estimate the cash flows for a fixed-income security, the next step is to determine the appropriate interest rate for discounting each cash flow. Before proceeding, we pause here to note that we will once again use the terms "interest rate," "discount rate," and "required yield" interchangeably throughout the chapter. The interest rate used to discount a particular security's cash flows will depend on three basic factors: (1) the level of benchmark interest rates (i.e., U.S. Treasury rates); (2) the risks that the market perceives the securityholder is exposed to; and (3) the compensation the market expects to receive for these risks.

The minimum interest rate that an investor should require is the yield available in the marketplace on a default-free cash flow. For bonds with dollar-

---

[1] While the probability of default of the U.S. government is not zero, it is close enough to that threshold to be safely ignored. Besides, if the U.S. government ever does default, we will have other things to worry about than valuing bonds.

denominated cash flows, yields on U.S. Treasury securities serve as benchmarks for default-free interest rates. In other countries as we will discuss later, the swaps curve serves as a benchmark for pricing spread product (e.g., corporate bonds). For now, we can think of the minimum interest rate that investors require as the yield on a comparable maturity Treasury security.

The additional compensation or spread over the yield on the Treasury issue that investors will require reflects the additional risks the investor faces by acquiring a security that is not issued by the U.S. government. These risks include default risk, liquidity risk, and the risks associated with any embedded options. These yield spreads (discussed in more detail in Chapter 5) will depend not only on the risks an individual issue is exposed to but also on the level of Treasury yields, the market's risk aversion, the business cycle, etc.

For each cash flow estimated, the same interest rate can be used to calculate the present value. This is the traditional approach to valuation and it serves as a useful starting point for our discussion. We discuss the traditional approach in the next section and use a single interest rate to determine present values. By doing this, however, we are implicitly assuming that the yield curve is flat. Since the yield curve is almost never flat and a coupon bond can be thought of as a package of zero-coupon bonds, it is more appropriate to value each cash flow using an interest rate specific to that cash flow. After the traditional approach to valuation is discussed, we will explain the proper approach to valuation using multiple interest rates and demonstrate why this must be the case.

Discounting the Expected Cash Flows

Once the expected (estimated) cash flows and the appropriate interest rate or interest rates that should be used to discount the cash flows are determined, the final step in the valuation process is to value the cash flows. As discussed in Chapter 1, the present value of an expected cash flow to be received t years from now using a discount rate i is:

$$\text{present value}_t = \frac{\text{expected cash flow in period } t}{(1 + i)^t}$$

The value of a financial asset is then the sum of the present value of all the expected cash flows. Specifically, assuming that there are N expected cash flows:

$$\text{value} = \text{present value}_1 + \text{present value}_2 + \ldots + \text{present value}_N$$

DETERMINING A BOND'S VALUE

Determining a bond's value involves computing the present value of the expected future cash flows using a discount rate that reflects market interest rates and the bond's risks. A bond's cash flows come in two forms — coupon interest payments and the repayment of principal at maturity. In practice, many bonds deliver semi-annual cash flows. Fortunately, as we saw in Chapter 3, this does not introduce any complexities into the calculation. Two simple adjustments are needed. First, we adjust the coupon payments by dividing the annual coupon payment by 2. Second, we adjust the discount rate by dividing the annual discount rate by 2. The time period t in the present value expression is treated in terms of 6-month periods as opposed to years.

To illustrate the process, let's value a 4-year, 6% coupon bond with a maturity value of $100. The coupon payments are $3 (0.06 × $100/2) every six months for the next eight periods. In addition, on the maturity date, the investor receives the repayment of principal ($100). The value of a non-amortizing bond can be divided in two components: (1) the present value of the coupon payments (i.e., an annuity) and (2) the present value of the maturity value (i.e., a lump sum). Therefore, when a single discount rate is employed, a bond's value can be thought of as the sum of two presents values — an annuity and a lump sum

The adjustment for the discount rate is easy to accomplish but tricky to interpret. For example, if an annual discount rate of 6% is used, how do we obtain the semiannual discount rate? We will simply use one-half the annual rate, 3.0% (6%/2). How can this be? From Chapter 1, we know that a 3.0% semiannual rate is *not* a 6% effective annual rate. As we will see in the next chapter, the *convention* in the bond market is to quote annual interest rates that are just double the semiannual rates. This convention will be explained more fully later when we discuss yield to maturity. For now, accept on faith that one-half the discount rate is used as a semiannual discount rate in the balance of the chapter.

We now have everything in place to value a semiannual coupon-paying bond. Recall, the present value of an annuity is equal to:

$$\text{annuity payment} \times \left[\frac{1 - \dfrac{1}{(1 + r)^{\text{no. of years}}}}{r} \right]$$

where r is the *annual* discount rate.

Applying this formula to a semiannual-pay bond, the annuity payment is one half the annual coupon payment and the number of periods is double the number of years to maturity. Accordingly, the present value of the coupon payments can be expressed as:

$$\text{semiannual coupon payment} \times \left[\frac{1 - \dfrac{1}{(1 + i)^{\text{no. of years} \times 2}}}{i} \right]$$

where i is the *semiannual* discount rate ($r/2$). Notice that in the formula, for the number of periods we use the number of years multiplied by 2 since a period in our illustration is six months.

The present value of the maturity value is just the present value of a lump sum and is equal to

$$\text{present value of the maturity value } = \frac{\$100}{(1+i)^{\text{no. of years} \times 2}}$$

We will value our 4-year, 6% coupon bond under three different scenarios. These scenarios are defined by the relationship between the discount rate or required yield and the coupon rate. In the first scenario, we will consider the case when the annual discount rate and the coupon rate are equal. For the second scenario we will value the bond when the discount rate is greater than the coupon rate. The last scenario assumes the discount rate is less than the coupon rate.

Valuing a Bond When the Discount Rate and Coupon Rate are Equal

Now let's turn our attention to the 4-year 6% coupon bond and assume the annual discount is 6% and therefore (for reasons mentioned above) the semiannual discount rate is one half this rate (3%) and will be applicable for calculating the present value to all of the cash flows. Note that the coupon rate and the discount rate are the same. The relevant data are summarized below:

semiannual coupon payment $=$ $3 (per $100 of par value)
semiannual discount rate (i) $=$ 3% (6%/2)
number of years to maturity $=$ 4

To determine the present value of the coupon payments, we compute the following expression:

$$\$3 \times \left[\frac{1 - \dfrac{1}{(1.03)^{4 \times 2}}}{0.03} \right] = \$21.0591$$

Simply put, this number tells us how much the coupon payments contribute to the bond's value. In addition, the bondholder receives the maturity value when the bond matures so the present value of the maturity value must be added to the present value of the coupon payments. The present value of the maturity value is

$$\text{present value of the maturity value } = \frac{\$100}{(1.03)^{4 \times 2}} = \$78.9409$$

This number ($78.9409) tells us how much the bond's maturity value contributes to the bond's value. The bond's value is the sum of these two present values which in this case is $100 ($21.0591 + $78.9409).

When an option-free bond is issued, the coupon rate and the term to maturity are fixed. Consequently, as yields change in the market, bond prices will move in the opposite direction, as we will see in the next two scenarios. Generally, a bond's coupon rate at the time of issuance is set at approximately the required yield demanded by the market for comparable bonds. By comparable, we mean bonds that have the same maturity and the same risk exposure. The price of an option-free coupon bond at issuance will then be approximately equal to its par value. In the example presented above, when the required yield is equal to the coupon rate, the bond's price is its par value ($100).

Valuing a Bond When the Discount Rate is Greater Than the Coupon Rate

We now take up the case when the discount rate is greater than the coupon rate. Suppose now that the relevant discount rate for our 4-year, 6% coupon bond is 7%. The data are summarized below:

$$\text{semiannual coupon payment} = \$3 \text{ (per \$100 of par value)}$$
$$\text{semiannual discount rate } (i) = 3.5\% \text{ (7\%/2)}$$
$$\text{number of years to maturity} = 4$$

Note that the only number that has changed from the previous scenario is the semiannual discount rate which has increased from 3% to 3.5%. We compute the present value of the coupon payments in the same manner as before:

$$\$3 \times \left[\frac{1 - \dfrac{1}{(1.035)^{4 \times 2}}}{0.035} \right] = \$20.6219$$

This number tells us that the coupon payments contribute $20.6219 to the bond's value.

The present value of the maturity value is

$$\text{present value of the maturity value} = \frac{\$100}{(1.035)^{4 \times 2}} = \$75.9412$$

This number ($75.9412) tells us how much the maturity value contributes to the bond's value. The bond's value is then $96.5631 ($20.6219 + $75.9412). The price is less than par value and the bond is said to be trading at a *discount*. This will occur when the fixed coupon rate a bond offers (6%) is less than the required yield demanded by the market (the 7% discount rate). A discount bond has an inferior coupon rate relative to new comparable bonds being issued at par so its price must drop so as to bid up to the required yield of 7%. If the discount bond is held to maturity, the investor will experience a capital gain that just offsets the lower the current coupon rate so that it appears equally attractive to new comparable bonds issued at par.[2]

---

[2] We are ignoring the differential tax treatment of interest and capital gains/losses.

Valuing a Bond When the Discount Rate is Less Than the Coupon Rate

The final scenario is when the discount rate is less than the coupon rate. Suppose that the relevant discount rate for our 4-year, 6% coupon bond is 5%. The data are summarized below:

semiannual coupon payment $= \$3$ (per \$100 of par value)
semiannual discount rate (i) $= 2.5\%$ (5%/2)
number of years to maturity $= 4$

Once again the only number that has changed for the scenario presented above is the semiannual discount rate, 2.5%. We compute the present value of the coupon payments in the same manner as before:

$$\$3 \times \left[\dfrac{1 - \dfrac{1}{(1.025)^{4 \times 2}}}{0.025} \right] = \$21.5104$$

This number tells us that the coupon payments contribute \$21.5104 to the bond's value.

The present value of the maturity value is

$$\text{present value of the maturity value} = \dfrac{\$100}{(1.025)^{4 \times 2}} = \$82.0747$$

Once again, this number (\$82.0747) tells us how much the bond's maturity value contributes to the bond's value. The bond's value is then \$103.5851 (\$21.5104 + \$82.0747). That is, the price is greater than par value and the bond is said to be trading at a *premium*. This will occur when the fixed coupon rate a bond offers (6%) is greater than the required yield demanded by the market (the 5% discount rate). Accordingly, a premium bond carries a higher coupon rate than new bonds (otherwise the same) being issued today at par so the price will be bid up and the required yield will fall until it equals 5%. If the premium bond is held to maturity, the investor will experience a capital loss that just offsets the benefits of the higher coupon rate so that it will appear equally attractive to new comparable bonds issued at par.[3]

THE PRICE/DISCOUNT RATE RELATIONSHIP

The preceding three scenarios illustrate an important general property of present value. The higher (lower) the discount rate, the lower (higher) the present value.

---

[3] We are ignoring the differential tax effects once again.

Since the value of a security is the present value of the expected future cash flows, this property carries over to the value of a security: the higher (lower) the discount rate, the lower (higher) a security's value. We can summarize the relationship between the coupon rate, the required market yield, and the bond's price relative to its par value as follows:

coupon rate = yield required by market ⇒ price = par value
coupon rate < yield required by market ⇒ price < par value (discount)
coupon rate > yield required by market ⇒ price > par value (premium)

Exhibit 1 depicts this inverse relationship between an option-free bond's price and its discount rate (i.e., required yield). We saw this exhibit in Chapter 1 when we discussed the present value of a single cash flow and we return to this relationship once more. There are two things to infer from the price/discount rate relationship depicted in the exhibit. First, the relationship is downward sloping. This is simply the inverse relationship between present values and discount rates at work. Second, the relationship is represented as a curve rather than a straight line. In fact, the shape of the curve in Exhibit 1 is referred to as *convex*. By convex, it simply means the curve is "bowed in" relative to the origin. This second observation raises two questions about the convex or curved shape of the price/discount rate relationship. First, why is it curved? Second, what is the import of the curvature?

As noted in Chapter 1, the answer to the first question is mathematical. The answer lies in the denominator of the bond pricing formula. Since we are raising one plus the discount rate to powers greater than one, it should not be surprising that the relationship between the level of the price and the level of the discount rate is not linear.

Exhibit 1: Price/Discount Rate Relationship for an Option-Free Bond

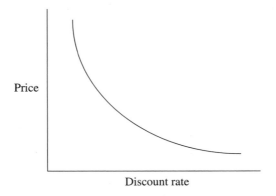

As for the importance of the curvature to bond investors, let's consider what happens to bond prices in both falling and rising interest rate environments. First, what happens to bond prices as interest rates fall? The answer is obvious — bond prices rise. How about the rate at which they rise? If the price/discount rate relationship was linear, as interest rates fell, bond prices would rise at a constant rate. However, the relationship is not linear, it is curved and curved inward. Accordingly, when interest rates fall, bond prices *increase* at an *increasing* rate. Now, let's consider what happens when interest rates rise. Of course, bond prices fall. How about the rate at which bond prices fall? Once again, if the price/discount rate relationship were linear, as interest rates rose, bond prices would fall at a constant rate. Since it curved inward, when interest rates rise, bond prices *decrease* at a *decreasing* rate. In Chapter 11, we will explore more fully the implications of the curvature or convexity of the price/discount rate relationship.

TIME PATH OF BOND

As a bond moves towards its maturity date, its value changes. More specifically, assuming that the discount rate does not change, a bond's value:

1. decreases over time if the bond is selling at a premium
2. increases over time if the bond is selling at a discount
3. is unchanged if the bond is selling at par value[4]

At the maturity date, the bond's value is equal to its par or maturity value. So, as a bond's maturity approaches, the price of a discount bond will rise to its par value and a premium bond will fall to its par value — a characteristic sometimes referred to as "pull to par value."

Time Path of a Premium Bond

To illustrate what happens to a bond selling at a premium, consider once again the 4-year 6% coupon bond. When the discount rate is 5%, the bond's price is $103.5851. Suppose that one year later, the discount rate is still 5%. There are only six cash flows remaining since the bond is now a 3-year security. We compute the present value of the coupon payments in the same way as before:

$$\$3 \times \left[\frac{1 - \dfrac{1}{(1.025)^{3 \times 2}}}{0.025} \right] = \$16.5244$$

---

[4] We are assuming the bond is valued on its coupon anniversary dates. We will relax this assumption shortly and consider what happens to a par bond between coupon payment dates.

The present value of the maturity value is

$$\text{present value of the maturity value} = \frac{\$100}{(1.025)^{3 \times 2}} = \$86.2297$$

The bond's value is then $102.7541 ($21.5104 + $82.0747).

As the bond moves toward maturity with no change in the discount rate, the price has declined from $103.5851 to $102.7541. What are the mechanics of this result? The value of a coupon bond can thought of as the sum of two present values — the present value of the coupon payments and the present value of the maturity value. What happens to each of these present values as the bond moves toward maturity with no change in the discount rate? The present value of the coupon payments falls for the simple reason that there are fewer coupon payments remaining. Correspondingly, the present value of the maturity value rises because it is one year closer to the present. What is the net effect? The present value of the coupon payments fall by more than the present value of the maturity value rises so the bond's value declines or is pulled down to par.

The intuition for the result reveals a great deal about bond valuation. Why does the present value of the coupon payments fall by more than the present value of the maturity value rises? Recall why a coupon bond sells at a premium in the first place. The answer is because it offers a higher coupon rate (6%) than new comparable bonds issued at par (5%). So, a premium bond's value is driven by its relatively high coupon payments. As the premium bond marches toward maturity and these coupon payments are delivered to investors, there are fewer and fewer "high coupon" payments remaining. So, the bond's premium must shrink and the bond price declines toward par.

Time Path of a Discount Bond

Now suppose our 4-year, 6% coupon bond is selling at a discount. When the discount rate is 7%, the bond's price is $96.5630. Suppose that one year later, the discount rate is still 7%. We compute the present value of the coupon payments as shown below:

$$\$3 \times \left[\frac{1 - \dfrac{1}{(1.035)^{3 \times 2}}}{0.035} \right] = \$15.9857$$

The present value of the maturity value is

$$\text{present value of the maturity value} = \frac{\$100}{(1.035)^{3 \times 2}} = \$81.3501$$

The bond's price increases from $96.5630 to $97.3357. Let's review the present value mechanics for this result. The present value of a discount bond's coupon payments falls for the same reason as before — as we march toward maturity, there are fewer coupon payments remaining so the present value of the remaining coupon payments must decline. As for the present value of the maturity value, it rises just like before and for the same reason — it is closer to the present. What is the net effect of these two forces for a discount bond? The present value of the maturity value rises by more than the present value of the coupon payments declines so the bond's value rises.

Why does the present value of the maturity value rise by more than the present value of the coupon payments falls? A coupon bond sells at a discount because it offers a lower coupon rate (6%) than new comparable bonds issued at par (7%). So, relative to a bond selling at par, the repayment of the principal at maturity is a relatively more important cash flow. To be sure, it is the capital gain we obtain from this payment if the bond is held to maturity that offsets the below current coupon interest payments. As the discount bond moves toward maturity, the receipt of the maturity value gets closer and closer. So, the discount must shrink and the bond's value rises toward par.

The Pull to Par Value

To illustrate how the value of a bond changes as it moves towards maturity, consider the following three 10-year bonds for which the yield required by the market is 7%: a premium bond (8% coupon selling for 107.1062), a discount bond (6% coupon selling for 92.8938), and a par bond (7% coupon). Exhibit 2 shows the value of each bond as it moves towards maturity assuming that the 7% yield required by the market does not change. Notice the pull downward to par value for the premium bond and the pull upward to par value for the discount bond. Exhibit 3 is a graph showing how each bond's value changes as the maturity date approaches assuming the yield remains at 7%. Note that if the discount rate does not change, a par bond's value will change as the bond marches towards maturity. As we will see shortly, this is only true if we value the bond on coupon payment dates.

Exhibit 2: Movement of a Premium, Discount, and Par Bond as a Bond Moves Toward Maturity*

Term to Maturity in Years	Premium Bond 8% Coupon	Discount Bond 6% Coupon	Par Bond 7% Coupon
10	107.1062	92.8938	100.00
9	106.5480	93.4052	100.00
8	106.0471	93.9529	100.00
7	105.4603	94.5397	100.00
6	104.8317	95.1683	100.00
5	104.1583	95.8417	100.00
4	103.4370	96.5630	100.00
3	102.6643	97.3357	100.00
2	101.8365	98.1635	100.00
1	100.9498	99.0502	100.00
0	100.0000	100.0000	100.00

* All bonds selling to yield 7%.

Exhibit 3: Time Path of Three Bonds

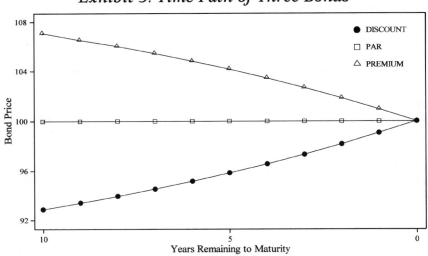

The Impact of Changing Discount Rates

In practice, of course, the discount rate will change over time. So the bond's value will change due to both the change in the discount rate and the change in the bond's cash flow as it marches toward maturity. For example, suppose that the discount rate for the 4-year 6% coupon bond is 7% so that the bond is selling for $96.5630. One year later, suppose that the discount rate appropriate for a 3-year, 6% coupon bond increases from 7% to 8%. The bond's price will decline from $96.5630 to $94.7579. If the discount rate had not increased, the price would have increased to $97.3357. The price decline of $1.8051 ($96.5630 − $94.7579) can be decomposed as follows:

Price change attributable to moving to maturity (no change in discount rate)	$0.7727 (97.3357 − 96.5630)
Price change attribute to an increase in the discount rate from 7% to 8%	−$2.5778 (94.7579 − 97.3357)
Total price change	−$1.8051

VALUING A ZERO-COUPON BOND

For a zero-coupon bond, there is only one cash flow — the repayment of principal at maturity. The value of a zero-coupon bond that matures N years from now is

$$\frac{\text{Maturity value}}{(1 + i)^{\text{no. of years} \times 2}}$$

where i is the semiannual discount rate.

The expression presented above states that the price of a zero-coupon bond is simply the present value of the maturity value. In the present value computation, why is the number of periods used for discounting rather than the number of years to the bond's maturity when there are no semiannual coupon payments? We do this in order to make the valuation of a zero-coupon bond consistent with the valuation of a coupon bond. In other words, both coupon and zero-coupon bonds are valued using semiannual compounding.

To illustrate, the value of a 10-year zero-coupon bond with a maturity value of $100 discounted at a 6.4% interest rate is $53.2606, as presented below:

$$i = 032 = (0.064/2)$$
$$N = 10$$

$$\frac{\$100}{(1.032)^{10 \times 2}} = \$53.2606$$

VALUING A BOND BETWEEN COUPON PAYMENTS

In our discussion of bond valuation to this point, we have assumed that the bonds are valued on their coupon payment dates (i.e., the next coupon payment is one full period away). For bonds with semiannual coupon payments, this occurs only twice a year. Our task now is to describe how bonds are valued on the other 363 or 364 days of the year.

In order to value a bond with the settlement date between coupon payments, we must answer three questions. First, how many days are there until the next coupon payment date? From Chapter 3, we know the answer depends on the day count convention for the bond being valued. Second, how should we compute the present value of the cash flows received over the fractional period? Third, how much must the buyer compensate the seller for the coupon earned over the fractional period? This is accrued interest that we computed in Chapter 3. In the next two sections, we will answer these three questions in order to determine the full price and the clean price of a coupon bond.

Computing the Full Price

When valuing a bond purchased with a settlement date between coupon payment dates, the first step is to determine the fractional periods between the settlement date and the next coupon date. Using the appropriate day count convention, this is determined as follows:

$$w \text{ periods} = \frac{\text{days between settlement date and next coupon payment date}}{\text{days in the coupon period}}$$

Then the present value of each expected future cash flow to be received t periods from now using a discount rate i assuming the next coupon payment is w periods from now (settlement date) is:

$$\text{present value}_t = \frac{\text{expected cash flow}}{(1+i)^{t-1+w}}$$

Note for the first coupon payment subsequent to the settlement date, $t=1$ so the exponent is just w. This procedure for calculating the present value when a bond is purchased between coupon payments is called the "Street method." In the Street method, as can be seen in the expression above, coupon interest is compounded over the fractional period w.[5]

To illustrate this calculation, suppose that a U.S. Treasury note maturing June 15, 2001 is purchased with a settlement date of January 27, 2000. This note's coupon rate is 5.5% and it has coupon payment dates of June 15 and December 15. As a result, the next coupon payment is June 15, 2000, while the previous coupon payment was December 15, 1999. There are three cash flows remaining — June 15, 2000, December 15, 2000, and June 15, 2001. The final cash flow represents the last coupon payment and the maturity value of $100. Also assume the following:

1. actual/actual day count convention
2. 140 days between the settlement date and the next coupon payment date
3. 183 days in the coupon period

Then w is 0.7659 periods (140/183). The present value of each cash flow assuming that each is discounted at a 6.1% annual discount rate is

$$\textit{Period 1: } \text{present value}_1 = \frac{\$2.75}{(1.0305)^{0.7650}} = \$2.6875$$

$$\textit{Period 2: } \text{present value}_2 = \frac{\$2.75}{(1.0305)^{1.7650}} = \$2.6080$$

$$\textit{Period 3: } \text{present value}_3 = \frac{\$102.75}{(1.0305)^{2.7650}} = \$94.5593$$

The sum of the present values of the cash flows is $99.8548. This price is referred to as the *full price* (or the *dirty price*).

It is the full price the bond's buyer pays the seller at delivery. However, the very next cash flow received and included in the present value calculation was not earned by the bond's buyer. A portion of the next coupon payment is the *accrued interest*. From Chapter 3, we know that accrued interest is the portion of a bond's next coupon payment that the bond's seller is entitled to depending on the amount of time the bond was held by the seller. Recall, the buyer recovers the accrued interest when the next coupon payment is delivered.

---

[5] The "Treasury method" treats coupon interest over the fractional period as simple interest.

Computing the Accrued Interest and the Clean Price

The last step in this process is to find the bond's value without accrued interest (called the *clean price* or simply *price*). To do this, the accrued interest must be computed. The first step is to determine the number of days in the accrued interest period (i.e., the number of days between the last coupon payment date and the settlement date) using the appropriate day count convention. For ease of exposition, we will assume in the example that follows that the actual/actual calendar is used. We will also assume there are only two bondholders in a given coupon period — the buyer and the seller.

As an illustration, we return to the previous example with the 5.5% coupon Treasury note. Since there are 183 days in the coupon period and 140 days from the settlement date to the next coupon period, there are 43 days (183 − 140) in the accrued interest period. Therefore, the percentage of the next coupon payment that is accrued interest is:

$$\frac{43}{183} = 0.2350 = 23.50\%$$

Of course, this is the same percentage found by simply subtracting w from 1. In our example, w was 0.7650. Then, 1 − 0.7650 = 0.2350.

Given the value of w, the amount of accrued interest (AI) is equal to:

$$AI = \text{semiannual coupon payment} \times (1 - w)$$

Accordingly, using a 5.5% Treasury note with a settlement date of January 27, 2000, the portion of the next coupon payment that is accrued interest is:

$$\$2.75 \times (1 - 0.7650) = \$0.64625 \text{ (per \$100 of par value)}$$

Once we know the full price and the accrued interest, we can determine the clean price. The clean price is the price that quoted in the market and represents the bond's value to the new bondholder. The clean price is computed as follows

$$\text{clean price} = \text{full price} - \text{accrued interest}$$

In our illustration, the clean price is

$$99.2086 = \$99.8548 - \$0.64625$$

Note that in computing the full price the present value of the next coupon payment is computed. However, the buyer pays the seller the accrued interest now despite the fact that it will not be recovered until the next coupon payment date. To make this concrete, suppose one sells a bond such that the settlement date is halfway between the coupon payment dates. In this case $w = 0.50$. Accordingly, the seller will be entitled to one-half of the next coupon payment which would not otherwise be received for another three months. Thus, when calculating the clean price, we subtract "too much" accrued interest — one-half the coupon payment rather than the present value of one-half the coupon payment. Of course, this is the market convention for calculating accrued interest but it does introduce a curious twist in bond valuation.

Time Path of a Par Bond Between Coupon Payment Dates

What path does a par bond's clean price take between coupon payment dates if the discount rate is unchanged? The answer is presented in Exhibit 4. When a bond's coupon rate and discount rate are the same, a bond will be valued at a slight discount to par between coupon payment dates. The clean price of a "par bond" is at a discount to par because of the market's convention for calculating accrued interest.

Two final points. First, this effect is small and this can be seen by observing the scale on the vertical axis of the exhibit. Second, why is the discount to par small at the beginning of the coupon period, gradually gets larger, and then becomes small as the next coupon payment date is approached? The answer lies in the difference between the accrued interest and the present value of the accrued interest. At the beginning of the period, the difference between the accrued interest and present value of the accrued interest is large on a relative basis but the accrued interest (to this point) is small. As a result, this difference will have only a small impact on the price. Furthermore, as we move through the coupon period, the accrued interest gets increasingly larger but the difference between the accrued interest and present value of the accrued interest is getting progressively smaller on a relative basis because the next coupon payment is getting closer to the present. Thus, we should see the largest discount to par about halfway between the coupon payment dates where the these two effects — the size of the accrued interest and the difference the accrued interest and its present value — are both at half-strength. We see in Exhibit 4 that this is true.

Exhibit 4: Time Path of a Par Bond

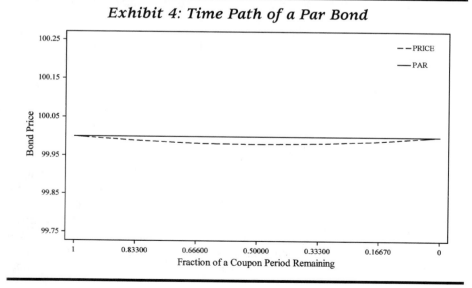

Exhibit 5: Cash Flows for Three 10-Year Hypothetical Treasury Securities

Per $100 of Par Value

Each period is six months

Period	Coupon Rate		
	8%	6%	0%
1-19	$4	$3	$0
20	$104	$103	$100

TRADITIONAL APPROACH TO VALUATION

The traditional approach to valuation is to discount every cash flow of a fixed-income security by the same interest rate (or discount rate). For example, consider the three hypothetical 10-year Treasury securities shown in Exhibit 5: an 8% coupon bond, a 6% coupon bond, and a zero-coupon bond. The cash flows for each bond are shown in the exhibit. Since the cash flows of all three bonds are viewed as default free, the traditional practice is to use the same discount rate to calculate the present value of all three bonds and use the same discount rate for the cash flow for each period. The discount rate used is the yield for the on-the-run issue obtained from the Treasury yield curve. For example, suppose that the yield for the 10-year on-the-run Treasury issue is 7%. Then, the traditional approach is to discount each cash flow of each bond using a discount rate of 7% appropriately adjusted for the frequency of the coupon payments.

For a non-Treasury security, a premium or yield spread is added to the on-the-run Treasury yield. In the traditional approach, the yield spread is the same regardless of when a cash flow is to be received. For a 10-year non-Treasury security, suppose that 55 basis points is the appropriate yield spread. Then all cash flows would be discounted at the yield for the on-the-run 10-year Treasury issue of 7% plus 55 basis points.

THE ARBITRAGE-FREE VALUATION APPROACH

As just noted, the traditional approach to valuation is to discount every cash flow of a fixed-income security with the same interest or discount rate (i.e., assuming that the yield curve is flat). For example, consider a 10-year U.S. Treasury note with a 6% coupon rate. The cash flows per $100 of par value would be 9 payments of $3.00 every six months and $103 ten 6-month periods from now. The *arbitrage-free valuation approach* views the 10-year, 6% coupon Treasury note as a package of zero-coupon instruments whose maturity value is the amount of the cash flow and whose maturity date coincides with the date the cash flow is to be received. Thus, the 10-year, 6% coupon Treasury issue should be viewed as a package of 20 zero-coupon instruments that mature every six months for the next

ten years. This approach to valuation does not allow a market participant to realize an arbitrage profit by stripping or reconstituting Treasury bonds.

The difference between the traditional valuation approach and the arbitrage-free approach is illustrated in Exhibit 6, which presents how the three bonds
whose cash flows are depicted in Exhibit 5 should be valued. With the traditional
approach, the discount rate for all bonds is the yield on a 10-year Treasury taken
from the Treasury par yield curve. With the arbitrage-free approach, cash flows
are discounted using spot rates taken from the Treasury spot rate curve that corre-
spond to the maturity date of the cash flow. We call the bond's value based on
spot rates the *arbitrage-free value.*

Valuation Using Treasury Spot Rates

To illustrate how Treasury spot rates are used to compute the arbitrage-free value
of a Treasury security, we will use the hypothetical Treasury spot rates shown in
the fourth column of Exhibit 7 to value an 8%, 10-year Treasury security. The
present value of each period's cash flow is shown in the last column. The sum of
the present values is the arbitrage-free value for the Treasury security. For the 8%,
10-year Treasury it is $107.002.

Exhibit 6: Comparison of Traditional Approach and Arbitrage-Free Approach in Valuing a Treasury Security
Each period is six months

| Period | Discount (Base Interest) Rate | | Cash Flows For* | | |
	Traditional Approach	Arbitrage-Free Approach	8%	6%	0%
1	10-year Treasury rate	1-period Treasury spot rate	$4	$3	$0
2	10-year Treasury rate	2-period Treasury spot rate	4	3	0
3	10-year Treasury rate	3-period Treasury spot rate	4	3	0
4	10-year Treasury rate	4-period Treasury spot rate	4	3	0
5	10-year Treasury rate	5-period Treasury spot rate	4	3	0
6	10-year Treasury rate	6-period Treasury spot rate	4	3	0
7	10-year Treasury rate	7-period Treasury spot rate	4	3	0
8	10-year Treasury rate	8-period Treasury spot rate	4	3	0
9	10-year Treasury rate	9-period Treasury spot rate	4	3	0
10	10-year Treasury rate	10-period Treasury spot rate	4	3	0
11	10-year Treasury rate	11-period Treasury spot rate	4	3	0
12	10-year Treasury rate	12-period Treasury spot rate	4	3	0
13	10-year Treasury rate	13-period Treasury spot rate	4	3	0
14	10-year Treasury rate	14-period Treasury spot rate	4	3	0
15	10-year Treasury rate	15-period Treasury spot rate	4	3	0
16	10-year Treasury rate	16-period Treasury spot rate	4	3	0
17	10-year Treasury rate	17-period Treasury spot rate	4	3	0
18	10-year Treasury rate	18-period Treasury spot rate	4	3	0
19	10-year Treasury rate	19-period Treasury spot rate	4	3	0
20	10-year Treasury rate	20-period Treasury spot rate	104	103	100

* Per $100 of par value.

Exhibit 7: Determination of the Arbitrage-Free Value of an 8% 10-Year Treasury

Period	Years	Cash Flow ($)	Spot Rate (%)	Present Value ($)
1	0.5	4	6.05	3.8826
2	1.0	4	6.15	3.7649
3	1.5	4	6.21	3.6494
4	2.0	4	6.26	3.5361
5	2.5	4	6.29	3.4263
6	3.0	4	6.37	3.3141
7	3.5	4	6.38	3.2107
8	4.0	4	6.40	3.1090
9	4.5	4	6.41	3.0113
10	5.0	4	6.48	2.9079
11	5.5	4	6.49	2.8151
12	6.0	4	6.53	2.7203
13	6.5	4	6.63	2.6178
14	7.0	4	6.78	2.5082
15	7.5	4	6.79	2.4242
16	8.0	4	6.81	2.3410
17	8.5	4	6.84	2.2583
18	9.0	4	6.93	2.1666
19	9.5	4	7.05	2.0711
20	10.0	104	7.20	51.2670
			Total	107.0018

As a second illustration, suppose that a 6% coupon 10-year Treasury bond is being valued based on the Treasury spot rates shown in Exhibit 7. The arbitrage-free value of this bond is $92.5751, as shown in Exhibit 8.

In the next chapter we discuss yield measures. The yield to maturity is a measure that would be computed for this bond. We will not show how it is computed in this chapter, but simply state the result. The yield to maturity is 7.0471%. Notice that the spot rates are used to obtain the price and the price is then used to compute a conventional yield measure. It is important to understand that there are an infinite number of spot rate curves that can generate the same price of $92.5751 and therefore the same yield. This is true because the yield to maturity is a complicated average of the spot rates.

Reason for Using Treasury Spot Rates

Thus far, we have simply asserted that the value of a Treasury security should be based on discounting each cash flow using the corresponding Treasury spot rate. But what if market participants value a security using just the yield for the on-the-run Treasury with a maturity equal to the maturity of the Treasury security being valued? Let's see why the value of a Treasury security should trade close to its arbitrage-free value.

Exhibit 8: Determination of the Arbitrage-Free Value of an 6% 10-Year Treasury

Period	Years	Cash Flow ($)	Spot Rate (%)	Present Value ($)
1	0.5	3	6.05	2.9119
2	1.0	3	6.15	2.8237
3	1.5	3	6.21	2.7370
4	2.0	3	6.26	2.6520
5	2.5	3	6.29	2.5697
6	3.0	3	6.37	2.4855
7	3.5	3	6.38	2.4080
8	4.0	3	6.40	2.3318
9	4.5	3	6.41	2.2585
10	5.0	3	6.48	2.1809
11	5.5	3	6.49	2.1114
12	6.0	3	6.53	2.0403
13	6.5	3	6.63	1.9633
14	7.0	3	6.78	1.8811
15	7.5	3	6.79	1.8181
16	8.0	3	6.81	1.7557
17	8.5	3	6.84	1.6937
18	9.0	3	6.93	1.6249
19	9.5	3	7.05	1.5533
20	10.0	103	7.20	50.7741
			Total	92.5751

Stripping and the Arbitrage-Free Valuation

The key to the arbitrage-free valuation approach is the existence of the Treasury strips market. As explained in Chapter 2, a dealer has the ability to take apart the cash flows of a Treasury coupon security (i.e., strip the security) and create zero-coupon securities. These zero-coupon securities, which we called *Treasury strips*, can be sold to investors.[6] At what interest rate or yield can these Treasury strips be sold to investors? They can be sold at the Treasury spot rates. If the market price of a Treasury security is less than its value using the arbitrage-free valuation approach, then a dealer can buy the Treasury security, strip it, and sell off the individual Treasury strips so as to generate greater proceeds than the cost of purchasing the Treasury security. The resulting profit is an *arbitrage profit*. Since, as we will see, the value determined by using the Treasury spot rates does not allow for the generation of an arbitrage profit, this is referred to as an "arbitrage-free" approach.

To illustrate this, suppose that the yield for the on-the-run 10-year Treasury issue is 7.08%. Suppose that the 8% coupon 10-year Treasury issue is valued using the traditional approach based on 7.08%. Exhibit 9 shows that the value based on discounting all the cash flows at 7.08% is $106.5141.

---

[6] All 10-year notes and 30-year bonds issued on or after February 15, 1985 can be stripped. All notes of less than 10 years to maturity issued on or after September 30, 1997 can be stripped.

Exhibit 9: Price of an 8% 10-Year Treasury Valued at a 7.08% Discount Rate

Period	Years	Cash Flow ($)	Discount Rate (%)	Present Value ($)
1	0.5	4	7.08	3.8632
2	1.0	4	7.08	3.7312
3	1.5	4	7.08	3.6036
4	2.0	4	7.08	3.4804
5	2.5	4	7.08	3.3614
6	3.0	4	7.08	3.2465
7	3.5	4	7.08	3.1355
8	4.0	4	7.08	3.0283
9	4.5	4	7.08	2.9247
10	5.0	4	7.08	2.8247
11	5.5	4	7.08	2.7282
12	6.0	4	7.08	2.6349
13	6.5	4	7.08	2.5448
14	7.0	4	7.08	2.4578
15	7.5	4	7.08	2.3738
16	8.0	4	7.08	2.2926
17	8.5	4	7.08	2.2142
18	9.0	4	7.08	2.1385
19	9.5	4	7.08	2.0654
20	10.0	104	7.08	51.8645
			Total	106.5141

Consider what would happen if the market priced the security at $106.5141. The value based on the Treasury spot rates (Exhibit 7) is $107.002. What can the dealer do? The dealer can buy the 8% 10-year issue for $106.5141, strip it, and sell the Treasury strips at the spot rates shown in Exhibit 7. By doing so, the proceeds that will be received by the dealer are $107.002. This results in an arbitrage profit of $0.4879 (= $107.002 − $106.5141). Dealers recognizing this arbitrage opportunity will bid up the price of the 8% 10-year Treasury issue in order to acquire it and strip it. At what point will the arbitrage profit disappear? When the security is priced at $107.002, the value that we said is the arbitrage-free value.[7]

To understand in more detail where this arbitrage profit is coming from, look at Exhibit 10. The third column shows how much each cash flow can be sold for by the dealer if it is stripped. The values in the third column are simply the present values in Exhibit 7 based on discounting the cash flows at the Treasury spot rates. The fourth column shows how much the dealer is effectively purchasing the cash flow for if each cash flow is discounted at 7.08%. This is taken from the last column in Exhibit 9. The sum of the arbitrage profit from each stripped cash flow is the total arbitrage profit and is contained in the last column of Exhibit 10.

---

[7] We are ignoring transaction costs. However, strictly speaking, the arbitrage profits will be bid down to the amount of transaction costs.

Exhibit 10: Arbitrage Profit from Stripping the 8% 10-Year Treasury

Period	Years	Sell for	Buy for	Arbitrage profit
1	0.5	3.8836	3.8632	0.0193
2	1.0	3.7649	3.7312	0.0337
3	1.5	3.6494	3.6036	0.0458
4	2.0	3.5361	3.4804	0.0557
5	2.5	3.4263	3.3614	0.6486
6	3.0	3.3141	3.2465	0.0676
7	3.5	3.3107	3.1355	0.0752
8	4.0	3.1090	3.0283	0.0807
9	4.5	3.0113	2.9247	0.0866
10	5.0	2.9079	2.8247	0.0832
11	5.5	2.8151	2.7282	0.0867
12	6.0	2.7203	2.6349	0.0854
13	6.5	2.6178	2.5448	0.0730
14	7.0	2.5082	2.4578	0.0504
15	7.5	2.4242	2.3738	0.0504
16	8.0	2.3410	2.2926	0.0484
17	8.5	2.2583	2.2142	0.0441
18	9.0	2.1666	2.1385	0.0281
19	9.5	2.0711	2.0654	0.0057
20	10.0	51.2670	51.8645	−0.5975
		107.0018	106.5141	0.4877

Reconstitution and Arbitrage-Free Valuation

We have just demonstrated how coupon stripping of a Treasury issue will force the market value to be close to the value as determined by the arbitrage-free valuation approach when the market price is less than the arbitrage-free value (i.e., the whole is worth less than the sum of the parts). What happens when a Treasury issue's market price is greater than the arbitrage-free value? Obviously, a dealer will not want to strip the Treasury issue since the proceeds generated from stripping will be less than the cost of purchasing the issue.

When such situations occur, the dealer can purchase a package of Treasury strips so as to create a synthetic Treasury coupon security that is worth more than the same maturity and same coupon Treasury issue. This process is called *reconstitution*.[8]

All securities including Treasury securities are assigned a standard identification number called a CUSIP number.[9] Each coupon and principal payment of a coupon Treasury security has a CUSIP number. All coupon payments (*interest strips*) that are payable on the same day (say May 15) have the same generic CUSIP number even when stripped from different Treasury issues. How-

---

[8] The U.S. Treasury permitted reconstitution beginning in May 1987.
[9] CUSIP is an acronym for Committee on Uniform Security Identification Procedures.

ever, the principal payment (i.e., *principal strip*) for any note or bond has a unique CUSIP number. Thus, coupon strips are interchangeable parts while principal strips are not.

To illustrate this process, consider the 6% 10-year Treasury issue whose arbitrage-free value was computed in Exhibit 8. The arbitrage-free value is $92.5751. Exhibit 11 shows the price assuming the traditional approach where all the cash flows are discounted at a 7% discount rate. The price is $92.8938. Under these circumstances, the dealer will purchase the Treasury strip for each 6-month period at the prices shown in Exhibit 8 and sell short the 6% 10-year Treasury coupon issue whose cash flows are being replicated. By doing so, the dealer has the cash flow of a 6% coupon 10-year Treasury security at a cost of $92.5751, thereby generating an arbitrage profit of $0.3187 ($92.8938 − $92.5751). The cash flows from the package of Treasury strips purchased is used to make the payments for the Treasury coupon security shorted. Actually, in practice this can be done in a more efficient manner using a procedure for reconstitution provided by the Department of the Treasury.

What forces the market price to the arbitrage-free value of $92.5751? As dealers sell short the Treasury coupon issue (6% 10-year issue), these actions drive down the price of the issue. When the price is driven down to $92.5751, the arbitrage profit no longer exists.

Exhibit 11: Price of an 6% 10-Year Treasury Valued at a 7% Discount Rate

Period	Years	Cash Flow ($)	Discount Rate (%)	Present Value ($)
1	0.5	3	7	2.8986
2	1.0	3	7	2.8001
3	1.5	3	7	2.7058
4	2.0	3	7	2.6143
5	2.5	3	7	2.5259
6	3.0	3	7	2.4405
7	3.5	3	7	2.3580
8	4.0	3	7	2.2782
9	4.5	3	7	2.2012
10	5.0	3	7	2.1268
11	5.5	3	7	2.0548
12	6.0	3	7	1.9854
13	6.5	3	7	1.9182
14	7.0	3	7	1.8533
15	7.5	3	7	1.7907
16	8.0	3	7	1.7301
17	8.5	3	7	1.6716
18	9.0	3	7	1.6151
19	9.5	3	7	1.5605
20	10.0	103	7	51.7643
			Total	92.8938

Thus the process of stripping and reconstitution assures that the price of a Treasury issue will not depart materially (depending on transaction costs) from its arbitrage-free value.

Credit Spreads and the Valuation of Non-Treasury Securities

The Treasury spot rates can be used to value any default-free security. For a non-Treasury security, the theoretical value is not as easy to determine. The value of a non-Treasury security is found by discounting the cash flows by the Treasury spot rates plus a yield spread which reflects the additional risks (e.g., default risk, liquidity risks, the risk associated with any embedded options, and so on).

The spot rate used to discount the cash flow of a non-Treasury security can be the Treasury spot rate plus a constant credit spread. For example, suppose the 6-month Treasury spot rate is 6.05% and the 10-year Treasury spot rate is 7.20%. Also suppose that a suitable credit spread is 100 basis points. Then a 7.05% spot rate is used to discount a 6-month cash flow of a non-Treasury bond and a 8.20% discount rate is used to discount a 10-year cash flow. (Remember that when each semiannual cash flow is discounted, the discount rate used is one-half the spot rate: 3.525% for the 6-month spot rate and 4.10% for the 10-year spot rate.)

The drawback of this approach is that there is no reason to expect the credit spread to be the same regardless of when the cash flow is expected to be received. Consequently, the credit spread may vary with a bond's term to maturity. In other words, there is a *term structure of credit spreads.*

Dealer firms typically estimate the term structure of credit spreads for each credit rating and market sector. Typically, the credit spread increases with maturity. In addition, the shape of the term structure is not the same for all credit ratings. Typically, the lower the credit rating, the steeper the term structure of credit spreads.

When the relevant credit spreads for a given credit rating and market sector are added to the Treasury spot rates, the resulting term structure is used to value the bonds of issuers with that credit rating in that market sector.[10] This term structure is referred to as the *benchmark spot rate curve* or *benchmark zero-coupon rate curve.*

For example, Exhibit 12 reproduces the Treasury spot rate curve in Exhibit 7. Also shown in the exhibit is a hypothetical term structure of credit spread for a non-Treasury security. The resulting benchmark spot rate curve is in the next-to-the-last column. Like before, it is this spot rate curve that is used to value the securities of issuers that have the same credit rating and are in the same market sector. This is done in Exhibit 12 for a hypothetical 8% 10-year issue. The arbitrage-free value is $101.763. Notice that the theoretical value is less than that for an otherwise comparable Treasury security. The arbitrage-free value for an 8% 10-year Treasury is $107.0018 (see Exhibit 7).

---

[10] A good example is Bloomberg's fair market curves (function FMC).

Exhibit 12: Calculation of Arbitrage-Free Value of a Hypothetical 8% 10-Year Non-Treasury Security Using Benchmark Spot Rate Curve

Period	Years	Cash Flow ($)	Treasury Spot Rate (%)	Credit Spread (%)	Benchmark Spot (%)	Present Value ($)
1	0.5	4	6.05	0.30	6.35	3.8769
2	1.0	4	6.15	0.33	6.48	3.7529
3	1.5	4	6.21	0.34	6.55	3.6314
4	2.0	4	6.26	0.37	6.63	3.5108
5	2.5	4	6.29	0.42	6.71	3.3916
6	3.0	4	6.37	0.43	6.80	3.2729
7	3.5	4	6.38	0.44	6.82	3.1632
8	4.0	4	6.40	0.45	6.85	3.0553
9	4.5	4	6.41	0.46	6.87	2.9516
10	5.0	4	6.48	0.52	7.00	2.8357
11	5.5	4	6.49	0.53	7.02	2.7369
12	6.0	4	6.53	0.55	7.08	2.6349
13	6.5	4	6.63	0.58	7.21	2.5241
14	7.0	4	6.78	0.59	7.37	2.4101
15	7.5	4	6.79	0.63	7.42	2.3161
16	8.0	4	6.81	0.64	7.45	2.2281
17	8.5	4	6.84	0.69	7.53	2.1340
18	9.0	4	6.93	0.73	7.66	2.0335
19	9.5	4	7.05	0.77	7.82	1.9301
20	10.0	104	7.20	0.82	8.02	47.3731
					Total	101.763

As an additional illustration, Exhibit 13 presents a Bloomberg screen (function FMCS) containing the term structure of credit spreads for four sectors of the corporate bond market as of November 28, 2000. These sectors include AAA (1), AA1 (2), A1 (5), and A1 (8) industrial bonds. Generally, credit spreads increase with maturity. This is a typical shape for the term structure of credit spreads. Moreover, the shape of the term structure is not the same for all credit ratings. Typically, the lower the credit rating, the steeper the term structure of credit spreads. Both of the tendencies are evident in Exhibit 14 which presents a Bloomberg graph of these credit spreads as a function of maturity.

Exhibit 13: Credit Spreads of Corporate Bonds by Maturity and Credit Rating

1   DG15 Govt **FMCS**
Hit <MENU> for list of curves.
SPREADS TO ACTIVE U.S. GOVTS   Page 1/ 3

	1	2	5	8		
3MO	39	48	64	104		
6MO	37	43	60	100		
1YR	40	44	64	100		
2YR	69	73	92	134		
3YR	77	81	102	148		
4YR	85	90	118	164		
5YR	98	107	134	181		
7YR	97	112	139	190		
10YR	114	138	164	215		
20YR	109	132	168	216		
30YR	126	147	191	235		

Currency ■

+ indicates curve floats intraday with benchmark curve

+	1: US$ Industrials AAA	+	8: US$ Industrials BBB1
+	2: US$ Industrials AA1		
+	5: US$ Industrials A1		

Copyright 2000 BLOOMBERG L.P.   Frankfurt:69-920410 Hong Kong:2-977-6000 London:207-330-7500 New York:212-318-2000
Princeton:609-279-3000   Singapore:65-212-1000   Sydney:2-9777-8686   Tokyo:3-3201-8900   Sao Paulo:11-3048-4500
1464-169-0 28-Nov-00 16:51:50

Bloomberg
PROFESSIONAL

Source: Bloomberg

Exhibit 14: Term Structure of Credit Spreads

Page   DG15 Govt **FMCS**
Hit <MENU> for list of curves.
SPREADS TO ACTIVE U.S. GOVTS   Page 2/ 3

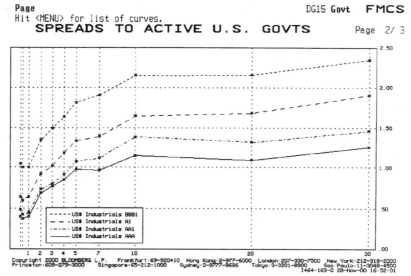

Copyright 2000 BLOOMBERG L.P.   Frankfurt:69-920410 Hong Kong:2-977-6000 London:207-330-7500 New York:212-318-2000
Princeton:609-279-3000   Singapore:65-212-1000   Sydney:2-9777-8686   Tokyo:3-3201-8900   Sao Paulo:11-3048-4500
1464-169-0 28-Nov-00 16:52:01

Bloomberg
PROFESSIONAL

Source: Bloomberg

Chapter 5

Yield Measures

A bond's yield is a measure of its *potential* return. Market participants commonly assess a security's relative value by calculating a yield or some yield spread. There are a number of yield measures that are quoted in the market. These measures are based on certain assumptions necessary to carry out the calculation. However, they also limit effectiveness of a yield measure in gauging relative value. In this chapter, we will explain the various yield and yield spread measures as well as document their limitations.

SOURCES OF RETURN

The dollar return an investor expects to receive comes from three potential sources:

1. the periodic interest payments made by the issuer (i.e., coupon payments)
2. any capital gain (or capital loss, which is a negative dollar return) when the bond matures, is sold by the investor, or is called by the issuer
3. income earned from reinvestment of the bond's interim cash flows (i.e., coupon payments and principal repayments.)

In order to be a useful indicator of a bond's potential return, a yield measure should account for all three of these potential sources of dollar return in a reasonable way. We will begin our discussion by examining the three return sources in more detail.

We will illustrate the sources of dollar returns using an example. On the afternoon of July 5, 2000, the on-the-run 5-year Treasury note was trading at 102-20+ assuming next day settlement (i.e., $102.6406 per $100 of par value). The security description (DES) screen from Bloomberg is presented in Exhibit 1. This note carries a coupon rate of 6.75% and matures on May 15, 2005. Coupon payments are delivered on May 15 and November 15. Suppose the $1 million of par value of these 5-year notes are purchased on July 5, 2000. If this position is held to maturity, what are the three sources of dollar returns? These numbers can be found on yield analysis (YA) screen from Bloomberg in Exhibit 2.

Periodic Interest Payments

The most obvious source of dollar return is the periodic coupon interest payments. For the $1 million par value of this 5-year note, the semiannual coupon

91

payments consist of 10 payments of $33,750 with the first occurring on November 15, 2000. Since this note has a settlement date between coupon periods, the buyer pays the seller accrued interest. There are 52 days between the date the bond was issued (May 15, 2000) and the bond's settlement date of July 6, 2000. In addition, there are 184 days in the coupon period. At settlement, the buyer will pay the seller $9,538.04 (per $1 million in par value) in accrued interest which is calculated as follows

$$\$33,750 \times (52/184) = \$9,538.04$$

The accrued interest is located on the right-hand side of the screen under "PAYMENT INVOICE" and is labeled "52 DAYS ACCRUED INT."

For a zero-coupon bond, there are no interim coupon payments so the return from this source is zero. This is true even though the investor is effectively receiving interest by purchasing the instrument at a discount to its par value and realizing interest at the maturity date when the investor receives the repayment of principal.

Exhibit 1: Bloomberg Security Description Screen for a 5-Year Treasury Note

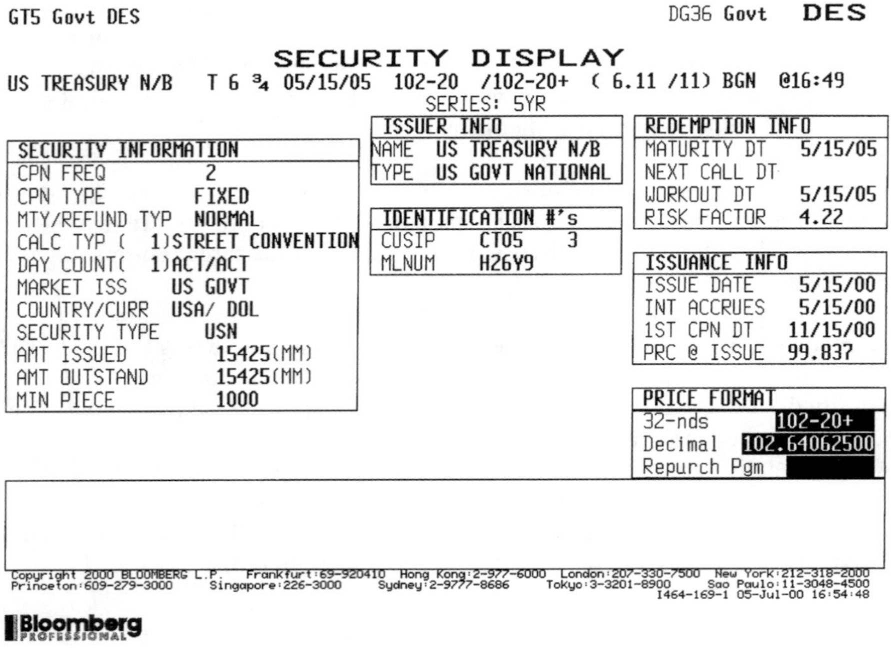

GT5 Govt DES   DG36 Govt   **DES**

SECURITY DISPLAY

US TREASURY N/B   T 6 ¾ 05/15/05 102-20 /102-20+ (6.11 /11) BGN @16:49

SERIES: 5YR

SECURITY INFORMATION		ISSUER INFO		REDEMPTION INFO	
CPN FREQ	2	NAME US TREASURY N/B		MATURITY DT	5/15/05
CPN TYPE	FIXED	TYPE US GOVT NATIONAL		NEXT CALL DT	
MTY/REFUND TYP	NORMAL			WORKOUT DT	5/15/05
CALC TYP (1)STREET CONVENTION		IDENTIFICATION #'s		RISK FACTOR	4.22
DAY COUNT(1)ACT/ACT		CUSIP CT05 3			
MARKET ISS US GOVT		MLNUM H26Y9		ISSUANCE INFO	
COUNTRY/CURR USA/ DOL				ISSUE DATE	5/15/00
SECURITY TYPE USN				INT ACCRUES	5/15/00
AMT ISSUED 15425(MM)				1ST CPN DT	11/15/00
AMT OUTSTAND 15425(MM)				PRC @ ISSUE	99.837
MIN PIECE 1000					

PRICE FORMAT
32-nds   102-20+
Decimal 102.64062500
Repurch Pgm

Bloomberg PROFESSIONAL

Source: Bloomberg

Exhibit 2: Bloomberg Yield Analysis Screen for a 5-Year Treasury Note

```
GT5  Govt YA                                          DG36 Govt  YA
Bond Matures on a SUNDAY
                        YIELD  ANALYSIS          CUSIP     CT05    3
US TREASURY N/B    T 6 ¾ 05/15/05   102-20  /102-20+  ( 6.11 /11) BGN  @16:49
PRICE  102-20+                 SETTLEMENT  DATE  7/ 6/2000
YIELD                  MATURITY   CASHFLOW  ANALYSIS
CALCULATIONS           5/15/2005  To  5/15/2005WORKOUT   1000M FACE
STREET CONVENTION              6.111  PAYMENT  INVOICE
TREASURY CONVENTION            6.109  PRINCIPAL[RND(Y/N)N]   1026406.25
TRUE YIELD                     6.108   52 DAYS ACCRUED INT      9538.04
EQUIVALENT  1/YEAR COMPOUND    6.205  TOTAL                  1035944.29
JAPANESE YIELD (SIMPLE)        6.046          INCOME
PROCEEDS/MMKT EQUIVALENT              REDEMPTION VALUE       1000000.00
                                      COUPON PAYMENT          337500.00
REPO EQUIVALENT                6.374  INTEREST @ 6.111%        50397.77
EFFECTIVE  @ 6.111 RATE(%)     6.111  TOTAL                  1387897.77
TAXED: INC 39.60% CG 28.00%    3.692          RETURN
*ISSUE PRICE = 99.837.  BOND PURCHASED WITH PREMIUM.*
                                      GROSS PROFIT            351953.48
SENSITIVITY  ANALYSIS                 RETURN  (SIMPLE INT)       6.111
CNV DURATION(YEARS)            4.195
ADJ/MOD DURATION               4.071  FURTHER  ANALYSIS
RISK                           4.217  HIT 1 <GO> COST OF CARRY
CONVEXITY                      0.202  HIT 2 <GO> PRICE/YIELD TABLE
DOLLAR VALUE OF A  0.01        0.04217 HIT 3 <GO> TOTAL RETURN
YIELD VALUE OF A   0 32        0.00741
Copyright 2000 BLOOMBERG L.P.  Frankfurt:69-920410  Hong Kong:2-977-6000  London:207-330-7500  New York:212-318-2000
Princeton:609-279-3000   Singapore:226-3000   Sydney:2-9777-8686   Tokyo:3-3201-8900   Sao Paulo:11-3048-4500
                                                                    I464-169-1 05-Jul-00 16:55:18
```

Bloomberg
PROFESSIONAL

Source: Bloomberg

Capital Gain or Loss[1]

The investor's tenure as a bond's owner ends as a result of one of the following circumstances. First, the investor may simply sell the bond and will receive the bond's prevailing market price plus accrued interest. Next, the issuer may call the bond in which case the investor receives the call price plus accrued interest or the investor may put the bond and receive the put price plus accrued interest. Lastly, if the bond matures, the investor will receive the maturity value plus the final coupon payment. Regardless of the reason, if the proceeds received are greater than the investor's initial purchase price, a capital gain is generated which is an additional source of dollar return. Similarly, if the proceeds received are less than the investor's initial purchase price, a capital loss is generated which is a negative dollar return. For the 5-year note described above, the purchase price is $1,035,944.29 (i.e., the clean price plus accrued interest). Thus, if the investor holds this note until the maturity date of May 15, 2005, the investor will generate a capital loss of $35,944.29 ($1,000,000 − $1,035,944.29).

---

[1] The definition of capital gain or loss here is different from that defined for tax purposes.

Reinvestment Income

The source of dollar return called *reinvestment income* represents the interest earned from reinvesting the bond's interim cash flows (interest and/or principal payments) until the bond is removed from the investor's portfolio. With the exception of zero-coupon bonds, fixed income securities deliver coupon payments that can be reinvested. Moreover, amortizing securities (e.g., mortgage-backed and asset-backed securities) make periodic principal repayments which can also be invested.

As an example, if $1 million of the 5-year note is held to maturity, the investor will receive $337,500 in coupon payments over the next 10 semiannual periods. The total coupon payments can be found on the left-hand side of the YA screen in Exhibit 2 and are labeled "COUPON PAYMENT." Suppose an investor can reinvest each of these 10 coupon payments at say 6.111% compounded semiannually.[2] The reinvestment income can be determined using the future value of an ordinary annuity formula from Chapter 1. Recall the general formula for the future value of an ordinary annuity when payments occur m times per year is

$$FV_n = A\left[\frac{(1 + i)^n - 1}{i}\right]$$

where

A = Amount of the annuity ($)
i = Periodic interest rate which is the annual interest rate divided by m (in decimal form)
n = $N \times m$

Accordingly, the future value of 10 semiannual payments of $33,750 to be received plus the interest earned by investing the payments at 6.111% compounded semiannually is found as follows:

A = 33,750
m = 2
i = 0.030555 (0.06111/2)
N = 5
n = 10 (5 × 2)

therefore,

$$FV_{10} = \$33,750\left[\frac{(1.030555)^{10} - 1}{0.030555}\right]$$

$$= \$33,750(11.49322) = \$387,896.30$$

Thus, the coupon payments and reinvestment income together are $387,896.30. The reinvestment income alone is $50,396.30 which is found by subtracting the

---

[2] This interest rate was not chosen arbitrarily; the 5-year note's yield to maturity (discussed shortly) is 6.111%.

total coupon payments ($387,896.30 − $337,500). This number (with rounding error) matches the reinvestment income (labeled as "INTEREST @ 6.111%") presented in the YA screen in Exhibit 2. Note that this function allows the user to input alternative interest rates to determine the reinvestment income.

TRADITIONAL YIELD MEASURES

There are several yield measures commonly quoted by dealers and traders in the bond market. Among the more prominent are *current yield, yield to maturity, yield to call, yield to put, yield to worst,* and *cash flow yield.* In this section, we will demonstrate how to compute various yield measures for a bond given its price. We will also highlight their limitations as measures of potential return. This discussion will pave the way for a more useful yield measure for determining the potential return from investing in a bond, total return, which will be discussed in Chapter 10.

Current Yield

The *current yield* of a bond is calculated by dividing the security's annual dollar coupon payment by the market price. The formula for the current yield is

$$\text{Current yield} = \frac{\text{Annual dollar coupon payment}}{\text{Price}}$$

To illustrate the calculation, consider a 7.45% coupon bond issued by Ford Motor Co. in July 1999 that matures on July 16, 2031. The Security Description screen from Bloomberg is presented in Exhibit 3. Moreover, the Bloomberg's YA (yield analysis) screen is displayed in Exhibit 4. The market price of this bond is 94.697251. The current yield is located underneath the price and is 7.867%. The current yield calculation is shown below

$$\text{Annual dollar coupon payment} = \$100 \times 0.0745 = \$7.45$$

$$\text{Current yield} = \frac{\$7.45}{\$94.697251} = 0.07867 = 7.867\%$$

Current yield possesses a number of drawbacks as a potential return measure. Current yield considers only coupon interest and no other source of return that will affect an investor's yield. To see this, assume the current yield is a yield to perpetuity, the annual dollar coupon payment is a perpetual annuity payment, and the security's price is the present value of the perpetual annuity. By rearranging terms such that the price equals the annual coupon payment divided by the current yield, we obtain the present value of a perpetual annuity formula discussed in Chapter 1 as shown below

$$\$94.697251 = \frac{\$7.45}{0.07867}$$

Exhibit 3: Bloomberg Security Description for a Ford Motor Co. Bond

13   DG36 Corp **DES**

```
SECURITY  DESCRIPTION            Page 1/ 1       ████████
FORD MOTOR CO    F 7.45 07/16/31   94.37051/94.69725 (7.94/7.91) BGN  MATRIX
┌─ISSUER INFORMATION──────────┬─IDENTIFIERS──────────┬─1) Additional Sec Info─┐
│Name FORD MOTOR COMPANY       │Common    009984194   │2) Identifiers          │
│Type Auto-Cars/Light Trucks   │ISIN    US345370CA64  │3) Ratings              │
│Market of Issue GLOBAL        │CUSIP      345370CA6  │4) Fees/Restrictions    │
├─SECURITY INFORMATION─────────┼─RATINGS──────────────┤5) Prospectus           │
│Country US        Currency USD│Moody's      A2       │6) Sec. Specific News   │
│Collateral Type NOTES         │S&P          A        │7) Involved Parties     │
│Calc Typ(   1)STREET CONVENTION│FI          A+       │8) Custom Notes         │
│Maturity   7/16/2031 Series   ├─ISSUE SIZE───────────┤9) Issuer Information    │
│NORMAL                        │Amt Issued            │10) ALLQ                │
│Coupon   7.45        FIXED    │USD  1,800,000   (M)  │11) Pricing Sources     │
│S/A          30/360           │Amt Outstanding       │12) Prospectus Request  │
│Announcement Dt  7/ 8/99      │USD  1,800,000   (M)  │13) Related Securities  │
│Int. Accrual Dt  7/16/99      │Min Piece/Increment   │14) Issuer Web Page     │
│1st Settle Date  7/16/99      │   1,000.00/ 1,000.00 │                        │
│1st Coupon Date  1/16/00      │Par Amount   1,000.00 │                        │
│Iss Pr  99.0490 Reoffer  99.049├─BOOK RUNNER/EXCHANGE─┤                        │
│SPR @ FPR  140.0 vs T 5 ¼ 11/28│BEAR,ML,SSB          │65) Old DES             │
│HAVE PROSPECTUS    DTC         │LUXEMBOURG            │66) Send as Attachment  │
└──────────────────────────────┴──────────────────────┴────────────────────────┘
GLOBAL LANDMARK SECURITIES (GlobLS). UNSEC'D. ALSO SINGAPORE SE.
```

Copyright 2000 BLOOMBERG L.P.   Frankfurt:69-920410 Hong Kong:2-977-6000 London:207-330-7500 New York:212-318-2000
Princeton:609-279-3000   Singapore:226-3000   Sydney:2-9777-8686   Tokyo:3-3201-8900   Sao Paulo:11-3048-4500
                                                                              1464-169-1 05-Jul-00 17:30:18

Bloomberg
PROFESSIONAL

Source: Bloomberg

Simply put, the current yield assumes that the bond delivers a perpetual annuity. As such, current yield ignores the capital gain that the investor will realize if the bond is held to maturity as well as any reinvestment income.

Yield to Maturity

The most common measure of yield in the bond market is the *yield to maturity*. The yield to maturity is simply a bond's internal rate of return. Specifically, the yield to maturity is the interest rate that will make the present value of the bond's cash flows equal to its market price plus accrued interest (i.e., the full price). To find the yield to maturity, we must first determine the bond's expected future cash flows. Then we search by trial and error for the interest rate that will make the present value of the bond's cash flows equal to the market price plus accrued interest.

To illustrate, consider once again the 7.45% coupon Ford Motor Co. bond described in Exhibit 3. From the yield analysis screen in Exhibit 4, we can locate the full price of the bond under the heading "Payment Invoice" on the right-hand side of the screen. The clean price (labeled "PRINCIPAL") is $946,972.51 for $1 million face value. Next, the accrued interest is $36,008.33 which is computed as follows using 30/360 day count convention:

Exhibit 4: Bloomberg Yield Analysis Screen for a Ford Motor Co. Bond

```
1                                                    DG36 Corp   YA
Enter all values and hit <GO>.
                       YIELD ANALYSIS           CUSIP:345370CA
FORD MOTOR CO      F 7.45 07/16/31   94.37051/94.69725  (7.94/7.91) BGN  MATRIX
PRICE        94.697251        SETTLEMENT DATE 7/10/2000
current yield   7.867        W ORST       CASHFLOW ANALYSIS
YIELD              MATURITY  7/16/2031   TO 7/16/31   WORKOUT    1000M FACE
CALCULATIONS    7/16/2031 @100.000    PAYMENT INVOICE
 STREET CONVENTION         7.911    7.911
 U.S. GOVT EQUIVALENT      7.911    7.911  PRINCIPAL              946972.51
 TRUE YIELD                7.910    7.910  174 DAYS ACCRUED INT    36008.33
 EQUIVALENT 1/YR COMPOUND  8.067    8.067  TOTAL                  982980.84
 JAPANESE YIELD (SIMPLE)   8.047    8.047        I N C O M E
 PROCEEDS/MMKT(ACT/360)                    REDEMPTION VALUE      1000000.00
                                           COUPON PAYMENT        2346750.00
 A F T E R   T A X :                       INTEREST @ 7.911%     7558362.3
 INCOME 39.60% CAPITAL 20.00%   4.816  4.816 TOTAL              10905112.30
                                                 R E T U R N
   SENSITIVITY ANALYSIS          GROSS PROFIT          9922131.46
 CNV  DURATION (YEARS)   11.621  11.621  RETURN      2 /YR COMP   7.911
      ADJ/MOD DURATION   11.179  11.179    FURTHER ANALYSIS
      RISK               10.988  10.988  HIT 1 <GO> TOTAL RETURN
      CONVEXITY           2.183   2.183  HIT 2 <GO> PRICE TABLE
 PRICE VALUE OF A  0.01  0.10988 0.10988
 YIELD VALUE OF A  0 32  0.00284 0.00284
Copyright 2000 BLOOMBERG L.P.   Frankfurt:69-920410 Hong Kong:2-977-6000 London:207-330-7500 New York:212-318-2000
Princeton:609-279-3000  Singapore:226-3000   Sydney:2-9777-8686   Tokyo:3-3201-8900   Sao Paulo:11-3048-4500
                                                            I464-169-1 05-Jul-00 17:09:31
Bloomberg
PROFESSIONAL
```

Source: Bloomberg

$$\$36,008.33 = (0.0745 \times \$1,000,000)/2 \times (174/180)$$

Accordingly, the full price is $982,980.84 (labeled "TOTAL") for $1 million face value. The cash flows of the bond are (1) 63 payments every six months of $37,250 and (2) a payment of $1,000,000 63 six-month periods from now. The interest rate that makes the present value of these cash flows equal to $982,980.84 is 3.995%. Hence, 3.995% is the *semiannual* yield to maturity.

The market convention adopted to annualize the semiannual yield to maturity is to double it and call the resulting number the yield to maturity. Thus, the yield to maturity for the Ford Motor Co. bond is 7.911% (2 × 3.995%). The yield to maturity computed using this convention — doubling the semiannual yield — is called a *bond-equivalent yield*.

Important Relationships

In Chapter 4, we explained the relationship between the coupon rate, the required yield, and a bond's price relative to its par value (i.e., discount, premium, or par value). If a bond is held to maturity, we know that the yield to maturity is the required yield. We restate these relationships substituting yield to maturity for required yield as shown below:

Bond selling at	Relationship
Par	coupon rate = yield to maturity
Discount	coupon rate < yield to maturity
Premium	coupon rate > yield to maturity

The following relationships between the price of a bond (relative to par), coupon rate, current yield, and yield to maturity also hold:

Bond price selling at	Relationship
Par	coupon rate = current yield = yield to maturity
Discount	coupon rate < current yield < yield to maturity
Premium	coupon rate > current yield > yield to maturity

A quick example will illustrate these relationships. For a 10-year 7% coupon and a $100 maturity value, it is easy to verify that when the bond is selling at $100, the coupon rate, current yield, and yield to maturity are all 7%. If the bond is selling at $93.2048, the yield to maturity is 8%. The current yield is 7.5103% ($7/93.2048) and is less than the yield to maturity because it ignores the built-in capital gain if the bond is held to maturity. The coupon rate is 7% which is the lowest of the three measures for this bond. Conversely, if the bond is selling at $107.4387, the yield to maturity is 6%. The current yield of 6.5153% ($7/107.4387) is higher than the yield to maturity because it ignores the built-in capital loss if the bond is held to maturity. The coupon rate is 7% which is higher than the current yield.

Related Yield to Maturity Measures
Let us return to Exhibit 4 and locate the yield to maturity on the YA screen. For this bond, Bloomberg presents the yield to maturity calculated three slightly different ways. First, the standard yield to maturity calculation for a corporate bond using a 30/360 day count convention is labeled "STREET CONVENTION" in the "YIELD CALCULATIONS" box on the left side of the screen. This is the bond-equivalent yield of 7.911% as described above. Next, the yield measure labeled "U.S. GOVT EQUIVALENT" is the yield to maturity calculated using the day count convention for coupon Treasuries, actual/actual. The last yield to maturity measure is labeled "TRUE YIELD" and is the yield calculated with coupon dates moved from a non-business day (e.g., weekend or holiday) to the next valid business day.

The Bond-Equivalent Yield Convention
The convention that was developed in the bond market to convert a semiannual yield into an annual yield is to double the semiannual yield. As we have discussed, this is called a bond-equivalent yield. Generally, when one doubles a semiannual yield (or semiannual return) to obtain an annual measure, one is said to be computing the measure on a bond-equivalent basis.

The convention raises two obvious questions. First, why is the practice of simply doubling a semiannual yield followed? Second, would it not be more appropriate to compute the effective annual yield by compounding the semiannual yield in a manner described in Chapter 1?

The first question is easily dispatched. The bond-equivalent yield is simply a convention that is well-ingrained in the workings of the bond market. There is no danger with a convention unless it is used improperly. Naturally, market participants recognize that a yield (or return) is computed on a semiannual basis by convention and adjust accordingly when using the number such as comparing non-U.S. bonds that pay interest annually[3] and amortizing securities that pay interest monthly.[4]

The answer to the second question is that it is true that computing an effective annual yield would be better. However, the question is moot. Once we discover the limitations of yield measures in general, we will question whether or not an investor should ever make an investment decision using either a bond-equivalent yield or an effective annual yield measure. That is, once we identify the major limitations with yield measures, how we annualize a semiannual yield will be of trifling importance.

Limitations of the Yield to Maturity Measure

At first blush, the yield to maturity appears to be an informative measure of a bond's potential return. It considers not only the coupon income but any capital gain or loss that will be realized by holding the bond to maturity. The yield to maturity recognizes the timing of the cash flows. It also considers the third source of dollar return that we discussed at the beginning of the chapter — reinvestment income. However, when calculating yield to maturity, we are implicitly assuming that the coupon payments can be reinvested at an interest equal to the semiannual yield to maturity.[5]

The following illustration demonstrates this. In what follows, the analysis will be cast in terms of dollars. Be sure to keep in mind the distinction between *total future dollars* which are equal to all dollars that the bond investor expects to receive (including the recovery of the principal) and the *total dollar return* which is equal to the dollars the investor expects to realize from the three sources of return, namely, coupon payments, capital gain/loss, and reinvestment income.

Let's illustrate the distinction between total future dollars and total dollar return with a simple example. Suppose one invested $100 for ten years at 7% compounded semiannually (i.e., 3.5% every six months). What is the total future dollars that will result from this investment? This is nothing more than asking for the future value of a single cash flow invested at 3.5% for 20 six-month periods. The total future dollars generated are $198.98, as shown below

$$\text{Total future dollars} = \$100(1.035)^{20} = \$198.98$$

---

[3] This will be explained later in the chapter.

[4] We will see this when we discuss cash flow yield later in this chapter.

[5] This assumes that the bond in question pays semiannual cash flows. If the bond pays annual cash flows, the cash flows must be reinvested at the annual yield to maturity.

The total future dollars of this investment ($198.98) are comprised of the return of principal $100 and the total interest of $98.98. If we subtract the amount invested ($100) from the total future dollars, the difference is $98.98, which is the total dollar return.

Consider a hypothetical 10-year bond selling at par ($100) with a coupon rate of 7%. Assume the bond delivers coupon payments semiannually. The yield to maturity for this bond is 7%. Suppose an investor buys this bond, holds it to maturity, and receives the maturity value of $100. In addition, the investor receives 20 semiannual coupon payments of $3.50 and can reinvest them every six months that they received at a semiannual rate of 3.5%. What are the total future dollars assuming a 7% reinvestment rate? As demonstrated above, an investment of $100 must generate $198.98 in order to generate a yield of 7% compounded semiannually. Alternatively, the bond investment of $100 must deliver a total dollar return of $98.98.

Let us partition the total dollar return for this bond into its three components: coupon payments, capital gain/loss, and reinvestment income. The coupon payments contribute $70 ($3.5 × 20) of the total dollar return. The capital gain/loss component is zero because the bond is purchased at par and held to maturity. Lastly, the remainder of the total dollar return ($28.98) must be due to reinvestment income.

To verify this, this par bond's total dollar return of $98.98 is driven by two sources of dollar return — coupon payments and reinvestment income. Recall from the beginning of the chapter, the reinvestment income can be determined using the future value of an ordinary annuity formula given in Chapter 1. Accordingly, the future value of 20 semiannual payments of $3.50 to be received plus the interest earned by investing the payments at 7% compounded semiannually is found as follows:

$$A = \$3.50$$
$$m = 2$$
$$i = 0.035 \ (0.07/2)$$
$$N = 10$$
$$n = 20 \ (10 \times 2)$$

therefore,

$$FV_{20} = \$3.50 \left[\frac{(1.035)^{20} - 1}{0.035} \right]$$
$$= \$3.50(27.27968) = \$98.98$$

Thus, the coupon payments and reinvestment income together are $98.98 which agrees with total dollar return from our earlier calculation. The reinvestment income alone is $28.28 ($98.98 − $70).

To summarize, in order to generate at 7% return over the 10 years until maturity, an investor must generate a total dollar return of $98.98. How plausible is this? If the bond does not default, the investor will receive all the coupon payments ($70) and the repayment of principal at maturity ($0 capital gain). How about the reinvestment income of $28.28? Of course, obtaining this amount depends on being able to reinvest at a 7% rate compounded semiannually all coupon payments over the next 10 years.

Clearly, the investor will only realize the yield to maturity that is computed at the time of purchase if the following two assumptions hold:

> *Assumption 1:* the coupon payments can be reinvested at the yield to maturity
> *Assumption 2:* the bond is held to maturity

With respect to the first assumption, the risk that an investor faces is that future interest rates will be less than the yield to maturity at the time the bond is purchased. This risk is called *reinvestment risk.* As for the second assumption, if the bond is not held to maturity, it may have to be sold for less than its purchase price, resulting in a return that is less than the yield to maturity. This risk is called *interest rate risk.*

Factors Affecting Reinvestment Risk

There are two characteristics of a bond that affect the degree of reinvestment risk. First, for a given yield to maturity and a given non-zero coupon rate, the longer the maturity the more the bond's total return is dependent on reinvestment income to realize the yield to maturity at the time of purchase. The implication is that the yield to maturity measure for long-term coupon bonds tells us little about the potential return an investor may realize if the bond is held to maturity. For long-term bonds, the reinvestment income component will be the most important source of total dollar return. As an example, for the Ford Motor Co. bond in Exhibit 4, the reinvestment income component is 76.18% of the total dollar return, using information from the "INCOME" box of the YA screen.

The second bond characteristic that affects reinvestment income is the coupon rate. For a coupon bond of a given maturity and yield to maturity, the higher the coupon rate, the more dependent the bond's total dollar return will be on the reinvestment of the coupon payments in order to produce the yield to maturity at the time of purchase. In other words, holding maturity and yield to maturity constant, a bond selling at a premium will be more dependent on reinvestment income than a bond selling at par. This is true because the reinvestment income must offset the capital loss realized by holding the premium bond to maturity. Conversely, a bond selling at a discount depends less on reinvestment income than a bond selling at par because a portion of the return is derived from the capital gain that is realized from maturing the bond. For a zero-coupon bond, none of the bond's total dollar return is dependent on reinvestment income. Hence, a zero-coupon bond has no reinvestment risk if held to maturity.

Exhibit 5: Bloomberg Security Description Screen for a Fannie Mae Bond

13   DG36 **Corp**   **DES**

```
SECURITY DESCRIPTION                    Page 1/ 2    ▮▮▮▮▮▮▮
FANNIE MAE        FNMA7.1 10/18/04   98.88644/98.88644  (7.40/7.40) BFV  @17:45
┌─ISSUER INFORMATION────────┬─IDENTIFIERS──────────┬─ 1) Additional Sec Info
│ Name FANNIE MAE           │ CUSIP      31359MFA6 │  2) Call Schedule
│ Type Sovereign Agency     │ ISIN    US31359MFA62 │  3) Identifiers
│ Market of Issue GLOBAL    │ BB number   EC1902732│  4) Ratings
├─SECURITY INFORMATION──────┼─RATINGS──────────────┤  5) Fees/Restrictions
│ Country US      Currency USD│ Moody's     Aaa    │  6) Sec. Specific News
│ Collateral Type NOTES     │ S&P         NA       │  7) Involved Parties
│ Calc Typ(  1)STREET CONVENTION│ Composite AAA     │  8) Custom Notes
│ ▐Maturity▌ 10/18/2004 Series│ ISSUE SIZE         │  9) Pricing Sources
│ CALLABLE   CALL 10/18/01@ 100.00│ Amt Issued     │ 10) Prospectus Request
│ ▐Coupon▌ 7.1      FIXED   │ USD  1,050,000  (M)  │ 11) Related Securities
│ S/A        30/360         │ Amt Outstanding      │ 12) Issuer Web Page
│ Announcement Dt 10/14/99  │ USD  1,050,000  (M)  │
│ Int. Accrual Dt 10/18/99  │ Min Piece/Increment  │
│ 1st Settle Date 10/18/99  │   1,000.00/  1,000.00│
│ 1st Coupon Date   4/18/00 │ Par Amount   1,000.00│
│ Iss Pr  99.9750           │ BOOK RUNNER/EXCHANGE │
│ SPR @ ISS  105.0 vs T 6 08/15/04│ CSFB,LEH,ML     │ 65) Old DES
│ HAVE PROSPECTUS           │                      │ 66) Send as Attachment
BENCHMARK NOTES. UNSEC'D. BOOK-ENTRY. ADD'L $250MM ISS'D 12/6/99 @ 100.13 FOR
SETTLEMENT ON 12/8/99. ADD'L $250MM ISS'D 12/22/99.
Copyright 2000 BLOOMBERG L.P.   Frankfurt:69-920410  Hong Kong:2-977-6000  London:207-330-7500  New York:212-318-2000
Princeton:609-279-3000   Singapore:226-3000   Sydney:2-9777-8686   Tokyo:3-3201-8900   Sao Paulo:11-3048-4500
                                                                      1464-169-1 05-Jul-00 17:44:43
▌Bloomberg
 PROFESSIONAL
```

Source: Bloomberg

YIELD TO CALL

For callable bonds, the market convention is to calculate a yield to call in addition to a yield to maturity. A callable bond may be called at more than one price and these prices are specified in a call price schedule. The yield to call assumes that the issuer will call the bond at some call date and the call price is then specified in the call schedule

The procedure for calculating the yield to call is the same as that for the yield to maturity: determine the interest rate that will make the present value of the expected cash flows equal to the market price plus accrued interest. The expected cash flows are the coupon payments to a particular call date in the future and the call price.

To illustrate the various yield to call measures, consider a callable bond with a 7.1% coupon issued by Fannie Mae. The security description screen (DES) from Bloomberg is presented in Exhibit 5. The bond matures on October 28, 2004 and the first and only call date is October 18, 2001. This Fannie Mae issue has a

European-style embedded call option (i.e., the option can only exercised on one date and then ceases to exist) as is common with agency debenture issues. The call price is 100. Exhibit 6 presents the yields to call (YTC) screen. Using a settlement date of July 6, 2000, the various yield measures are presented.

Yield to Custom

Yield to custom computes a yield to call for a call date and a price specified by the user. Typically, a bond does not have one call price but a call schedule which sets forth the call price based on when the issuer can exercise the call option. Bloomberg's YTC screen allows the user to select any call date in the future to compute a yield to call for the designated bond. The call price according to the call schedule for the particular date selected will be used in the yield calculation.

Yield to Next Call

Yield to next call is the yield to call for the next call date after the current settlement date. For the Fannie Mae bond, the next call date is the first and only call date, 10/18/2001. The yield to next call is 8.016%. Specifically, a semiannual interest rate of 4.008% makes the present value of the three coupon payments of $3.55 (per $100 of par value) and the call price of $100 (i.e., the bond's cash flows assuming it will be called on 10/18/2001) equal to the current market price of $98.88644 plus the accrued interest.

Exhibit 6: Bloomberg Yields to Call Screen for a Fannie Mae Bond

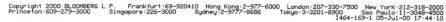

```
4                                            DG36 Corp   YTC
  Enter all values and hit <GO>.
           YIELDS  TO  CALL              Page 1 of  1
FANNIE MAE      FNMA7.1 10/18/04   98.88644/98.88644  (7.40/7.40) BFV  @17:44
  Settlement Date      7/ 6/2000       Price   98.88644    CUSIP: 31359MFA
  Yield To Maturity   10/18/2004 @REDM 100      7.404
  Yield to Custom     10/18/2004 @REDM 100      7.404 blend N wght  0.0%
  Yield to Next Call  10/18/2001 @REDM 100      8.016  CNV Duration
  Yield To Refunding  10/18/2001 @REDM 100      8.016    & Risk Calc
  Yield to Worst Call 10/18/2004 @REDM 100      7.404 B.A.Yield

                              Treas  Treas  Adjusted Risk
       Date      Price   Yield Curve  Spread Duration Factor
     10/18/01  100.0000  8.016 6.121   1.895  1.185   1.190
     10/18/04  100.0000  7.404 6.142   1.261  3.577   3.592
```

Source: Bloomberg

Yield to Refunding

Yield to refunding is employed when bonds are currently callable but have some restrictions on the source of funds used to buy back the debt when a call is exercised. Namely, if a debt issue contains some refunding protection, bonds cannot be called for a certain period of time with the proceeds of other debt issues sold at a lower cost of money. As a result, the bondholder is afforded some protection if interest rates decline and the issuer can obtain lower cost funds to pay off the debt. It should be stressed that the bonds can be called with funds derived from other sources (e.g., cash on hand) during the refunded-protected period. The refunding date is the first date the bond can be called using lower cost debt. Given this backdrop, the yield to refunding is the discount rate (appropriately annualized) that discounts the cash flows to the first refunding date back to the bond's market price. Since the Fannie Mae issue in Exhibit 6 is only callable on October 18, 2001, the yield to next call and yield to refunding are one in the same.

YIELD TO PUT

When a bond is putable, the yield to the first put date is calculated and called the *yield to put*. This yield is the interest rate that will make the present value of the bond's cash flows to the first put date equal to the clean price plus accrued interest. As with all yield measures that are internal rates of return (e.g., yield to maturity and yield to call), yield to put assumes that any interim coupon payments can be reinvested at the calculated yield. Moreover, the yield to put assumes that the put will be exercised on the first possible date; that is the investor will put the bond back to the issuer and receive the put price plus the accrued interest.

For example, suppose that a 7% coupon bond maturing in five years is putable at par in two years and the bond's price is $103.39. The cash flows for this bond if the put is exercised in two years are: (1) 4 coupon payments of $3.50 every six months and (2) the $100 put price in four 6-month periods from now. The semiannual interest rate that will make the present value of the cash flows equal to the price of $103.39 is 2.5968%. Therefore, 2.5968% is the semiannual yield to put and 5.1968% is the yield to put on a bond-equivalent basis.

YIELD TO WORST

A yield can be calculated for every possible call (or put) date. Additionally, a yield to maturity can be calculated. The lowest of all these possible yields is called the *yield to worst*. For the Fannie Mae callable bond shown in Exhibit 5 there is one call date and the yield to call is 8.016% (see Exhibit 6). The yield to maturity is 7.404%. Therefore, the yield to worst is the minimum of these yields, 7.404% in our example.

CASH FLOW YIELD

As discussed in Chapter 7, mortgage-backed and asset-backed securities are backed by a pool of loans or receivables. For example, mortgage-backed securities are backed by a pool of mortgage loans. The cash flows for these securities include principal repayment as well as interest. Uncertainty in the cash flows arises because the individual borrowers whose loans comprise the pool usually have the option to prepay the loan in whole or in part usually without penalty prior to the scheduled principal repayment date. Thus, a mortgaged-backed or asset-backed security has an embedded short position in a prepayment option. Owing to this prepayment option, it is necessary to assume the rate at which prepayments will occur in order to project the security's cash flows. The assumed rate is called the *prepayment rate* or *prepayment speed.*

A yield can be calculated given the projected cash flows based on an assumed prepayment rate. The yield is the interest rate that will make the present value of the assumed cash flows equal to the clean price plus accrued interest. A yield calculated in this manner is called a *cash flow yield.*

The cash flows for mortgaged-backed and asset-backed securities are often delivered monthly rather than semiannually. Accordingly, the interest rate that will make the present value of the assumed cash flows (interest and principal payments) equal to the market price plus accrued interest is a monthly yield. This monthly yield is then annualized using the following convention.

First, the semiannual effective yield is computed from the monthly yield by compounding it for six months as follows:

$$\text{effective semiannual yield} = (1 + \text{monthly yield})^6 - 1$$

Second, the effective semiannual yield is doubled to obtain the annual cash flow yield on a bond-equivalent basis. Specifically,

$$\text{cash flow yield} = 2 \times \text{effective semiannual yield} = 2[(1 + \text{monthly yield})^6 - 1]$$

For example, if the monthly yield is 0.63%, then:

$$\text{cash flow yield} = 2[(1.0063)^6 - 1] = 7.6801\%$$

Thus, the cash flow yield on a bond-equivalent basis is 7.6801%.

Although it is commonly quoted by market participants, the cash flow yield suffers from limitations similar to the yield to maturity. These shortcomings include: (1) the projected cash flows assume that the prepayment speed will be realized, (2) the projected cash flows are assumed to be reinvested at the cash flow yield, and (3) the mortgage-backed or asset-backed security is assumed to be held until the final payoff of all the loans in the pool based on some prepayment assumption. If the cash flows are reinvested at rate lower than the cash flow yield (i.e., reinvestment risk) or if actual prepayments differ from those projected, then the cash flow yield will not be realized. Mortgage-backed and asset-backed securities are particularly sensitive to reinvestment risk since payments are usually monthly and include principal repayments as well as interest.

PORTFOLIO YIELD MEASURES

Intuitively, the yield on a portfolio of bonds is the discount rate that makes the present value of the portfolio's expected future cash flows equal to the portfolio's total market value. Thus, in principle, we calculate the portfolio yield in the same manner as the yield to maturity on a single bond. In other words, the portfolio yield is the portfolio's internal rate of return.

Portfolio Internal Rate of Return

A portfolio's internal rate of return is computed by first forecasting the cash flows for all the bonds that comprise the portfolio and then finding the interest rate that will make the present value of the cash flows equal to the portfolio market value.

To illustrate how to calculate a portfolio's internal rate of return, we will use a use a three-bond portfolio presented Exhibit 7. Bond A is a 5-year 6% coupon bond with a maturity value of $20 million. Next, Bond B is a 2-year 5.25% coupon bond with a maturity value of $10 million. Finally, Bond C is a 4-year, 5.50% coupon bond with a maturity value of $30 million. The market values and yields to maturity of these bonds are also presented.

The cash flows for each bond in the portfolio and for the entire portfolio are presented in Exhibit 8. Suppose the total market value of this portfolio is $58,705,521. The internal rate of return for this three-bond portfolio is found via iteration and is the interest rate that makes the present value of the portfolio's cash flows shown in the last column of Exhibit 8 equal to $58,705,521. If the semiannual interest rate of 3.1522% is used, the present value of the portfolio's cash flows equals $56,511,509. The portfolio's internal rate of return on a bond-equivalent basis is found by doubling 3.1522% which is 6.3044%.

An additional comment is warranted. The portfolio internal rate of return carries the same baggage as yield to maturity which we discussed earlier in the chapter. Namely, the portfolio's cash flows can be reinvested at the internal rate of return and the investor will hold the portfolio until the maturity date of the longest bond in the portfolio.

Exhibit 7: Bond Portfolio with Three Issues

Bond	Coupon Rate (%)	Maturity (in years)	Par Value (in dollars)	Market Value (in dollars)	Yield to Maturity (%)
A	6.00%	5	$20,000,000	$19,578,880	6.5%
B	5.25%	2	$10,000,000	$9,860,609	6.0%
C	5.50%	4	$30,000,000	$29,266,032	6.2%

Exhibit 8: Cash Flows for a Three-Bond Portfolio

Period	Bond A ($)	Bond B ($)	Bond C ($)	Portfolio ($)
1	600,000	262,500	825,000	1,687,500
2	600,000	262,500	825,000	1,687,500
3	600,000	262,500	825,000	1,687,500
4	600,000	10,262,500	825,000	11,687,500
5	600,000		825,000	1,425,000
6	600,000		825,000	1,425,000
7	600,000		825,000	1,425,000
8	600,000		30,825,000	31,425,000
9	600,000			600,000
10	20,600,000			20,600,000

Approximating a Portfolio's Internal Rate of Return

In practice, a portfolio's internal rate of return is usually approximated by taking the weighted average of the yields of the individual bonds in the portfolio. There are two common methods for weighting individual bond yields to arrive at a weighted-average portfolio yield. One method uses market values while the other uses dollar duration.

Using Market Value Weights

The simplest and least meaningful method for calculating a portfolio yield is to weight individual bond yields using the market values. In general, if we let

w_i = market value of security i relative to the portfolio's total market value

y_i = yield on security i

K = number of securities in the portfolio

then, the market-value-weighted yield is

$$w_1 y_1 + w_2 y_2 + w_3 y_3 + \ldots + w_K y_K$$

Consider the following three-bond portfolio displayed in Exhibit 7. The total market value of the portfolio is $58,705,521, K is equal to 3 and

$w_1 = 19,578,880/58,705,521 \ = 0.334$ $y_1 = 6.5\%$

$w_2 = \ \ 9,860,609/58,705,521 \ = 0.168$ $y_2 = 6.0\%$

$w_3 = 29,266,032/58,705,521 \ = 0.498$ $y_3 = 6.2\%$

The market-value-weighted yield is then

$$0.334(6.5\%) + 0.168(6.0\%) + 0.498(6.2\%) = 6.2666\%$$

While the market-value-weighted portfolio yield has considerable intuitive appeal, it can differ substantially from a portfolio's internal rate of return. Moreover, it tells us little about the portfolio's potential return. To see this, suppose that a portfolio consists of two zero-coupon bonds — a 6-month zero yielding 10% and a 20-year zero yielding 7%. Suppose further that 98% of the portfolio is invested in the 6-month zero while the remaining 2% is invested in the 20-year zero. The market-value-weighted portfolio yield is 9.94%. How should this yield be interpreted? Under what set of circumstances and over what investment horizon could a portfolio manager expect to earn 9.94%? Since the answer to these questions is we do not know, the market-value-weighted portfolio yield is not very useful in bond portfolio management.

Using Dollar Duration Weights

The other method for approximating a portfolio yield is to use dollar durations. A bond's dollar duration tells us the approximate dollar price change for a 100 basis point change in yield. Dollar duration is a measure of a bond's interest rate risk. The procedure for calculating dollar duration will be explained in Chapter 11. The dollar duration for each bond in our hypothetical portfolio is presented in Exhibit 9.

We illustrate the calculation of a portfolio yield by weighting individual bond yields using the dollar duration. In general, if we let

w_i = dollar duration of security i relative to the portfolio's total dollar duration which is simply the sum of the individual bond's dollar durations

y_i = yield on security i

K = number of securities in the portfolio

then, the dollar-duration-weighted yield is

$$w_1y_1 + w_2y_2 + w_3y_3 + \ldots + w_Ky_K$$

Consider the three-bond portfolio displayed in Exhibit 9. The total dollar duration of the portfolio is $2,048,831.26, K is equal to 3 and

$$w_1 = 831,534.61/2,048,831.26 \quad = 0.4058 \qquad y_1 = 6.5\%$$
$$w_2 = 184,176.45/2,028,831.26 \quad = 0.0899 \qquad y_2 = 6.0\%$$
$$w_3 = 1,033,120.20/2,028,831.26 = 0.5043 \qquad y_3 = 6.2\%$$

The dollar-duration-weighted yield is then

$$0.4058(6.5\%) + 0.0899(6.0\%) + 0.5043(6.2\%) = 6.3038\%$$

Exhibit 9: Dollar Durations for a Three-bond Portfolio

Bond	Dollar Duration	Yield to Maturity
A	831,534.61	6.5%
B	184,176.45	6.0%
C	1,033,120.20	6.2%
Total Dollar Duration	2,048,831.26	

Recall, the portfolio's internal rate of return is 6.3044%, so the dollar-duration-weighted yield is indeed a close approximation.

YIELD MEASURES FOR U.S. TREASURY BILLS

U.S. Treasury bills, like many money market instruments, are discount securities (e.g., agency discount notes, commercial paper). Unlike bonds that pay coupon interest, Treasury bills are akin to zero-coupon bonds in that they are sold at a discount from their face value and are redeemed for full face value at maturity. In addition, Treasury bills use an ACT/360 day count convention as do most money market instruments. For these reasons, we devote this section to a description of yield measures for U.S. Treasury bills.

Yield on a Bank Discount Basis

The convention for quoting bids and offers is different for Treasury bills and Treasury coupon securities. Bids/offers on bills are quoted in a special way. Treasury bill values are quoted on a *bank discount basis*, not on a price basis. The *yield on a bank discount basis* is computed as follows:

$$Y_d = \frac{D}{F} \times \frac{360}{t}$$

where

$\quad Y_d$ = annualized yield on a bank discount basis (expressed as a decimal)
$\quad D$ = dollar discount, which is equal to the difference between the face value and the price
$\quad F$ = face value
$\quad t$ = number of days remaining to maturity

As an example, suppose a Treasury bill has 91 days to maturity and a face value of $100. Suppose this bill is trading at a price of $98.5846. The dollar discount, D, is computed as follows

$$D = \$100 - \$98.5846 = \$1.4054$$

Therefore, the annualized yield on a bank discount basis (expressed as a decimal) is

$$Y_d = \frac{\$1.4054}{\$100} \times \frac{360}{91} = 5.56\%$$

Given the yield on a bank discount basis, the price of a Treasury bill is found by first solving the formula for Y_d given the dollar discount (D), as follows:

$$D = Y_d \times F \times (t/360)$$

The price is then

$$price = F - D$$

As an example, suppose a 91-day bill with a face value of $100 has a yield on a bank discount basis of 5.56%. Then D is equal to

$$D = 0.0556 \times \$100 \times 91/360 = \$1.4054$$

Therefore,

$$price = \$100 - \$1.4054 = \$98.5946$$

There are two reasons why the quoted yield on a bank discount basis is not a meaningful measure of the potential return from holding a Treasury bill. First, the measure is based on a face-value investment rather than on the actual dollar amount invested. Second, the yield is annualized according to a 360-day rather than a 365-day year, making it difficult to compare Treasury bill yields with Treasury notes and bonds which pay interest on a 365-day basis. The use of 360 days for a year is a day count convention for most money market instruments. Despite its shortcomings as a measure of potential return, this is the method that dealers have adopted to quote Treasury bills. Many dealer quote sheets and some other reporting services provide two other yield measures that attempt to make the quoted yield comparable to that for a coupon bond and interest-bearing money market instruments — the CD equivalent yield and the bond equivalent yield.

CD Equivalent Yield

The *CD equivalent yield* (also called the *money market equivalent yield*) makes the quoted yield on a Treasury bill more comparable to yield quotations on other money market instruments that pay interest on a 360-day basis. It does this by taking into consideration the price of the Treasury bill (i.e., the amount invested) rather than its face value. The formula for the CD equivalent yield is

$$\text{CD equivalent yield} = \frac{360 Y_d}{360 - t(Y_d)}$$

To illustrate the calculation of the CD equivalent yield, once again we use the information from Bloomberg. Exhibit 10 presents the PX1 Governments screen. Data for the most recently issued bills and when-issued bills (WIB) appear in the box in the upper left-hand corner. The first and second columns indicate the issue and its maturity date. In the third column, there is an arrow indicating an up or down tick for the last trade. The fourth column indicates the current bid/ask rates. A bond-equivalent yield using the ask yield/price is reported in column (5) and will be explained shortly. The last column shows the change in bank discount yields based on the previous day's closing rates as of the time posted.

Using the data from Exhibit 10 for the 91-day bill that matures on May 18, 2000, the ask rate on a bank discount basis is 5.56%. The CD equivalent yield is computed as follows:

$$\text{CD equivalent yield} = \frac{360(0.0556)}{360 - 91(0.0556)} = 0.05639 = 5.639\%$$

Bond-Equivalent Yield

The measure that seeks to make the Treasury bill quote comparable to coupon Treasuries is the *bond-equivalent yield* as discussed earlier in the chapter. This yield measure makes the quoted yield on a Treasury bill more comparable to yields on Treasury notes and bonds that use an actual/actual day count convention. The calculations depend on whether the Treasury bill has 182 days or less to maturity or more than 182 days.

Bills with Less Than 182 Days to Maturity

To convert the yield on a bank discount to a bond-equivalent yield for a bill with less than 182 days to maturity, we use the following formula:

$$\text{Bond-equivalent yield} = \frac{T(Y_d)}{360 - t(Y_d)}$$

Exhibit 10: Bloomberg PX1 Screen

<HELP> for explanation, <MENU> for similar functions.   DG36 Govt   **PX1**
Hit PAGE FWD for off-the-run Bills, Notes, and Bonds.
17:15   **CURRENTS/WHEN ISSUED**   **Bloomberg**
                                                        GENERIC

TREASURY BILLS									
1)3Mo	5/18/00 ↑	5.57/56	5.73	+.01	16) 5¹₄	2/29	↑ 85-13+/15+	6.35	+ 19
2)WIB	5/25/00 ↓	5.61/59	5.76		17) 6¹₈	8/29	↑ 97-08 /10	6.33	+ 18+
3)6Mo	8/17/00 ↓	5.76/75	6.02	+.04	18) 6¹₄	5/30 ₃₀ᵧᵣ	↑100-13 /14	6.22	+ 20+
4)WIB	8/24/00 ↑	5.77/75	6.02						
5)1Yr	2/01/01 ↓	5.88/87	6.24	+.04					

					19)TII . 5 YR		↓ 98-29+/31+	4.07	--
NOTES/BONDS					20)TII 10 YR		↑ 99-19 /21	·4.29	+ 01
6) 5⁷₈	11/01	↓ 98-19+/21+	6.6?	– 03+	21)TII 30 YR		↓ 91-22 /22	4.38-3-11	
7) 6¹₈	12/01	↓ 99-00 /02	6.66	– 03					
8) 6³₈	1/02 ₂ᵧᵣ	↓ 99-14+/15	6.67	– 03+					
9) WI	2 YR	↓	6.65/64	99.74 +5.80					

					OTHER MARKETS				
10) 5¹₄	5/04	↓ 94-17 /19	6.73	– 05+	22)US Long(CBT)	16:30 s	94-05	+ 15	
11) 6	8/04	↓ 97-02 /04	6.75	– 05+	23)10Y Fut(CBT)	16:30 s	94-18	– 07	
12) 5⁷₈	11/04 ₅ᵧᵣ	↓ 96-16+/17	6.74	– 05+	24)5Yr Fut(CBT)	16:28 s	96-28	– 06	
					25)EURO$ (IMM)	17:03 s	93.7275	-.0325	
					26)Fed Funds	17:12 ↑	5.6250	-.0625	
13) 5¹₂	5/09	↓ 91-20 /22	6.72	– 02	27)S&P 500 Ind	17:00 ↑	1388.25	+.58	
14) 6	8/09	↑ 95-08+/10+	6.67	– 06+	28)DowJones Ind	16:03 ↑	10514.57	-46.84	
15) 6¹₂	2/10 ₁₀ᵧᵣ	↓ 99-16 /17	6.56	– 05	29)Gold (CMX)	yd	303.80	--	
					30)Crude Oil	yd	29.46	--	

Copyright 2000 BLOOMBERG L.P.   Frankfurt:69-920410   Hong Kong:2-977-6000   London:171-330-7500   New York:212-318-2000
Princeton:609-279-3000   Singapore:226-3000   Sydney:2-9777-8686   Tokyo:3-3201-8900   Sao Paulo:11-3048-4500
                                                                                    1464-169-0 17-Feb-00 17:14:26

Bloomberg
PROFESSIONAL

Source: Bloomberg

where T is the actual number of days in the calendar year (i.e., 365 or 366). As an example, using the same Treasury bill with 91 days to maturity, a face value of $1,000 would be quoted at 5.56% on a bank discount basis, the bond-equivalent yield is calculated as follows:

$$\text{Bond-equivalent yield} = \frac{366(0.0556)}{360 - 91(0.0556)} = 0.05733 = 5.733\%$$

This number matches the bond-equivalent yield shown in the Bloomberg screen in Exhibit 9. Note that we used 366 in the numerator because the year 2000 is a leap year. Second, the formula for the bond-equivalent yield presented above assumes that the current maturity of the Treasury bill in question is 182 days or less.

Bills with More Than 182 Days to Maturity

When a Treasury bill has a current maturity of more than 182 days, converting a yield on a bank discount basis into a bond-equivalent yield is more involved. Specifically, the calculation must reflect the fact that a Treasury bill is a discount instrument while a coupon Treasury delivers one coupon payment that can be reinvested.

In order to make this adjustment, we assume that interest is paid after six months at a rate equal to the Treasury bill's bond-equivalent yield (BEY) and that this interest is reinvested at this rate. We can express this mathematically using the following notation:

P = price of the Treasury bill
BEY = bond-equivalent yield
t = number of days until the bill's maturity

Then,

$P[1 + (BEY/2)]$ = future value obtained by the investor if the P (price of the Treasury bill) is invested for six months at one-half the BEY

$(BEY/365)[t - (365/2)][1 + (BEY/2)]P$ = the amount earned by the investor (on a simple interest basis) if the proceeds are reinvested at the BEY for the Treasury bill's remaining days to maturity

Assuming a face value for the bill of $100, then

$$P[1 + (BEY/2)] + (BEY/365)[t - (365/2)][1 + (BEY/2)]P = 100$$

This expression can be written more compactly as

$$P[1 + (BEY/2)][(1 + (BEY/2))(2t/365 - 1)] = 100$$

Expanding this expression, we obtain

$$(2t/365 - 1)\text{BEY}^2 + (4t/365)\text{BEY} + 4(1 - 100/P) = 0$$

The expression above is a quadratic equation which is an equation which can be written in the form:

$$ax^2 + bx + c = 0$$

which can be solved as follows:

$$x = \frac{-b \pm [b^2 - 4ac]^{1/2}}{2a}$$

Thus, to find the a Treasury bill's bond-equivalent yield if its current maturity is greater than 182 days, we solve for BEY using the quadratic formula.

$$\text{BEY} = \frac{\dfrac{-2 \times t}{T} + 2\left[\left(\dfrac{t}{T}\right)^2 - \left(\dfrac{2 \times t}{T} - 1\right) \times \left(1 - \dfrac{100}{P}\right)\right]^{1/2}}{\dfrac{2 \times t}{T} - 1}$$

As an example, let's use the 52-week bill in Exhibit 10 with a bank discount yield (ask rate) of 5.87%. The price of this bill would be 94.0647 (per $100 of face value). This bill matures on February 1, 2001, so as of February 17, 2000 there would be 350 days to maturity. Since the year 2000 is a leap year, $T = 366$. Substituting this information in the expression above gives the bond-equivalent yield for this 52-week bill:

$$\text{BEY} = \frac{\dfrac{-2 \times 350}{366} + 2\left[\left(\dfrac{350}{366}\right)^2 - \left(\dfrac{2 \times 350}{366} - 1\right) \times \left(1 - \dfrac{100}{94.2931}\right)\right]^{1/2}}{\dfrac{2 \times 350}{366} - 1}$$

$$= 0.0624 = 6.24\%$$

This agrees with the bond-equivalent yield calculated by Bloomberg as reported in Exhibit 10.

YIELD SPREAD MEASURES RELATIVE TO A SPOT RATE CURVE

Traditional yield spread analysis for a non-Treasury security involves calculating the difference between the risky bond's yield and the yield on a comparable maturity benchmark Treasury security. As an illustration, let's use the 7.45% coupon Ford Motor Co. bond described in Exhibit 3 that matures on July 16, 2031.

Bloomberg's Yield & Spread Analysis screen (function YAS) is presented in Exhibit 11. The yield spreads against the benchmark U.S. Treasury yield curve appear in a box at the bottom left-hand corner of the screen. Using a settlement date of July 10, 2000, the yield spread is 205 basis points versus the 6.25% coupon Treasury bond with a maturity date of May 15, 2030. The yield spread is simply the difference between the yields to maturity of these two bonds (7.91% − 5.86%). This yield spread measure is referred to as the *nominal spread*.

The nominal spread measure has several drawbacks. For now, the most important is that the nominal spread fails to account for the term structure of spot rates for both bonds. Moreover, as we will see in Chapter 6 when we discuss the valuation of bonds with embedded options (e.g., callable bonds), the nominal spread does not take into consideration the fact that expected interest rate volatility may alter the non-Treasury bond's expected future cash flows. We will focus here only on the first drawback and pose an alternative spread measure that incorporates the spot rate curve. In Chapter 6 we will discuss another spread measure, the option-adjusted spread (OAS), for bonds with embedded options.

Exhibit 11: Bloomberg Yield and Spread Analysis Screen for Ford Motor Co. Bond

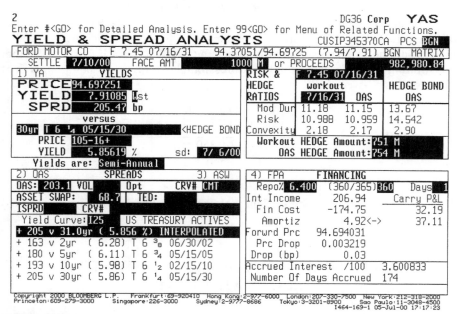

Exhibit 12: Determination of the Z-Spread for an 7% 5-Year Non-Treasury Issue Selling at $101.9576 to Yield 6.5347%

Period	Years	Cash Flow ($)	Spot Rate (%)	Present value ($) assuming a spread of		
				100 bp	120 bp	150 bp
1	0.5	3.50	4.20	3.4113	3.4080	3.4030
2	1.0	3.50	4.33	3.3207	3.3142	3.3045
3	1.5	3.50	4.39	3.2793	3.2222	3.2081
4	2.0	3.50	4.44	3.1438	3.1315	3.1133
5	2.5	3.50	4.51	3.0553	3.0405	3.0184
6	3.0	3.50	4.54	2.9708	2.9535	2.9278
7	3.5	3.50	4.58	2.8868	2.8672	2.8381
8	4.0	3.50	4.73	2.7921	2.7705	2.7384
9	4.5	3.50	4.90	2.6942	2.6708	2.6360
10	5.0	103.50	5.11	76.6037	75.8643	74.7699
			Total	104.110	103.243	101.958

Zero-Volatility Spread

The *zero-volatility spread*, also referred to as the *Z-spread* or *static spread*, is a measure of the spread that the investor would realize over the entire Treasury spot rate curve if the bond were held to maturity. Unlike the nominal spread, it is not a spread at one point on the yield curve. The Z-spread is the spread that will make the present value of the cash flows from the non-Treasury bond, when discounted at the Treasury rate plus the spread, equal to the non-Treasury bond's market price plus accrued interest. A trial-and-error procedure is used to compute the Z-spread.

To illustrate how this is done, consider the following two 5-year bonds:

Issue	Coupon	Price	Yield to maturity
Treasury	5.055%	100.0000	5.0550%
Non-Treasury	7.000%	101.9576	6.5348%

The nominal spread for the non-Treasury bond is 147.98 basis points. Let's use the information presented in Exhibit 12 to determine the Z-spread. The third column in Exhibit 12 shows the cash flows for the 7% 5-year non-Treasury issue. The fourth column is a hypothetical Treasury spot rate curve that we will employ in this example. The goal is to determine the spread that, when added to all the Treasury spot rates, will produce a present value for the non-Treasury bond equal to its market price of $101.9576.

Suppose we select a spread of 100 basis points. To each Treasury spot rate shown in the fourth column of Exhibit 12, 100 basis points are added. So, for example, the 1-year (period 2) spot rate is 5.33% (4.33% plus 1%). The spot rate plus 100 basis points is used to calculate the present values as shown in the fifth column.[6] The total present value in the fifth column is $104.110. Because the

---

[6] The discount rate used to compute the present value of each cash flow in the third column is found by adding the assumed spread to the spot rate and then dividing by 2.

present value is not equal to the non-Treasury issue's price of ($101.9576), the Z-spread is not 100 basis points. If a spread of 120 basis points is tried, it can be seen from the next-to-the-last column of Exhibit 12 that the present value is $103.243; again, because this is not equal to the non-Treasury issue's price, 120 basis points is not the Z-spread. The last column of Exhibit 11 shows the present value when a 150 basis point spread is used. The present value of the cash flows is equal to the non-Treasury issue's price. Accordingly, 150 basis points is the Z-spread, compared to the nominal spread of 147.98 basis points.

What does the Z-spread represent for this non-Treasury security? Since the Z-spread is relative to the benchmark Treasury spot rate curve, it represents a spread required by the market to compensate for all the risks of holding the non-Treasury bond versus a Treasury security with the same maturity. These risks include the non-Treasury's credit risk, liquidity risk, and the risks associated with any embedded options.

Divergence Between Z-Spread and Nominal Spread

Generally, the divergence is a function of the term structure's shape and the security's characteristics. Among the relevant security characteristics are coupon rate, term to maturity, and type of principal repayment provision — non-amortizing versus amortizing. The steeper the term structure, the greater will be the divergence. For standard coupon-paying bonds with a bullet maturity (i.e., a single payment of principal), the Z-spread and the nominal spread will usually not differ significantly. For monthly-pay amortizing securities the divergence can be substantial in a steep yield curve environment.

Z-Spread Relative to Any Benchmark

A Z-spread can be calculated relative to any benchmark spot rate curve in the same manner. The question arises: what does the Z-spread mean when the benchmark is not the Treasury spot rate curve (i.e., default-free spot rate curve)? This is especially true in Europe where swaps curves are commonly used as a benchmark for pricing.[7] When the Treasury spot rate curve is the benchmark, we indicated that the Z-spread for non-Treasury issues captured credit risk, liquidity risk, and any option risks. When the benchmark is the spot rate curve for the issuer, for example, the Z-spread reflects the spread attributable to the issue's liquidity risk and any option risks.

Accordingly, when a Z-spread is cited, it must be cited relative to some benchmark spot rate curve. This is essential because it indicates the credit and sector risks that are being considered when the Z-spread is calculated. While Z-spreads are typically calculated in the United States using Treasury securities as the benchmark interest rates, this is usually not the case elsewhere. Vendors of analytical systems such Bloomberg commonly allow the user to select a benchmark.

---

[7] We will discuss swaps and swap rates in Chapter 12.

Chapter 6

Valuation of Bonds with Embedded Options

In Chapter 4, we discussed the valuation of option-free bonds. These are bonds where neither the issuer nor the investor has the option to alter a bond's cash flows. In this chapter we will explain how to value bonds with embedded options.

OVERVIEW OF THE VALUATION OF BONDS WITH EMBEDDED OPTIONS

To develop an analytical framework for valuing a bond with an embedded option, it is necessary to decompose a bond into its component parts. Consider, for example, the most common bond with an embedded option, a callable bond. A callable bond is a bond in which the bondholder has sold the issuer an option (more specifically, a call option) that allows the issuer to repurchase the contractual cash flows of the bond from the time of the bond's first call date until the maturity date.

Consider the following two bonds: (1) a callable bond with an 8% coupon, 20 years to maturity, and callable in five years at 104 and (2) a 10-year 9% coupon bond callable immediately at par. For the first bond, the bondholder owns a 5-year option-free bond and has sold a call option granting the issuer the right to call away from the bondholder 15 years of cash flows five years from now for a price of 104. The investor who owns the second bond has a 10-year option-free bond and has sold a call option granting the issuer the right to immediately call the entire 10-year contractual cash flows, or any cash flows remaining at the time the issue is called, for 100.

Effectively, the owner of a callable bond is entering into two separate transactions. First, the investor buys an option-free bond from the issuer for which he pays some price. Then, the investor sells the issuer a call option for which he/she receives the option price. Therefore, we can summarize the position of a callable bondholder as follows:

long a callable bond = long an option-free bond + sold a call option

In terms of value, the value of a callable bond is therefore equal to the value of the two component parts. That is,

value of a callable bond = value of an option-free bond − value of a call option

The reason the call option's value is subtracted from the value of the option-free bond is that when the bondholder sells a call option, he/she receives the option price. Actually, the position is more complicated than we just described. The issuer may be entitled to call the bond at the first call date and anytime thereafter, or at the first call date and any subsequent coupon anniversary date. Thus the investor has effectively sold an American-type call option to the issuer, but the call price may vary with the date the call option is exercised. This is because the call schedule for a bond may have a different call price depending on the call date. Moreover, the underlying bond for the call option is the remaining coupon payments that would have been made by the issuer had the bond not been called. For exposition purposes, it is easier to understand the principles associated with the investment characteristics of callable bonds by describing the investor's position as long an option-free bond and short a call option.

The same logic applies to putable bonds. In the case of a putable bond, the bondholder has the right to sell the bond to the issuer at a designated price and time. A putable bond can be broken into two separate transactions. First, the investor buys an option-free bond. Second, the investor buys a put option from the issuer that allows the investor to sell the bond to the issuer. Therefore, the position of a putable bondholder can be described as:

long a putable bond = long an option-free bond + long a put option

In terms of value,

value of a putable bond = value of an option-free bond + value of a put option

OPTION-ADJUSTED SPREAD AND OPTION COST

Before presenting the valuation models, we will discuss two measures that are derived from a valuation model — option-adjusted spread and option cost.

Option-Adjusted Spread

What an investor seeks to do is to buy a security whose value is greater than its price. A valuation model such as the two described later in this chapter allows an investor to estimate the theoretical value of a security, which at this point would be sufficient to determine the fairness of the price of the security. That is, the investor can say that this bond is 1 point cheap or 2 points cheap, and so on.

A valuation model need not stop here, however. Instead, it can convert the divergence between the security's price observed in the market and the theoretical value derived from the model into a yield spread measure. This step is necessary because many market participants find it more convenient to think in terms of yield spread than price differences.

Exhibit 1: Bond Valuation Models

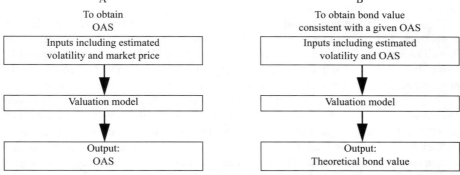

The *option-adjusted spread* (OAS) was developed as a yield spread measure to convert dollar differences between value and price. Thus, basically, the OAS is used to reconcile value with market price. But what is it a "spread" over? As we shall see when we describe the two valuation methodologies, the OAS is a spread over some benchmark curve. The benchmark curve itself is not a single curve, but a series of curves that allow for changes in interest rates.

The reason that the resulting spread is referred to as "option-adjusted" is because the cash flows of the security whose value we seek are adjusted to reflect any embedded options. In contrast, as explained in the previous chapter the zero-volatility spread does not consider how the cash flows will change when interest rates change in the future. That is, the zero-volatility spread assumes that interest rate volatility is zero. Consequently, the zero-volatility spread is also referred to as the *static spread*.

While the product of a valuation model is the OAS, the process can be worked in reverse. For a specified OAS, the valuation model can determine the theoretical value of the security that is consistent with that OAS. This is depicted in Exhibit 1.

Option Cost

The implied cost of the option embedded in any security can be obtained by calculating the difference between the OAS at the assumed volatility of interest rates and the zero-volatility spread. That is,

option cost = zero-volatility spread − option-adjusted spread

The reason that the option cost is measured in this way is as follows. In an environment of no interest rate changes, the investor would earn the zero-volatility spread. When future interest rates are uncertain, the spread is different because of the embedded option; the OAS reflects the spread after adjusting for this option.

Therefore, the option cost is the difference between the spread that would be earned in a static interest rate environment (the zero-volatility spread) and the spread after adjusting for the option (the OAS).

For callable bonds and mortgage passthrough securities, the option cost is positive. This is because the borrower's ability to alter the cash flow will result in an OAS that is less than the zero-volatility spread. In the case of a putable bond, the OAS is greater than the zero-volatility spread so that the option cost is negative. This occurs because of the investor's ability to alter the cash flow.

In general, when the option cost is positive, this means that the investor has sold or is short an option. This is true for callable bonds and mortgage passthrough securities. A negative value for the option cost means that the investor has purchased or is long an option. A putable bond is an example of a security with a negative option cost. There are certain securities in the mortgage-backed securities market that also have an option cost that is negative.

While the option cost as described above is measured in basis points, it can be translated into a dollar price.

LATTICE MODEL

There are several models that have been proposed to value bonds with embedded options. Of interest to us are those models that provide an "arbitrage-free value" for a security. In Chapter 4 we saw that an arbitrage-free value for an option-free bond was obtained by first generating the spot rates (or forward rates). The spot rates are the rates that would produce a value for each on-the-run Treasury issue that is equal to its observed market price. In developing the interest rates that should be used to value a bond with an embedded option, the same principle applies. That is, no matter how complex the valuation model, when each on-the-run Treasury issue is valued using the model, the value produced should be equal to the on-the-run issue's market price. This is because it is assumed that the on-the-run issues are fairly priced.

The first complication in building a model to value bonds with embedded options is that the future cash flows will depend on what happens to interest rates in the future. This means that future interest rates must be considered. This is incorporated into a valuation model by considering how interest rates can change based on some assumed interest rate volatility. In Chapter 13 we will explain what interest rate volatility is and how it is estimated. Given the assumed interest rate volatility, an interest rate "tree" representing possible future interest rates consistent with the volatility assumption can be constructed. Since the interest rate tree looks like a lattice, these valuation models are commonly referred to as *lattice models*. It is from the interest rate tree (or lattice) that two important elements in the valuation process are obtained. First, the interest rates on the tree are used to generate the cash flows taking into account the embedded option. Second, the interest rates on the tree are used to compute the present value of the cash flows.

For a given interest rate volatility, there are several interest rate models that have been used in practice to construct an interest rate tree. An *interest rate model* is a probabilistic description of how interest rates can change over the life of the bond. An interest rate model does this by making an assumption about the relationship between the level of short-term interest rates and the interest rate volatility as measured by the standard deviation. A discussion of the various interest rate models that have been suggested in the finance literature and that are used by practitioners in developing valuation models is beyond the scope of this chapter. What is important to understand is that the interest rate models commonly used are based on how short-term interest rates can evolve (i.e., change) over time. Consequently, these interest rate models are referred to as *one-factor models*, where "factor" means only one interest rate is being modeled over time. More complex models consider how more than one interest rate changes over time. For example, an interest rate model can specify how the short-term interest rate and the long-term interest rate can change over time. Such a model is called a *two-factor model*.

Given an interest rate model and an interest rate volatility assumption, it can be assumed that interest rates can realize one of two possible rates in the next period. A valuation model that makes this assumption in creating an interest rate tree is called a *binomial lattice model*, or simply *binomial model*. There are valuation models that assume that interest rates can take on three possible rates in the next period and these models are called *trinomial lattice models*, or simply *trinomial models*. There are even more complex models that assume in creating an interest rate tree that more than three possible rates in the next period can be realized. Regardless of the assumption about how many possible rates can be realized in the next period, the interest rate tree generated must produce a value for the on-the-run Treasury issue that is equal to its observed market price — that is, it must produce an arbitrage-free value. Moreover, the intuition and the methodology for using the interest rate tree (i.e., the backward induction methodology described later) are the same.

Once an interest rate tree is generated that (1) is consistent with both the interest rate volatility assumption and the interest rate model, and (2) generates the observed market price for each on-the-run issue, the next step is to use the interest rate tree to value a bond with an embedded option. The complexity here is that a set of rules must be introduced to determine, for any period, when the embedded option will be exercised. For a callable bond, these rules are called the "call rules." The rules vary from model builder to model builder.

At this stage, all of this sounds terribly complicated. While the building of a model to value bonds with embedded options is more complex than building a model to value option-free bonds, the basic principles are the same. In the case of valuing an option-free bond, the model that is built is simply a set of spot rates that are used to value cash flows. The spot rates will produce an arbitrage-free value. For a model to value a bond with embedded options, the interest rate tree is used to value future cash flows and the interest rate tree is combined with the call rules to generate the future cash flows. Again, the interest rate tree will produce an arbitrage-free value.

Let's move from theory to practice. Only a few practitioners will develop their own model to value bonds with embedded options. Instead, it is typical for a portfolio manager or analyst to use a model developed by either a dealer firm or a vendor of analytical systems. A fair question is then: Why bother covering a valuation model that is readily available from a third-party? The answer is that a valuation model should not be a black box to portfolio managers and analysts. The models in practice share all of the principles described in this chapter, but differ with respect to certain assumptions that can produce quite different results. The reasons for these differences in valuation must be understood. Moreover, third-party models give the user a choice of changing the assumptions. A user who has not "walked through" a valuation model has no appreciation of the significance of these assumptions and therefore of how to assess the impact of these assumptions on the value produced by the model. There is always "modeling risk" when we use the output of a valuation model. This is the risk that the underlying assumptions of a model may be incorrect. Understanding a valuation model permits the user to effectively determine the significance of an assumption.

An example of understanding the assumptions of a model is the volatility used. Suppose that the market price of a bond is $89. Suppose further that a valuation model produces a value for a bond with an embedded option of $90 based on a 12% interest rate volatility assumption. Then, according to the valuation model, this bond is cheap by one point. However, suppose that the same model produces a value of $87 if a 15% volatility is assumed. This tells the portfolio manager or analyst that the bond is two points rich. Which is correct?

Below we will use the binomial model to demonstrate all of the issues and assumptions associated with valuing a bond with embedded options. Specifically, it is used to value agency debentures, corporates, and municipal bond structures with embedded options. The reason it is not used to value mortgage-backed securities and certain types of asset-backed securities will be explained when we describe the Monte Carlo simulation valuation model in Chapter 8.

BINOMIAL MODEL

To illustrate the binomial valuation methodology, we start with the on-the-run yield curve for the particular issuer whose bonds we want to value. The starting point is the Treasury's on-the-run yield curve. To obtain a particular issuer's on-the-run yield curve, an appropriate credit spread is added to each on-the-run Treasury issue. The credit spread need not be constant for all maturities. For example, as explained in the Chapter 4, the credit spread may increase with maturity.

In our illustration, we use the hypothetical on-the-run issues for an issuer shown in Exhibit 2. Each bond is trading at par value (100) so the coupon rate is equal to the yield to maturity. We will simplify the illustration by assuming annual-pay bonds. Using the bootstrapping methodology explained in Chapter 2, the spot rates are those shown in the last column of Exhibit 2.

Exhibit 2: On-the-Run Yield Curve and Spot Rates for an Issuer

Maturity (Years)	Yield to Maturity (%)	Market Price ($)	Spot Rate (%)
1	3.5	100	3.5000
2	4.2	100	4.2147
3	4.7	100	4.7345
4	5.2	100	5.2707

Exhibit 3: Four-Year Binomial Interest Rate Tree

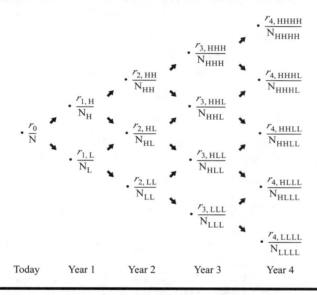

Today   Year 1   Year 2   Year 3   Year 4

Binomial Interest Rate Tree[1]

Once we allow for embedded options, consideration must be given to interest rate volatility. This can be done by introducing a *binomial interest rate tree*. This tree is nothing more than a graphical depiction of the 1-period or short rates over time based on some assumption about interest rate volatility. How this tree is constructed is illustrated below.

Exhibit 3 provides an example of a binomial interest rate tree. In this tree, each node (bold circle) represents a time period that is equal to one year from the node to its left. Each node is labeled with an N, representing node, and a subscript that indicates the path that the 1-year rate took to get to that node. L represents the lower of the two 1-year rates and H represents the higher of the two 1-year rates. For example, node N_{HH} means to get to that node the following path

---

[1] The model described in this section was presented in Andrew J. Kalotay, George O. Williams, and Frank J. Fabozzi, "A Model for the Valuation of Bonds and Embedded Options," *Financial Analysts Journal* (May-June 1993), pp. 35-46.

for 1-year rates occurred: the 1-year rate realized is the higher of the two rates in the first year and then the higher of the 1-year rates in the second year.[2]

Look first at the point denoted by just N in Exhibit 3. This is the root of the tree and is nothing more than the current 1-year spot rate, or equivalently the current 1-year rate, which we denote by r_0. What we have assumed in creating this tree is that the 1-year rate can take on two possible rates the next period and the two rates have the same probability of occurring. One rate will be higher than the other. It is assumed that the 1-year rate can evolve over time based on a random process called a lognormal random walk with a certain volatility.

We use the following notation to describe the tree in Year 1. Let

σ = assumed volatility of the 1-year rate

$r_{1,L}$ = the lower 1-year rate one year from now

$r_{1,H}$ = the higher 1-year rate one year from now

The relationship between $r_{1,L}$ and $r_{1,H}$ is as follows:

$$r_{1,H} = r_{1,L}(e^{2\sigma})$$

where e is the base of the natural logarithm 2.71828.

For example, suppose that $r_{1,L}$ is 4.4448% and σ is 10% per year, then:

$$r_{1,H} = 4.4448\%(e^{2\times0.10}) = 5.4289\%$$

In Year 2, there are three possible values for the 1-year rate, which we will denote as follows:

$r_{2,LL}$ = 1-year rate in Year 2 assuming the lower rate in Year 1 and the lower rate in Year 2

$r_{2,HH}$ = 1-year rate in Year 2 assuming the higher rate in Year 1 and the higher rate in Year 2

$r_{2,HL}$ = 1-year rate in Year 2 assuming the higher rate in Year 1 and the lower rate in Year 2 or equivalently the lower rate in Year 1 and the higher rate in Year 2

The relationship between $r_{2,LL}$ and the other two 1-year rates is as follows:

$$r_{2,HH} = r_{2,LL}(e^{4\sigma}) \text{ and } r_{2,HL} = r_{2,LL}(e^{2\sigma})$$

So, for example, if $r_{2,LL}$ is 4.6958%, then assuming once again that σ is 10%, then

$$r_{2,HH} = 4.6958\%(e^{4\times0.10}) = 7.0053\%$$

and

$$r_{2,HL} = 4.6958\%(e^{4\times0.10}) = 5.7354\%$$

---

[2] Note that N_{HL} is equivalent to N_{LH} in the second year and that in the third year N_{HHL} is equivalent to N_{HLH} and N_{LHH} and that N_{HLL} is equivalent to N_{LLH}. We have simply selected one label for a node rather than clutter up the exhibit.

Exhibit 4: Four-Year Binomial Interest Rate Tree with 1-Year Rates*

Today	Year 1	Year 2	Year 3	Year 4

* r_t equals forward 1-year lower rate

In Year 3, there are four possible values for the 1-year rate, which are denoted as follows: $r_{3,HHH}$, $r_{3,HHL}$, $r_{3,HLL}$, and $r_{3,LLL}$, and whose first three rates are related to the last as follows:

$$r_{3,HHH} = (e^{6\sigma})\, r_{3,LLL}$$
$$r_{3,HHL} = (e^{4\sigma})\, r_{3,LLL}$$
$$r_{3,HLL} = (e^{2\sigma})\, r_{3,LLL}$$

Exhibit 3 shows the notation for a 4-year binomial interest rate tree. We can simplify the notation by letting r_t be the 1-year rate t years from now for the lower rate since all the other short rates t years from now depend on that rate. Exhibit 4 shows the interest rate tree using this simplified notation.

Before we go on to show how to use this binomial interest rate tree to value bonds, let's focus on two issues here. First, what does the volatility parameter σ represent? Second, how do we find the value of the bond at each node?

Volatility and the Standard Deviation

It can be shown that the standard deviation of the 1-year rate is equal to $r_0\sigma$.[3] The standard deviation is a statistical measure of volatility. In Chapter 13 we explain how it is estimated. It is important to see that the process that we assumed gener-

---

[3] This can be seen by noting that $e^{2\sigma} \approx 1 + 2\sigma$. Then the standard deviation of the 1-year rate is

$$\frac{re^{2\sigma} - r}{2} \approx \frac{r + 2\sigma r - r}{2} = \sigma r$$

ates the binomial interest rate tree (or equivalently the short rates), implies that volatility is measured relative to the current level of rates. For example, if σ is 10% and the 1-year rate (r_0) is 4%, then the standard deviation of the 1-year rate is 4% $\times$ 10% = 0.4% or 40 basis points. However, if the current 1-year rate is 12%, the standard deviation of the 1-year rate would be 12% $\times$ 10% or 120 basis points.

Determining the Value at a Node

To find the value of the bond at a node, we first calculate the bond's value at the two nodes to the right of the node we are interested in. For example, in Exhibit 4, suppose we want to determine the bond's value at node N_H. The bond's value at node N_{HH} and N_{HL} must be determined. Hold aside for now how we get these two values because as we will see, the process involves starting from the last year in the tree and working backwards to get the final solution we want, so these two values will be known.

Effectively what we are saying is that if we are at some node, then the value at that node will depend on the future cash flows. In turn, the future cash flows depend on (1) the bond's value one year from now and (2) the coupon payment one year from now. The latter is known. The former depends on whether the 1-year rate is the higher or lower rate. The bond's value depending on whether the rate is the higher or lower rate is reported at the two nodes to the right of the node that is the focus of our attention. So, the cash flow at a node will be either (1) the bond's value if the short rate is the higher rate plus the coupon payment, or (2) the bond's value if the short rate is the lower rate plus the coupon payment. For example, suppose that we are interested in the bond's value at N_H. The cash flow will be either the bond's value at N_{HH} plus the coupon payment, or the bond's value at N_{HL} plus the coupon payment.

To get the bond's value at a node we follow the fundamental rule for valuation: the value is the present value of the expected cash flows. The appropriate discount rate to use is the 1-year rate at the node. Now there are two present values in this case: the present value if the 1-year rate is the higher rate and one if it is the lower rate. Since it is assumed that the probability of both outcomes is equal, an average of the two present values is computed. This is illustrated in Exhibit 5 for any node assuming that the 1-year rate is r^* at the node where the valuation is sought and letting:

V_H = the bond's value for the higher 1-year rate
V_L = the bond's value for the lower 1-year rate
C = coupon payment

Using our notation, the cash flow at a node is either:

$V_H + C$ for the higher 1-year rate

$V_L + C$ for the lower 1-year rate

Exhibit 5: Calculating the Value at a Node

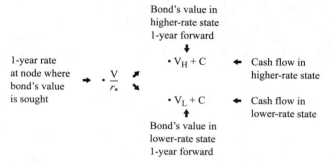

Bond's value in
higher-rate state
1-year forward
↓

1-year rate
at node where $\cdot \dfrac{V}{r_*}$ ↗ $\cdot$ V$_H$ + C   ← Cash flow in
bond's value   higher-rate state
is sought   ↘

                                $\cdot$ V$_L$ + C   ← Cash flow in
                                ↑   lower-rate state
                        Bond's value in
                        lower-rate state
                        1-year forward

Exhibit 6: The 1-Year Rates for Year 1 Using the 2-Year 4.2% On-the-Run Issue: First Trial

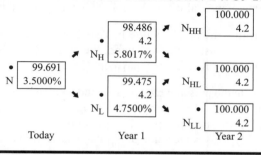

	Today	Year 1	Year 2

N · 99.691 / 3.5000%

N$_H$ · 98.486 / 4.2 / 5.8017%

N$_{HH}$ · 100.000 / 4.2

N$_L$ · 99.475 / 4.2 / 4.7500%

N$_{HL}$ · 100.000 / 4.2

N$_{LL}$ · 100.000 / 4.2

The present value of these two cash flows using the 1-year rate at the node, r_*, is:

$$\frac{V_H + C}{(1 + r_*)} = \text{present value for the higher 1-year rate}$$

$$\frac{V_L + C}{(1 + r_*)} = \text{present value for the lower 1-year rate}$$

Then, the value of the bond at the node is found as follows:

$$\text{value at a node} = \frac{1}{2}\left[\frac{V_H + C}{(1 + r_*)} + \frac{V_L + C}{(1 + r_*)}\right]$$

Constructing the Binomial Interest Rate Tree

To see how to construct the binomial interest rate tree, let's use the assumed on-the-run yields in Exhibit 2. We will assume that volatility, σ, is 10% and construct a 2-year tree using the 2-year bond with a coupon rate of 4.2%.

Exhibit 6 shows a more detailed binomial interest rate with the cash flow shown at each node. We'll see how all the values reported in the exhibit are obtained. The root rate for the tree, r_0, is simply the current 1-year rate, 3.5%.

In the first year there are two possible 1-year rates, the higher rate and the lower rate. What we want to find is the two 1-year rates that will be consistent with the volatility assumption, the process that is assumed to generate the short rates, and the observed market value of the bond. There is no simple formula for this. It must be found by an iterative process (i.e., trial-and-error). The steps are described and illustrated below.

Step 1: Select a value for r_1. Recall that r_1 is the lower 1-year rate. In this first trial, we *arbitrarily* selected a value of 4.75%.

Step 2: Determine the corresponding value for the higher 1-year rate. As explained earlier, this rate is related to the lower 1-year rate as follows: $r_1 e^{2\sigma}$. Since r_1 is 4.75%, the higher 1-year rate is 5.8017% ($= 4.75\%\ e^{2\times0.10}$). This value is reported in Exhibit 6 at node N_H

Step 3: Compute the bond value's in Year 1. This value is determined as follows:

    3a. Determine the bond's value in Year 2. In our example, this is simple. Since we are using a 2-year bond, the bond's value is its maturity value ($100) plus its final coupon payment ($4.2). Thus, it is $104.2.

    3b. Calculate the present value of the bond's value found in 3a for the higher rate in Year 2. The appropriate discount rate is the higher 1-year rate, 5.8017% in our example. The present value is $98.486 ($= \$104.2/1.058017$). This is the value of V_H that we referred to earlier.

    3c. Calculate the present value of the bond's value found in 3a for the lower rate. The discount rate assumed for the lower 1-year rate is 4.75%. The present value is $99.475 ($= \$104.2/1.0475$) and is the value of V_L.

    3d. Add the coupon to both V_H and V_L to get the cash flow at N_H and N_L, respectively. In our example we have $102.686 for the higher rate and $103.675 for the lower rate.

    3e. Calculate the present value of the two values using the 1-year rate r_*. At this point in the valuation, r_* is the root rate, 3.50%. Therefore,

$$\frac{V_H + C}{1 + r_*} = \frac{\$102.686}{1.035} = \$99.213$$

and

$$\frac{V_L + C}{1 + r_*} = \frac{\$103.675}{1.035} = \$100.169$$

Step 4: Calculate the average present value of the two cash flows in Step 3. This is the value we referred to earlier as

$$\text{value at a node} = \frac{1}{2}\left[\frac{V_H + C}{(1 + r_*)} + \frac{V_L + C}{(1 + r_*)}\right]$$

In our example, we have

$$\text{value at a node} = \frac{1}{2}(\$99.213 + \$100.169) = \$99.691$$

Step 5: Compare the value in Step 4 to the bond's market value. If the two values are the same, then the r_1 used in this trial is the one we seek. This is the 1-year rate that would then be used in the binomial interest rate tree for the lower rate and to obtain the corresponding higher rate. If, instead, the value found in Step 4 is not equal to the market value of the bond, this means that the value r_1 in this trial is not the 1-year rate that is consistent with (1) the volatility assumption, (2) the process assumed to generate the 1-year rate, and (3) the observed market value of the bond. In this case, the five steps are repeated with a different value for r_1.

When r_1 is 4.75%, a value of $99.691 results in Step 4 which is less than the observed market price of $100. Therefore, 4.75% is too high and the five steps must be repeated trying a lower rate for r_1.

Let's jump right to the correct rate for r_1 in this example and rework Steps 1 through 5. This occurs when r_1 is 4.4448%. The corresponding binomial interest rate tree is shown in Exhibit 7.

Step 1: In this trial we select a value of 4.4448% for r_1, the lower 1-year rate.

Step 2: The corresponding value for the higher 1-year rate is 5.4289% (= 4.4448% $e^{2\times0.10}$).

Step 3: The bond's value in Year 1 is determined as follows:

3a. The bond's value in Year 2 is $104.2, just as in the first trial.

Exhibit 7: The 1-Year Rates for Year 1 Using the 2-Year 4.2% On-the-Run Issue

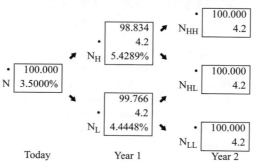

3b. The present value of the bond's value found in *3a* for the higher 1-year rate, V_H, is $98.834 (= $104.2/1.054289).

3c. The present value of the bond's value found in *3a* for the lower 1-year rate, V_L, is $99.766 (= $104.2/1.044448).

3d. Adding the coupon to V_H and V_L, we get $103.034 as the cash flow for the higher rate and $103.966 as the cash flow for the lower rate.

3e. The present value of the two cash flows using the 1-year rate at the node to the left, 3.5%, gives

$$\frac{V_H + C}{1 + r_*} = \frac{\$103.034}{1.035} = \$99.550$$

and,

$$\frac{V_L + C}{1 + r_*} = \frac{\$103.966}{1.035} = \$100.450$$

Step 4: The average present value is $100, which is the value at the node.

Step 5: Since the average present value is equal to the observed market price of $100, r_1 or $r_{1,L}$ is 4.4448% and $r_{1,H}$ is 5.4289%.

We can "grow" this tree for one more year by determining r_2. Now we will use the 3-year on-the-run issue, the 4.7% coupon bond, to get r_2. The same five steps are used in an iterative process to find the 1-year rates in the tree in Year 2. Our objective is now to find the value of r_2 that will produce a bond value of $100 (since the 3-year on-the-run issue has a market price of $100) and is consistent with (1) a volatility assumption of 10%, (2) a current 1-year rate of 3.5%, and (3) the two rates one year from now of 4.4448% (the lower rate) and 5.4289% (the higher rate).

We explain how this is done using Exhibit 8. Let's look at how we get the information in the exhibit. The maturity value and coupon payment are shown in the boxes at the four nodes at Year 3. Since the 3-year on-the-run issue has a maturity value of $100 and a coupon payment of $4.7, these values are the same in the box shown at each node. For the three nodes at Year 2 the coupon payment of $4.7 is shown. Unknown at these three nodes are (1) the three rates in Year 2 and (2) the value of the bond at Year 2. For the two nodes in Year 1, the coupon payment is known, as are the 1-year rates. These are the rates found earlier. The value of the bond, which depends on the bond values at the nodes to the right, is unknown at these two nodes. All of the unknown values are indicated by a question mark.

Exhibit 8: Information for Deriving the 1-Year Rates for Year 2 Using the 3-Year 4.7% On-the-Run Issue

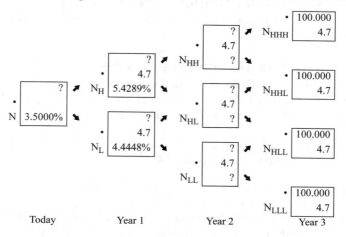

Exhibit 9: The 1-Year Rates for Year 2 Using the 3-Year 4.7% On-the-Run Issue

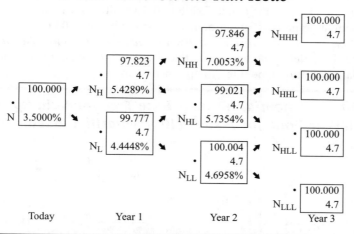

Exhibit 9 is the same as Exhibit 8 but complete with the values previously unknown. As can be seen from Exhibit 9, the value of r_2, or equivalently $r_{2,LL}$, which will produce the desired result is 4.6958%. We showed earlier that the corresponding rates $r_{2,HL}$ and $r_{2,HH}$ would be 5.7354% and 7.0053%, respectively. To verify that these are the 1-year rates in Year 2, work backwards from the four nodes at Year 3 of the tree in Exhibit 9. For example, the value in the box at N_{HH} is found by taking the value of $104.7 at the two nodes to its right and discounting at 7.0053%. The value is $97.846. (Since it is the same value for both nodes to the right, it is also the average value.) Similarly, the value in the box at N_{HL} is found by discounting $104.70 by 5.7354% and at N_{LL} by discounting at 4.6958%. The same procedure used in Exhibits 6 and 7 is used to get the values at the other nodes.

Valuing an Option-Free Bond with the Tree

Now consider an option-free bond with four years remaining to maturity and a coupon rate of 6.5%. The value of this bond can be calculated by discounting the cash flow at the spot rates in Exhibit 2 as shown below:

$$\frac{\$6.5}{(1.035)^1} + \frac{\$6.5}{(1.042147)^2} + \frac{\$6.5}{(1.047345)^3} + \frac{\$100 + \$6.5}{(1.052707)^4} = \$104.643$$

An option-free bond that is valued using the binomial interest rate tree should have the same value as discounting by the spot rates.

Exhibit 10 shows the 1-year rates or binomial interest rate tree that can then be used to value any bond for this issuer with a maturity up to four years. To illustrate how to use the binomial interest rate tree, consider once again the 6.5% option-free bond with three years remaining to maturity. Also assume that the issuer's on-the-run yield curve is the one in Exhibit 2, hence the appropriate binomial interest rate tree is the one in Exhibit 10. Exhibit 11 shows the various values in the discounting process, and produces a bond value of $104.643.

This value is identical to the bond value found when we discounted at the spot rates. This clearly demonstrates that the valuation model is consistent with the standard valuation model for an option-free bond.

Exhibit 10: Binomial Interest Rate Tree for Valuing Up to a 4-Year Bond for Issuer (10% Volatility Assumed)

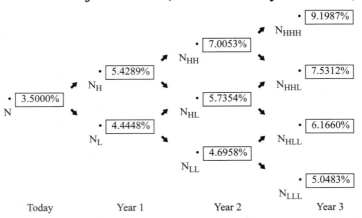

Exhibit 11: Valuing an Option-Free Bond with Four Years to Maturity and a Coupon Rate of 6.5% (10% Volatility Assumed)

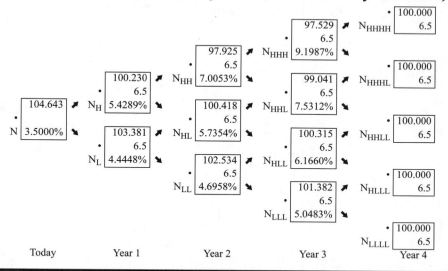

Valuing a Callable Bond

Now we will demonstrate how the binomial interest rate tree can be applied to value a callable bond. The valuation process proceeds in the same fashion as in the case of an option-free bond, but with one exception: when the call option may be exercised by the issuer, the bond value at a node must be changed to reflect the lesser of its values if it is not called (i.e., the value obtained by applying the recursive valuation formula described above) and the call price.

For example, consider a 6.5% corporate bond with four years remaining to maturity that is callable in one year at $100. Exhibit 12 shows two values at each node of the binomial interest rate tree. The discounting process explained above is used to calculate the first of the two values at each node. The second value is the value based on whether the issue will be called. For simplicity, let's assume that this issuer calls the issue if it exceeds the call price. Then, in Exhibit 12 at nodes N_L, N_H, N_{LL}, N_{HL}, N_{LLL}, and N_{HLL} the values from the recursive valuation formula are $101.968, $100.032, $101.723, $100.270, $101.382, and $100.315, respectively. These values exceed the assumed call price ($100) and therefore the second value is $100 rather than the calculated value. It is the second value that is used in subsequent calculations. The root of the tree indicates that the value for this callable bond is $102.899.

The question that we have not addressed in our illustration, which is nonetheless important, is the circumstances under which the issuer will call the bond. A detailed explanation of the call rule is beyond the scope of this chapter. Basically, it involves determining when it would be economic for the issuer on an after-tax basis to call the issue.

Exhibit 12: Valuing a Callable Bond with Four Years to Maturity, a Coupon Rate of 6.5%, and Callable in One Year at 100 (10% Volatility Assumed)

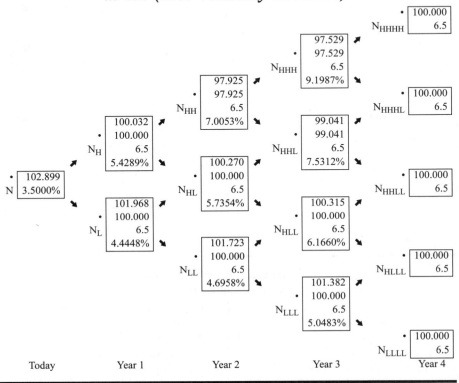

Suppose instead that the call price schedule is $102 in Year 1, $101 in Year 2, and $100 in Year 3. Also assume that the bond will not be called unless it exceeds the call price for that year. Exhibit 13 shows the value at each node and the value of the callable bond. The call price schedule results in a greater value for the callable bond, $103.942 compared to $102.899 when the call price is $100 in each year.

Determining the Call Option Value

The value of a callable bond is equal to the value of an option-free bond minus the value of the call option. This means that:

value of a call option
= value of an option-free bond − value of a callable bond

We have just seen how the value of an option-free bond and the value of a callable bond can be determined. The difference between the two values is, therefore, the value of the call option.

Exhibit 13: Valuing a Callable Bond with Four Years to Maturity, a Coupon Rate of 6.5%, and with a Call Price Schedule (10% Volatility Assumed)

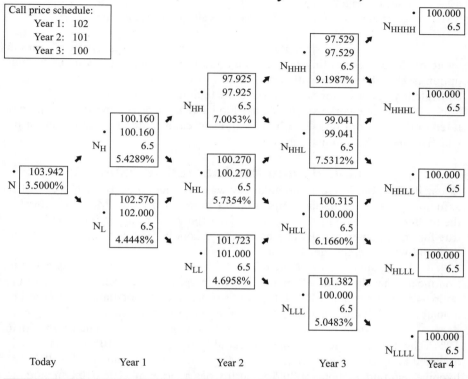

In our illustration, the value of the option-free bond is $104.643. If the call price is $100 in each year, the value of the callable bond is $102.899. Therefore, the value of the call option is $1.744 (= $104.634 − $102.899).

Extension to Other Embedded Options

The bond valuation framework presented here can be used to analyze other embedded options such as put options, caps and floors on floating-rate notes, and the optional accelerated redemption granted to an issuer in fulfilling its sinking fund requirement.

For example, let's consider a putable bond. Suppose that a 6.5% coupon bond with four years remaining to maturity is putable in one year at par ($100). Also assume that the appropriate binomial interest rate tree for this issuer is the one in Exhibit 10. It can be demonstrated that the value of this putable bond is $105.327.

Since the value of a putable bond can be expressed as the value of an option-free bond plus the value of a put option on that bond, this means that:

value of a put option
   = value of an option-free bond − value of a putable bond

In our example, since the value of the putable bond is $105.327 and the value of the corresponding option-free bond is $104.643, the value of the put option is −$0.684. The negative sign indicates the issuer has sold the option, or equivalently, the investor has purchased the option.

The framework can also be used to value a bond with multiple or interrelated embedded options. The bond values at each node are altered based on whether one of the options is exercised.

Volatility and the Theoretical Value

In our illustration, interest rate volatility was assumed to be 10%. The volatility assumption has an important impact on the theoretical value. More specifically, the higher the expected volatility, the higher the value of an option. The same is true for an option embedded in a bond. Correspondingly, this affects the value of the bond with an embedded option.

For example, for a callable bond, a higher interest rate volatility assumption means that the value of the call option increases and, since the value of the option-free bond is not affected, the value of the callable bond must be lower. For a putable bond, higher interest rate volatility means that its value will be higher.

To illustrate this, suppose that a 20% volatility is assumed rather than 10%. The value of the hypothetical callable bond is $102.108 if volatility is assumed to be 20% compared to $102.899 if volatility is assumed to be 10%. The hypothetical putable bond at 20% volatility has a value of $106.010 compared to $105.327 at 10% volatility.

In the construction of the binomial interest rate, it was assumed that volatility is the same for each year. The methodology can be extended to incorporate a term structure of volatility.

Option-Adjusted Spread

Suppose the market price of the 4-year 6.5% callable bond is $102.218 and the theoretical value assuming 10% volatility is $102.899. This means that this bond is cheap by $0.681 according to the valuation model. The option-adjusted spread is the constant spread that, when added to all the 1-year rates on the binomial interest rate tree, will make the arbitrage-free value (i.e., the value produced by the binomial model) equal to the market price.

In our illustration, if the market price is $102.218, the OAS would be the constant spread added to every rate in Exhibit 10 that will make the arbitrage-free value equal to $102.218. The solution in this case would be 35 basis points. This can be verified in Exhibit 14 which shows the value of this issue by adding 35 basis points to each rate.

As with the value of a bond with an embedded option, the OAS will depend on the volatility assumption. For a given bond price, the higher the interest rate volatility assumed, the lower the OAS for a callable bond. For example, if volatility is 20% rather than 10%, the OAS would be –6 basis points. This illustration clearly demonstrates the importance of the volatility assumption. Assuming volatility of 10%, the OAS is 35 basis points. At 20% volatility, the OAS declines and in this case is negative and therefore the bond is overvalued relative to the model.

How do we interpret the OAS? In general, a nominal spread between two yields reflects differences in the:

1. credit risk of the two issues
2. liquidity risk of the two issues
3. option risk of the two issues

Exhibit 14: Demonstration that the Option-Adjusted Spread is 35 Basis Points for a 6.5% Callable Bond Selling at 102.218 (Assuming 10% Volatility)

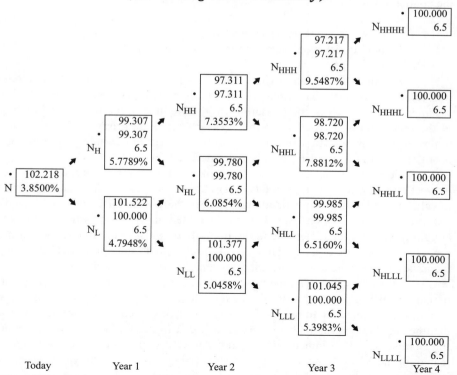

For example, if one of the issues is a non-U.S. Treasury issue with an embedded option and the benchmark interest rates are the rates for the U.S. Treasury on-the-run securities, then the nominal spread is a measure of the difference due to the:

1. credit risk of the non-Treasury issue
2. liquidity risk associated with the non-Treasury issue
3. option risk associated with the non-Treasury issue that is not present in Treasury issues

What the OAS seeks to do is remove from the nominal spread the amount that is due to the option risk. The measure is called an OAS because (1) it is a spread and (2) it adjusts the cash flows for the option when computing the spread to the benchmark interest rates. The second point can be seen from Exhibits 12 and 13. Notice that at each node the value obtained from the backward induction method is adjusted based on the call option and the call rule. Thus, the resulting spread is "option adjusted."

Consequently, if the Treasury on-the-run issues are used as the benchmark, because the call option has been taken into account, the OAS is measuring the compensation for the:

1. credit risk of the non-Treasury issue
2. liquidity risk associated with the non-Treasury issue

So, for example, an OAS of 160 basis points for a callable BBB industrial issue would mean that based on the valuation model (including the volatility assumption), the OAS is compensation for the credit risk and the lower liquidity of the industrial issue relative to the Treasury benchmark issues. The OAS has removed the compensation for the call feature present in the industrial issue that is not present in the Treasury benchmark interest rates.

However, suppose that the benchmark interest rates are the on-the-run interest rates for the issuer, as in our illustration of how to use the binomial model to value a bond with an embedded option. Then there is no difference in the credit risk between the benchmark interest rates and the non-Treasury issue. That is, the OAS reflects only the difference in the liquidity of an issue relative to the on-the-run issues. The valuation has removed the spread due to the option risk and using the issuer's own benchmark interest rates removes the credit risk.

Suppose instead that the benchmark interest rates used are not of that particular issuer but the on-the-run issues for issuers in the same sector of the bond market and the same credit rating of the issue being analyzed. For example, suppose that the callable bond issue being analyzed is that issued by the XYZ Manufacturing Company, a BBB industrial company. An on-the-run yield curve can be estimated for the XYZ Manufacturing Company. Using that on-the-run yield curve, the

OAS reflects the difference in the liquidity risk between the particular callable bond of the XYZ Manufacturing Company analyzed and the on-the-run issues of the XYZ Manufacturing Company. However, if instead the benchmark interest rates used to value the callable bond of the XYZ Manufacturing Company are those of a generic BBB industrial company, the OAS reflects (1) the difference between the liquidity risk of the XYZ Manufacturing Company's callable bond and that of a generic BBB industrial company and (2) differences between event risk/credit risk specific to XYZ Manufacturing Company's issue beyond generic BBB credit risk.

Consequently, we know that an OAS is a spread after adjusting for the embedded option. But we know nothing else until the benchmark interest rates are identified. Without knowing the benchmark used — Treasury on-the-run yield curve, an issuer's on-the-run yield curve, or a generic on-the-run yield curve for issuers in the same sector of the bond market and of the same credit rating — we cannot interpret what the OAS is providing compensation for. Some market participants might view this as unrealistic since most of the time the on-the-run Treasury yield curve is used and therefore the OAS reflects credit risk and liquidity risk. However, vendors of analytical system and most dealer models allow an investor to specify the benchmark interest rates to be used. The default feature in these systems (i.e., what the model uses as the benchmark interest rates if the investor does not specify the benchmark) is the Treasury on-the-run yield curve.

So, once an investor is told what the OAS of a particular bond is, the first question should be: Relative to what benchmark interest rates? This is particularly important in non-U.S. markets where the OAS concept is beginning to be used with greater frequency. It also means that comparing OAS values across global markets is difficult because different benchmark interest rates are being used and therefore the OAS is capturing different risks.

Funded investors — that is, investors who borrow funds and seek to earn a spread over their funding costs — use the London interbank offered rate (LIBOR) as their benchmark interest rates. Most funded investors borrow funds at a spread over LIBOR. Consequently, if a yield curve for LIBOR is used as the benchmark interest rates, the OAS reflects a spread relative to their funding cost. The OAS reflects credit risk relative to the credit risk associated with LIBOR and liquidity risk of the issue. So, if a callable bond has an OAS of 80 basis points and the LIBOR yield curve is the benchmark, then the OAS is compensation relative to LIBOR after adjusting for the embedded call option. A funded investor will then compare the OAS to the spread it must pay over its funding costs. So, if an investor's funding cost is 25 basis points over LIBOR, then a callable bond with an OAS of 80 basis points would be acceptable. Whether or not a funded investor would purchase the callable bond depends on whether or not the credit risk and the liquidity risk are acceptable and whether or not the compensation for these risks (as measured by the OAS) in the opinion of the investor is adequate.

Finally, let's take a closer look at the interpretation of the OAS as a spread relative to benchmark interest rates. This does *not* mean that it is a spread over one maturity for the benchmark interest rates. For example, consider the 35 basis point OAS for the 4-year 6.5% callable issue. The yield for the 4-year on-the-run issue is 5.2%. An OAS of 35 basis points does *not* mean that this callable issue is offering an option-adjusted *yield* of 5.55% (5.2% plus 35 basis points). Rather, to understand how it is spread off the benchmark interest rates, look at Exhibit 14.

First, the benchmark interest rates are used to construct the interest rate at each node of the interest rate tree. Next, recall that the rate at each node in the interest rate tree is the 1-year forward rate. (In general, they are the 1-period forward rates). Now, to get the OAS we must determine the spread that must be added to each of the 1-year forward rates in the interest rate tree so that the backward induction method will produce a value equal to the market value. So, while it is often stated that the OAS is a spread relative to the benchmark interest rates, strictly speaking, it is a spread over the 1-period forward rates in the interest rate tree that are constructed from the benchmark interest rates.

Chapter 7

Cash Flow for Mortgage-Backed Securities and Amortizing Asset-Backed Securities

A major sector of the fixed income market is the mortgage-backed securities market. Mortgage-backed securities are securities backed by a pool of mortgage loans. The pool of loans is referred to as the *collateral*. Loans that are included in the pool are said to have been *securitized*. While residential mortgage loans are by far the largest type of asset that has been securitized, other assets (consumer and business loans and receivables) have been securitized. The largest sectors of the asset-backed securities market in the United States are securities backed by credit card receivables, auto loans, home equity loans, manufactured housing loans, student loans, Small Business Administration loans, and collateralized bond obligations. Since home equity loans and manufactured housing loans are backed by real estate property, the securities backed by them are referred to as *real estate-backed asset-backed securities*. Other asset-backed securities include securities backed by home improvement loans, health care receivables, agricultural equipment loans, equipment leases, commercial mortgage loans, music royalty receivables, movie royalty receivables, and municipal parking ticket receivables. The list is continually expanding.

In this chapter, we will demonstrate how to compute the cash flow of mortgage-backed and amortizing asset-backed securities. We will also show how certain types of products are created or "structured" by redistributing the cash flow from the collateral among different bond classes. Throughout this chapter it is assumed that the reader is familiar with the products in the mortgage-backed and asset-backed securities market.

CASH FLOW OF MORTGAGE-BACKED SECURITIES

Mortgage-backed securities include mortgage passthrough securities, collateralized mortgage obligations, and stripped mortgage-backed securities. We begin with the cash flow for the basic product in the mortgage-backed securities market, the mortgage loan. From there we show how to compute the cash flow for mortgage-backed securities.

141

The Mortgage Loan

The basic product of a mortgage-backed security is the mortgage loan. There are many types of mortgage designs used throughout the world. A mortgage design is a specification of the interest rate, term of the mortgage, and the manner in which the borrowed funds are repaid. In the United States, the alternative mortgage designs include (1) fixed rate, level-payment, fully amortized mortgages, (2) adjustable-rate mortgages, (3) balloon mortgages, (4) growing equity mortgages, (5) reverse mortgages, and (6) tiered payment mortgages. In this chapter we will focus on the most common mortgage design in the United States — the fixed-rate, level-payment, fully amortized mortgage.

Cash Flow of a Fixed-Rate, Level-Payment, Fully Amortized Mortgage

The basic idea behind the design of the fixed-rate, level-payment, fully amortized mortgage is that the borrower pays equal installments over the term of the mortgage such that at the end of the term of the mortgage, the loan has been fully amortized. The payments include principal repayment and interest.

Each monthly mortgage payment for this mortgage design is due on the first of each month and consists of:

1. interest of $\frac{1}{12}$ of the fixed annual interest rate times the amount of the outstanding mortgage balance at the beginning of the previous month, and
2. a repayment of a portion of the outstanding mortgage balance (principal).

The difference between the monthly mortgage payment and the portion of the payment that represents interest equals the amount that is applied to reduce the outstanding mortgage balance. This amount is referred to as the *amortization*. We shall also refer to it as the *scheduled principal repayment*.

In a level-payment, fixed-rate, fully amortized mortgage, the monthly mortgage payment is designed so that after the last scheduled monthly mortgage payment is made, the amount of the outstanding mortgage balance is zero (i.e., the mortgage is fully repaid). There are some types of mortgage design where the scheduled payments will not fully pay off the mortgage balance when the last mortgage payment is made. Instead, there is an outstanding balance that must be made by the borrower.

Calculation of the Monthly Mortgage Payment

The calculation of the monthly mortgage payment for a level-payment, fixed-rate, fully amortized mortgage is simply an application of the present value of an annuity given in Chapter 1. We know that:

$$PV = A \left[\frac{1 - \left[\dfrac{1}{(1+i)^n} \right]}{i} \right]$$

where

PV = present value of an annuity (\$)
A = amount of the annuity (\$)
i = periodic interest rate
n = number of periods

For a level-payment, fixed-rate, fully amortized mortgage, the above formula can be expressed as

$$MB_0 = MP \left[\frac{1 - \left[\frac{1}{(1+i)^n} \right]}{i} \right] \qquad (1)$$

where

MB_0 = PV = original mortgage balance (\$)
MP = A = monthly mortgage payment (\$)
i = simple monthly interest rate (annual interest rate/12)
n = number of months

Solving for the monthly mortgage payment (MP) gives

$$MP = MB_0 \left[\frac{i(1+i)^n}{[(1+i)^n - 1]} \right]$$

For example, for a 30-year (360-month), \$100,000 mortgage with an 8.125% mortgage rate, we have the following:

MB_0 = \$100,000
i = 0.0067708 (= 0.08125/12)
n = 360 (= 30 × 12)

Substituting these values into equation (1), we get

$$MP = \$100,000 \left[\frac{0.0067708(1.0067708)^{360}}{[(1.0067708)^{360} - 1]} \right] = \$742.50$$

Amortization Schedule To illustrate this mortgage design, consider a 30-year (360-month), \$100,000 mortgage with an 8.125% mortgage rate. We just showed that the monthly mortgage payment would be \$742.50. Exhibit 1 shows for selected months how each monthly mortgage payment is divided between interest and scheduled principal repayment. Exhibit 1 is called an *amortization schedule*. At the beginning of month 1, the mortgage balance is \$100,000, the amount of the original loan. The mortgage payment for month 1 includes interest on the \$100,000 borrowed for the month. Since the interest rate is 8.125%, the monthly interest rate is 0.0067708 (0.08125 divided by 12). Interest for month 1 is therefore \$677.08 (\$100,000 times 0.0067708). The \$65.41 difference between the monthly mortgage payment of $742.50 and the interest of $677.08 is the portion of the monthly mortgage payment that represents the scheduled principal repayment. It is also referred to as the scheduled amortization and we shall use the terms *scheduled principal repayment* and *scheduled amortization* interchangeably throughout this chapter. This $65.41 in month 1 reduces the mortgage balance.

Exhibit 1: Amortization Schedule for a Level-Payment, Fixed-Rate, Fully Amortized Mortgage

Mortgage loan: $100,000   Monthly payment: $742.50
Mortgage rate: 8.125%   Term of loan: 30 years (360 months)

Month	Beginning of Month Mortgage Balance	Mortgage Payment	Interest	Scheduled Repayment	End of Month Mortgage Balance
1	$100,000.00	$742.50	$677.08	$65.41	$99,934.59
2	99,934.59	742.50	676.64	65.86	99,868.73
3	99,868.73	742.50	676.19	66.30	99,802.43
4	99,802.43	742.50	675.75	66.75	99,735.68
...	...	...	...	...	...
25	98,301.53	742.50	665.58	76.91	98,224.62
26	98,224.62	742.50	665.06	77.43	98,147.19
27	98,147.19	742.50	664.54	77.96	98,069.23
...	...	...	...	...	...
74	93,849.98	742.50	635.44	107.05	93,742.93
75	93,742.93	742.50	634.72	107.78	93,635.15
76	93,635.15	742.50	633.99	108.51	93,526.64
...	...	...	...	...	...
141	84,811.77	742.50	574.25	168.25	84,643.52
142	84,643.52	742.50	573.11	169.39	84,474.13
143	84,474.13	742.50	571.96	170.54	84,303.59
...	...	...	...	...	...
184	76,446.29	742.50	517.61	224.89	76,221.40
185	76,221.40	742.50	516.08	226.41	75,994.99
186	75,994.99	742.50	514.55	227.95	75,767.04
...	...	...	...	...	...
233	63,430.19	742.50	429.48	313.02	63,117.17
234	63,117.17	742.50	427.36	315.14	62,802.03
235	62,802.03	742.50	425.22	317.28	62,484.75
...	...	...	...	...	...
289	42,200.92	742.50	285.74	456.76	41,744.15
290	41,744.15	742.50	282.64	459.85	41,284.30
291	41,284.30	742.50	279.53	462.97	40,821.33
...	...	...	...	...	...
321	25,941.42	742.50	175.65	566.85	25,374.57
322	25,374.57	742.50	171.81	570.69	24,803.88
323	24,803.88	742.50	167.94	574.55	24,229.32
...	...	...	...	...	...
358	2,197.66	742.50	14.88	727.62	1,470.05
359	1,470.05	742.50	9.95	732.54	737.50
360	737.50	742.50	4.99	737.50	0.00

Exhibit 2: Monthly Split Between Interest and Principal

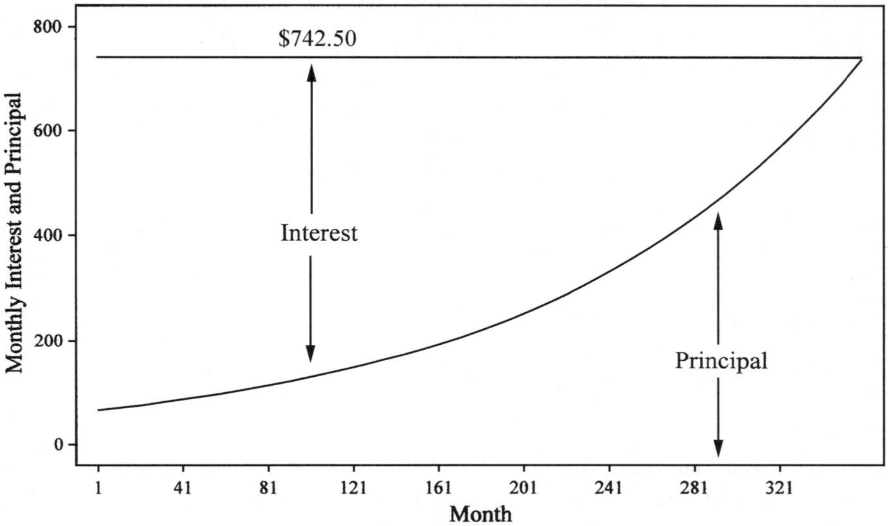

30-year, $100,000 mortgage with an 8.125% mortgage rate

The mortgage balance at the end of month 1 (beginning of month 2) is then $99,934.59 ($100,000 minus $65.41). The interest for the second monthly mortgage payment is $676.64, the monthly interest rate (0.0067708) times the mortgage balance at the beginning of month 2 ($99,934.59). The difference between the $742.50 monthly mortgage payment and the $676.64 interest is $65.86, representing the amount of the mortgage balance paid off with that monthly mortgage payment. Notice that the mortgage payment in month 360 — the final payment — is sufficient to pay off the remaining mortgage balance.

As Exhibit 1 clearly shows, the portion of the monthly mortgage payment applied to interest declines each month and the portion applied to principal repayment increases. The reason for this is that as the mortgage balance is reduced with each monthly mortgage payment, the interest on the mortgage balance declines. Since the monthly mortgage payment is a fixed dollar amount, an increasingly larger portion of the monthly payment is applied to reduce the mortgage balance outstanding in each subsequent month. Exhibit 2 presents a graphical depiction of this process.

Calculating the Monthly Mortgage Balance, Scheduled Principal Repayment, and Interest

It is not necessary to construct an amortization schedule such as Exhibit 1 in order to determine the remaining monthly mortgage balance. Instead, the next three formulas can be used:

Mortgage balance at the end of month t (MB_t):

$$MB_t = MB_0 \left[\frac{[(1+i)^n - (1+i)^t]}{[(1+i)^n - 1]} \right] \qquad (2)$$

where n is the original number of months of the mortgage

Scheduled principal repayment for month t (P_t)

$$P_t = MB_0 \left[\frac{i(1+i)^{t-1}}{[(1+i)^n - 1]} \right] \qquad (3)$$

Interest for month t (I_t)

$$I_t = MB_0 \left[\frac{i[(1+i)^n - (1+i)^{t-1}]}{[(1+i)^n - 1]} \right] \qquad (4)$$

To illustrate these formulas, consider month 186 for the mortgage whose amortization schedule is shown in Exhibit 1. We know that

$$MB_0 = \$100,000 \quad i = 0.0067708 \quad n = 360 \quad t = 186$$

Mortgage balance at the end of month 186 is

$$MB_{186} = \$100,000 \left[\frac{[(1.0067708)^{360} - (1.0067708)^{186}]}{[(1.0067708)^{360} - 1]} \right] = \$75,767$$

Scheduled principal repayment for month 186

$$P_{186} = \$100,000 \left[\frac{0.0067708(1.0067708)^{185}}{[(1.0067708)^{360} - 1]} \right] = \$227.95$$

Interest for month 186

$$I_{186} = MB_0 \left[\frac{0.0067708[(1.0067708)^{360} - (1.0067708)^{185}]}{[(1.0067708)^{360} - 1]} \right] = \$514.55$$

These values agree with the values shown in Exhibit 1 for month 186.

Cash Flow and Servicing Fee Every mortgage loan must be serviced. Servicing of a mortgage loan involves collecting monthly payments and forwarding proceeds to owners of the loan; sending payment notices to mortgagors; reminding mortgagors when payments are overdue; maintaining records of principal balances; administering an escrow balance for real estate taxes and insurance purposes; initiating foreclosure proceedings if necessary; and, furnishing tax information to borrowers (i.e., mortgagors) when applicable.

The servicing fee is a portion of the mortgage rate. If the mortgage rate is 8.125% and the servicing fee is 50 basis points, then the investor receives interest of 7.625%. The interest rate that the investor receives is said to be the *net interest* or *net coupon*. The servicing fee is commonly called the *servicing spread*.

Prepayments and Cash Flow Uncertainty Our illustration of the cash flow from a level-payment, fixed-rate, fully amortized mortgage assumes that the homeowner does not pay off any portion of the mortgage balance prior to the scheduled due date. But homeowners do pay off all or part of their mortgage balance prior to the maturity date. A payment made in excess of the monthly mortgage payment is called a *prepayment*. The prepayment could be to pay off the entire outstanding balance or a partial paydown of the mortgage balance. When a prepayment is not for the entire outstanding balance it is called a *curtailment*. A prepayment can be voluntarily by the borrower. If the borrower defaults and the loan is prepaid from the proceeds from the collateral for the loan, the prepayment is said to be an *involuntary prepayment*.

The effect of prepayments is that the amount and timing of the cash flow from a mortgage loan are not known with certainty. This risk is referred to as *prepayment risk*. For example, all that the investor in a $100,000, 8.125% 30-year mortgage knows is that as long as the loan is outstanding and the borrower does not default, interest will be received and the principal will be repaid at the scheduled date each month; then at the end of the 30 years, the investor would have received $100,000 in principal payments. What the investor does not know — the uncertainty — is for how long the loan will be outstanding, and therefore what the timing of the principal payments will be. This is true for all mortgage loans, not just the level-payment, fixed-rate, fully amortized mortgage.

Most mortgages have no prepayment penalty. That is, the outstanding loan balance can be repaid at par. In 1996, mortgages with prepayment penalties were originated. The purpose of the penalty is to deter prepayment when interest rates decline. A prepayment penalty mortgage has the following structure. There is a period of time over which if the loan is prepaid in full or in excess of a certain amount of the outstanding balance, there is a prepayment penalty. This period is referred to as the *lockout period* or *penalty period*. During the penalty period, the borrower may prepay up to a specified amount of the outstanding balance without a penalty. The amount of the penalty is specified in terms of the number of months of interest that must be paid.

Mortgage Passthrough Securities

A mortgage passthrough security is a security created when one or more holders of mortgages form a collection (pool) of mortgages and sell shares or participation certificates in the pool. A pool may consist of several thousand or only a few mortgages.

The cash flow of a mortgage passthrough security depends on the cash flow of the underlying pool of mortgages. As we explained earlier, the cash flow consists of monthly mortgage payments representing interest, the scheduled repayment of principal, and any prepayments.

Payments are made to security holders each month. However, neither the amount nor the timing of the cash flow from the pool of mortgages is identical to that of the cash flow passed through to investors. The monthly cash flow for a passthrough is less than the monthly cash flow of the underlying pool of mortgages by an amount equal to servicing and other fees. The other fees are those charged by the issuer or guarantor of the passthrough for guaranteeing the issue. The coupon rate on a passthrough, called the *passthrough coupon rate*, is less than the mortgage rate on the underlying pool of mortgages by an amount equal to the servicing and guaranteeing fees.

The timing of the cash flow is also different. The monthly mortgage payment is due from each mortgagor on the first day of each month, but there is a delay in passing through the corresponding monthly cash flow to the security holders. The length of the delay varies by the type of passthrough security.

Weighted Average Coupon and Weighted Average Maturity

Not all of the mortgages that are included in a pool of mortgages that are securitized have the same mortgage rate and the same maturity. Consequently, when describing a passthrough security, a *weighted average coupon rate* and a *weighted average maturity* are determined.

A weighted average coupon rate, or WAC, is found by weighting the mortgage rate of each mortgage loan in the pool by the percentage of the mortgage outstanding relative to the amount of all the mortgages in the pool. A weighted average maturity, or WAM, is found by weighting the remaining number of months to maturity for each mortgage loan in the pool by the amount of the outstanding mortgage balance.

For example, suppose a mortgage pool has just five loans and the outstanding mortgage balance, mortgage rate, and months remaining to maturity of each loan are as follows:

Loan	Outstanding mortgage balance	Weight in pool	Mortgage rate	Months remaining
1	$125,000	22.12%	7.50%	275
2	$85,000	15.04%	7.20%	260
3	$175,000	30.97%	7.00%	290
4	$110,000	19.47%	7.80%	285
5	$70,000	12.39%	6.90%	270
Total	$565,000	100.00%		

The WAC for this mortgage pool is:

$$0.2212\,(7.5\%) + 0.1504\,(7.2\%) + 0.3097\,(7.0\%) + 0.1947\,(7.8\%)$$
$$+ 0.1239\,(6.90\%) = 7.28\%$$

The WAM for this mortgage pool is

$$0.2212\ (275) + 0.1504\ (260) + 0.3097\ (290) + 0.1947\ (285)$$
$$+ 0.1239\ (270) = 279 \text{ months (rounded)}$$

Pool Factor and Price

The *pool factor* indicates the percentage of the initial mortgage balance still outstanding. So, a pool factor of 90 means that 90% of the original mortgage pool balance is outstanding. The pool factor is reported by the issuer of the passthrough each month.

The dollar price paid for just the principal is found as follows, given the agreed upon price, par value, and the month's pool factor provided by the issuer:

price × par value × pool factor

For example, if the parties agree to a price of 92 for $1 million par value for a passthrough with a pool factor of 0.85, then the dollar price paid by the buyer in addition to accrued interest is:

$$0.92 \times \$1,000,000 \times 0.85 = \$782,000$$

Prepayment Conventions and Cash Flow

Estimating the cash flow from a passthrough requires making an assumption about future prepayments. The conventions have been used as a benchmark for prepayment rates — conditional prepayment rate, Public Securities Association prepayment benchmark, and prospectus prepayment curve.

Conditional Prepayment Rate

One convention for describing the pattern of prepayments and the cash flow of a mortgage-backed security, as well as many asset-backed securities, assumes that some fraction of the remaining principal in the pool is prepaid each month for the remaining term of the loan. The prepayment rate assumed for a pool, called the *conditional prepayment rate* (CPR), is based on the characteristics of the pool (including its historical prepayment experience) and the current and expected future economic environment.

The CPR is an annual prepayment rate. To estimate monthly prepayments, the CPR must be converted into a monthly prepayment rate, commonly referred to as the *single-monthly mortality rate* (SMM). The following formula is used to calculate the SMM for a given CPR:[1]

$$SMM = 1 - (1 - CPR)^{1/12}$$

For example, suppose that the CPR is 6%. The corresponding SMM is:

---

[1] The reason why the SMM is not found by simply dividing the CPR by 12 is that there are scheduled principal repayments that are occurring.

$$\text{SMM} = 1 - (1 - 0.06)^{1/12} = 1 - (0.94)^{0.08333} = 0.005143$$

An SMM of w% means that approximately w% of the remaining mortgage balance at the beginning of the month, less the scheduled principal repayment, will prepay that month. That is,

prepayment for month t = SMM × (beginning mortgage balance for month t
 − scheduled principal repayment for month t)

That is, the prepayment for a month is found by first determining the amount that is available to be prepaid. This amount is equal to the outstanding balance at the beginning of the month less the amount of the scheduled principal repayment for that month. It is to this adjusted amount that the SMM is applied to obtain the prepayment for the month.

For example, suppose that an investor owns a passthrough in which the remaining mortgage balance at the beginning of some month is $290 million. Assuming that the SMM is 0.5143% and the scheduled principal repayment is $3 million, the estimated prepayment for the month is:

$$0.005143 \times (\$290,000,000 - \$3,000,000) = \$1,476,041$$

PSA Prepayment Benchmark The *Public Securities Association (PSA) prepayment benchmark* is expressed as a monthly series of CPRs. The PSA benchmark assumes that prepayment rates are low for newly originated mortgages and then will speed up as the mortgages become seasoned. The PSA benchmark assumes the following prepayment rates for 30-year mortgages: (1) a CPR of 0.2% for the first month, increased by 0.2% per year per month for the next 30 months until it reaches 6% per year, and (2) a 6% CPR for the remaining months.

This benchmark, referred to as "100% PSA" or simply "100 PSA," is graphically depicted in Exhibit 3. Mathematically, 100 PSA can be expressed as follows:

if $t < 30$ then CPR = 6% $(t/30)$
if $t \geq 30$ then CPR = 6%

where t is the number of months since the mortgages were originated.

Slower or faster speeds are then referred to as some percentage of PSA. For example, "50 PSA" means one-half the CPR of the PSA prepayment benchmark; "150 PSA" means 1.5 times the CPR of the PSA prepayment benchmark; "300 PSA" means three times the CPR of the prepayment benchmark. This is illustrated graphically in Exhibit 4 for 50 PSA, 100 PSA, and 150 PSA. A prepayment rate of 0 PSA means that no *prepayments* are assumed. While there are no prepayments at 0 PSA, there are scheduled principal repayments.

Exhibit 3: Graphical Depiction of 100 PSA

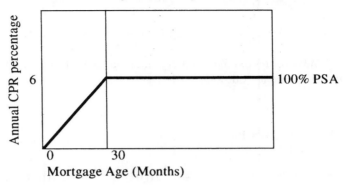

Exhibit 4: Graphical Depiction of 50 PSA, 100 PSA, and 300 PSA

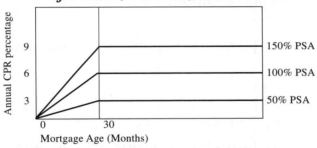

In constructing a schedule for monthly prepayments, the CPR (an annual rate) must be converted into a monthly prepayment rate (an SMM). The conversion is done using equation (1). For example, the SMMs for month 5, month 20, and months 31 through 360 assuming 100 PSA are calculated as follows:

for month 5:

$$CPR = 6\% \, (5/30) = 1\% = 0.01$$
$$SMM = 1 - (1 - 0.01)^{1/12} = 1 - (0.99)^{0.083333} = 0.000837$$

for month 20:

$$CPR = 6\% \, (20/30) = 4\% = 0.04$$
$$SMM = 1 - (1 - 0.04)^{1/12} = 1 - (0.96)^{0.083333} = 0.003396$$

for months 31-360:

$$CPR = 6\%$$
$$SMM = 1 - (1 - 0.06)^{1/12} = 1 - (0.94)^{0.083333} = 0.005143$$

The SMMs for month 5, month 20, and months 31 through 360, assuming 165 PSA, are computed as follows:

for month 5:

$$CPR = 6\% \ (5/30) = 1\% = 0.01$$
$$165 \ PSA = 1.65 \ (0.01) = 0.0165$$

$$SMM = 1 - (1 - 0.0165)^{1/12} = 1 - (0.9835)^{0.08333} = 0.001386$$

for month 20:

$$CPR = 6\% \ (20/30) = 4\% = 0.04$$
$$165 \ PSA = 1.65 \ (.04) = 0.066$$

$$SMM = 1 - (1 - 0.066)^{1/12} = 1 - (0.934)^{0.08333} = 0.005674$$

for months 31-360:

$$CPR = 6\%$$
$$165 \ PSA = 1.65 \ (0.06) = 0.099$$

$$SMM = 1 - (1 - 0.099)^{1/12} = 1 - (0.901)^{0.08333} = 0.008650$$

Notice that the SMM assuming 165 PSA is not just 1.65 times the SMM assuming 100 PSA. It is the CPR that is a multiple of the CPR assuming 100 PSA.

It is also important to note that the CPRs and corresponding SMMs apply to a mortgage pool *based on the number of months since origination.* For example, if a mortgage pool has loans that were originally 30-year (360-month) mortgage loans and the WAM is currently 357 months, this means that the mortgage pool is seasoned three months. So, in determining prepayments for the next month, the CPR and SMM that are applicable are those for month 4.

The PSA benchmark is commonly referred to as a prepayment model, suggesting that it can be used to estimate prepayments. Characterization of this benchmark as a prepayment model is wrong. It is simply a market convention regarding the expected pattern of prepayments.

The PSA benchmark is commonly used for agency passthrough securities — that is, passthroughs issued by the Government National Mortgage Association (Ginnie Mae), the Federal Home Loan Mortgage Corporation ("Freddie Mac"), and the Federal National Mortgage Association ("Fannie Mae"). Exhibit 5 presents historical (i.e., actual) prepayment statistics for Fannie Mae 30-year (conventional) collateral as of November 6, 2000 using Bloomberg's PFN function. The one-month historical prepayment rate is displayed in terms of both CPR and PSA for each coupon rate.

Prospectus Prepayment Curve Issuers of nonagency mortgage-backed securities have developed prepayment models for their loans. In the prospectus of an offering a base case prepayment assumption is made — the initial speed and the amount of time until the collateral is expected to be seasoned. Thus, the prepayment benchmark is issuer specific. The benchmark speed in the prospectus is called the *prospectus prepayment curve* or PPC. As with the PSA benchmark described earlier, slower or faster prepayments speeds are a multiple of the PPC. For example, the PPC for a particular nonagency deal might state the following:

> ... a 100% Prepayment Assumption assumes conditional prepayment rates of 1.5% per annum of the then outstanding principal balance of the mortgage loans in the first month of the life of the loans and an additional 0.5% per annum in each month thereafter until month 20. Beginning in month 20, 100% Prepayment Assumption assumes a conditional prepayment rate of 11% per annum each month.

Exhibit 5: Prepayment Statistics for Fannie Mae Collateral

Page   DG15 Mtge   **PFN**

Bloomberg   FANNIE MAE Historical Prepayments   Page 2 of 5
MBS

Fannie Mae Conventional - 30 Year

AS OF 11/06/00	One Month Historical Prepayments (Aggregate)							
	------- Nov 00 Factors -------				------- Previous Month -------			
COUPON	CPR	PSA	OUTST $MM	POOLS	CPR	PSA	OUTST $MM	POOLS
5.00	4.3	82	45.00	45	9.9	195	45.24	45
5.50	4.5	91	3854.48	861	5.2	109	3873.48	860
6.00	6.1	123	90067.09	11105	6.0	125	90619.14	11100
6.50	7.6	146	206756.90	29374	7.4	144	207916.99	29266
7.00	8.5	172	162840.42	37365	8.3	168	159340.88	36963
7.50	8.2	225	123586.90	35574	7.7	207	116228.77	34882
8.00	11.4	333	59099.92	29615	10.0	292	57301.73	29303
8.50	18.7	458	16396.10	18697	18.5	452	16176.33	18639
9.00	22.2	460	6717.96	15737	19.6	403	6679.64	15783
9.50	18.9	323	2972.55	12027	16.0	272	3003.91	12110
10.00	19.4	327	1417.22	6514	16.5	277	1435.57	6572
10.50	21.2	356	397.38	1832	18.6	311	405.43	1849
11.00	16.1	270	133.87	1080	15.5	259	136.29	1089

Copyright 2000 BLOOMBERG L.P.   Frankfurt:69-920410 Hong Kong:2-977-6000 London:207-330-7500 New York:212-318-2000
Princeton:609-279-3000   Singapore:65-212-1000   Sydney:2-9777-8686   Tokyo:3-3201-8900   Sao Paulo:11-3048-4500
                                                                        1464-169-0 28-Nov-00 17:59:50

Bloomberg
PROFESSIONAL

Source: Bloomberg

For this deal, 100% PPC, 80% PPC, and 150% PPC would then be:

Month	100% PCC (%)	80% PCC (%)	150% PPC (%)
1	1.5	1.2	2.3
2	2.0	1.6	3.0
3	2.5	2.0	3.8
4	3.0	2.4	4.5
5	3.5	2.8	5.3
6	4.0	3.2	6.0
7	4.5	3.6	6.8
8	5.0	4.0	7.5
9	5.5	4.4	8.3
10	6.0	4.8	9.0
11	6.5	5.2	9.8
12	7.0	5.6	10.5
13	7.5	6.0	11.3
14	8.0	6.4	12.0
15	8.5	6.8	12.8
16	9.0	7.2	13.5
17	9.5	7.6	14.3
18	10.0	8.0	15.0
19	10.5	8.4	15.8
20	11.0	8.8	16.5

Unlike the PSA prepayment benchmark, the PPC is not generic. By this it is meant that the PPC is issuer specific. In contrast, the PSA prepayment benchmark has been applied to any type of collateral issued by an agency for any type of loan design. This feature of the PPC is important for an investor to keep in mind when comparing the prepayment characteristics and investment characteristics of the collateral between issuers and issues (new and seasoned).

Monthly Cash Flow Construction for a Passthrough Security Based on a PSA Assumption

We now show how to construct a monthly cash flow for a hypothetical passthrough given a PSA assumption. For the purpose of this illustration, the underlying mortgages for this hypothetical passthrough are assumed to be fixed-rate, level-payment, fully amortized mortgages with a weighted average coupon (WAC) rate of 8.125%. It will be assumed that the passthrough rate is 7.5% with a weighted average maturity (WAM) of 357 months.

Exhibit 6 shows the cash flow for selected months assuming 100 PSA. The cash flow is broken down into three components: (1) interest (based on the passthrough rate), (2) the regularly scheduled principal repayment (i.e., scheduled amortization), and (3) prepayments based on 100 PSA.

Let's walk through Exhibit 6 column by column.

Column 1: This is the number of months until the cash flow is to be received.

Exhibit 6: Monthly Cash Flow for a $400 Million Passthrough with a 7.5% Passthrough Rate, a WAC of 8.125%, and a WAM of 357 Months Assuming 100 PSA

(1) Months from Now	(2) Months Seasoned*	(3) Outstanding Balance	(4) SMM	(5) Mortgage Payment	(6) Net Interest	(7) Scheduled Principal	(8) Prepayment	(9) Total Principal	(10) Cash Flow
1	4	$400,000,000	0.00067	$2,975,868	$2,500,000	$267,535	$267,470	$535,005	$3,035,005
2	5	399,464,995	0.00084	2,973,877	2,496,656	269,166	334,198	603,364	3,100,020
3	6	398,861,631	0.00101	2,971,387	2,492,885	270,762	400,800	671,562	3,164,447
4	7	398,190,069	0.00117	2,968,399	2,488,688	272,321	467,243	739,564	3,228,252
5	8	397,450,505	0.00134	2,964,914	2,484,066	273,843	533,493	807,335	3,291,401
6	9	396,643,170	0.00151	2,960,931	2,479,020	275,327	599,514	874,841	3,353,860
7	10	395,768,329	0.00168	2,956,453	2,473,552	276,772	665,273	942,045	3,415,597
8	11	394,826,284	0.00185	2,951,480	2,467,664	278,177	730,736	1,008,913	3,476,577
9	12	393,817,371	0.00202	2,946,013	2,461,359	279,542	795,869	1,075,410	3,536,769
10	13	392,741,961	0.00219	2,940,056	2,454,637	280,865	860,637	1,141,502	3,596,140
11	14	391,600,459	0.00236	2,933,608	2,447,503	282,147	925,008	1,207,155	3,654,658
27	30	364,808,016	0.00514	2,766,461	2,280,050	296,406	1,874,688	2,171,094	4,451,144
28	31	362,636,921	0.00514	2,752,233	2,266,481	296,879	1,863,519	2,160,398	4,426,879
29	32	360,476,523	0.00514	2,738,078	2,252,978	297,351	1,852,406	2,149,758	4,402,736
30	33	358,326,766	0.00514	2,723,996	2,239,542	297,825	1,841,347	2,139,173	4,378,715
100	103	231,249,776	0.00514	1,898,682	1,445,311	332,928	1,187,608	1,520,537	2,965,848
101	104	229,729,239	0.00514	1,888,917	1,435,808	333,459	1,179,785	1,513,244	2,949,052
102	105	228,215,995	0.00514	1,879,202	1,426,350	333,990	1,172,000	1,505,990	2,932,340
103	106	226,710,004	0.00514	1,869,538	1,416,938	334,522	1,164,252	1,498,774	2,915,712
104	107	225,211,230	0.00514	1,859,923	1,407,570	335,055	1,156,541	1,491,596	2,899,166
105	108	223,719,634	0.00514	1,850,357	1,398,248	335,589	1,148,867	1,484,456	2,882,703
200	203	109,791,339	0.00514	1,133,751	686,196	390,372	562,651	953,023	1,639,219
201	204	108,838,316	0.00514	1,127,920	680,239	390,994	557,746	948,740	1,628,980
202	205	107,889,576	0.00514	1,122,119	674,310	391,617	552,863	944,480	1,618,790
203	206	106,945,096	0.00514	1,116,348	668,407	392,241	548,003	940,243	1,608,650
300	303	32,383,611	0.00514	676,991	202,398	457,727	164,195	621,923	824,320
301	304	31,761,689	0.00514	673,510	198,511	458,457	160,993	619,449	817,960
302	305	31,142,239	0.00514	670,046	194,639	459,187	157,803	616,990	811,629
303	306	30,525,249	0.00514	666,600	190,783	459,918	154,626	614,545	805,328
352	355	3,034,311	0.00514	517,770	18,964	497,226	13,048	510,274	529,238
353	356	2,524,037	0.00514	515,107	15,775	498,018	10,420	508,437	524,213
354	357	2,015,600	0.00514	512,458	12,597	498,811	7,801	506,612	519,209
355	358	1,508,988	0.00514	509,823	9,431	499,606	5,191	504,797	514,228
356	359	1,004,191	0.00514	507,201	6,276	500,401	2,591	502,992	509,269
357	360	501,199	0.00514	504,592	3,132	501,199	0	501,199	504,331

* Since the WAM is 357 months, the underlying mortgage pool is seasoned an average of three months, and therefore based on 100 PSA, the CPR is 0.8% in month 1 and the pool seasons at 6% in month 27.

Column 2: This is the number of months of seasoning. Since the WAM for this mortgage pool is 357 months, this means that the loans are seasoned an average of 3 months (360 months − 357 months).

Column 3: This column gives the outstanding mortgage balance at the beginning of the month. It is equal to the outstanding balance at the beginning of the previous month reduced by the total principal payment in the previous month.

Column 4: This column shows the SMM based on the number of months the loans are seasoned — the number of months shown in Column (2). For example, for the first month shown in the exhibit, the loans are seasoned three months going into that month. Therefore, the CPR used is the CPR that corresponds to four months. From the PSA benchmark, the CPR is 0.8% (4 times 0.2%). The corresponding SMM is 0.00067. The mortgage pool becomes fully seasoned in Column (1) corresponding to month 27 because by that time the loans are seasoned 30 months. When the loans are fully seasoned the CPR at 100 PSA is 6% and the corresponding SMM is 0.00514.

Column 5: The total monthly mortgage payment is shown in this column. Notice that the total monthly mortgage payment declines over time as prepayments reduce the mortgage balance outstanding. There is a formula to determine what the monthly mortgage balance will be for each month given prepayments that will be presented later.

Column 6: The *net* monthly interest (i.e., amount available to pay bondholders after the servicing fee) is found in this column. This value is determined by multiplying the outstanding mortgage balance at the beginning of the month by the passthrough rate of 7.5% and then dividing by 12.

Column 7: This column gives the scheduled principal repayment (i.e., scheduled amortization). This is the difference between the total monthly mortgage payment [the amount shown in Column (5)] and the gross coupon interest for the month. The gross coupon interest is found by multiplying 8.125% by the outstanding mortgage balance at the beginning of the month and then dividing by 12.

Column 8: The prepayment for the month is reported in this column. The prepayment is found by using equation (2). For example, in month 100, the beginning mortgage balance is $231,249,776, the scheduled principal payment is $332,928, and the SMM at 100 PSA is 0.00514301 (only 0.00514 is shown in the exhibit to save space), so the prepayment is:

$$0.00514301 \times (\$231{,}249{,}776 - \$332{,}928) = \$1{,}187{,}608$$

Column 9: The total principal payment, which is the sum of columns (7) and (8), is shown in this column.

Column 10: The projected monthly cash flow for this passthrough is shown in this last column. The monthly cash flow is the sum of the interest paid [Column (6)] and the total principal payments for the month [Column (9)].

Let's look at what happens to the cash flow for this passthrough if a different PSA assumption is made. Suppose that instead of 100 PSA, 165 PSA is assumed. That is, prepayments are assumed to be faster. Exhibit 7 shows the cash flow for this passthrough based on 165 PSA. Notice that the cash flows are greater in the early years compared to Exhibit 6 because prepayments are higher. The cash flows in later years are smaller for 165 PSA compared to 100 PSA because of the higher prepayments in the earlier years.

Exhibit 7: Monthly Cash Flow for a $400 Million Passthrough with a 7.5% Passthrough Rate, a WAC of 8.125%, and a WAM of 357 Months Assuming 165 PSA

(1)	(2)	(3)	(4)	(5)	(6)	(7)	(8)	(9)	(10)
Month	Months Seasoned*	Outstanding Balance	SMM	Mortgage Payment	Net Interest	Scheduled Principal	Prepayment	Total Principal	Cash Flow
1	4	$400,000,000	0.00111	$2,975,868	$2,500,000	$267,535	$442,389	$709,923	$3,209,923
2	5	399,290,077	0.00139	2,972,575	2,495,563	269,048	552,847	821,896	3,317,459
3	6	398,468,181	0.00167	2,968,456	2,490,426	270,495	663,065	933,560	3,423,986
4	7	397,534,621	0.00195	2,963,513	2,484,591	271,873	772,949	1,044,822	3,529,413
5	8	396,489,799	0.00223	2,957,747	2,478,061	273,181	882,405	1,155,586	3,633,647
6	9	395,334,213	0.00251	2,951,160	2,470,839	274,418	991,341	1,265,759	3,736,598
7	10	394,068,454	0.00279	2,943,755	2,462,928	275,583	1,099,664	1,375,246	3,838,174
8	11	392,693,208	0.00308	2,935,534	2,454,333	276,674	1,207,280	1,483,954	3,938,287
9	12	391,209,254	0.00336	2,926,503	2,445,058	277,690	1,314,099	1,591,789	4,036,847
10	13	389,617,464	0.00365	2,916,666	2,435,109	278,631	1,420,029	1,698,659	4,133,769
11	14	387,918,805	0.00393	2,906,028	2,424,493	279,494	1,524,979	1,804,473	4,228,965
27	30	347,334,116	0.00865	2,633,950	2,170,838	282,209	3,001,955	3,284,164	5,455,002
28	31	344,049,952	0.00865	2,611,167	2,150,312	281,662	2,973,553	3,255,215	5,405,527
29	32	340,794,737	0.00865	2,588,581	2,129,967	281,116	2,945,400	3,226,516	5,356,483
30	33	337,568,221	0.00865	2,566,190	2,109,801	280,572	2,917,496	3,198,067	5,307,869
100	103	170,142,350	0.00865	1,396,958	1,063,390	244,953	1,469,591	1,714,544	2,777,933
101	104	168,427,806	0.00865	1,384,875	1,052,674	244,478	1,454,765	1,699,243	2,751,916
102	105	166,728,563	0.00865	1,372,896	1,042,054	244,004	1,440,071	1,684,075	2,726,128
103	106	165,044,489	0.00865	1,361,020	1,031,528	243,531	1,425,508	1,669,039	2,700,567
104	107	163,375,450	0.00865	1,349,248	1,021,097	243,060	1,411,075	1,654,134	2,675,231
105	108	161,721,315	0.00865	1,337,577	1,010,758	242,589	1,396,771	1,639,359	2,650,118
200	203	56,746,664	0.00865	585,990	354,667	201,767	489,106	690,874	1,045,540
201	204	56,055,790	0.00865	580,921	350,349	201,377	483,134	684,510	1,034,859
202	205	55,371,280	0.00865	575,896	346,070	200,986	477,216	678,202	1,024,273
203	206	54,693,077	0.00865	570,915	341,832	200,597	471,353	671,950	1,013,782
300	303	11,758,141	0.00865	245,808	73,488	166,196	100,269	266,465	339,953
301	304	11,491,677	0.00865	243,682	71,823	165,874	97,967	263,841	335,664
302	305	11,227,836	0.00865	241,574	70,174	165,552	95,687	261,240	331,414
303	306	10,966,596	0.00865	239,485	68,541	165,232	93,430	258,662	327,203
352	355	916,910	0.00865	156,460	5,731	150,252	6,631	156,883	162,614
353	356	760,027	0.00865	155,107	4,750	149,961	5,277	155,238	159,988
354	357	604,789	0.00865	153,765	3,780	149,670	3,937	153,607	157,387
355	358	451,182	0.00865	152,435	2,820	149,380	2,611	151,991	154,811
356	359	299,191	0.00865	151,117	1,870	149,091	1,298	150,389	152,259
357	360	148,802	0.00865	149,809	930	148,802	0	148,802	149,732

* Since the WAM is 357 months, the underlying mortgage pool is seasoned an average of three months, and therefore based on 165 PSA, the CPR is 0.8% × 1.65 in month 1 and the pool seasons at 6% × 1.65 in month 27.

Formulas for Computing the Projected Monthly Cash Flow

The following formulas can be used to calculate the projected monthly cash flow for a given month based on some assumed prepayment rate or rates. First, the projected monthly principal payments for month t

$$PMP_t = PMB_{t-1} \left[\frac{i(1+i)^{n-t+1}}{[(1+i)^{n-t+1} - 1]} \right] \tag{5}$$

where

PMP_t = projected monthly principal payments for month t

PMB_{t-1} = projected mortgage balance at the end of month $t-1$ given prepayments have occurred in the past (which is the projected mortgage balance at the beginning of month t).

All of the other notation is the same as in the formulas presented earlier in this chapter.

Next, to compute the portion of the projected monthly mortgage payment that is interest, the following formula should be used

$$PI_t = i[PMB_{t-1}] \tag{6}$$

where

PI_t = projected monthly interest for month t

Equation (6) states that the projected monthly interest is found by multiplying the projected mortgage balance at the end of the previous month by the monthly mortgage interest rate.

The projected monthly interest rate can be divided into two parts: (1) the projected net monthly interest rate after the servicing fee and (2) the servicing fee. The formula for each is given below:

$$PNI_t = (i - sf)[PMB_{t-1}] \tag{7}$$

where

PNI_t = projected interest net of servicing fee for month t

sf = servicing fee rate

$$PSF_t = sf[PMB_{t-1}] \tag{8}$$

where

PSF_t = projected servicing fee for month t

The projected monthly scheduled principal repayment is found by subtracting from the projected monthly mortgage repayment the projected monthly interest. That is,

$$PSP_t = PMP_t - PI_t \qquad (9)$$

where

PSP_t = projected monthly scheduled principal repayment for month t

As explained earlier, the projected monthly principal prepayment is found by multiplying the SMM by the difference between the outstanding balance at the beginning of the month (the ending balance in the previous month) and the projected scheduled principal repayment for the month. That is,

$$PPR_t = SMM_t [PMB_{t-1} - PSP_t] \qquad (10)$$

where

PPR_t = projected monthly principal prepayment for month t
SMM_t = assumed single monthly mortality rate for month t

The cash flow to the investor is then the sum of (1) the projected monthly interest net of the servicing fee, (2) the projected monthly scheduled principal repayment, and (3) the projected principal prepayment for the month. That is,

$$CF_t = PNI_t + PSP_t + PPR_t$$

Average Life

The stated maturity of a mortgage passthrough security is not a useful measure. Instead, market participants calculate the *average life* (or *weighted average life*) of a mortgage-backed security. This is the average time to receipt of principal payments (scheduled principal repayments and projected prepayments). Mathematically, the average life is expressed as follows:

$$\text{Average life} = \sum_{t=1}^{T} \frac{t \times \text{Projected principal received at time } t}{12 \times \text{Total principal}}$$

where T is the number of months.

The average life of a passthrough depends on the prepayment assumption. To see this, the average life is shown below for different prepayment speeds for the passthrough we used to illustrate the cash flow for 100 PSA and 165 PSA in Exhibits 6 and 7:

PSA speed	50	100	165	200	300	400	500	600	700
Average life (years)	15.11	11.66	8.76	7.68	5.63	4.44	3.68	3.16	2.78

Collateralized Mortgage Obligations

As we noted, there is prepayment risk associated with investing in a mortgage passthrough security. However, by redistributing the cash flow from the underlying collateral of mortgage-related products (passthrough securities or a pool of loans) to different bond classes, securities that have different exposure to prepayment risk and therefore different risk/return patterns than the mortgage-related product from which they were created can be structured. The bond classes or securities that are created are called *tranches*. Similarly, when the underlying collateral exposes the investor to credit risk, the credit risk can be redistributed among tranches with different levels of priority.

When the cash flows of mortgage-related products are redistributed to different bond classes, the resulting securities are called *collateralized mortgage obligations* (CMOs). The creation of a CMO cannot eliminate prepayment or credit risk; it can only distribute the various forms of these risk among different classes of bondholders (i.e., investors in the tranches). A CMO is also referred to as a *paythrough security*.

CMOs are issued by the same agencies that issue passthrough securities. These CMOs are referred to as *agency CMOs*. Because there is no perceived credit risk, the creation of an agency CMO involves redistributing the prepayment risk. For nonagency CMOs, it is necessary to redistribute both prepayment risk and credit risk.

Creating Agency CMOs

There is a wide range of agency CMO tranches. Our purpose here is not to describe the various types of tranches. Rather, the primary focus is to demonstrate how they are created by redistributing the cash flow from the collateral. This is referred to as *structuring the deal*. A discussion of the motivation for the creation of the different types of CMO tranches is beyond the scope of this chapter.[2]

Sequential-Pay Tranches

The first CMO was structured so that each class of bonds would be retired sequentially. Such structures are referred to as sequential-pay CMOs.

To illustrate a sequential-pay CMO, we discuss Deal 1, a hypothetical deal made up to illustrate how a deal can be structured. The collateral for this hypothetical CMO is a hypothetical passthrough with a total par value of $400 million and the following characteristics: (1) the passthrough coupon rate is 7.5%, (2) the weighted average coupon (WAC) is 8.125%, and (3) the weighted average maturity (WAM) is 357 months. This is the same passthrough that we used to describe the cash flow of a passthrough based on some PSA assumption (Exhibits 6 and 7).

---

[2] For an explanation of the motivation, see Frank J. Fabozzi and Chuck Ramsey, *Collateralized Mortgage Obligations: Third Edition* (New Hope, PA: Frank J. Fabozzi Associates, 1999).

Exhibit 8: Deal 1 - A Hypothetical 4-Tranche Sequential-Pay Structure

Tranche	Par Amount ($)	Coupon Rate (%)
A	194,500,000	7.5
B	36,000,000	7.5
C	96,500,000	7.5
D	73,000,000	7.5
Total	400,000,000	

Payment rules:

1. *For payment of monthly coupon interest:* Disburse monthly coupon interest to each tranche on the basis of the amount of principal outstanding for each tranche at the beginning of the month.

2. *For disbursement of principal payments:* Disburse principal payments to tranche A until it is completely paid off. After tranche A is completely paid off, disburse principal payments to tranche B until it is completely paid off. After tranche B is completely paid off, disburse principal payments to tranche C until it is completely paid off. After tranche C is completely paid off, disburse principal payments to tranche D until it is completely paid off.

From this $400 million of collateral, four bond classes or tranches are created. Their characteristics are summarized in Exhibit 8. The total par value of the four tranches is equal to the par value of the collateral (i.e., the passthrough security). In this simple structure, the coupon rate is the same for each tranche and also the same as the coupon rate on the collateral. There is no reason why this must be so, and, in fact, typically the coupon rate varies by tranche.

A CMO is created by redistributing the cash flow — interest and principal — to the different tranches based on a set of payment rules. The payment rules at the bottom of Exhibit 8 describe how the cash flow from the passthrough (i.e., collateral) is to be distributed to the four tranches. There are separate rules for the distribution of the coupon interest and the payment of principal (the principal being the total of the regularly scheduled principal repayment and any prepayments).

While the payment rules for the disbursement of the principal payments are known, the precise amount of the principal in each month is not. This will depend on the cash flow, and therefore principal payments, of the collateral, which depends on the actual prepayment rate of the collateral. An assumed PSA speed allows the cash flow to be projected. Exhibit 9 shows the cash flow (interest, regularly scheduled principal repayment, and prepayments) assuming 165 PSA. Assuming that the collateral does prepay at 165 PSA, the cash flow available to all four tranches of Deal 1 will be precisely the cash flow shown in Exhibit 9.

To demonstrate how the payment rules for Deal 1 work, Exhibit 9 shows the cash flow for selected months assuming the collateral prepays at 165 PSA. For each tranche, the exhibit shows: (1) the balance at the end of the month, (2) the principal paid down (regularly scheduled principal repayment plus prepayments), and (3) interest. In month 1, the cash flow for the collateral consists of a principal payment of $709,923 and an interest payment of $2.5 million (0.075 times $400 million divided by 12). The interest payment is distributed to the four tranches based on the amount of the par value outstanding. So, for example, tranche A receives $1,215,625 (0.075 times $194,500,000 divided by 12) of the $2.5 million. The principal, however, is all distributed to tranche A. Therefore, the cash flow for tranche A in month 1 is $1,925,548. The principal balance at the end of month 1 for tranche A is $193,790,076 (the original principal balance of $194,500,000 less the principal payment of $709,923). No principal payment is distributed to the three other tranches because there is still a principal balance outstanding for tranche A. This will be true for months 2 through 80. The cash flow for tranche A for each month is found by adding the amounts shown in the "Principal" and "Interest" columns. So, for tranche A, the cash flow in month 8 is $1,483,954 plus $1,169,958, or $2,653,912. The cash flow from months 82 on is zero based on 165 PSA.

Exhibit 9: Monthly Cash Flow for Selected Months for Deal 1 Assuming 165 PSA

Month	Tranche A			Tranche B		
	Balance ($)	Principal ($)	Interest ($)	Balance ($)	Principal ($)	Interest ($)
1	194,500,000	709,923	1,215,625	36,000,000	0	225,000
2	193,790,077	821,896	1,211,188	36,000,000	0	225,000
3	192,968,181	933,560	1,206,051	36,000,000	0	225,000
4	192,034,621	1,044,822	1,200,216	36,000,000	0	225,000
5	190,989,799	1,155,586	1,193,686	36,000,000	0	225,000
6	189,834,213	1,265,759	1,186,464	36,000,000	0	225,000
7	188,568,454	1,375,246	1,178,553	36,000,000	0	225,000
8	187,193,208	1,483,954	1,169,958	36,000,000	0	225,000
9	185,709,254	1,591,789	1,160,683	36,000,000	0	225,000
10	184,117,464	1,698,659	1,150,734	36,000,000	0	225,000
11	182,418,805	1,804,473	1,140,118	36,000,000	0	225,000
12	180,614,332	1,909,139	1,128,840	36,000,000	0	225,000
75	12,893,479	2,143,974	80,584	36,000,000	0	225,000
76	10,749,504	2,124,935	67,184	36,000,000	0	225,000
77	8,624,569	2,106,062	53,904	36,000,000	0	225,000
78	6,518,507	2,087,353	40,741	36,000,000	0	225,000
79	4,431,154	2,068,807	27,695	36,000,000	0	225,000
80	2,362,347	2,050,422	14,765	36,000,000	0	225,000
81	311,926	311,926	1,950	36,000,000	1,720,271	225,000
82	0	0	0	34,279,729	2,014,130	214,248
83	0	0	0	32,265,599	1,996,221	201,660
84	0	0	0	30,269,378	1,978,468	189,184
85	0	0	0	28,290,911	1,960,869	176,818
95	0	0	0	9,449,331	1,793,089	59,058
96	0	0	0	7,656,242	1,777,104	47,852
97	0	0	0	5,879,138	1,761,258	36,745
98	0	0	0	4,117,879	1,745,550	25,737
99	0	0	0	2,372,329	1,729,979	14,827
100	0	0	0	642,350	642,350	4,015
101	0	0	0	0	0	0

Exhibit 9 (Continued)

Month	Tranche C Balance ($)	Principal ($)	Interest ($)	Tranche D Balance ($)	Principal ($)	Interest ($)
1	96,500,000	0	603,125	73,000,000	0	456,250
2	96,500,000	0	603,125	73,000,000	0	456,250
3	96,500,000	0	603,125	73,000,000	0	456,250
4	96,500,000	0	603,125	73,000,000	0	456,250
5	96,500,000	0	603,125	73,000,000	0	456,250
6	96,500,000	0	603,125	73,000,000	0	456,250
7	96,500,000	0	603,125	73,000,000	0	456,250
8	96,500,000	0	603,125	73,000,000	0	456,250
9	96,500,000	0	603,125	73,000,000	0	456,250
10	96,500,000	0	603,125	73,000,000	0	456,250
11	96,500,000	0	603,125	73,000,000	0	456,250
12	96,500,000	0	603,125	73,000,000	0	456,250
95	96,500,000	0	603,125	73,000,000	0	456,250
96	96,500,000	0	603,125	73,000,000	0	456,250
97	96,500,000	0	603,125	73,000,000	0	456,250
98	96,500,000	0	603,125	73,000,000	0	456,250
99	96,500,000	0	603,125	73,000,000	0	456,250
100	96,500,000	1,072,194	603,125	73,000,000	0	456,250
101	95,427,806	1,699,243	596,424	73,000,000	0	456,250
102	93,728,563	1,684,075	585,804	73,000,000	0	456,250
103	92,044,489	1,669,039	575,278	73,000,000	0	456,250
104	90,375,450	1,654,134	564,847	73,000,000	0	456,250
105	88,721,315	1,639,359	554,508	73,000,000	0	456,250
175	3,260,287	869,602	20,377	73,000,000	0	456,250
176	2,390,685	861,673	14,942	73,000,000	0	456,250
177	1,529,013	853,813	9,556	73,000,000	0	456,250
178	675,199	675,199	4,220	73,000,000	170,824	456,250
179	0	0	0	72,829,176	838,300	455,182
180	0	0	0	71,990,876	830,646	449,943
181	0	0	0	71,160,230	823,058	444,751
182	0	0	0	70,337,173	815,536	439,607
183	0	0	0	69,521,637	808,081	434,510
184	0	0	0	68,713,556	800,690	429,460
185	0	0	0	67,912,866	793,365	424,455
350	0	0	0	1,235,674	160,220	7,723
351	0	0	0	1,075,454	158,544	6,722
352	0	0	0	916,910	156,883	5,731
353	0	0	0	760,027	155,238	4,750
354	0	0	0	604,789	153,607	3,780
355	0	0	0	451,182	151,991	2,820
356	0	0	0	299,191	150,389	1,870
357	0	0	0	148,802	148,802	930

Note: The cash flow for a tranche in each month is the sum of the principal and interest.

After month 81, the principal balance will be zero for tranche A. For the collateral, the cash flow in month 81 is $3,318,521, consisting of a principal payment of $2,032,197 and interest of $1,286,325. At the beginning of month 81 (end of month 80), the principal balance for tranche A is $311,926. Therefore, $311,926 of the $2,032,196 of the principal payment from the collateral will be disbursed to tranche A. After this payment is made, no additional principal payments are made to this tranche as the principal balance is zero. The remaining principal payment from the collateral, $1,720,271, is distributed to tranche B. Based on an assumed prepayment speed of 165 PSA, tranche B then begins receiving principal payments in month 81. The cash flow for tranche B for each month is found by adding the amounts shown in the "Principal" and "Interest" columns. For months 1 though 80, the cash flow is just the interest. There is no cash flow after month 100 for tranche B.

Exhibit 9 shows that tranche B is fully paid off by month 100, when tranche C begins to receive principal payments. Tranche C is not fully paid off until month 178, at which time tranche D begins receiving the remaining principal payments. The maturity (i.e., the time until the principal is fully paid off) for these four tranches assuming 165 PSA would be 81 months for tranche A, 100 months for tranche B, 178 months for tranche C, and 357 months for tranche D. The cash flow for each month for tranches C and D is found by adding the principal and the interest for the month.

The *principal pay down window* for a tranche is the time period between the beginning and the ending of the principal payments to that tranche. So, for example, for tranche A, the principal pay down window would be month 1 to month 81 assuming 165 PSA. For tranche B, it is from month 81 to month 100. The window is also specified in terms of the length of the time from the beginning of the principal pay down window to the end of the principal pay down window. For tranche A, the window would be stated as 81 months, for tranche B 20 months. In confirmation of trades involving CMOs, the principal pay down window is specified in terms of the initial month that principal is expected to be received to the final month that principal is expected to be received.

Accrual Bonds In Deal 1, the payment rules for interest provide for all tranches to be paid interest each month. In many sequential-pay CMO structures, at least one tranche does not receive current interest. Instead, the interest for that tranche would accrue and be added to the principal balance. Such a tranche is commonly referred to as an *accrual tranche* or a *Z bond*. The interest that would have been paid to the accrual tranche is then used to pay off the principal balance of earlier tranches.

To see this, consider Deal 2, a hypothetical CMO structure with the same collateral as Deal 1 and with four tranches, each with a coupon rate of 7.5%. The difference is in the last tranche, Z, which is an accrual tranche. The structure for Deal 2 is shown in Exhibit 10. Exhibit 11 shows the cash flow for selected months for tranches A and B. Let's look at month 1 and compare it to month 1 in Exhibit 9. Both cash flows are based on 165 PSA. The principal payment from the collateral is $709,923. In Deal 1, this is the principal paydown for tranche A. In Deal 2, the interest for tranche Z, $456,250, is not paid to that tranche but instead is used to pay down the principal of tranche A. So, the principal payment to tranche A in Exhibit 11 is $1,166,173, the collateral's principal payment of $709,923 plus the interest of $456,250 that was diverted from tranche Z.

The expected final maturity for tranches A, B, and C has shortened as a result of the inclusion of tranche Z. The final payout for tranche A is 64 months rather than 81 months; for tranche B it is 77 months rather than 100 months; and, for tranche C it is 113 months rather than 178 months.

Floating-Rate Tranches A floating-rate tranche can be created from a fixed-rate tranche by creating a floater and an inverse floater combination. We will illustrate the creation of a floating-rate tranche and an inverse floating-rate tranche using the hypothetical CMO structure Deal 2 — the 4-tranche sequential-pay structure with an accrual tranche. We can select any of the tranches from which to create a floating-rate and inverse floating-rate tranche. In fact, we can create these two securities for more than one of the four tranches or for only a portion of one tranche.

In this case, we create a floater and an inverse floater from tranche C. The par value for this tranche is $96.5 million, and we create two tranches that have a combined par value of $96.5 million. We refer to this CMO structure with a floater and an inverse floater as Deal 3. It has five tranches, designated A, B, FL, IFL, and Z, where FL is the floating-rate tranche and IFL is the inverse floating-rate tranche. Exhibit 12 describes Deal 3. Any reference rate can be used to create a floater and the corresponding inverse floater. The reference rate for setting the coupon rate for FL and IFL in Deal 3 is 1-month LIBOR.

Exhibit 10: Deal 2 – A Hypothetical 4-Tranche Sequential-Pay Structure with an Accrual Bond Class

Tranche	Par Amount ($)	Coupon Rate (%)
A	194,500,000	7.5
B	36,000,000	7.5
C	96,500,000	7.5
Z (Accrual)	73,000,000	7.5
Total	400,000,000	

Payment rules:

1. *For payment of monthly coupon interest:* Disburse monthly coupon interest to tranches A, B. and C on the basis of the amount of principal outstanding for each tranche at the beginning of the month. For tranche Z, accrue the interest based on the principal plus accrued interest in the previous month. The interest for tranche Z is to be paid to the earlier tranches as a principal paydown.

2. *For disbursement of principal payments:* Disburse principal payments to tranche A until it is completely paid off. After tranche A is completely paid off, disburse principal payments to tranche B until it is completely paid off. After tranche B is completely paid off, disburse principal payments to tranche C until it is completely paid off. After tranche C is completely paid off, disburse principal payments to tranche Z until the original principal balance plus accrued interest is completely paid off.

Exhibit 11: Monthly Cash Flow for Selected Months for Tranches A and B for Deal 2 Assuming 165 PSA

	Tranche A			Tranche B		
Month	Balance ($)	Principal ($)	Interest ($)	Balance ($)	Principal ($)	Interest ($)
1	194,500,000	1,166,173	1,215,625	36,000,000	0	225,000
2	193,333,827	1,280,997	1,208,336	36,000,000	0	225,000
3	192,052,829	1,395,531	1,200,330	36,000,000	0	225,000
4	190,657,298	1,509,680	1,191,608	36,000,000	0	225,000
5	189,147,619	1,623,350	1,182,173	36,000,000	0	225,000
6	187,524,269	1,736,446	1,172,027	36,000,000	0	225,000
7	185,787,823	1,848,875	1,161,174	36,000,000	0	225,000
8	183,938,947	1,960,543	1,149,618	36,000,000	0	225,000
9	181,978,404	2,071,357	1,137,365	36,000,000	0	225,000
10	179,907,047	2,181,225	1,124,419	36,000,000	0	225,000
11	177,725,822	2,290,054	1,110,786	36,000,000	0	225,000
12	175,435,768	2,397,755	1,096,474	36,000,000	0	225,000
60	15,023,406	3,109,398	93,896	36,000,000	0	225,000
61	11,914,007	3,091,812	74,463	36,000,000	0	225,000
62	8,822,195	3,074,441	55,139	36,000,000	0	225,000
63	5,747,754	3,057,282	35,923	36,000,000	0	225,000
64	2,690,472	2,690,472	16,815	36,000,000	349,863	225,000
65	0	0	0	35,650,137	3,023,598	222,813
66	0	0	0	32,626,540	3,007,069	203,916
67	0	0	0	29,619,470	2,990,748	185,122
68	0	0	0	26,628,722	2,974,633	166,430
69	0	0	0	23,654,089	2,958,722	147,838
70	0	0	0	20,695,367	2,943,014	129,346
71	0	0	0	17,752,353	2,927,508	110,952
72	0	0	0	14,824,845	2,912,203	92,655
73	0	0	0	11,912,642	2,897,096	74,454
74	0	0	0	9,015,546	2,882,187	56,347
75	0	0	0	6,133,358	2,867,475	38,333
76	0	0	0	3,265,883	2,852,958	20,412
77	0	0	0	412,925	412,925	2,581
78	0	0	0	0	0	0
79	0	0	0	0	0	0
80	0	0	0	0	0	0

The amount of the par value of the floating-rate tranche will be some portion of the $96.5 million. There are an infinite number of ways to slice up the $96.5 million between the floater and inverse floater, and final partitioning will be driven by the demands of investors. In Deal 3, we made the floater from $72,375,000 or 75% of the $96.5 million. The coupon formula for the floater is 1-month LIBOR plus 50 basis points. So, for example, if LIBOR is 3.75% at the reset date, the coupon rate on the floater is 3.75% + 0.5%, or 4.25%. There is a cap on the coupon rate for the floater (discussed later).

Exhibit 12: Deal 3 — A Hypothetical 5-Tranche Sequential-Pay Structure with Floater, Inverse Floater, and Accrual Bond Classes

Tranche	Par Amount ($)	Coupon Rate (%)
A	194,500,000	7.50
B	36,000,000	7.50
FL	72,375,000	1-month LIBOR + 0.50
IFL	24,125,000	28.50 − 3 × (1-month LIBOR)
Z (Accrual)	73,000,000	7.50
Total	400,000,000	

Payment rules:

1. *For payment of monthly coupon interest:* Disburse monthly coupon interest to tranches A, B, FL, and IFL on the basis of the amount of principal outstanding at the beginning of the month. For tranche Z, accrue the interest based on the principal plus accrued interest in the previous month. The interest for tranche Z is to be paid to the earlier tranches as a principal paydown. The maximum coupon rate for FL is 10%; the minimum coupon rate for IFL is 0%

2. *For disbursement of principal payments:* Disburse principal payments to tranche A until it is completely paid off. After tranche A is completely paid off, disburse principal payments to tranche B until it is completely paid off. After tranche B is completely paid off, disburse principal payments to tranches FL and IFL until they are completely paid off. The principal payments between tranches FL and IFL should be made in the following way: 75% to tranche FL and 25% to tranche IFL. After tranches FL and IFI are completely paid off, disburse principal payments to tranche Z until the original principal balance plus accrued interest are completely paid off.

Unlike a floating-rate note in the corporate bond market whose principal is unchanged over the life of the instrument, the floater's principal balance declines over time as principal payments are made. The principal payments to the floater are determined by the principal payments from the tranche from which the floater is created. In our CMO structure, this is tranche C.

Since the floater's par value is $72,375,000 of the $96.5 million, the balance is par value for the inverse floater. Assuming that 1-month LIBOR is the reference rate, the coupon formula for the inverse floater takes the following form:

$$K - L \times (\text{1-month LIBOR})$$

In FJF-03, K is set at 28.50% and L at 3. Thus, if 1-month LIBOR is 3.75%, the coupon rate for the month is:

$$28.50\% - 3 \times (3.75\%) = 17.25\%$$

K is the cap or maximum coupon rate for the inverse floater. In Deal 3, the cap for the inverse floater is 28.50%. The determination of the inverse floater's cap rate is based on (1) the amount of interest that would have been paid to the tranche from which the floater and the inverse floater were created, tranche C in our hypothetical deal, and (2) the coupon rate for the floater if 1-month LIBOR is zero. Let's see how the 28.5% for the inverse floater is determined.

The total interest to be paid to tranche C, if it was not split into the floater and the inverse floater, is the principal of $96,500,000 times 7.5%, or $7,237,500. The maximum interest for the inverse floater occurs if 1-month LIBOR is zero. In that case, the coupon rate for the floater is

$$1\text{-month LIBOR} + 0.5\% = 0.5\%$$

Since the floater receives 0.5% on its principal of $72,375,000, the floater's interest is $361,875. The remainder of the interest of $7,237,500 from tranche C goes to the inverse floater. That is, the inverse floater's interest is $6,875,625 (= $7,237,500 − $361,875). Since the inverse floater's principal is $24,125,000, the cap rate for the inverse floater is

$$\frac{\$6,875,625}{\$24,125,000} = 28.5\%$$

In general, the formula for the cap rate on the inverse floater, K, is

$$K = \frac{\text{inverse floater interest when reference rate for floater is zero}}{\text{principal for inverse floater}}$$

The L or multiple in the coupon formula to determine the coupon rate for the inverse floater is called the leverage. The higher the leverage, the more the inverse floater's coupon rate changes for a given change in 1-month LIBOR. For example, a coupon leverage of 3 means that a 1-basis point change in 1-month LIBOR will change the coupon rate on the inverse floater by 3 basis points. As in the case of the floater, the principal paydown of an inverse floater will be a proportionate amount of the principal paydown of tranche C.

Because 1-month LIBOR is always positive, the coupon rate paid to the floater cannot be negative. If there are no restrictions placed on the coupon rate for the inverse floater, however, it is possible for its coupon rate to be negative. To prevent this, a floor, or minimum, is placed on the coupon rate. In most structures, the floor is set at zero. Once a floor is set for the inverse floater, a cap or ceiling is imposed on the floater.

In Deal 3, a floor of zero is set for the inverse floater. The floor results in a cap or maximum coupon rate for the floater of 10%. This is determined as follows. If the floor for the inverse floater is zero, this means that the inverse floater receives no interest. All of the interest that would have been paid to tranche C, $7,237,500, would then be paid to the floater. Since the floater's principal is $72,375,000, the cap rate on the floater is $7,237,500/$72,375,000, or 10%.

In general, the cap rate for the floater assuming a floor of zero for inverse floater is determined as follows:

$$\text{cap rate for floater} = \frac{\text{collateral tranche interest}}{\text{principal for floater}}$$

The cap for the floater and the inverse floater, the floor for the inverse floater, the leverage, and the floater's spread are not determined independently.

Any cap or floor imposed on the coupon rate for the floater and the inverse floater must be selected so that the weighted average coupon rate does not exceed the collateral tranche's coupon rate.

Planned Amortization Class Tranches In a planned amortization class tranche there is a principal repayment schedule that must be satisfied. PAC bond-holders have priority over all other classes in the CMO structure in receiving principal payments from the collateral. The greater certainty of the cash flow for the PAC bonds comes at the expense of the non-PAC tranches, called the support tranches or companion tranches. It is these tranches that absorb the prepayment risk.

To illustrate how to create a PAC bond, we will use as collateral the $400 million passthrough with a coupon rate of 7.5%, an 8.125% WAC, and a WAM of 357 months. The creation requires the specification of two PSA prepayment rates — a lower PSA prepayment assumption and an upper PSA prepayment assumption. In our illustration the lower PSA prepayment assumption will be 90 PSA and the upper PSA prepayment assumption will be 300 PSA. A natural question is: How does one select the lower and upper PSA prepayment assumptions? These are dictated by market conditions. For our purpose here, how it is determined is not important. The lower and upper PSA prepayment assumptions are referred to as the initial PAC collar or the initial PAC band. In our illustration the initial PAC collar is 90-300 PSA.

The second column of Exhibit 13 shows the principal payment (regularly scheduled principal repayment plus prepayments) for selected months assuming a prepayment speed of 90 PSA, and the next column shows the principal payments for selected months assuming that the passthrough prepays at 300 PSA.

The last column of Exhibit 13 gives the minimum principal payment if the collateral prepays at 90 PSA or 300 PSA for months 1 to 349. (After month 349, the outstanding principal balance will be paid off if the prepayment speed is between 90 PSA and 300 PSA.) For example, in the first month, the principal payment would be $508,169.52 if the collateral prepays at 90 PSA and $1,075,931.20 if the collateral prepays at 300 PSA. Thus, the minimum principal payment is $508,169.52, as reported in the last column of Exhibit 13. In month 103, the minimum principal payment is also the amount if the prepayment speed is 90 PSA, $1,446,761, compared to $1,458,618.04 for 300 PSA. In month 104, however, a prepayment speed of 300 PSA would produce a principal payment of $1,433,539.23, which is less than the principal payment of $1,440,825.55 assuming 90 PSA. So, $1,433,539.23 is reported in the last column of Exhibit 13. From month 104 on, the minimum principal payment is the one that would result assuming a prepayment speed of 300 PSA.

In fact, if the collateral prepays at any one speed between 90 PSA and 300 PSA over its life, the minimum principal payment would be the amount reported in the last column of Exhibit 13. For example, if we had included principal payment figures assuming a prepayment speed of 200 PSA, the minimum principal payment would not change: from month 1 through month 103, the minimum principal payment is that generated from 90 PSA, but from month 104 on, the minimum principal payment is that generated from 300 PSA.

Exhibit 13: Monthly Principal Payment for $400 Million, 7.5% Coupon Passthrough with an 8.125% WAC and a 357 WAM Assuming Prepayment Rates of 90 PSA and 300 PSA

Month	At 90% PSA ($)	At 300% PSA	Minimum Principal Payment Available to PAC Investors — the PAC Schedule ($)
1	508,169.52	1,075,931.20	508,169.52
2	569,843.43	1,279,412.11	569,843.43
3	631,377.11	1,482,194.45	631,377.11
4	692,741.89	1 683,966.17	692,741.89
5	753,909.12	1,884,414.62	753,909.12
6	814,850.22	2,083,227.31	814,850.22
7	875,536.68	2,280,092.68	875,536.68
8	935,940.10	2,474,700.92	935,940.10
9	996,032.19	2,666,744.77	996,032.19
10	1,055,784.82	2,855,920.32	1,055,784.82
11	1,115,170.01	3,041,927.81	1,115,170.01
12	1,174,160.00	3,224,472.44	1,174,160.00
13	1,232,727.22	3,403,265.17	1,232,727.22
14	1,290,844.32	3,578,023.49	1,290,844.32
15	1,348,484.24	3,748,472.23	1,348,484.24
16	1,405,620.17	3,914,344.26	1,405,620.17
17	1,462,225.60	4,075,381.29	1,462,225.60
18	1,518,274.36	4,231,334.57	1,518,274.36
101	1,458,719.34	1,510,072.17	1,458,719.34
102	1,452,725.55	1,484,126.59	1,452,725.55
103	1,446,761.00	1,458,618.04	1,446,761.00
104	1,440,825.55	1,433,539.23	1,433,539.23
105	1,434,919.07	1,408,883.01	1,408,883.01
211	949,482.58	213,309.00	213,309.00
212	946,033.34	209,409.09	209,409.09
213	942,601.99	205,577.05	205,577.05
346	618,684.59	13,269.17	13,269.17
347	617,071.58	12,944.51	12,944.51
348	615,468.65	12,626.21	12,626.21
349	613,875.77	12,314.16	3,432.32
350	612,292.88	12,008.25	0
351	610,719.96	11,708.38	0
352	609,156.96	11,414.42	0
353	607,603.S4	11,126.28	0
354	606,060.57	10,843.85	0
355	604,527.09	10,567.02	0
356	603,003.38	10,295.70	0
357	601,489.39	10,029.78	0

This characteristic of the collateral allows for the creation of a PAC tranche, assuming that the collateral prepays over its life at a speed between 90 PSA to 300 PSA. A schedule of principal repayments that the PAC bondholders are entitled to receive before any other tranche in the CMO structure is specified. The monthly schedule of principal repayments is specified in the last column of Exhibit 13, which shows the minimum principal payment. That is, it is this minimum principal payment in each month that is the principal repayment schedule (i.e., planned amortization schedule) for investors in the PAC tranche. While there is no assurance that the collateral will prepay at a constant speed between these two speeds over its life, a PAC tranche can be structured to assume that it will.

Most CMO PAC structures have more than one PAC tranche that are typically retired in sequence just as with the basic sequential-pay structure described earlier.

Support Tranches The support tranches are the bonds that provide prepayment protection for the PAC tranches. Consequently, support tranches expose investors to the greatest level of prepayment risk. The support tranche typically is divided into different tranches. All the tranches we have discussed earlier are available, including sequential-pay support tranches, floater and inverse floater support tranches, and accrual support tranches.

The support tranche can even be partitioned to create support tranches with a schedule of principal payments. That is, support tranches that are PAC tranches can be created. In a structure with a PAC tranche and a support tranche with a PAC schedule of principal payments, the former is called a PAC I tranche or Level I PAC tranche and the latter a PAC II tranche or Level II PAC tranche or scheduled tranche (often denoted SCH in a prospectus). While PAC II tranches have greater prepayment protection than the support tranches without a schedule of principal repayments, the prepayment protection is less than that provided PAC I tranches.

The support tranche without a principal repayment schedule can be used to create any type of tranche. In fact, a portion of the non-PAC II support tranche can be given a schedule of principal repayments. This tranche would be called a *PAC III tranche* or a *Level III PAC tranche*. While it provides protection against prepayments for the PAC I and PAC II tranches and is therefore subject to considerable prepayment risk, such a tranche has greater protection than the support tranche without a schedule of principal repayments.

Creation of a Nonagency CMO Using the Senior-Subordinated Structure

Nonagency securities can be either passthroughs or CMOs. In the agency market, CMOs are created from pools of passthrough securities. In the nonagency market, a CMO can be created from either a pool of passthroughs or unsecuritized mortgage loans. It is uncommon for nonconforming mortgage loans to be securitized as passthroughs and then carve up a pool of passthroughs to create a CMO. Instead, in the nonagency market a CMO is typically carved out of mortgage loans that have *not* been securitized as passthroughs. Since a mortgage loan not securitized as a passthrough is called a "whole loan," nonagency CMOs are commonly referred to as *whole-loan CMOs*.

The major difference between agency and nonagency securities is due to guarantees. With a nonagency security there is no explicit or implicit government guarantee of payment of interest and principal as there is with an agency security. The absence of any such guarantee means that the investor in a nonagency security is exposed to credit risk. The nationally recognized statistical rating organizations rate nonagency securities.

Because of the credit risk, all nonagency securities are credit enhanced. Credit enhancement means that additional support against defaults must be obtained. The amount of credit enhancement needed is determined relative to a specific rating desired for a security from a rating agency. There are two general types of credit enhancement mechanisms: external and internal. *External credit enhancements* involve third party guarantees, such as a corporate guarantee, insurance, and letters of credit. *Internal credit enhancements* include excess servicing spread, reserve funds, overcollateralization, and senior-subordinated structures. The particular enhancements selected by the issuer to obtain the desired credit rating will depend on the relative cost of each enhancement.

Here our goal is simply to show how a non-agency CMO is created using the senior-subordinated structure. In this structure there is a senior tranche and at least one junior or subordinated tranche. For example, suppose a deal has $300 million of mortgage loans. The structure might look as follows:

senior tranche $270 million
subordinated tranche $30 million

This means that the first $30 million of losses are absorbed by the subordinated tranche.

There is no reason why there must be only one subordinated tranche. The structure can have more than one subordinated tranche. For example, the structure could be as follows:

senior tranche $270 million
subordinated tranche 1 $22 million
subordinated tranche 2 $8 million

In this structure, the subordinate tranches 1 and 2 are called the *non-senior tranches*. The senior tranche still has protection up to $30 million as in the previous structure with only one subordinated tranche. In the second structure, the first $8 million of losses is absorbed by the subordinated tranche 2. Hence, this tranche is referred to as the *first loss tranche*. Subordinated tranche 1 has protection of up to $8 million in losses, the protection provided by the first loss tranche.

The basic concern in the senior-subordinate structure is that while the subordinated tranches provide a certain level of credit protection for the senior tranche at the closing of the deal, the level of protection changes over time due to prepayments. The objective after the deal closes is to distribute any prepayments such that the credit protection for the senior tranche does not deteriorate over time.

There is a well developed mechanism used to address this concern called the *shifting interest mechanism*. Here is how it works. The percentage of the mortgage balance of the subordinate tranche to that of the mortgage balance for the entire deal is called the *level of subordination* or the *subordinate interest*. The higher the percentage, the greater the level of protection for the senior tranches. The subordinate interest changes after the deal is closed due to prepayments. That is, the subordinate interest shifts (hence the term "shifting interest"). The purpose of a shifting interest mechanism is to allocate prepayments so that the subordinate interest is maintained at an acceptable level to protect the senior tranche. In effect, by paying down the senior tranche more quickly, the amount of subordination is maintained at the desired level.

The prospectus will provide the shifting interest percentage schedule for calculating the senior prepayment percentage (the percentage of prepayments paid to the senior tranche). For mortgage loans, a commonly used shifting interest percentage schedule is as follows:

Year after issuance	Senior prepayment percentage
1-5	100
6	70
7	60
8	40
9	20
after year 9	0

So, for example, if prepayments in some month before the end of the fifth year is $2 million, the amount paid to the senior tranche is $2 million and no prepayments are made to the subordinated tranches. If prepayments in some month in the eighth year are $2 million, the senior tranche is paid $800,000 (40% × $2 million).

The shifting interest percentage schedule given in the prospectus is the "base" schedule. The set of shifting interest percentages can change over time depending on the performance of the collateral. If the performance is such that the credit protection for the senior tranche has deteriorated because credit losses have reduced the subordinate tranches, the base shifting interest percentages are overridden and a higher allocation of prepayments is made to the senior tranche.[3]

It is important to understand that the presence of a shifting interest mechanism results in a trade-off between credit risk and the risk that the senior tranche's average life will shorten. The shifting interest mechanism reduces the credit risk to the senior tranche. However, because the senior tranche receives a larger share of any prepayments, it increases the risk that the average life will shorten.

---

[3] Performance analysis of the collateral is undertaken by the trustee for determining whether or not to override the base schedule. The performance analysis is in terms of tests and if the collateral fails any of the tests, this will trigger an override of the base schedule.

In projecting the cash flow for a nonagency mortgage-backed security, it is necessary to project defaults and recoveries. We discuss the various measures used in the industry when we discuss the cash flow for amortizing asset-backed securities.

Stripped Mortgage-Backed Securities

A mortgage passthrough security divides the cash flow from the underlying pool of mortgages on a pro rata basis to the certificate holders. A stripped mortgage-backed security is created by altering that distribution of principal and interest from a pro rata distribution to an unequal distribution. The result is that the securities created will have a price/yield relationship that is different from the price/yield relationship of the underlying passthrough security.

In the most common type of stripped mortgage-backed securities all the interest is allocated to one class (called the *interest only* or IO class) and all the principal to the other class (called the principal only or PO class). The IO class receives no principal payments. These securities are also referred to as *mortgage strips*. The POs are called *principal-only mortgage strips* and the IOs are called *interest-only mortgage strips*.

The cash flow for an PO and IO are projected based on some prepayment assumption. For example, for the passthrough whose cash flow is shown in Exhibit 6 (based on an assumed 100 PSA), the cash flow for the PO is shown in Column (9) (the column labeled "Total principal") while the cash flow for the IO is shown in Column (6) (the column labeled "Net Interest"). The corresponding columns in Exhibit 7 show the cash flow for the PO and IO based on 165 PSA.

AMORTIZING ASSET-BACKED SECURITIES

The collateral for an asset-backed security can be classified as either amortizing or non-amortizing assets. *Amortizing assets* are loans in which the borrower's periodic payment consists of scheduled principal repayment and interest payments over the life of the loan. The schedule for the repayment of the principal is shown in the amortization table. The standard residential mortgage loan falls into this category (see, for example, Exhibit 1). Auto loans and certain types of home equity loans (specifically, closed-end home equity loans) are amortizing assets. Prepayments are any excess payment over the scheduled principal repayment. There are passthough and paythrough structures. The senior-subordinated structure is commonly used.

In contrast to amortizing assets, *non-amortizing assets* do not have a schedule for the periodic payments that the individual borrower must make. Instead, a non-amortizing asset is one in which the borrower must make a minimum periodic payment. If that payment is less than the interest on the outstanding loan balance, the shortfall is added to the outstanding loan balance. If the periodic payment is greater than the interest on the outstanding loan balance, then the difference is applied to the reduction of the outstanding loan balance. There is no schedule of principal repayments (i.e., no amortization schedule) for a non-amortizing asset. Consequently, the concept of a prepayment does not apply. Credit card receivables and certain types of home equity loans described later in this chapter are examples of non-amortizing assets.[4]

For an amortizing asset, projection of the cash flow requires projecting prepayments. One factor that may affect prepayments is the prevailing level of interest rates relative to the interest rate on the loan. In projecting prepayments it is critical to determine the extent to which borrowers take advantage of a decline in interest rates below the loan rate in order to refinance the loan. As we will see when we discuss valuation modeling for asset-backed securities in the next chapter, whether or not borrowers will take advantage of refinancing when rates decline will determine the valuation methodology.

As with nonagency mortgage-backed securities, modeling defaults for the collateral is critical in estimating the cash flows of an asset-backed security. Proceeds that are recovered in the event of a default of a loan prior to the scheduled principal repayment date of an amortizing asset represent a prepayment and are referred to as an involuntary prepayment. Projecting prepayments for amortizing assets requires an assumption of the default rate and the recovery rate. For a non-amortizing asset, while the concept of a prepayment does not exist, a projection of defaults is still necessary to project how much will be recovered and when.

The analysis of prepayments can be performed on a pool level or a loan level. In pool-level analysis it is assumed that all loans comprising the collateral are identical. For an amortizing asset, the amortization schedule is based on the gross weighted average coupon (GWAC) and weighted average maturity (WAM) for that single loan. Pool-level analysis is appropriate where the underlying loans are homogeneous. Loan-level analysis involves amortizing each loan (or group of homogeneous loans).

Prepayment Measures

The most common measure that is used in the market for measuring prepayments for amortizing asset-backed securities is the conditional prepayment rate and the corresponding single mortality rate. A PPC is provided in the prospectus of most offerings.

The major amortizing asset-backed security type that does not use the CPR/SMM convention is auto loan-backed securities. Prepayments for these securities are measured in terms of the *absolute prepayment speed* (ABS). The ABS is the monthly prepayment expressed as a percentage of the original collateral amount. As explained in the previous chapter, the SMM (monthly CPR) expresses prepayments based on the prior month's balance.

---

[4] There may be prepayments at the structure level due to the payoff of a deal as a result of a rapid amortization trigger.

There is a mathematical relationship between the SMM and the ABS measures. Letting M denote the number of months after loan origination, the SMM rate can be calculated from the ABS rate using the following formula:

$$SMM = \frac{ABS}{1 - [ABS \times (M - 1)]}$$

where the ABS and SMM rates are expressed in decimal form.

For example, if the ABS rate is 1.5% (i.e., 0.015) at month 14 after origination, then the SMM rate is 1.86%, as shown below:

$$SMM = \frac{0.015}{1 - [0.015 \times (14 - 1)]} = 0.0186 = 1.86\%$$

The ABS rate can be calculated from the SMM rate using the following formula:

$$ABS = \frac{SMM}{1 + [SMM \times (M - 1)]}$$

For example, if the SMM rate at month 9 after origination is 1.3%, then the ABS rate is:

$$ABS = \frac{0.013}{1 + [0.013 \times (9 - 1)]} = 0.0118 = 1.18\%$$

Historically, when measured in terms of SMM rate, auto loans have experienced SMMs that increase as the loans season.

Default and Loss Measures

In computing prepayments for a pool of loans, voluntary and involuntary prepayments are added. An involuntary prepayment is a result of a default by the borrower. When a borrower's loan is classified as delinquent, the servicer will use its collection methods to obtain the delinquent contractual payments from the borrower. If these collection efforts fail, then after a specified number of days in the delinquency status, the loan is declared to be in default. If the loan is secured by an asset, the defaulted loan does not result in an immediate loss. Instead, the servicer will seek to repossess or foreclose on the asset for the loan and sell it at fair market value. It is when the asset is sold that a determination of the loss can be made based on the proceeds received from the sale after taking into consideration the fees and costs associated with liquidation.

In fact, a loan classified as a defaulted loan can be reclassified as a performing loan if the borrower makes good on all contractual payments. Moreover, a loan classified as in default can result in no loss if the proceeds received are greater than or equal to the loan balance. Thus, it is important to understand that there is a difference between a default and a loss. Consequently, there is a default rate and loss rate associated with a pool of loans. Unfortunately, oftentimes this distinction between default rates and loss rates is not made and the terms are used interchangeably.

It should also be understood that when computing the prepayment rate due to defaults, the entire defaulted loan balance is used as the amount of the prepayment. When computing losses for a pool, only the loss based on the liquidation value after considering the associated costs is used.

For loan pools a *loss curve* is projected. The construction of this loss curve depends on three factors: (1) the default rate, (2) the estimated time between a loan being classified in default and the receipt of liquidation proceeds (i.e., the liquidation timeline), and (3) the extent of the loss relative to the unpaid principal balance. The extent of the loss is measured in terms of the *loss of severity* which is computed by dividing the liquidation proceeds after associated costs by the unpaid principal balance for the liquidated loan.

Conditional Default Rate

Despite the difference between defaults and losses, participants in the mortgage-backed and asset-backed securities market discuss involuntary prepayments in terms of a *conditional default rate* (CDR). The conditional default rate for a month is measured as follows:

$$\text{CDR} = 1 - \left(1 - \frac{\text{unpaid principal balance of defaulted loans for month}}{\text{loan balance in previous month} - \text{scheduled repayments}}\right)^{12}$$

Given the difference between defaults and losses, the CDR is effectively the rate at which defaulted loans are being removed from the loan pool. In practice, the CDR is assumed to ramp up and then plateau just as in the case of voluntary prepayments.

Default Rates

There are two commonly used measures of default rates for a pool of loans reported by issuers. For these measures, default is defined as an event (as determined by the servicer) when the borrower no longer makes contractual payments and remains in this status until the asset is liquidated. The first is the *monthly loss*. It is measured in terms of the *remaining* pool balance. Specifically, the monthly loss is computed as follows:

$$\text{monthly loss} = \frac{\text{unpaid principal balance of defaulted loans for month}}{\text{principal balance in the previous month}}$$

The above measure is then annualized.

The second measure is the *cumulative default rate* and it reflects the total defaults to date relative to the original principal balance. That is,

$$\text{cumulative default rate} = \frac{\text{unpaid principal balance of defaulted loans to date}}{\text{original principal balance}}$$

Chapter 8

Valuation of Mortgage-Backed and Asset-Backed Securities

I n this chapter we show how to value mortgage-backed and asset-backed securities. We begin by reviewing the conventional framework — static cash flow yield analysis — and its limitations. Then we discuss a more advanced technology, the Monte Carlo valuation model and a byproduct of the model, the option-adjusted spread analysis. The static cash flow yield methodology is the simplest of the two valuation technologies to apply, although it may offer little insight into the relative value of a mortgage-backed or asset-backed security. The option-adjusted spread technology while far superior in valuation is based on assumptions that must be recognized by an investor and the sensitivity of the security's value to changes in those assumptions must be tested.

STATIC CASH FLOW YIELD ANALYSIS

As explained in Chapter 1, the yield on any financial instrument is the interest rate that makes the present value of the expected cash flow equal to its market price plus accrued interest. For mortgage-backed and asset-backed securities, the yield calculated is called a *cash flow yield*. The problem in calculating the cash flow yield of a mortgage-backed and asset-backed security is that because of prepayments (voluntary and involuntary) the cash flow is unknown. Consequently, to determine a cash flow yield some assumption about the prepayment rate must be made.

The cash flow for a mortgage-backed and asset-backed security is typically monthly. The convention is to compare the yield on a mortgage-backed security to that of a Treasury coupon security by calculating the MBS's bond-equivalent yield. As explained in Chapter 5, the bond-equivalent yield for a Treasury coupon security is found by doubling the semiannual yield. However, it is incorrect to follow that convention for mortgage-backed and asset-backed securities because the investor has the opportunity to generate greater interest by reinvesting the more frequent cash flows. The market practice/convention is to calculate a yield so as to make it comparable to the yield to maturity on a bond-equivalent yield basis. The formula for annualizing the monthly cash flow yield for a mortgage-backed security is as follows:

$$\text{bond-equivalent yield} = 2[(1 + i_M)^6 - 1]$$

where i_M is the monthly interest rate that will equate the present value of the projected monthly cash flow to the market price (plus accrued interest) of the security.

As we explained in Chapter 5, all yield measures suffer from problems that limit their use in assessing a security's potential return. The yield to maturity has two major shortcomings as a measure of a bond's potential return. To realize the stated yield to maturity, the investor must: (1) reinvest the coupon payments at a rate equal to the yield to maturity, and (2) hold the bond to the maturity date. The reinvestment of the coupon payments is critical and for long-term bonds can be as much as 80% of the bond's return. The risk of having to reinvest the interest payments at less than the computed yield is called *reinvestment risk*. The risk associated with having to sell the security prior to the maturity date is called *interest rate risk*.

These shortcomings are equally applicable to the cash flow yield measure: (1) the projected cash flows are assumed to be reinvested at the cash flow yield, and (2) the mortgage-backed and asset-backed security is assumed to be held until the final payout based on some prepayment assumption. The importance of reinvestment risk, the risk that the cash flow will have to be reinvested at a rate lower than the cash flow yield, is particularly important for mortgage-backed and asset-backed securities because payments are monthly and both interest and principal (regularly scheduled repayments and prepayments) must be reinvested. Moreover, an additional assumption is that the projected cash flow is actually realized. If the prepayment experience is different from the prepayment rate assumed, the cash flow yield will not be realized.

Given the computed cash flow yield and the average life for a mortgage-backed or asset- backed security based on some prepayment assumption, the next step is to compare the yield to the yield for a comparable Treasury security. "Comparable" is typically defined as a Treasury security with the same maturity as the average life of the security. The difference between the cash flow yield and the yield on a comparable Treasury security is called a *nominal spread*. We described this measure in Chapter 5.

Unfortunately, it is the nominal spread that some investors will use as a measure of relative value. However, this spread masks the fact that a portion of the nominal spread is compensation for accepting prepayment risk. For example, CMO support tranches are offered at large nominal spreads. However, the spread embodies the substantial prepayment risk associated with support tranches. An investor who buys solely on the basis of nominal spread — dubbed a "yield hog" — fails to determine whether that nominal spread offers potential compensation given the substantial prepayment risk faced by the holder of a support tranche.

Instead of nominal spread, investors need a measure that indicates the potential compensation after adjusting for prepayment risk. This measure is called the *option-adjusted spread* (OAS). In Chapter 6 we demonstrated how this measure is computed within the context of the lattice model. Below we will explain how this measure is computed using the model employed for mortgage-backed securities and certain types of asset-backed securities.

MONTE CARLO SIMULATION/OAS

In fixed income valuation modeling, there are two methodologies commonly used to value securities with embedded options — the lattice model and the Monte Carlo model. The lattice model was explained in Chapter 6. The Monte Carlo simulation model involves simulating a sufficiently large number of potential interest rate paths in order to assess the value of a security along these different paths. This model is the most flexible of the two valuation methodologies for valuing interest rate sensitive instruments where the history of interest rates is important. Mortgage-backed and some asset-backed securities are commonly valued using this model. As explained below, a byproduct of a valuation model is the OAS.

Interest Rate History and Path-Dependent Cash Flows

For some fixed income securities and derivative instruments, the periodic cash flows are *path-dependent*. This means that the cash flow received in one period is determined not only by the current interest rate level, but also by the path that interest rates took to get to the current level.

In the case of mortgage passthrough securities (or simply, passthroughs), prepayments are path-dependent because this month's prepayment rate depends on whether there have been prior opportunities to refinance since the underlying mortgages were originated. Unlike passthroughs, the decision as to whether a corporate issuer will elect to refund an issue when the current rate is below the issue's coupon rate is not dependent on how rates evolved over time to reach the current level.

Moreover, in the case of securities backed by adjustable-rate mortgages (ARMs), prepayments are not only path-dependent but the periodic coupon rate depends on the history of the reference rate upon which the coupon rate is determined. This is because ARMs have periodic caps and floors as well as a lifetime cap and floor. For example, an ARM whose coupon rate resets annually could have the following restriction on the coupon rate: (1) the rate cannot change by more than 200 basis points each year and (2) the rate cannot be more than 500 basis points from the initial coupon rate.

Pools of passthroughs are used as collateral for the creation of collateralized mortgage obligations (CMOs) as discussed in the previous chapter. Consequently, for CMOs there are typically two sources of path dependency in a tranche's cash flows. First, the collateral prepayments are path-dependent as discussed above. Second, the cash flow to be received in the current month by a tranche depends on the outstanding balances of the other tranches in the deal. Thus, we need the history of prepayments to calculate these balances.

Valuing Mortgage-Backed Securities[1]

Conceptually, the valuation of passthroughs using the Monte Carlo method is simple. In practice, however, it is very complex. The simulation involves generating a set of cash flows based on simulated future mortgage refinancing rates, which in turn imply simulated prepayment rates.

Valuation modeling for CMOs is similar to valuation modeling for passthroughs, although the difficulties are amplified because the issuer has sliced and diced both the prepayment and interest rate risk into smaller pieces and distributed these risks among the tranches. The sensitivity of the passthroughs comprising the collateral to these two risks is not transmitted equally to every tranche. Some of the tranches wind up more sensitive to prepayment and interest rate risk than the collateral, while some of them are much less sensitive.

Using Simulation to Generate Interest Rate Paths and Cash Flows

The typical model that Wall Street firms and commercial vendors use to generate random interest rate paths takes as input today's term structure of interest rates and a volatility assumption. The term structure of interest rates is the theoretical spot rate (or zero coupon) curve implied by today's Treasury securities which serve as a benchmark. The volatility assumption determines the dispersion of future interest rates in the simulation. The simulations should be calibrated to the market so that the average simulated price of a zero-coupon Treasury bond equals today's actual price.

Each model has its own model of the evolution of future interest rates and its own volatility assumptions. Typically, there are no important differences in the interest rate models of dealer firms and vendors, although their volatility assumptions can be significantly different.

The random paths of interest rates should be generated from an arbitrage-free model of the future term structure of interest rates. By arbitrage-free it is meant that the model replicates today's term structure of interest rates, an input of the model, and that for all future dates there is no possible arbitrage within the model.

The simulation works by generating many scenarios of future interest rate paths. In each month of the scenario, a monthly interest rate and a mortgage refinancing rate are generated. The monthly interest rates are used to discount the projected cash flows in the scenario. The mortgage refinancing rate is needed to determine the cash flow because it represents the opportunity cost the mortgagor is facing at that time.

If the refinancing rates are high relative to the mortgagor's original coupon rate (i.e., the rate on the mortgagor's loan), the mortgagor will have less incentive to refinance, or even a positive disincentive (i.e., the homeowner will avoid moving in order to avoid refinancing). If the refinancing rate is low relative to the mortgagor's original coupon rate, the mortgagor has an incentive to refinance.

---

[1] Portions of the material in this section and the one to follow are adapted from Frank J. Fabozzi, Scott F. Richard, and David S. Horowitz, "Valuation of CMOs," Chapter 6 in Frank J. Fabozzi (ed.), *Advances in the Valuation and Management of Mortgage-Backed Securities* (New Hope, PA: Frank J. Fabozzi Associates, 1998).

Exhibit 1: Simulated Paths of 1-Month Future Interest Rates

Month	Interest Rate Path Number						
	1	2	3	...	n	...	N
1	$f_1(1)$	$f_1(2)$	$f_1(3)$	...	$f_1(n)$	...	$f_1(N)$
2	$f_2(1)$	$f_2(2)$	$f_2(3)$	...	$f_2(n)$	...	$f_2(N)$
3	$f_3(1)$	$f_3(2)$	$f_3(3)$	...	$f_3(n)$	...	$f_3(N)$
t	$f_t(1)$	$f_t(2)$	$f_t(3)$	...	$f_t(n)$	...	$f_t(N)$
358	$f_{358}(1)$	$f_{358}(2)$	$f_{358}(3)$	...	$f_{358}(n)$	...	$f_{358}(N)$
359	$f_{359}(1)$	$f_{359}(2)$	$f_{359}(3)$	...	$f_{359}(n)$	...	$f_{359}(N)$
360	$f_{360}(1)$	$f_{360}(2)$	$f_{360}(3)$	...	$f_{360}(n)$	...	$f_{360}(N)$

Notation:

   $f_t(n)$ = 1-month future interest rate for month t on path n
   N = total number of interest rate paths

Exhibit 2: Simulated Paths of Mortgage Refinancing Rates

Month	Interest Rate Path Number						
	1	2	3	...	n	...	N
1	$r_1(1)$	$r_1(2)$	$r_1(3)$	...	$r_1(n)$	...	$r_1(N)$
2	$r_2(1)$	$r_2(2)$	$r_2(3)$	...	$r_2(n)$	...	$r_2(N)$
3	$r_3(1)$	$r_3(2)$	$r_3(3)$	...	$r_3(n)$	...	$r_3(N)$
t	$r_t(1)$	$r_t(2)$	$r_t(3)$	...	$r_t(n)$	...	$r_t(N)$
358	$r_{358}(1)$	$r_{358}(2)$	$r_{358}(3)$	...	$r_{358}(n)$	...	$r_{358}(N)$
359	$r_{359}(1)$	$r_{359}(2)$	$r_{359}(3)$	...	$r_{359}(n)$	...	$r_{359}(N)$
360	$r_{360}(1)$	$r_{360}(2)$	$r_{360}(3)$	...	$r_{360}(n)$	...	$r_{360}(N)$

Notation:

   $r_t(n)$ = mortgage refinancing rate for month t on path n
   N = total number of interest rate paths

Prepayments (voluntary and involuntary) are projected by feeding the refinancing rate and loan characteristics, such as age, into a prepayment model. Given the projected prepayments, the cash flow along an interest rate path can be determined.

To make this process more concrete, consider a newly issued mortgage passthrough security with a maturity of 360 months. Exhibit 1 shows N simulated interest rate path scenarios. Each scenario consists of a path of 360 simulated 1-month future interest rates. Just how many paths should be generated is explained later. Exhibit 2 shows the paths of simulated mortgage refinancing rates corresponding to the scenarios shown in Exhibit 1. Assuming these mortgage refinancing rates, the cash flow for each scenario path is shown in Exhibit 3.

Calculating the Present Value for a Scenario Interest Rate Path

Given the cash flow on an interest rate path, its present value can be calculated. The discount rate for determining the present value is the simulated spot rate for each month on the interest rate path plus an appropriate spread. The spot rate on a path can be determined from the simulated future monthly rates in Exhibit 1. The relationship that holds between the simulated spot rate for month T on path n and the simulated future 1-month rates is:[2]

$$z_T(n) = \{[1 + f_1(n)][1 + f_2(n)]...[1 + f_T(n)]\}^{1/T} - 1$$

where

$z_T(n)$ = simulated spot rate for month T on path n

$f_j(n)$ = simulated future 1-month rate for month j on path n

Consequently, the interest rate path for the simulated future 1-month rates can be converted to the interest rate path for the simulated monthly spot rates as shown in Exhibit 4.

Therefore, the present value of the cash flow for month T on interest rate path n discounted at the simulated spot rate for month T plus some spread is:

$$PV[C_T(n)] = \frac{C_T(n)}{[1 + z_T(n) + K]^{1/T}}$$

where

$PV[C_T(n)]$ = present value of cash flow for month T on path n

$C_T(n)$ = cash flow for month T on path n

$z_T(n)$ = spot rate for month T on path n

K = spread

Exhibit 3: Simulated Cash Flow on Each of the Interest Rate Paths

| Month | Interest Rate Path Number | | | | | | |
	1	2	3	...	n	...	N
1	$C_1(1)$	$C_1(2)$	$C_1(3)$	...	$C_1(n)$	...	$C_1(N)$
2	$C_2(1)$	$C_2(2)$	$C_2(3)$	...	$C_2(n)$	...	$C_2(N)$
3	$C_3(1)$	$C_3(2)$	$C_3(3)$	...	$C_3(n)$	...	$C_3(N)$
t	$C_t(1)$	$C_t(2)$	$C_t(3)$	...	$C_t(n)$	...	$C_t(N)$
358	$C_{358}(1)$	$C_{358}(2)$	$C_{358}(3)$	...	$C_{358}(n)$	...	$C_{358}(N)$
359	$C_{359}(1)$	$C_{359}(2)$	$C_{359}(3)$	...	$C_{359}(n)$	...	$C_{359}(N)$
360	$C_{360}(1)$	$C_{360}(2)$	$C_{360}(3)$	...	$C_{360}(n)$	...	$C_{360}(N)$

Notation:

$C_t(n)$ = cash flow for month t on path n

N = total number of interest rate paths

[2] This is the same equation we saw in Chapter 2 when we examined the relationship between long-term spot rates and short-term forward rates.

Exhibit 4: Simulated Paths of Monthly Spot Rates

Month	Interest Rate Path Number						
	1	2	3	...	n	...	N
1	$z_1(1)$	$z_1(2)$	$z_1(3)$	...	$z_1(n)$	...	$z_1(N)$
2	$z_2(1)$	$z_2(2)$	$z_2(3)$	...	$z_2(n)$	...	$z_2(N)$
3	$z_3(1)$	$z_3(2)$	$z_3(3)$	...	$z_3(n)$	...	$z_3(N)$
t	$z_t(1)$	$z_t(2)$	$z_t(3)$	...	$z_t(n)$	...	$z_t(N)$
358	$z_{358}(1)$	$z_{358}(2)$	$z_{358}(3)$	...	$z_{358}(n)$	...	$z_{358}(N)$
359	$z_{359}(1)$	$z_{359}(2)$	$z_{359}(3)$	...	$z_{359}(n)$	...	$z_{359}(N)$
360	$z_{360}(1)$	$z_{360}(2)$	$z_{360}(3)$	...	$z_{360}(n)$	...	$z_{360}(N)$

Notation:

$z_t(n)$ = spot rate for month t on path n

N = total number of interest rate paths

The present value for path n is the sum of the present values of the cash flows for each month on path n. That is,

$$PV[\text{Path}(n)] = PV[C_1(n)] + PV[C_2(n)] + ... + PV[C_{360}(n)]$$

where $PV[\text{Path}(n)]$ is the present value of interest rate path n.

Determining the Theoretical Value

The present value of a given interest rate path is the theoretical value of a passthrough if that path was actually realized. The theoretical value of the passthrough can be determined by calculating the average of the theoretical values of all the interest rate paths. That is,

$$\text{Theoretical value} = \frac{PV[\text{Path}(1)] + PV[\text{Path}(2)] + ... + PV[\text{Path}(N)]}{N}$$

where N is the number of interest rate paths.

This procedure for valuing a passthrough is also followed for a CMO tranche. The cash flow for each month on each interest rate path is found according to the principal repayment and interest distribution rules of the deal. In order to do this, a model for reverse engineering a CMO deal is needed.

Option-Adjusted Spread

In the Monte Carlo model, the *option-adjusted spread* (OAS) is the spread that, when added to all the spot rates on all interest rate paths, will make the average present value of the paths equal to the observed market price (plus accrued interest). Mathematically, OAS is the value for K (the spread) that will satisfy the following condition:

$$\frac{PV[Path(1)] + PV[Path(2)] + \dots + PV[Path(N)]}{N} = \text{market price}$$

where N is the number of interest rate paths. The left-hand side of the above equation looks identical to that of the equation for the theoretical value. The difference is that the objective is to determine what spread, K, will make the model produce a theoretical value equal to the market price.

The procedure for determining the OAS is straightforward and involves the same search algorithm explained for the zero-volatility spread. The next question, then, is how to interpret the OAS. Basically, the OAS is used to reconcile value with market price. On the left-hand side of the previous equation is the market's statement: the price of a structured product. The average present value over all the paths on the right-hand side of the equation is the model's output, which we refer to as the theoretical value. Thus, OAS tells us the *mean* adjustment that must be made to the set of future interest rates used for discounting the cash flows of a structured product to obtain its market price.

Some Technical Issues

In the binomial method for valuing bonds, the interest rate tree is constructed so that it is arbitrage free. That is, if any on-the-run issue is valued, the value produced by the model is equal to the market price. This means that the tree is calibrated to the market. In contrast, in our discussion of the Monte Carlo method, there is no mechanism that we have described above that will assure that the valuation model will produce a value for an on-the-run Treasury security (the benchmark in the case of agency mortgage-backed securities) equal to the market price. In practice, this is accomplished by adding a *drift term* to the short-term return generating process (Exhibit 1) so that the value produced by the Monte Carlo method for all on-the-run Treasury securities is equal to their market price.[3] A technical explanation of this process is beyond the scope of this chapter.[4]

There is also another adjustment made to the interest rate paths. Restrictions on interest rate movements must be built into the model to prevent interest rates from reaching levels that are believed to be unreasonable (e.g., an interest rate of zero or an interest rate of 30%). This is done by incorporating *mean reversion* into the model. By this it is meant that at some point, the interest rate is forced toward some estimated average (mean) value.

The specification of the relationship between short-term rates and refinancing rates is necessary. Empirical evidence on the relationship is also necessary. More specifically, the correlation between the short-term and long-term rates must be estimated.

---

[3] This is equivalent to saying that the OAS produced by the model is zero.

[4] For an explanation of how this is done, see Lakhbir S. Hayre and Kenneth Lauterbach, "Stochastic Valuation of Debt Securities," in Frank J. Fabozzi (ed.), *Managing Institutional Assets* (New York: Harper & Row, 1990), pp. 321-364.

The number of interest rate paths determines how "good" the estimate is, not relative to the truth but relative to the valuation model used. The more paths, the more the theoretical value tends to settle down. It is a statistical sampling problem. Most Monte Carlo models employ some form of *variance reduction* to cut down on the number of sample paths necessary to get a good statistical sample. Variance reduction techniques allow us to obtain value estimates within a tick. By this we mean that if the model is used to generate more scenarios, value estimates from the model will not change by more than a tick. So, for example, if 1,024 paths are used to obtain the estimate value for a tranche, there is little more information to be had from the OAS model by generating more than that number of paths. (For some very sensitive CMO tranches, more paths may be needed to estimate value within one tick.)

To reduce computational time, a statistical methodology has been used by vendors that involves the analysis of a small number of interest rate paths. Basically, the methodology is as follows. A large number of paths of interest rates are generated. Using a statistical technique, these paths can be reduced to a small representative number of interest rate paths. These interest rate paths are called *representative paths*. The security is then valued on each representative path. The value of the security is then the weighted average of the representative path values. The weight used for a representative path is determined by the percentage of the interest rate paths it represents. This approach is called the *representative path method*.

For example, suppose that 3,000 interest rate paths are generated and that these paths can be reduced to 10 representative paths. Suppose further that the percentage of the 3,000 interest rate paths for each representative path and the present value for each representative path for some CMO tranche is as follows:

Representative path	Percentage interest rate paths (%)	Present value
1	20	85
2	18	70
3	12	60
4	10	90
5	10	80
6	10	65
7	5	95
8	5	83
9	5	60
10	5	52

The theoretical value of this CMO tranche is 74.8, as shown below:

$$85 \ (0.20) + 70 \ (0.18) + 60 \ (0.12) + 90 \ (0.10) + 80 \ (0.10) + 65 \ (0.10)$$
$$+ \ 95 \ (0.05) + 83 \ (0.05) + 60 \ (0.05) + 52 \ (0.05) = 74.8$$

Distribution of Path Present Values

The Monte Carlo method is a commonly used management science tool in business. It is employed when the outcome of a business decision depends on the outcome of several random variables. The product of the simulation is the average value and the probability distribution of the possible outcomes.

Unfortunately, the use of Monte Carlo simulation to value fixed income securities has been limited to just the reporting of the average value, which is referred to as the theoretical value of the security. This means that all of the information about the distribution of the path's present values is ignored. Yet, this information is quite valuable.

For example, consider a well protected PAC bond. The distribution of the present value for the paths should be concentrated around the theoretical value. That is, the standard deviation should be small. In contrast, for a support tranche, the distribution of the present value for the paths could be wide, or equivalently, the standard deviation could be large.

Therefore, before using the theoretical value for a mortgage-backed security generated from the Monte Carlo method, a portfolio manager should ask for information about the distribution of the path's present values.

OAS versus the Benchmark

It is important to make sure that OAS is interpreted relative to the benchmark selected. While in our illustrations we have used the on-the-run Treasury rates as the benchmark, many funded investors will use LIBOR as the benchmark. As explained in Chapter 2, a spot rate curve can be created for LIBOR using boot-strapping.

To see the impact of the benchmark on the computed OAS, the table below shows the OAS computed in November 1999 for a 15-year 6.5% FNMA TBA passthrough (seasoned and unseasoned) and a 30-year 6.5% FNMA TBA using the on-the-run Treasuries and LIBOR:[5]

Issue: 6.5% coupon FNMA TBA	Average life	OAS (bps) benchmark	
		Treasuries	LIBOR
15-year unseasoned	5.9 years	70	−10
15-year seasoned (1994 production)	4.0 years	75	1
30-year	9.5 years	87	−2

As can be seen from the table, the selection of the benchmark has a dramatic impact on the computed OAS. It cannot be overemphasized that the user of an OAS number should make sure that the benchmark is known, as well as the volatility assumption.

Illustrations

We will use two deals to show how CMOs can be analyzed using the Monte Carlo model/OAS procedure discussed above — a simple CMO structure and a PAC/support structure.[6]

---

[5] The table is reported in the November 16, 1999 issue of PaineWebber's *Mortgage Strategist*, p. 10. The values reported were computed on Bloomberg.

Exhibit 5: OAS Analysis of FHLMC 1915 Classes A, B, and C
(As of 3/10/98)

All three tranches were trading at a premium as of the date of the analysis.

Base Case (Assumes 13% Interest Rate Volatility

	OAS (in basis points)	Option Cost (in basis points)	Z-Spread (in basis points)	Effective Duration (in years)
Collateral	51	67	118	1.2
Tranche				
A	32	51	83	0.9
B	33	82	115	2.9
C	46	70	116	6.7

Prepayments at 80% and 120% of Prepayment Model
(Assumes 13% Interest Rate Volatility)

	New OAS (in basis points)		Change in Price per $100 par (holding OAS constant)	
	80%	120%	80%	120%
Collateral	63	40	$0.45	−$0.32
Tranche				
A	40	23	0.17	−0.13
B	43	22	0.54	−0.43
C	58	36	0.97	−0.63

Interest Rate Volatility of 9% and 17%

	New OAS (in basis points)		Change in Price per $100 par (holding OAS constant)	
	9%	17%	9%	17%
Collateral	79	21	$1.03	−$0.94
Tranche				
A	52	10	0.37	−0.37
B	66	−3	1.63	−1.50
C	77	15	2.44	−2.08

Simple CMO Structure

The simple structure analyzed is Freddie Mac (FHLMC) 1915. It is a simple sequential-pay CMO bond structure. The structure includes eight tranches, A, B, C, D, E, F, G, and S. The focus of our analysis is on tranches A, B, and C. All three tranches were priced at a premium.

The top panel of Exhibit 5 shows the OAS, the option cost, and effective duration[7] for the collateral and the three tranches in the CMO structure. However, tranche A had the smallest effective duration and tranche C had the largest effective duration. The OAS for the collateral is 51 basis points. Since the option cost is 67 basis points, the zero-volatility spread is 118 basis points (51 basis points plus 67 basis points).

---

[6] These illustrations are from Fabozzi, Richard, and Horowitz, "Valuation of CMOs."

[7] We explain how to compute the effective duration in Chapter 11.

At the time this analysis was performed, March 10, 1998, the Treasury yield curve was not steep. As explained earlier, when the yield curve is relatively flat the zero-volatility spread will not differ significantly from the nominal spread. Thus, for the three tranches shown in Exhibit 5, the zero-volatility spread is 83 basis points for A, 115 basis points for B, and 116 basis points for C.

Notice that the tranches did not share the OAS equally. The same is true for the option cost. Both the Z-spread and the option cost increase as the effective duration increases. Whether or not any of these tranches were attractive investments requires a comparison to other tranches in the market with the same effective duration. While not presented here, all three tranches offered an OAS similar to other sequential-pay tranches with the same effective duration available in the market when the analysis was performed. On a relative basis (i.e., relative to the other tranches analyzed in the deal), the only tranche where there appears to be a bit of a bargain is tranche C. A portfolio manager contemplating the purchase of this last cash flow tranche can see that C offers a higher OAS than B and appears to bear less of the risk (i.e., has lower option cost), as measured by the option cost. The problem portfolio managers may face is that they might not be able to go out as long on the yield curve as tranche C because of effective duration, maturity, and average life constraints relative to their liabilities, for example.

Now let's consider modeling risk. Examination of the sensitivity of the tranches to changes in prepayments and interest rate volatility will help us to understand the interaction of the tranches in the structure and who is bearing the risk. How the deal behaves under various scenarios should reinforce and be consistent with the valuation (i.e., a tranche may look "cheap" for a reason).

We begin with prepayments. Specifically, we keep the same interest rate paths as those used to get the OAS in the base case (the top panel of Exhibit 5), but reduce the prepayment rate on each interest rate path to 80% of the projected rate. As can be seen in the second panel of Exhibit 5, slowing down prepayments increases the OAS and price for the collateral. The exhibit reports two results of the sensitivity analysis. First, it indicates the change in the OAS. Second, it indicates the change in the price, holding the OAS constant at the base case.

To see how a portfolio manager can use the information in the second panel, consider tranche A. At 80% of the prepayment speed, the OAS for this tranche increases from 32 basis points to 40 basis points. If the OAS is held constant, the panel indicates that the buyer of tranche A would gain $0.17 per $100 of par value.

Notice that for all of the tranches reported in Exhibit 5 there is a gain from a slowdown in prepayments. This is because all of the sequential tranches in this deal are priced over par. (An investor in a tranche priced at a premium benefits from a slowdown in prepayments because the investor receives the higher coupon for a longer period and postpones the capital loss resulting from a prepayment.) Also notice that while the changes in OAS are about the same for the different tranches, the changes in price are quite different. This arises because the shorter tranches have less duration. Therefore, their prices do not move as much from a change in OAS as a longer average life tranche. A portfolio manager who is willing to go to the long end of the yield curve, such as tranche C, would realize the most benefit from the slowdown in prepayments.

Also shown in the second panel of the exhibit is the second part of our experiment to test the sensitivity of prepayments: the prepayment rate is assumed to be 120% of the base case. The collateral loses money in this scenario because it is trading above par. This is reflected in the OAS of the collateral which declines from 51 basis points to 40 basis points. Now look at the three tranches. They all lost money because the tranches were all at a premium and the speeding up of prepayments adversely affects the tranches.

Before looking at the last panel that shows the effect of a change in interest rate volatility on the OAS, let's review the relationship between expected interest rate volatility and the value of a mortgage-backed security. Recall that the investor in a mortgage-backed security has sold an option to homeowners (borrowers). Thus, the investor is short an option and the value of an option depends on expected interest rate volatility. When expected interest rate volatility decreases, the value of the option embedded in a mortgage-backed security decreases and therefore the value of a mortgage-backed security increases. The opposite is true when expected interest rate volatility increases — the value of the embedded option increases and the value of a mortgage-backed security decreases.

Now let's look at the sensitivity to the interest rate volatility assumption, 13% in the base case. Two experiments are performed: reducing the volatility assumption to 9% and increasing it to 17%. These results are reported in the third panel of Exhibit 5.

Reducing the volatility to 9% increases the dollar price of the collateral by $1.03 and increases the OAS from 51 in the base case to 79 basis points. However, this $1.03 increase in the price of the collateral is not equally distributed among the three tranches. Most of the increase in value is realized by the longer tranches. The OAS gain for each of the tranches follows more or less the effective durations of those tranches. This makes sense, because the longer the duration, the greater the risk, and when volatility declines, the reward is greater for the accepted risk. At the higher level of assumed interest rate volatility of 17%, the collateral is severely affected. The longer the duration, the greater the loss. These results for a decrease and an increase in interest rate volatility are consistent with what we explained earlier.

Using the Monte Carlo simulation/OAS analysis, a fair conclusion that can be made about this simple structure is: what you see is what you get. The only surprise in this structure is the lower option cost in tranche C. In general, however, a portfolio manager willing to extend duration gets paid for that risk in this structure.

Exhibit 6: Summary of Federal Home Loan Mortgage Corporation — Multiclass Mortgage Participation Certificates (Guaranteed), Series 1706

Total Issue: $300,000,000   Issue Date: 2/18/94

Tranche	Original Balance ($)	Coupon (%)	Stated Maturity	Original Issue Pricing (225% PSA Assumed)	
				Average Life (yrs)	Expected Maturity
PAC Tranches					
C (PAC Bond)	25,500,000	5.25	4/15/14	3.5	6/15/98
D (PAC Bond)	9,150,000	5.65	8/15/15	4.5	1/15/99
E (PAC Bond)	31,650,000	6.00	1/15/19	5.8	1/15/01
G (PAC Bond)	30,750,000	6.25	8/15/21	7.9	5/15/03
H (PAC Bond)	27,450,000	6.50	6/15/23	10.9	10/15/07
J (PAC Bond)	5,220,000	6.50	10/15/23	14.4	9/15/09
K (PAC Bond)	7,612,000	7.00	3/15/24	18.8	5/15/19
Support Tranches					
LA (SCH Bond)	26,673,000	7.00	11/15/21	3.5	3/15/02
LB (SCH Bond)	36,087,000	7.00	6/15/23	3.5	9/15/02
M (SCH Bond)	18,738,000	7.00	3/15/24	11.2	10/15/08

PAC/Support Tranche Structure

Now let's look at how to apply the methodology to a more complicated CMO structure, FHLMC Series 1706. The collateral (i.e., pool of passthroughs) for this structure is Freddie Mac 7s (7% coupon rate). A partial summary of the deal is provided in Exhibit 6. That is, only the tranches we will be discussing in this section are shown in the exhibit.

While this deal looks complicated, it is relatively simple compared to many deals that are issued. Nonetheless, it brings out all the key points about application of OAS analysis, specifically, the fact that most deals include cheap bonds, expensive bonds, and fairly priced bonds. The OAS analysis helps identify how a tranche should be classified. A more proper analysis would compare the OAS for each tranche to a similar duration tranche available in the market.

All of the tranches in Exhibit 6 were discussed in the last chapter. At issuance, there were 10 PAC tranches, three scheduled tranches, a floating-rate support tranche, and an inverse floating-rate support. Recall that the "scheduled tranches" are support tranches with a schedule, also referred to as "PAC II tranches."

The first two PAC tranches in the deal, tranche A and tranche B, were paid off at the time of the analysis. The other PAC tranches were still available at the time of the analysis. The prepayment protection for the PAC tranches is provided by the support tranches. The support tranches in this deal that are shown in Exhibit 6 are tranches LA, LB, and M. There were other support tranches not shown in Exhibit 6. LA is the shortest average life support tranche (a scheduled (SCH) bond).

The collateral for this deal was trading at a premium. That is, the home-owners (borrowers) were paying a higher mortgage rate than available in the market at the time of the analysis. This meant that the value of the collateral would increase if prepayments slow down but would decrease if prepayments increase. What is important to note, however, is that a tranche could be trading at a discount, par, or premium even though the collateral is priced at a premium. For example, PAC C had a low coupon rate at the time of the analysis and therefore was trading at a discount. Thus, while the collateral (which was selling at a premium) loses value from an increase in prepayments, a discount tranche such as tranche C would increase in value if prepayments increase. (Recall that in the simple structure analyzed earlier, the collateral and all the tranches were trading at a premium.)

The top panel of Exhibit 7 shows the base case OAS, the option cost, and the effective duration for the collateral and tranches in Exhibit 6. The collateral OAS is 60 basis points, and the option cost is 44 basis points. The Z-spread of the collateral to the Treasury spot curve is 104 basis points.

The 60 basis points of OAS did not get equally distributed among the tranches — as was the case with the simple structure analyzed earlier. Tranche LB, the scheduled support, did not realize a good OAS allocation, only 29 basis points, and had an extremely high option cost. Given the prepayment uncertainty associated with this tranche, its OAS would be expected to be higher. The reason for the low OAS is that this tranche was priced so that its cash flow yield is high. Using the Z-spread as a proxy for the nominal spread (i.e., spread over the Treasury yield curve), the 103 basis point spread for tranche LB is high given that this appears to be a short average life tranche. Consequently, "yield buyers" (i.e., investors with a preference for high nominal yield, who may not be attentive to compensation for prepayment risk) probably bid aggressively for this tranche and thereby drove down its OAS, trading off "yield" for OAS. From a total return perspective, however, tranche LB should be avoided. It is a rich, or expensive, tranche. The other support tranche analyzed, tranche M, had an OAS of 72 basis points and at the time of this analysis was similar to that offered on comparable duration tranches available in the market.

The analysis reported in the top panel of Exhibit 7 helps us identify where the cheap tranches are in the deal. The long average life and effective duration tranches in the deal are the PAC tranches G, H, J, and K. These tranches have high OAS relative to the other tranches and low option cost. They appear to be the cheap tranches in the deal. These PAC tranches had well protected cash flows and exhibited positive convexity (i.e., these tranches lose less in an adverse scenario than they gain in a positive scenario).

The next two panels in Exhibit 7 show the sensitivity of the OAS and the price (holding OAS constant at the base case) to changes in the prepayment speed (80% and 120% of the base case) and to changes in volatility (9% and 17%). This analysis shows that the change in the prepayment speed does not affect the collateral significantly, while the change in the OAS (holding the price constant) and price (holding OAS constant) for each tranche can be significant.

Exhibit 7: OAS Analysis of FHLMC 1706 (As of 3/10/98)
Base Case (Assumes 13% Interest Rate Volatility)

	OAS (in basis points)	Option Cost (in basis points)	Z-Spread (in basis points)	Effective Duration (in years)
Collateral	60	44	104	2.6
PAC Tranches				
C (PAC)	15	0	15	0.2
D (PAC)	16	4	20	0.6
E (PAC)	26	4	30	1.7
G (PAC)	42	8	50	3.3
H (PAC)	50	12	62	4.9
J (PAC)	56	14	70	6.8
K (PAC)	57	11	68	8.6
Support Tranches				
LA (SCH)	39	12	51	1.4
LB (SCH)	29	74	103	1.2
M (SCH)	72	53	125	4.9

Prepayments at 80% and 120% of Prepayment Model
(Assumes 13% Interest Rate Volatility)

	Base Case OAS	New OAS (in basis points)		Change in Price per $100 par (holding OAS constant)	
		80%	120%	80%	120%
Collateral	60	63	57	$0.17	−$0.11
PAC Tranches					
C (PAC)	15	15	15	0.00	0.00
D (PAC)	16	16	16	0.00	0.00
E (PAC)	26	27	26	0.01	−0.01
G (PAC)	42	44	40	0.08	−0.08
H (PAC)	50	55	44	0.29	−0.27
J (PAC)	56	63	50	0.50	−0.47
K (PAC)	57	65	49	0.77	−0.76
Support Tranches					
LA (SCH)	39	31	39	−0.12	0.00
LB (SCH)	29	39	18	0.38	−0.19
M (SCH)	72	71	76	−0.07	0.18

Interest Rate Volatility of 9% and 17%

	Base Case OAS	New OAS (in basis points)		Change in Price per $100 par (holding OAS constant)	
		9%	17%	9%	17%
Collateral	60	81	35	$0.96	−$0.94
PAC Tranches					
C (PAC)	15	15	15	0.00	0.00
D (PAC)	16	16	16	0.00	0.00
E (PAC)	26	27	24	0.02	−0.04
G (PAC)	42	48	34	0.21	−0.27
H (PAC)	50	58	35	0.48	−0.72
J (PAC)	56	66	41	0.70	−1.05
K (PAC)	57	66	44	0.82	−1.19
Support Tranches					
LA (SCH)	39	47	24	0.09	−0.18
LB (SCH)	29	58	−4	0.80	−0.82
M (SCH)	72	100	41	1.80	−1.72

Tranches C and D at the time of the analysis were priced at a discount with short average lives. The OAS and price of these two tranches were not affected by a slowing down or a speeding up of the prepayment model. Tranche H was a premium tranche with a medium-term average life at the time of the analysis. Because tranche H was trading at a premium, it benefits from a slowing in prepayments, as the bondholder will receive the coupon for a longer time. Faster prepayments represent an adverse scenario. The PAC tranches are quite well-protected. The longer average life PACs will actually benefit from a reduced prepayment rate because they will be earning the higher coupon interest longer. So, on an OAS basis, the earlier conclusion that the long PACs were allocated a good part of the deal's value holds up under our first stress test (i.e., changing prepayments).

The sensitivity of the collateral and the tranches to changes in volatility is shown in the third panel of Exhibit 7. A lower volatility increases the value of the collateral, while a higher volatility reduces its value. The long average life PACs continue to be fairly well-protected, whether the volatility is lower or higher. In the two volatility scenarios they continue to get a good OAS on a relative value basis, although not as much as in the base case if volatility is higher (but the OAS still looks like a reasonable value in this scenario). This reinforces the earlier conclusion concerning the investment merit of the long PACs in this deal. Note, however, that PAC tranches H, J, and K are more sensitive to the volatility assumption than tranches C, D, E, and G and therefore the investor is accepting greater volatility risk (i.e., the risk that volatility will change) with tranches H, J, and K relative to tranches C, D, E, and G.

Special Considerations in Valuing Asset-Backed Securities

The model that should be used for valuing an asset-backed security (ABS) depends on the characteristic of the loans or receivables backing the deal. An ABS can have one of the following three characteristics:

> *Characteristic 1:* The ABS does not have a prepayment option.
>
> *Characteristic 2:* The ABS has a prepayment option but borrowers do not exhibit a tendency to prepay when refinancing rates fall below the loan rate.
>
> *Characteristic 3:* The ABS has a prepayment option and borrowers are expected to prepay when refinancing rates fall below the loan rate.

An example of a Characteristic 1 type ABS is a security backed by credit card receivables. An example of a Characteristic 2 type ABS is a security backed by automobile loans. A security backed by closed-end home equity loans where the borrowers are of high quality (i.e., prime borrowers) is an example of a Characteristic 3 type ABS. There are some real-estate backed ABS where the verdict is still out as to the degree to which borrowers take advantage of refinancing opportunities. Specifically, these include securities backed by manufactured housing loans and securities backed by closed-end home equity loans to borrowers classified as low quality borrowers.

There are two possible approaches to valuing an ABS. They are the

1. zero-volatility spread (Z-spread) approach
2. option-adjusted spread (OAS) approach

For the Z-spread approach (discussed in Chapter 5) the interest rates used to discount the cash flows are the spot rates plus the zero-volatility spread. The value of an ABS is then the present value of the cash flows based on these discount rates. The Z-spread approach does not consider the prepayment option. Consequently, the Z-spread approach should be used to value Characteristic 1 type ABS. (In terms of the relationship between the Z-spread, OAS, and option cost discussed earlier in this chapter, this means that the value of the option is zero and therefore the Z-spread is equal to the OAS.) Since the Z-spread is equal to the OAS, the Z-spread approach to valuation can be used.

The Z-spread approach can also be used to value Characteristic 2 type ABS because while the borrowers do have a prepayment option, the option is not typically exercised when rates decline below the loan rate. Thus, as with Characteristic 1 type ABS, the Z-spread is equal to the OAS.

The OAS approach — which is considerably more computationally extensive than the Z-spread approach — is used to value securities where there is an embedded option and there is an expectation that the option is expected to be exercised if it makes economic sense for the borrower to do so. Consequently, the OAS approach is used to value Characteristic 3 type ABS. The choice is then whether to use the lattice model or the Monte Carlo simulation model. Since typically the cash flow for an ABS with a prepayment option is interest rate path dependent — as with a mortgage-backed security — the Monte Carlo simulation model is used.

When the Monte Carlo model must be employed for an ABS, then there are some modifications to the model relative to its application for valuing agency mortgage-backed securities. First, instead of the mortgage refinancing rate, the appropriate rate is the borrowing rate for comparable loans of the underlying loan pool. Moreover, an assumption must be made about the relationship between the relevant borrowing rate and the Treasury rate. Second, given the refinancing rates, the collateral's cash flows on each interest rate path can be generated. This requires a prepayment and default/recovery model to project involuntary prepayments.

Illustrations[8]

We will apply the Monte Carlo/OAS analysis to a home equity loan ABS, a manufactured housing ABS, agency passthrough securities, and an agency CMO.

---

[8] These illustrations are adapted from Frank J. Fabozzi, Shrikant Ramamurthy, and Laurent Gauthier, "Analysis of ABS," Chapter 28 in Frank J. Fabozzi (ed.), *Investing in Asset-Backed Securities* (New Hope, PA: Frank J. Fabozzi Associates, 2000).

Exhibits 8, 9, 10, and 11 provide information about these deals. The analysis was performed on April 14, 2000. Market implied volatility is assumed.[9]

Exhibit 8 shows the information for the home equity loan ABS — the Residential Asset Securities Corp. (RASC) issued in February 2000. The deal has six tranches. The weighted average life of the tranches is 3.2 years and the average option cost is 24 basis points per tranche.

Exhibit 9 shows the information for the Vanderbilt Mortgage and Finance manufactured housing loan deal issued in February 2000. The deal has six tranches with a weighted average life of 6.7 years. The average option cost is 18 basis points per tranche. Notice that the average option cost is lower than in the home equity loan deal. Also note that comparable tranches have lower option costs and a lower standard deviation for the average life in the manufactured housing deal versus the home equity loan deal as shown below:

Average life	Option cost		Average life Std. dev.	
	HEL	MH	HEL	MH
3-years	38	27	0.98	0.73
5-years	48	18	2.35	2.18

Information for several agency passthrough securities — Fannie Mae passthroughs with coupon rates from 6% to 8% — is shown in Exhibit 10. Notice from Exhibits 8, 9, and 10 that agency passthrough securities have higher option costs than the weighted average option costs of both the home equity loan deals and manufactured housing deals. Alternatively stated, there is more prepayment volatility in agency passthrough securities. The most relevant passthrough for comparison purposes would be the 8% coupon given that the price on this coupon security is comparable to both the home equity loan and manufactured housing loan structures that are presented — they are all slightly above par. The Fannie Mae 8% coupon passthrough has an option cost of 70 basis points versus 24 basis points on the home equity loan deal and 18 basis points on the manufactured housing loan deal.

The CMO deal analyzed is a Fannie Mae deal issued in January 2000 backed by 7% collateral. Information about the deal is presented in Exhibit 11. The weighted average option costs on the collateral as well as option costs on individual tranches are higher in the CMO deal than for the home equity loan deal and the manufactured housing loan deal.

The value of the options embedded in the bonds shown in Exhibits 8, 9, 10, and 11 are mainly driven by two factors: the sensitivity of prepayments to interest rates and the maturity of these options. On one extreme, manufactured housing prepayments are typically insensitive to interest rates, while agency mortgage borrowers are much more able to benefit from refinancing opportunities. Home equity loan borrowers — first-lien mortgages for sub-prime borrowers — are less able to profit from decreasing interest rates to refinance their loans.

---

[9] We will explain implied volatility in Chapter 13.

Exhibit 8: Analysis of Home-Equity Loan

Issuer	Residential Asset Securities Corp. (RASC)	Prepay. Assumption*	25 HEP
Deal Date	February 2000	Credit Support	Wrapped by AMBAC
Type	HEL REMIC	Volatility Assumption	Market implied

Class	Size ($ mm)	Type	Coupon (%)	Maturity	Avg. Life	Price	Yield (%)	Spread to WAL (bps)	Zero-vol Spd. (bps)	OAS** (bps)	Option Cost*** (bps)	Eff. Dur.	Eff. Conv.	St. Dev. of Avg. Life
A1	220	AAA Seq	7.615	1/15	0.9	100-11	6.585	40****	50	45	5	0.9	-0.3	0.10
A2	100	AAA Seq	7.700	6/21	2.0	100-00	7.525	110	113	93	20	2.1	-0.5	0.45
A3	105	AAA Seq	7.735	11/25	3.1	100-04	7.612	122	130	92	38	3.2	-0.7	0.98
A4	105	AAA Seq	8.040	11/28	5.1	100-16	7.915	163	175	127	48	4.7	-0.6	2.35
A5	55	AAA Seq	8.195	1/31	7.9	100-20	8.126	200	212	176	36	6.3	0.6	2.63
A6	65	AAA NAS	7.905	1/31	6.2	100-24	7.763	155	162	144	18	4.9	0.3	0.74
Weighted avg.			7.794		3.2	100.34	7.358				24	3.0		

Analysis as of 4/4/00

* Yields and spreads are computed relative to a constant prepayment assumption.

** OASs and durations are calculated by a Monte Carlo simulation of rates which utilizes Prudential Securities Inc.'s home equity loan prepayment model.

*** Option cost is defined as the difference between the OAS at market volatility and at zero volatility.

**** The spread to WAL for this class is lower than the OAS because the spread and OAS are computed at different prepayment speeds. The spread is computed at a constant prepayment speed assumption, while the OAS is computed assuming that prepayment speeds vary by time and interest-rate scenario.

Exhibit 9: Analysis of Manufactured Housing

Issuer   Vanderbilt Mortgage and Finance   Prepay. Assumption*   250 MHP
Deal Date   February 2000   Credit Support   Senior/sub structure
Type   MH REMIC   Volatility Assumption   Market implied

Class	Size ($ mm)	Type	Coupon (%)	Maturity	Avg. Life	Price	Yield (%)	Spread to WAL (bps)	Zero-vol Spd. (bps)	OAS** (bps)	Option Cost*** (bps)	Eff. Dur.	Eff. Conv.	St. Dev. of Avg. Life
A2	33.0	AAA Seq	7.580	8/12	3.0	100-16	7.434	103	105	78	27	2.4	-0.3	0.73
A3	32.0	AAA Seq	7.820	11/17	5.1	101-00	7.639	133	145	127	18	3.8	-0.2	2.18
A4	27.2	AAA Seq	7.955	12/24	9.2	101-20	7.877	169	190	175	15	5.8	-0.2	3.76
A5	9.1	AA Seq	8.195	11/32	12.0	102-12	7.989	200	220	212	8	7.9	0.2	3.18
M1	7.3	A Seq	8.635	11/32	8.7	101-16	8.502	240	254	239	15	6.3	0.3	1.53
B1	7.3	BBB Seq	9.250	9/15	6.1	100-09	9.330	310	314	292	22	4.7	0.0	0.54
B2	12.8	BBB Seq	9.250	11/32	10.2	99-02+	9.536	355	363	353	10	6.9	0.4	2.12
Weighted avg.			8.083		6.7	100.90	7.995				18	4.6		

Analysis as of 4/4/00

* Yields and spreads are computed relative to a constant prepayment assumption.
** OASs and durations are calculated by a Monte Carlo simulation of rates which utilizes Prudential Securities Inc.'s manufactured housing prepayment model.
*** Option cost is defined as the difference between the OAS at market volatility and at zero volatility.

Exhibit 10: Analysis of Agency Fixed-Rate MBS

Issuer Fannie Mae   Volatility Assumption Market implied

Class	Coupon (%)	Maturity	Avg. Life	Price	Yield (%)	Spread to WAL (bps)	Zero-vol Spd. (bps)	OAS* (bps)	Option Cost** (bps)	Eff. Dur.	Eff. Conv.
FNMA	6%	30-year	9.4	91-30	7.40	151	155	125	30	6.0	0.1
FNMA	6.5%	30-year	9.2	94-18	7.46	156	162	122	40	5.6	-0.1
FNMA	7%	30-year	8.7	96-27	7.59	166	174	122	52	5.1	-0.4
FNMA	7.5%	30-year	7.8	98-29	7.74	177	185	122	63	4.6	-0.8
FNMA	8%	30-year	6.7	100-23	7.86	183	194	124	70	3.9	-1.5

Analysis as of 4/4/00

* OASs and durations are calculated by a Monte Carlo simulation of rates which utilizes Prudential Securities Inc.'s Agency prepayment model.
** Option cost is defined as the difference between the OAS at market volatility and at zero volatility.

Exhibit 11: Analysis of Agency CMO

Issuer FNMA   Type Agency REMIC   Volatility Assumption Market implied

Deal Date January 2000   Prepay. Assumption* 153 PSA

Class	Size ($ mm)	Type	Coupon (%)	Maturity	Avg. Life	Price	Yield (%)	Spread to WAL (bps)	Zero-vol Spd. (bps)	OAS** (bps)	Option Cost*** (bps)	Eff. Dur.	Eff. Conv.	St. Dev. of Avg. Life
A	82.5	Seq	7%	4/28	5.6	98-02	7.50	135	148	98	50	3.8	-0.6	1.70
B	65.5	Seq	7%	1/26	3.9	98-20	7.43	120	130	84	46	3.0	-0.6	1.14
C	10.1	Seq	7%	5/27	10.5	96-01	7.64	175	178	122	56	6.2	-0.4	3.57
D	6.8	Seq	7%	4/28	13.1	95-04	7.67	180	193	137	56	7.3	0.1	4.31
VA	12.5	AD Seq	7%	8/10	5.8	99-04	7.23	110	118	107	11	4.0	0.1	0.48
VB	10.9	AD Seq	7%	12/15	13.0	96-22	7.47	160	173	139	34	7.1	0.8	2.40
Z	11.6	Z-Seq	7%	2/30	19.7	89-24	7.69	185	216	168	48	17.7	7.3	4.01
Weighted avg life:					6.8					Weighted avg OC	43			

Analysis as of 4/4/00

* Yields and spreads are computed relative to a constant prepayment assumption.
** OASs and durations are calculated by a Monte Carlo simulation of rates which utilizes Prudential Securities Inc.'s Agency prepayment model.
*** Option cost is defined as the difference between the OAS at market volatility and at zero volatility.

The maturity of the loans is important since the longer borrowers possess the option to prepay a loan, the more chances the option has to be exercised. In addition, depending on the seasoning of the underlying loans, prepayments may be more or less interest rate sensitive; after some time, borrowers are more able to refinance. Finally, very seasoned loans exhibit prepayment burnout: the most savvy borrowers have already refinanced if the opportunity presented itself, and the remaining ones are less inclined to do so.

In a structured transaction, depending on the sequencing of cash flows, the value of the option can vary. The very short tranches have low optionality given no seasoning. The highest optionality is on the 3- and 5-year structures where borrowers are at the top of the prepayment ramp and the collateral is slightly seasoned. The longest tranches have low optionality because of prepayment burnout.

Chapter 9

Analysis of Floating-Rate Securities

T he term "floating-rate security" covers several different types of securities with one common feature: the interest rate will vary over the instrument's life. The rate may be based on some market interest rate (e.g., LIBOR) or a constructed interest rate (e.g., Constant Maturity Treasury rate), a non-interest rate financial benchmark or price (e.g., CPI), or it can be determined at the issuer's discretion. Typically, floating-rate securities have coupons based on a short-term money market rate or index that resets more than once a year, such as weekly, monthly, quarterly, or semiannually. Usually, the term "adjustable-rate" or "variable-rate" security refers to those issues with coupons based mostly on a long-term interest rate or index and reset not more than annually. In this chapter, we will refer to both floating-rate securities and adjustable-rate securities as floating-rate securities or simply floaters.

Our focus in this chapter is on the analysis of floating-rate securities. In the first section, we describe the basic features of floaters. Next, we discuss the valuation of floaters without embedded options. In addition, we outline a framework of valuing floaters with embedded options. Most market participants use some "spread" measure to assess a floater's relative value. These measures include spread for life, adjusted simple margin, adjusted total margin, discount margin, and option-adjusted spread. In the last section of this chapter, we explain and illustrate these measures, highlighting their limitations.

GENERAL FEATURES OF FLOATERS

At one time it was fairly simple to describe the structure of a floater. The coupon rate was specified in terms of a simple coupon formula and there was typically a cap, and possibly a floor. In today's capital market there is a wide range of floating-rate structures. These structures have been created for issuers by financial engineers using certain derivative instruments (typically, swaps and options) combined with medium-term notes. The resulting floaters are referred to as *structured notes*. Also, financial engineers have created floaters in the mortgage-backed securities and asset-backed securities markets by slicing up cash flows from a pool of loans or receivables. Not surprisingly, floaters are created from a pool of loans or receivables that pay a floating rate. What is surprising is how financial engineers have created (without the use of derivatives) floaters when the underlying loans pay a fixed rate.

In this section we will describe the general features of floaters: the various coupon structures, caps and floors, principal repayment features, and early redemption features.

Coupon Structures

A floater is an instrument whose coupon rate is reset at designated dates in the future based on the value of some reference rate. The coupon rate can be determined by a coupon formula, by a schedule, or at the discretion of the issuer.

Coupon Formula

The typical formula that expresses the coupon rate in terms of the reference rate is:

Reference rate + Quoted margin

The *quoted margin* is the adjustment that the issuer agrees to make to the reference rate. For example, suppose that the reference rate is the 1-month London interbank offered rate (LIBOR) and that the quoted margin is 100 basis points. Then the coupon formula is:

1-month LIBOR + 100 basis points

So, if 1-month LIBOR on the coupon reset date is 5%, the coupon rate is reset for that period at 6% (5% plus 100 basis points).

The quoted margin need not be a positive value. The quoted margin could be subtracted from the reference rate. For example, the reference rate could be the yield on a 5-year Treasury security and the coupon rate could reset every six months based on the following coupon formula:

5-year Treasury yield − 90 basis points

The quoted margin is −90 basis points. So, if the 5-year Treasury yield is 7% on the coupon reset date, the coupon rate is 6.1% (7% minus 90 basis points).

Mismatched Floaters There is no requirement that the frequency with which the coupon is reset be equal to the frequency of the coupon payment. For example, consider the Wells Fargo & Company's Floating Rate Subordinated Capital Notes that matured in August 1, 1996. The coupon rate for this floater reset weekly at $\frac{1}{16}$ of 1% over 3-month LIBOR and payable quarterly. That is, the coupon rate resets a number of times during the period based on the reference rate applicable to the whole period. The reference rate was based on 3-month LIBOR, not 1-week LIBOR. Floaters with this characteristic are called *mismatched floaters*.

Inverse Floaters Typically, the coupon formula on floaters is such that the coupon rate increases when the reference rate increases, and decreases when the reference rate decreases. There are issues whose coupon rate moves in the opposite direction from the change in the reference rate. Such issues are called *inverse floaters* or *reverse floaters.*[1]

In the agency, corporate, and municipal markets inverse floaters are created as structured notes. Inverse floaters in the mortgage-backed securities market are common and are created without the use of derivatives, as discussed in Chapter 7.

The coupon formula for an inverse floater is:

$K - L \times$ (Reference rate)

When L is greater than 1, the security is referred to as a *leveraged inverse floater.*

For example, suppose that for a particular inverse floater K is 12% and L is 1. Then the coupon reset formula would be:

12% − Reference rate

Suppose that the reference rate is 1-month LIBOR, then the coupon formula would be

12% − 1-month LIBOR

If in some month 1-month LIBOR at the coupon reset date is 5%, the coupon rate for the period is 7%. If in the next month 1-month LIBOR declines to 4.5%, the coupon rate increases to 7.5%.

Notice that if 1-month LIBOR exceeded 12%, then the coupon formula would produce a negative coupon rate. To prevent this, there is a floor imposed on the coupon rate. Typically, the floor is zero. There is a cap on the inverse floater. This occurs if 1-month LIBOR is zero. In that unlikely event, the maximum coupon rate is 12% for our hypothetical inverse floater. In general, it will be the value of K in the coupon formula for an inverse floater.

Suppose instead that the coupon formula for an inverse floater whose reference rate is 1-month LIBOR is as follows:

28% − 3 × (1-month LIBOR)

If 1-month LIBOR at a reset date is 5%, then the coupon rate for that month is 13%. If in the next month 1-month LIBOR declines to 4%, the coupon rate increases to 16%. Thus, a decline in 1-month LIBOR of 100 basis points increases the coupon rate by 300 basis points. This is because the value for L in the coupon reset formula is 3. Assuming neither the cap nor the floor is reached, for each one basis point change in 1-month LIBOR the coupon rate changes by 3 basis points.

As an example, consider an inverse floater issued by the Federal Home Loan Bank in April 1999. This issue matures in April 2002 and delivers quarterly payments according to the following formula:

18% − 2.5 × (3-month LIBOR)

---

[1] These issues were also referred to as *yield curve notes*. For example, the General Motors Acceptance Corporation's Yield Curve Notes that were due April 15, 1993 were based on 15.25% minus 6-month LIBOR.

This inverse floater has a floor of 3% and a cap of 15.5%. Beginning July 29, 1999, this issue is callable at par with five business days notice.

Deleveraged Floaters The coupon rate for a deleveraged floater is computed as a fraction of the reference rate plus a fixed percentage. For example, Banker's Trust issued such a floater in April 1992 that matures in March 2003. This issue delivers quarterly coupon payments according to the following formula: 2.65% + 0.40 × (10-year Constant Maturity Treasury rate) with a floor of 6%.

Dual-Indexed Floaters The coupon rate for a dual-indexed floater is typically a fixed percentage plus the difference between two reference rates. For example, the Federal Home Loan Bank System issued a floater in July 1993 (matured in July 1996) whose coupon rate was the difference between the 10-year Constant Maturity Treasury rate and 3-month LIBOR plus 160 basis points. This issue reset and paid quarterly.

Range Notes A special type of floater is a *range note*. For this instrument, the coupon rate is equal to the reference rate as long as the reference rate is within a certain range at the reset date. If the reference rate is outside of the range, the coupon rate is zero for that period. The range note is a structured note.

For example, a 3-year range note might specify that the reference rate is 1-year LIBOR and that the coupon rate resets every year. The coupon rate for the year will be 1-year LIBOR as long as 1-year LIBOR at the coupon reset date falls within the range as specified below:

	Year 1	Year 2	Year 3
Lower limit of range	4.5%	5.25%	6.00%
Upper limit of range	5.5%	6.75%	7.50%

If 1-year LIBOR is outside of the range, the coupon rate is zero. For example, if in Year 1 1-year LIBOR is 5% at the coupon reset date, the coupon rate for the year is 5%. However, if 1-year LIBOR is 6%, the coupon rate for the year is zero since 1-year LIBOR is greater than the upper limit for Year 1 of 5.5%.

Consider a range note issued by Sallie Mae in August 1996 that matures in August 2003. This issue makes coupon payments quarterly. The investor earns 3-month LIBOR plus 155 basis points for every day during the quarter that 3-month LIBOR is between 3% and 9%. Interest will accrue at 0% for each day that 3-month LIBOR is outside this range. As a result, this range note has a floor of 0%.

Ratchet Bonds In 1998 a new adjustable-rate structure was brought to market by the Tennessee Valley Authority. This structure, referred to as a *ratchet bond*, has a coupon rate that adjusts periodically at a fixed spread over a non-money market reference rate such as the 10-year constant maturity Treasury. However, it can only adjust downward based on a coupon formula. Once the coupon rate is adjusted down, it cannot be readjusted up even if the reference rate subsequently increases. Basically, a ratchet bond is designed to replicate the cash flow pattern generated by a series of conventional callable bonds.

Floaters with a Changing Quoted Margin

Some issues provide for a change in the quoted margin at certain intervals over a floater's life. These issues are often referred to as *stepped spread floaters* because the quoted margin could either step to a higher or lower level over the security's life. For example, consider Standard Chartered Bank's floater that matures in December 2006. From issuance until December 2001, the coupon formula is 3-month LIBOR plus 40 basis points. From December 2001 until maturity, the quoted margin "steps up" to 90 basis points.

Some issues are on an "either or" basis. One such example is Barclays-American Corporation Floating Rate Subordinated Notes that were due November 1, 1990. Interest was payable quarterly and calculated monthly at the higher of (1) the prime rate minus 125 basis points or (2) the 30-day commercial paper rate plus 25 basis points. Other issues have their coupon rates determined through a Dutch auction procedure or remarketing process, with the applicable interest rate the one at which all sell orders and all buy orders are satisfied.

Reset Margin Determined at Issuer Discretion

There are floaters which require that the issuer reset the coupon rate so that the issue will trade at a predetermined price (typically above par). These issues are called *extendible reset bonds*. The coupon rate at the reset date may be the average of rates suggested by two investment banking firms. The new rate will then reflect: (1) the level of interest rates at the reset date, and (2) the margin required by market at the reset date. Notice the difference between an extendible reset bond and a typical floater that resets based on a coupon formula. For the latter, the coupon rate resets based on a known margin over some reference rate (i.e., the quoted margin). In contrast, the coupon rate on an extendible reset issue is reset based on the margin required by the market at the reset date as determined by the issuer or suggested by several investment banking firms.

For example, consider the Primerica Corporation's Extendible Notes that were due August 1, 1996. This issue was scheduled for an interest rate change on August 1, 1987. The coupon rate was 13.25%, but as market rates were considerably lower, the issuer set the rate from August 1, 1987 through July 31, 1992 at 8.40%, about 105% of the then 5-year Constant Maturity Treasury rate of 8.00%. The minimum percentage under the indenture was 102.5%. Apparently this rate was not satisfactory to the holders and many notes were either put back to the issuer during the first two weeks of July 1987 or the holders threatened to do so. In any event, several days prior to the commencement of the new rate and interest period a notice appeared in the newspaper of record announcing that the company "... is exercising its option under the terms of the Extendible Notes due 1996 to establish an interest rate higher than the rate previously announced..." The rate was increased to 8.875%, equal to 110.9% of the Constant Maturity Treasury.

Non-Interest Rate Indexes

While the reference rate for most floaters is an interest rate or an interest rate index, a wide variety of reference rates appear in coupon formulas. This is particularly true for structured notes. The coupon for a floater could be indexed to movements in foreign exchange rates, the price of a commodity (e.g., crude oil), movements in an equity index (e.g., the S&P 500), or movements in a bond index (e.g., the Merrill Lynch Corporate Bond Index). In fact, through financial engineering, issuers have been able to structure floaters with almost any reference rate. As an example, Merrill Lynch issued in April 1983 Stock Market Annual Reset Term Notes which mature in December 1999. These notes pay interest semiannually. The formula for the coupon rate is 0.65 multiplied by the annual return of the S&P MidCap 400 during the calendar year. These notes have a floor of 3% and a cap of 10%.

In several countries, there are government bonds whose coupon formula is tied to an inflation index. The U.S. Treasury in January 1997 began auctioning 10-year Treasury notes whose semiannual coupon interest depends on the rate of inflation as measured by the Consumer Price Index for All Urban Consumers (i.e., CPI-U). In the market, these issues are referred to as *Treasury Inflation-Protection Securities* (TIPS). The first such issue matures on January 15, 2007 and carries a coupon rate of 3.375%. The initial value of the CPI-U was 158.43548. On January 1, 1998, the CPI-U was 161.55484. Accordingly, the semiannual coupon payment (per $100 of par value) was computed as follows:

$$\$1.72027 = (0.03375/2) \times (161.55484/158.43548) \times \$100$$

For a conventional 10-year U.S. Treasury note with a fixed coupon rate the semiannual coupon payment would have been $1.68875 (per $100 of par value).

In 1997 corporations and agencies in the United States began issuing inflation-linked (or inflation-indexed) bonds. For example, in February 1997, J.P. Morgan & Company issued a 15-year bond that pays the CPI plus 400 basis points & Co. In the same month, the Federal Home Loan Bank issued a 5-year bond with a coupon rate equal to the CPI plus 315 basis points and a 10-year bond with a coupon rate equal to the CPI plus 337 basis points.

Caps and Floors

A floater may have a restriction on the maximum coupon rate that will be paid at any reset date. The maximum coupon rate is called a *cap*.[2] For example, suppose for our hypothetical floater whose coupon formula is 1-month LIBOR plus 100 basis points, there is a cap of 11%. If 1-month LIBOR is 10.5% at a coupon reset date, then the coupon formula would give a value of 11.5%. However, the cap restricts the coupon rate to 11%. Thus, for our hypothetical security, once 1-month LIBOR exceeds 10%, the coupon rate is capped at 11%.

---

[2] Many issues state that the maximum rate is 25% due to New York State's usury law but holders of $2.5 million or more of an issue are exempt from this.

Because a cap restricts the coupon rate from increasing, a cap is an unattractive feature for the investor. In contrast, there could be a minimum coupon rate specified for a floater. The minimum coupon rate is called a *floor*. If the coupon formula produces a coupon rate that is below the floor, the floor is paid instead. Thus, a floor is an attractive feature for the investor. For example, First Chicago (now 1st Chicago NBD Corp.) issued a floored floating-rate note in July 1993 that matures in July 2003. This issue delivers quarterly coupon payments and the coupon formula is 3-month LIBOR + 12.5 basis points with a minimum coupon rate of 4.25%.

Some issues have declining floors. For example, for a Citicorp floater issue that was due September 1, 1998, the minimum rate was 7.50% through August 31, 1983, then 7.00% through August 31, 1988, and then 6.50% to maturity.

A floater can have both a cap and floor. This feature is referred to as a *collar*. For example, the Economic Development Corporation issued a collared floater in February 1993 that makes semiannual coupon payments and matures in February 2003. The coupon formula is 6-month LIBOR with a minimum coupon rate of 5% and a maximum coupon rate of 8%. There are some issues that grant the issuer the right to convert the floater into a fixed coupon rate at some time. There are also some issues referred to as *drop-lock bonds*, which automatically change the floating coupon rate into a fixed coupon rate under certain circumstances.

Principal Repayment Features

A floater will either have a stated maturity date, or it may be a *perpetual*, also called *undated*, issue (i.e., it has no stated maturity date).[3] For floaters that do mature, the issuer agrees to repay the principal by the stated maturity date. The issuer can agree to repay the entire amount borrowed in one lump sum payment at the maturity date.

Amortizing Securities Fixed-income securities backed by pools of loans (mortgage-backed securities and asset-backed securities) often have a schedule of principal repayments. Such securities are said to be *amortizing securities*. For many loans, the payments are structured so that when the last loan payment is made, the entire amount owed is fully paid off.

Indexed Amortizing Notes Thus far in our description of floaters, we have explained how the coupon rate depends on the reference rate. There are notes where the coupon rate is fixed but the principal repayments are made prior to the stated maturity date based on the prevailing value for the reference rate. The principal payments are structured to accelerate when the reference rate is low. These structures are referred to as *indexed amortizing notes*. So, technically, while these instruments are not floaters in the sense that their coupon rate changes with a ref-

---

[3] For example, in April 1997, Sakura Capital Funding issued a perpetual floating-rate note with a coupon formula of 3-month LIBOR plus 90 basis points. The issue is callable in September 2002. However, if the issuer does not call the issue, the coupon rate steps up to 240 basis points over 3-month LIBOR.

erence rate, they can be viewed as "principal floaters" in that the principal repayment floats with a reference rate.

Early Redemption Features

Early redemption features grant the issuer and/or the investor an option to retire all or a portion of the outstanding principal prior to the stated maturity date. Below we describe these features.

Call and Prepayment Provisions

As with fixed-rate issues, a floater may be callable. The call option gives the issuer of the floater the right to retire the issue prior to the stated maturity date. The advantage of the call option to the issuer is that at some time in the future either (1) the general level of interest rates may fall so that the issuer can call the issue and replace it with a fixed-rate issue or (2) the required margin decreases so that the issuer can call the issue and replace it with a floater with a lower quoted margin. This right is a disadvantage to the investor in floaters since proceeds received must be reinvested at a lower interest rate or a lower margin. As a result, an issuer who wants to include this right as part of a floater offering must compensate investors by offering a higher quoted margin.

Unlike conventional fixed-rate issues, many have call features that permit the issuer to redeem the bonds only on specific dates, often the date on which the holder may put the bond. Others have fairly standard call features. Only a few of the issues have sinking funds requiring the periodic retirement of a portion of the issue.

For amortizing securities that are backed by loans and have a schedule of principal repayments, individual borrowers typically have the option to pay off all or part of their loan prior to the scheduled date. Any principal repayment prior to the scheduled date is called a *prepayment*. The right of borrowers to prepay is called the *prepayment option*. Basically, the prepayment option is the same as a call option. However, unlike a call option, there is not a call price that depends on when the borrower pays off the issue. Typically, the price at which a loan is prepaid is at par value. We discussed this feature of floaters in Chapter 7.

Put Provision

An issue with a *put provision* included in the indenture grants the security holder the right to sell the issue back to the issuer at a specified price on designated dates. The specified price is called the *put price*. The put feature in floaters varies. Some issues permit the holder to require the issuer to redeem the issue on any interest payment date. Others allow the put to be exercised only when the coupon is reset. In cases of extendible notes where the new terms, including the coupon and the interest period are reset only every few years, the put may be exercised only on those dates. The time required for prior notification to the issuer or its agent varies from as little as four days to as much as a couple of months.

The advantage of the put provision to the holder of the floater is that if after the issue date the margin required by the market for the issue to trade at par rises above the issue's quoted margin, the investor can force the issuer to redeem the floater at the put price and then reinvest the proceeds in a floater with a higher quoted margin.

VALUING A RISKY FLOATER

We begin our valuation discussion with the simplest possible case — a default risk-free floater with no embedded options. Suppose the floater pays cash flows quarterly and the coupon formula is 3-month LIBOR flat. The coupon reset and payment dates are assumed to coincide. Under these idealized circumstances, the floater's price will always equal par on the coupon reset dates. This result holds because the floater's new coupon rate is always reset to reflect the current market rate (e.g., 3-month LIBOR). Accordingly, on each coupon reset date, any change in interest rates (via the reference rate) is also reflected in the size of the floater's coupon payment.

The discussion is easily expanded to include risky floaters (e.g., corporate floaters) without a call feature or other embedded options. We will illustrate the valuation of a risky floater with a non-callable floating-rate note issued by Merrill Lynch (ticker symbol "MER 06/03") that matures June 24, 2003. The Security Description Screen (DES) from Bloomberg is presented in Exhibit 1. This floater delivers cash flows quarterly employing a coupon formula equal to 3-month LIBOR plus 15 basis points and does not possess a cap or a floor. As before, the coupon reset and payment dates are assumed to be the same. This floater pays a spread of 15 basis points above the reference rate (i.e., the quoted margin) to compensate the investor for the risks (e.g., default, liquidity, etc.) associated with this security. The quoted margin is established on the floater's issue date and is fixed to maturity. If the market's evaluation of the risk of holding the floater does not change, the risky floater will be repriced to par on each coupon reset date just as with the default-free floater. This result holds as long as the issuer's risk can be characterized by a constant markup over the risk-free rate.[4]

The more likely scenario, however, is that the market's perception of the security's risk will change over time. A perceived change in the floater's risk manifests itself in a divergence between the quoted margin (which is fixed at issue) and the spread the market requires for bearing the security's risks — henceforth, the *required margin*. When this divergence occurs, the risky floater will not be repriced to par on the coupon reset date. If the required margin increases (decreases) relative to the quoted margin, the floater will be repriced at a discount (premium) to par value.

---

[4] See Jess Yawitz, Howard Kaufold, Thomas Macirowski, and Michael Smirlock, "The Pricing and Duration of Floating-Rate Bonds," *The Journal of Portfolio Management* (Summer 1987), pp. 49-56.

Exhibit 1: Bloomberg Security Description of a Merrill Lynch Floater Maturing June 24, 2003

```
5                                              P066 Corp   D E S

SECURITY  DESCRIPTION              Page 1/ 3
MERRILL LYNCH    MER Float 06/03   N O T   P R I C E D
```

ISSUER INFORMATION	IDENTIFIERS		1) Additional Sec Info
Name MERRILL LYNCH & CO	Common	008850305	2) Floating Rates
Type Finance-Invest Bnkr/Brkr	ISIN	US590188JC35	3) Identifiers
Market of Issue GLOBAL	CUSIP	590188JC3	4) Ratings
SECURITY INFORMATION	RATINGS		5) Fees/Restrictions
Country USA Currency USD	Moody's	Aa3	6) Prospectus
Collateral Type NOTES	S&P	AA-	7) Sec. Specific News
Calc Typ (21) FLOAT RATE NOTE	FI	AA	8) Involved Parties
Maturity 6/24/2003 Series	ISSUE SIZE		9) Custom Notes
NORMAL	Amt Issued		10) Issuer Information
Coupon5.15 FLOATING QUARTLY	USD 750,000.00 (M)		11) Pricing Sources
QUARTL US LIB+15 ACT/360	Amt Outstanding		12) Prospectus Request
Announcement Dt 6/17/98	USD 750,000.00 (M)		
Int. Accrual Dt 6/24/98	Min Piece/Increment		
1st Settle Date 6/24/98	1,000.00/ 1,000.00		
1st Coupon Date 9/24/98	Par Amount 1,000.00		
Iss Pr 99.912 Reoffer 99.912	LEAD MANAGER/EXCHANGE		
	ML		65) Old DES
HAVE PROSPECTUS	LUXEMBOURG		66) Send as Attachment

```
CPN RATE=3MO US$LIBOR +15BP. UNSEC'D. DISC MARGIN: 17BP OVER 3MO LIBOR.
```

Source: Bloomberg Financial Markets

Intuitively, the pricing expression for a risky floater can be thought of as possessing two components: (1) a floater whose quoted margin and required margin are the same and (2) a "differential risk annuity" that delivers payments equal to the difference between the quoted margin and the required margin multiplied by the par value. Note it is the differential risk annuity that causes the floater's price to deviate from par on a coupon reset date. Specifically, if the required margin is above (below) the quoted margin, then the differential risk annuity will deliver negative (positive) cash flows and the floater's price will be reset at a discount (premium) to its par value.

We will illustrate this process using the Merrill Lynch floater from Exhibit 1. For ease of exposition, we will invoke some simplifying assumptions. First, the issue will be priced on a coupon reset date. Second, although this floater has an ACT/360 day-count convention, for simplicity we will assume that each quarter has 91 days. Third, we will assume initially that the LIBOR yield curve is flat such that all implied 3-month LIBOR forward rates are the same.[5] Note the same principles apply with equal force when these assumptions are relaxed.

Let's value the Merrill Lynch floater on June 24, 1999. From Exhibit 1, we know this floater's coupon rate is equal to 3-month plus 15 basis points and delivers cash flows quarterly. Since this floater matures on June 24, 2003, there

---

[5] We will relax this assumption shortly.

are 16 coupon payments remaining. Assume that 3-month LIBOR is 5% and will remain at that level until the floater's maturity. Finally, suppose the required margin is also 15 basis points so the quoted margin and the required margin are the same. Exhibit 2 illustrates the valuation process.

The first column in Exhibit 2 simply lists the quarterly periods. Next, column (2) lists the number of days in each quarterly coupon period assumed to be 91 days. Column (3) indicates the assumed current value of 3-month LIBOR. In period 0, 3-month LIBOR is the current 3-month spot rate. In periods 1 through 16, these rates are implied 3-month LIBOR forward rates derived from the current LIBOR yield curve.[6] For ease of exposition, we will call these rates *forward rates*. Recall for a floater, the coupon rate is set at the beginning of the period and paid at the end. For example, the coupon rate in the first period depends on the value of 3-month LIBOR at period 0 plus the quoted margin. In this first illustration, 3-month LIBOR is assumed to remain constant at 5%. Column (4) is the quoted margin of 15 basis points and remains fixed to maturity.

Exhibit 2: Valuing a Risk Floater When the Market's Required Margin Equals the Quoted Margin*

(1) Coupon Period	(2) Day Count	(3) Forward Rate (%)	(4) Quoted Margin (%)	(5) Cash Flow	(6) Required Margin (%)	(7) Discount Factor	(8) PV of Cash Flow
0	91	5.00				1.000000	
1	91	5.00	0.15	$1.301806	0.15	0.987149	$1.285076
2	91	5.00	0.15	1.301806	0.15	0.974464	1.268562
3	91	5.00	0.15	1.301806	0.15	0.961941	1.252260
4	91	5.00	0.15	1.301806	0.15	0.949579	1.236168
5	91	5.00	0.15	1.301806	0.15	0.937377	1.220282
6	91	5.00	0.15	1.301806	0.15	0.925331	1.204600
7	91	5.00	0.15	1.301806	0.15	0.913439	1.189120
8	91	5.00	0.15	1.301806	0.15	0.901701	1.173839
9	91	5.00	0.15	1.301806	0.15	0.890113	1.158755
10	91	5.00	0.15	1.301806	0.15	0.878675	1.143864
11	91	5.00	0.15	1.301806	0.15	0.867383	1.129164
12	91	5.00	0.15	1.301806	0.15	0.856237	1.114654
13	91	5.00	0.15	1.301806	0.15	0.845233	1.100329
14	91	5.00	0.15	1.301806	0.15	0.834371	1.086189
15	91	5.00	0.15	1.301806	0.15	0.823649	1.072231
16	91	5.00	0.15	101.301800	0.15	0.813065	82.264910
							Price = 100.000000

* Assumes 3-month LIBOR remains constant at 5%

---

[6] The implied LIBOR forward rates can also be determined using Eurodollar CD futures contracts as described in Chapter 12.

The cash flow is found by multiplying the coupon rate and the maturity value (assumed to be 100). However, the coupon rate (the forward rate in the previous period plus the quoted margin) must be adjusted for the number of days in the quarterly payment period. The formula to do so is:

$$\frac{\text{Coupon rate} \times \text{Number of days in period}}{360} \times 100$$

In addition to the projected cash flow, in period 16 the investor receives the maturity value of 100. The projected cash flows of the Merrill Lynch floater are shown in Column (5).

It is from the assumed values of 3-month LIBOR (i.e., the current spot rate and the implied forward rates) and the required margin in Column (6) that the discount rate that will be used to determine the present value of the cash flows will be calculated. The discount factor is found as follows:[7]

$$\frac{\text{Discount factor in the previous period}}{1 + (\text{Fwd. rate in previous period} + \text{Required margin}) \times \text{No. of days in period}/360}$$

The discount factors are shown in Column (7).

Finally, Column (8) is the present value of each of the cash flows and is computed by taking the product of the cash flow in Column (5) and the discount factor in Column (7). The floater's value is the sum of these present values and appears at the bottom of Column (8). Thus, a floater whose quoted margin and market's required margin are the same trades at par.

It is important to stress that this result holds *regardless of the path 3-month LIBOR takes in the future*. To see this, we replicate the process described in Exhibit 2 once again with one important exception. Rather than remaining constant, we assume that 3-month LIBOR forward rates increase by 1 basis point per quarter until the floater's maturity. These calculations are displayed in Exhibit 3. As before, the present value of the floater's projected cash flows is 100. When the market's required margin equals the quoted margin, any increase/decrease in the floater's projected cash flows will result in an offsetting increase/decrease in the floater's discount factors leaving the total present value of the cash flow equal to par.

Now let's consider the case when the required margin does not equal the quoted margin. A risky floater can be separated into two components.[8] Namely, a floater selling at par (i.e., the required margin equals the floater's quoted margin) and a "differential risk annuity" that causes the floater to deviate from par. A differential risk annuity is a series of constant payments (until a floater's maturity date) equal to the difference between the quoted margin and the required margin multiplied by the par value. A position in a risky floater can be described as a long position in a par floater and a long (short) position in a differential risk annuity. A

---

[7] The formulas presented below are adapted from Chapter 6 of Ravi E. Dattatreya, Raj E.S. Venkatesh, and Vijaya E. Venkatesh, *Interest Rate & Currency Swaps* (Chicago: Probus Publishing, 1994).

[8] See Steven I. Dym, "A Generalized Approach to Price and Duration of Non-Par Floating-Rate Notes," *The Journal of Portfolio Management* (Summer 1998), pp. 102-107.

long (short) position in the differential risk annuity indicates that the required margin has decreased (increased) since the floater's issue date. Accordingly, the price of a risky floater is equal to par plus the present value of the differential risk annuity when the required margin and the quoted margin are not the same.

To illustrate, we will value the same Merrill Lynch floater assuming that the required margin is now 20 basis points. For this to occur, some dimension of the floater's risk must have increased since the floater's issuance. Now in order to be reset to par, the Merrill Lynch floater would hypothetically have to possess a coupon rate equal to 3-month LIBOR plus 20 basis points. Since the quoted margin is fixed, the floater's price must fall to reflect the market's perceived increase in the security's risk.

Exhibit 4 illustrates the calculation. Once again for simplicity, we assume that 3-month LIBOR remains unchanged at 5% and there are 91 days in each coupon period. Since a risky floater can be thought of as par plus the differential risk annuity, all that is necessary is to take the present value of the annuity. Each annuity payment is computed as follows:

Differential risk annuity payment

$$= \frac{((\text{Quoted margin} - \text{Required margin}) \times \text{Number of days in period})}{360} \times 100$$

Exhibit 3: Valuing a Risk Floater When the Market's Required Margin Equals the Quoted Margin*

(1)	(2)	(3)	(4)	(5)	(6)	(7)	(8)
Coupon Period	Day Count	Forward Rate (%)	Quoted Margin (%)	Cash Flow	Required Margin (%)	Discount Factor	PV of Cash Flow
0	91	5.00				1.000000	
1	91	5.01	0.15	1.301806	0.15	0.987149	$1.285076
2	91	5.02	0.15	1.304333	0.15	0.974439	1.270994
3	91	5.03	0.15	1.306861	0.15	0.961869	1.257029
4	91	5.04	0.15	1.309389	0.15	0.949437	1.243182
5	91	5.05	0.15	1.311917	0.15	0.937143	1.229453
6	91	5.06	0.15	1.314444	0.15	0.924984	1.215840
7	91	5.07	0.15	1.316972	0.15	0.912961	1.202344
8	91	5.08	0.15	1.319500	0.15	0.901071	1.188963
9	91	5.09	0.15	1.322028	0.15	0.889314	1.175698
10	91	5.10	0.15	1.324556	0.15	0.877689	1.162547
11	91	5.11	0.15	1.327083	0.15	0.866194	1.149511
12	91	5.12	0.15	1.329611	0.15	0.854828	1.136588
13	91	5.13	0.15	1.332139	0.15	0.843590	1.123779
14	91	5.14	0.15	1.337194	0.15	0.832458	1.113159
15	91	5.15	0.15	1.339722	0.15	0.821453	1.100519
16	91	5.16	0.15	101.342300	0.15	0.810573	82.145320
						Price =	100.000000

* Assumes 3-month LIBOR increases 1 basis point per quarter until maturity.

Exhibit 4: Valuing the Differential Risk Annuity When the Market's Required Margin is Greater Than the Quoted Margin*

(1) Coupon Period	(2) Day Count	(3) Forward Rate (%)	(4) Quoted Margin	(5) Required Margin (%)	(6) Cash Flow	(7) Discount Factor	(8) PV of Cash Flow
0	91	5.00				1.000000	
1	91	5.00	0.15	0.20	−0.01264	0.987026	−0.01247
2	91	5.00	0.15	0.20	−0.01264	0.974221	−0.01231
3	91	5.00	0.15	0.20	−0.01264	0.961581	−0.01215
4	91	5.00	0.15	0.20	−0.01264	0.949106	−0.01200
5	91	5.00	0.15	0.20	−0.01264	0.936792	−0.01184
6	91	5.00	0.15	0.20	−0.01264	0.924638	−0.01169
7	91	5.00	0.15	0.20	−0.01264	0.912642	−0.01153
8	91	5.00	0.15	0.20	−0.01264	0.900801	−0.01139
9	91	5.00	0.15	0.20	−0.01264	0.889115	−0.01124
10	91	5.00	0.15	0.20	−0.01264	0.877579	−0.01109
11	91	5.00	0.15	0.20	−0.01264	0.866194	−0.01095
12	91	5.00	0.15	0.20	−0.01264	0.854956	−0.01081
13	91	5.00	0.15	0.20	−0.01264	0.843864	−0.01067
14	91	5.00	0.15	0.20	−0.01264	0.832915	−0.01053
15	91	5.00	0.15	0.20	−0.01264	0.822109	−0.01039
16	91	5.00	0.15	0.20	−0.01264	0.811443	−0.01026
						Total Present Value = −0.1813	

* Assumes 3-month LIBOR remains constant at 5%

The quoted margin and required margin are in Columns (4) and (5), respectively. These cash flows are contained in Column (6). The discount factors are computed as described previously with the exception of the larger required margin. The discount factors appear in Column (7). The present value of each cash flow is in Column (8) and is just the product of the cash flow (Column (6)) and its corresponding discount factor (Column (7)). The present value of the differential risk annuity is −0.1813 and is shown at the bottom of Column (8).

Once the present value of the differential risk annuity is determined, the price of the risky Merrill Lynch floater is simply the sum of 100 (price of the floater per $100 of par value when the quoted margin and required margin are the same) and the present value of the differential risk annuity. In our example,

Price of risky floater = 100 + (−0.1813) = 99.8187

When the required margin exceeds the quoted margin, the floater will be priced at a discount to par value. However, the size of the discount will depend on the assumed path 3-month LIBOR will take in the future.[9]

[9] Raymond J. Iwanowski, "An Investor's Guide to Floating-Rate Notes: Conventions, Mathematics, and Relative Valuation," Chapter 9 in Thomas S.Y. Ho (ed.), *Fixed Income Solutions* (Chicago: Irwin Professional Publishing, 1996).

Exhibit 5: Valuing the Differential Risk Annuity When the Market's Required Margin is Less Than the Quoted Margin*

(1) Coupon Period	(2) Day Count	(3) Forward Rate (%)	(4) Quoted Margin (%)	(5) Required Margin (%)	(6) Cash Flow	(7) Discount Factor	(8) PV of Cash Flow
0	91	5.00				1.000000	
1	91	5.00	0.15	0.10	0.01264	0.987272	0.01248
2	91	5.00	0.15	0.10	0.01264	0.974707	0.01232
3	91	5.00	0.15	0.10	0.01264	0.962301	0.01216
4	91	5.00	0.15	0.10	0.01264	0.950053	0.01201
5	91	5.00	0.15	0.10	0.01264	0.937961	0.01186
6	91	5.00	0.15	0.10	0.01264	0.926024	0.01170
7	91	5.00	0.15	0.10	0.01264	0.914237	0.01156
8	91	5.00	0.15	0.10	0.01264	0.902601	0.01141
9	91	5.00	0.15	0.10	0.01264	0.891113	0.01127
10	91	5.00	0.15	0.10	0.01264	0.879772	0.01112
11	91	5.00	0.15	0.10	0.01264	0.868574	0.01098
12	91	5.00	0.15	0.10	0.01264	0.857520	0.01084
13	91	5.00	0.15	0.10	0.01264	0.846605	0.01070
14	91	5.00	0.15	0.10	0.01264	0.835830	0.01056
15	91	5.00	0.15	0.10	0.01264	0.825192	0.01043
16	91	5.00	0.15	0.10	0.01264	0.814689	0.01030
						Total Present Value =	0.1817

* Assumes 3-month LIBOR remains constant at 5%

The next illustration takes up the case when the required margin is less than the quoted margin. For example, we will value the Merrill Lynch floater assuming the required margin is now 10 basis points and everything else is assumed to remain the same. Exhibit 5 presents the calculation of the differential risk annuity. Note the difference between the quoted margin (Column (4)) and the required margin (Column (5)) is positive and therefore produces a positive annuity payment (Column (6)). The discount factors (Column (7)) are computed as previously described except for the lower required margin. The present values of the differential risk annuity payments appear in Column (8) and their total appears at the bottom of the column.

In this instance, the price of the Merrill Lynch floater is given by:

Price of risky floater = 100 + 0.1817 = 100.1817

When the required margin is less than the quoted margin, the floater will be priced at a premium to par value. Note, the size of the premium is also interest-rate path dependent.

VALUATION OF FLOATERS WITH EMBEDDED OPTIONS

Given the underlying principles and concepts in the valuation process explained in Chapters 4 and 6, we turn our attention to the valuation of risky floaters with embedded options. As noted in Chapter 6, once recognition is given to an embedded option, a valuation model that incorporates the volatility of interest rates must be adopted. The lattice model (e.g., binomial tree) developed in Chapter 6 can be extended to floaters with embedded options (e.g., capped floater, range note, etc.). Recall, a lattice model permits interest rates to change each period based on a volatility assumption. Employing a lattice model to value floaters with embedded options involves adjusting the coupon rate at each node based on movements of the reference rate contained the coupon formula and whether or not the embedded options are in-the-money.[10]

MARGIN MEASURES

There are several yield spread measures or *margins* that are routinely used to evaluate floaters. The four margins commonly used are spread for life, adjusted simple margin, adjusted total margin, and discount margin. We will illustrate the calculations of these margins with a floating-rate note issued by Enron Corp. (ticker symbol "ENE 03/00") that matures March 30, 2000. This issue contains no embedded options. The floater has a coupon formula equal to 3-month LIBOR plus 45 basis points and delivers cash flows quarterly. The Yield Analysis screen (YA) from Bloomberg is presented in Exhibit 6. We will illustrate the calculation of each of the four margin measures in turn.

Exhibit 6: Bloomberg's Yield Analysis Screen for Enron Floater

```
2                                              DG41 Corp    Y A
  ENTER ALL VALUES AND HIT <GO>.
  ENRON CORP          ENE Float 03/00   N O T   P R I C E D
                      F L O A T I N G    R A T E    N O T E S
  ┌──────I N P U T S──────┬──────DATE   FIX RATE │ DATE   FIX RATE │ DATE   FIX RATE──┐
  │SETTLE DATE     4/20/99 │ 3/30/99  5.45000    │                 │                  │
  │MATURITY        3/30/00 │ 6/30/99             │                 │                  │
  │PREV PAY DATE   3/30/99 │                     │                 │                  │
  │NEXT PAY DATE   6/30/99 │                     │                 │                  │
  │REDEMPTION    100.0000  │                     │                 │                  │
  │CPN FREQUENCY       4   │                     │                 │                  │
  │REFIX FREQ          4   │                     │                 │                  │
  │BENCHMARK  US00  -3 MNTH │                    │                 │                  │
  │ASSUMED INDEX    5.0000 │                     │                 │                  │
  │QUOTED MARGIN   45.000  │                     │                 │                  │
  │REPO TO  6/30/99 4.9755 ├──FACE AMOUNT(M)       1000 │ M/M EQUIV TO NEXT FIX
  │INDEX TO 6/30/99 4.9755 │  PRINCIPAL       999900.00 │ PRICE @ FIX =   99.991
  │──────P R I C E S────── │  ACCRUED INTEREST  3179.17 │ ON  6/30/99-  71 DAYS
  │PRICE           99.99000│  TOTAL          1003079.17 │ CD(ACT/360) =    5.438
  │NEUTRAL PRICE   99.99089│                            │ FIX PRICES? (Y/N) N
  │ADJUSTED PRICE  99.90031│          M A R G I N S
  │ADJUSTED SIMPLE MARGIN    55.458 BPS  (  5.555) SPREAD FOR LIFE
  │ADJUSTED TOTAL MARGIN     55.957 BPS  (  5.560)    46.06 BPS
  │DISCOUNT MARGIN           46.231 BPS  (  5.462) VOLATILITY = 0.00

  Copyright 1999 BLOOMBERG L.P.  Frankfurt:69-920410  Hong Kong:2-977-6000  London:171-330-7500  New York:212-318-2000
  Princeton:609-279-3000    Singapore:226-3000    Sydney:2-9777-8686    Tokyo:3-3201-8900    Sao Paulo:11-3048-4500
                                                                       G279-532-3 15-Apr-99 17:34:08
```

Source: Bloomberg Financial Markets

---

[10] See Chapter 4 in Frank J. Fabozzi and Steven V. Mann, *Floating-Rate Securities* (New Hope, PA: Frank J. Fabozzi Associates, 2000).

Spread for Life

When a floater is selling at a premium/discount to par, a potential buyer of a floater will consider the premium or discount as an additional source of dollar return. *Spread for life* (also called *simple margin*) is a measure of potential return that accounts for the accretion (amortization) of the discount (premium) as well as the constant index spread over the security's remaining life. Spread for life is calculated using the following formula:

$$\text{Spread for life} = \left[\frac{100(100 - P)}{\text{Maturity}} + \text{Quoted margin} \right] \frac{100}{P} \tag{1}$$

where P is the market price (per \$100 of par value) and Maturity is in years using the appropriate day-count convention. The quoted margin is measured in basis points.

To illustrate this calculation, the Enron floater has a current coupon of 5.45, matures in 345 days or 0.9583 of a year using an ACT/360. Although there is no current market quote available for this floater as indicated by the words "NOT PRICED" at the top center of the screen, we will use the Bloomberg default price of 99.99 for the current market price P. The simple margin is calculated as follows

$$\text{Spread for life} = \left[\frac{100(100 - 99.99)}{0.9583} + 45 \right] \frac{100}{99.99} = 46.0481 \text{ basis points}$$

At the bottom of the YA screen in Exhibit 6 is a box labeled "MARGINS." The Enron floater's spread for life is 46.06. The slight difference between our calculation and Bloomberg's is likely due to rounding error. Note also that spread for life considers only the accretion/amortization of the discount/premium over the floater's remaining term to maturity and considers neither the level of the coupon rate nor the time value of money.

Adjusted Simple Margin

The *adjusted simple margin* (also called *effective margin*) is an adjustment to spread for life. This adjustment accounts for a one-time cost of carry effect when a floater is purchased with borrowed funds. Suppose a security dealer has purchased \$10 million of a particular floater. Naturally, the dealer has a number of alternative ways to finance the position — borrowing from a bank, repurchase agreement, etc. Regardless of the method selected, the dealer must make a one-time adjustment to the floater price to account for the cost of carry from the settlement date to the next coupon reset date. Given a particular financing rate, a carry-adjusted forward price can be determined as of the next coupon reset date. Once the carry-adjusted price is determined, the floater's adjusted price is simply the carry-adjusted price discounted to the settlement date by the reference rate. As before, the reference rate is assumed to remain constant until maturity. Note the cost of carry adjustment is simply an adjustment to the purchase price of the floater. If the cost of carry is positive (negative), the purchase price will be adjusted downward (upward). A floater's adjusted price is calculated as below:

$$\text{Adjusted price} = P - \frac{[(\text{Coupon rate})100 - (P + AI)rf]w}{[1 + (w)(rr_{\text{avg}})]} \tag{2}$$

where

Coupon rate = current coupon rate of the floater (in decimal)
P = market price (per \$100 of par value)
AI = accrued interest (per \$100 of par value)
rf = financing rate (e.g., the repo rate) (in decimal)

$$w = \frac{\text{Number of days between settlement and the next coupon payent}}{\text{Number of days in a year using the appropriate day-count}}$$

rr_{avg} = assumed (average) value for the reference rate until maturity (in decimal)

To illustrate this calculation, we revisit the Enron floater. The following information is taken from the YA screen in Exhibit 6. The market price of 99.99 is taken from the "PRICES" box on the left-hand side of the screen. For the coupon rate, we use 0.0545 (in decimal) which is located under "FIX RATE." The accrued interest is 0.3179 (per \$100 of par value). Under "INPUTS", we find the repo rate (0.049755) to the next coupon reset date. There are 71 days between the settlement date (4/20/99) and the next coupon reset date (6/30/99) and the day count is ACT/360. Given this information, $w = 71/360$ or 0.1972. Lastly, the assumed value of the reference rate until maturity (rr_{avg}) is simply the current value of the reference rate which is 0.05 (in decimal) and is labeled "ASSUMED INDEX" under the "INPUTS" section.

$$\text{Adjusted price} = 99.99 - \frac{[(0.0545)100 - (99.99 + 0.3179)0.049755]0.1972}{[1 + (0.1972)(0.05)]}$$

$$= 99.90033$$

The adjusted price as computed by Bloomberg is 99.90031 and is found under "PRICES."

Once the adjusted price is determined, the adjusted simple margin is computed using the formula below.

$$\text{Adjusted simple margin} = \left[\frac{100(100 - P_A)}{\text{Maturity}} + \text{Quoted margin}\right]\frac{100}{P_A} \tag{3}$$

where P_A is the adjusted price, Maturity is measured in years using the appropriate day-count convention, and Quoted margin is measured in basis points.

To compute the adjusted simple margin for the Enron floater, we gather the following information from Exhibit 6. We use the adjusted price of 99.90031 for P_A. There are 345 days between the settlement date (4/20/99) and the maturity date (3/30/00). Since the day count convention is ACT/360, the maturity is 345/360 or 0.9583. The quoted margin of 45 basis points is obtained from the "INPUTS" box. Plugging this information into equation (5), we obtain the adjusted simple margin.

$$\text{Adjusted simple margin} = \left[\frac{100(100 - 99.90031)}{0.9583} + 45\right]\frac{100}{99.90031} \qquad (4)$$

$$= 55.458 \text{ basis points}$$

The adjusted simple margin from Bloomberg is 55.458 which is also located in the "MARGINS" box at the bottom of Exhibit 6.

Adjusted Total Margin

The *adjusted total margin* (also called *total adjusted margin*) adds one additional refinement to the adjusted simple margin. Specifically, the adjusted total margin is the adjusted simple margin plus the interest earned by investing the difference between the floater's par value and the adjusted price.[11] The current value of the reference rate (i.e., the assumed index) is assumed to be the investment rate. The adjusted total margin is calculated using the following expression:

Adjusted total margin

$$= \left[\frac{100(100 - P_A)}{\text{Maturity}} + \text{Quoted margin} + 100(100 - P_A)rr_{avg}\right]\frac{100}{P_A} \qquad (5)$$

The notation used is the same as given above.

For the Enron floater we used in previous illustrations, the adjusted total margin is:

Adjusted total margin

$$= \left[\frac{100(100 - 99.90031)}{0.9583} + 45 + 100(100 - 99.90031)0.05\right]\frac{100}{99.90031}$$

$$= 55.957 \text{ basis points}$$

In Exhibit 6, Bloomberg's adjusted total margin is 55.957 which is obtained from the "MARGINS" box.

Discount Margin

One common method of measuring potential return that employs discounted cash flows is *discount margin*. This measure indicates the average spread or margin over the reference rate the investor can expect to earn over the security's life given a particular assumption of the path the reference rate will take to maturity. The assumption that the future levels of the reference rate are equal to today's level is the usual assumption. The procedure for calculating the discount margin is as follows:

---

[11] When the floater's adjusted price is greater than 100, the additional increment is negative and represents the interest forgone.

Exhibit 7: Calculation of the Discount Margin for a Floater

Floater: Maturity   =   6 years
Coupon rate   =   Reference rate + 80 basis points
Resets every 6 months
Maturity value   = $100

(1)	(2)	(3)	(4)	(5)	(6)	(7)	(8)
	Rate	Flow			Assumed Margin		
Period	(%)	($)*	80	84	88	96	100
1	10	5.40	$5.1233	$5.1224	$5.1214	$5.1195	$5.1185
2	10	5.40	4.8609	4.8590	4.8572	4.8535	4.8516
3	10	5.40	4.6118	4.6092	4.6066	4.6013	4.5987
4	10	5.40	4.3755	4.3722	4.3689	4.3623	4.3590
5	10	5.40	4.1514	4.1474	4.1435	4.1356	4.1317
6	10	5.40	3.9387	3.9342	3.9297	3.9208	3.9163
7	10	5.40	3.7369	3.7319	3.7270	3.7171	3.7122
8	10	5.40	3.5454	3.5401	3.5347	3.5240	3.5186
9	10	5.40	3.3638	3.3580	3.3523	3.3409	3.3352
10	10	5.40	3.1914	3.1854	3.1794	3.1673	3.1613
11	10	5.40	3.0279	3.0216	3.0153	3.0028	2.9965
12	10	105.40	56.0729	55.9454	55.8182	55.5647	55.4385
	Present value =		$100.00	$99.8269	$99.6541	$99.3098	$99.1381

* For periods 1-11: Cash flow = 100(Reference rate + 80 basis points) (0.5)
  For period 12: Cash flow = 100(Reference rate + 80 basis points) (0.5) + 100

Step 1. Determine the cash flows assuming that the reference rate does not change over the security's life.

Step 2. Select a margin.

Step 3. Discount the cash flows found in Step 1 by the current value of the reference rate plus the margin selected in Step 2.

Step 4. Compare the present value of the cash flows as calculated in Step 3 to the price. If the present value is equal to the security's price, the discount margin is the margin assumed in Step 2. If the present value is not equal to the security's price, go back to Step 2 and select a different margin.

For a security selling at par, the discount margin is simply the quoted margin.

For example, suppose that a 6-year floater selling for $99.3098 pays the reference rate plus a quoted margin of 80 basis points. The coupon resets every 6 months. Assume that the current value of the reference rate is 10%.

Exhibit 7 presents the calculation of the discount margin for this security. Each period in the security's life is enumerated in Column (1), while Column (2) shows the current value of the reference rate.[12] Column (3) sets forth the security's cash flows. For the first 11 periods, the cash flow is equal to the reference rate (10%) plus the quoted margin of 80 basis points multiplied by 100 and then

---

[12] For simplicity, we assume the coupon periods are of equal length.

divided by 2. In last 6-month period, the cash flow is \$105.40 — the final coupon payment of \$5.40 plus the maturity value of \$100. Different assumed margins appear at the top of the last five columns. The rows below the assumed margin indicate the present value of each period's cash flow for that particular value of assumed margin. Finally, the last row gives the total present value of the cash flows for each assumed margin.

For the five assumed margins, the present value of the cash flows is equal to the floater's price (\$99.3098) when the assumed margin is 96 basis points. Accordingly, the discount margin on a semiannual basis is 48 basis points and correspondingly 96 basis points on an annual basis. (Notice that the discount margin is 80 basis points (i.e., the quoted margin) when the floater is selling at par.)

Now that we have a sense about how to calculate discount margin, let's return to our Enron floater in Exhibit 6. The floater is trading at 99.99 with a coupon rate of 5.45% as of the last coupon reset date, 3/30/99. Accrued interest on this floater from the last coupon date (3/30/99) to the settlement date (4/20/00) is 0.3179 (per \$100 of par value) which appears in the box in the middle of the screen. Given this information, we know the floater's full price (i.e., flat price plus accrued interest) is 100.307917 (per \$100 of par value). In the box labeled "MARGINS" at the bottom of the screen, we see that the discount margin is 46.231 basis points. Accordingly, if we discount the floater's four remaining quarterly cash flows using an annual discount of 5.46321% (i.e., the reference rate plus the discount margin), we should recover the floater's full price of 100.307917 (per \$100 of par value).

The Enron floater has four remaining quarterly cash flows of \$1.3625 [(0.0545 × 100)/4] delivered on 6/30/99, 9/30/99, 12/30/99, and 3/30/99. In addition, on the day the floater matures (3/30/00) the investor will receive the floater's terminal cash flow of \$100 (per \$100 of par value). Since the floater is being valued between coupon payment dates, we determine the present value of cash flows received over fractional coupon periods using an ACT/360 day count convention. The present value calculation is as follows:

$$\frac{\$1.3625}{1.0546321^{71/360}} + \frac{\$1.3625}{1.0546321^{163/360}} + \frac{\$1.3625}{1.0546321^{254/360}} + \frac{\$101.3625}{1.0546321^{345/360}} = 100.3156$$

This calculation is within rounding error of Bloomberg's full price of 100.3079 (per \$100 of par value).

There are several drawbacks of the discount margin as a measure of potential return from holding a floater. First and most obvious, the measure assumes the reference rate will not change over the security's life. Second, the price of a floater for a given discount margin is sensitive to the path that the reference rate takes in the future except in the special case when the discount margin equals the quoted margin.

To see the significance of the second drawback, it is useful to partition the value of an option-free floater into two parts: (1) the present value of the security's cash flows (i.e., coupon payments and maturity value) if the discount margin equals the quoted margin and (2) the present value of an annuity which pays the difference between the quoted margin and the discount margin multiplied by 100 and divided by the number of periods per year.

$$P = 100 + \sum_{i=1}^{n} \frac{100(qm - dm)/m}{(1 + y_i + dm)^i} \tag{6}$$

where

P = price of the floater (per $100 of par value)
qm = quoted margin
dm = discount margin
y_i = assumed value of the reference rate in period i
n = number of periods until maturity
m = number of periods per year

In this framework, one can easily see as before that if the quoted margin is equal to the discount margin, the second term is zero and the floater will be valued at par. If the index spread is greater than (less than) the discount margin, the second term is positive (negative) and the floater will be valued at a premium (discount).

This framework is also quite useful for addressing the question: for a given discount margin, how does the present value of the floater's cash flows change given different assumptions about how the reference rate is expected to change in the future? [13] Consider a floater that pays interest semiannually with the following characteristics:

Maturity = 3 years
Coupon rate = 6-month LIBOR + 50 basis points
Maturity value = $100

For ease of exposition, assume that we value the security on its coupon anniversary date. Let's consider two paths that 6-month LIBOR can take in the next three years. In the first path, we assume that 6-month LIBOR will remain unchanged at say, 5.25%. In the second path, we assume that 6-month LIBOR will increase by 10 basis points each period for the next three years (i.e., 5.25%, 5.35%, 5.45%, 5.55%, 5.65%, 5.75%). Finally, we will value the floater assuming three different values (in basis points) for the discount margin: 0, 50 and 100. The values for the floaters associated with each discount margin and under each interest rate path are given in Exhibit 8.

---

[13] For further discussion, see Iwanowski, "An Investor's Guide to Floating-Rate Notes: Conventions, Mathematics, and Relative Valuation."

Exhibit 8: Bond Values Assuming Different Discounted Margins and Alternative Interest Rate Paths

	Assumed Interest Rate Path	
Discounted Margin	6-month LIBOR remains constant at 5.25%	6-month LIBOR increases 10 bp each period
100	98.6512	98.6549
50	100.0000	100.0000
0	101.3713	101.3676

There are several implications that we can draw from the results in Exhibit 8. First, as discussed previously, when the discount margin equals the quoted margin, the value of the floater equals 100 regardless of the assumed interest rate path. This result holds because any change in the discount rate is exactly offset by a corresponding increase/decrease in the coupon. In other words, the second term in equation (6)

$$\sum_{i=1}^{n} \frac{100(qm - dm)/m}{(1 + y_i + dm)^i} \tag{7}$$

is always equal to zero so the security will sell at par. However, when the discount margin differs from the quoted margin, the present value of the security's cash flows will depend on the assumed interest rate path.

For example, suppose the reference rate is expected to increase as in Exhibit 7. What happens to the size of the discount/premium of a floater? When the discount margin is less than the quoted margin, the second term in equation (6) will be smaller because the cash flows are growing at a slower rate than the discount rate. If this occurs, the security will have a smaller premium than under the assumption of an unchanged reference rate. Conversely, when the discount margin is larger than the quoted margin, the effect is reversed. A smaller discount and a higher price will result owing to the fact that the cash flows are growing at a faster rate than the discount rate. These effects are even more pronounced as the term to maturity increases. This illustration clearly demonstrates that the discount margin possesses an important shortcoming as a measure of relative value.

Option-Adjusted Spread

The spread measures discussed thus far fail to recognize any embedded options that may be present in a floater. A spread measure that takes into account embedded options is called an *option-adjusted spread*. Here is how it is computed.

We described earlier how to value a floater with an embedded option. In the binomial tree, the cash flows at any node are discounted at the appropriate rate on the binomial tree. The product of the valuation model is the theoretical value of the floater. The option-adjusted spread (OAS) enters the picture when we compare the security's theoretical value to the market price. Because of perceived differences in risk (default, liquidity, etc.) between the security being valued and the on-the-run benchmark securities used to construct the binomial tree, the theoretical value will usually differ from the market price. Suppose we are valuing a floater which is less liquid than the on-the-run benchmark securities. As a result, the floater's theoretical value (which ignores the difference in liquidity) is higher than its market price. We conclude the discount rates from the binomial tree used to determine the floater's theoretical value are "too low." The option-adjusted spread is the spread that is added to each discount rate in the tree so that the valuation model produces a value equal to the market price. The reason why the spread is "option adjusted" is because the cash flows shown in the binomial tree are those that result after they are adjusted for any embedded options. For example, if the floater has a cap, the cash flows in the binomial tree take into account the cap.

The interpretation of the option-adjusted spread depends on what the benchmark is. Sometimes the on-the-run yield curve employed is that of the issuer. Thus, the option-adjusted spread is the additional spread over the spot rates for the issuer after adjusting for the embedded options. Many times, however, the Treasury on-the-run yield curve is used to generate the binomial tree. In that case, the option-adjusted spread is the spread over the Treasury spot rate curve after adjusting for the embedded options. In fact, some vendors allow the user to generate a tree based on the LIBOR yield curve. When the LIBOR yield curve is the benchmark, the OAS is the spread over that curve after adjusting for the floater's embedded options. Some market participants prefer to use the LIBOR yield curve because they are interested in the spread over their LIBOR-based funding costs.

Despite its widespread use, the OAS has a number of limitations which we discussed in Chapter 8.

Chapter 10

Total Return

An investor who purchases a bond can expect to receive a *dollar* return from one or more of the following sources: (1) the coupon interest payments made by the issuer, (2) any capital gain (or capital loss — negative dollar return) when the bond matures, is called, is put, is refunded, or is sold, and (3) income from reinvestment of the coupon interest payments (i.e., interest on interest). Any measure of the potential return from holding a bond over some investment horizon should consider these three sources of dollar return. In Chapter 5, we explained why yield measures are limited with respect to assessing the potential performance over some investment horizon. In this chapter we set forth a framework to assess the potential performance of a bond or bond strategy — total return.

COMPUTING THE TOTAL RETURN

The *total return* considers all three sources of potential dollar return over the investor's investment horizon. It is the return (interest rate) that will make the proceeds (i.e., price plus accrued interest) invested grow to the projected total dollar return at the end of the investment horizon.[1] The total return requires the investor to specify:

- an investment horizon
- a reinvestment rate
- a price for the bond at the end of the investment horizon.

More formally, the steps for computing a total return over some investment horizon are as follows:

Step 1: Compute the total coupon payments plus the reinvestment income based on an assumed reinvestment rate. The reinvestment rate is one-half the annual interest rate that the investor assumes can be earned on the reinvestment of coupon interest payments.[2]

Step 2: Determine the projected sale price at the end of the investment horizon. We refer to this as the *horizon price*. In Chapter 4 we explained how the price of a bond is computed based on the term structure of default-free interest rates (i.e., the

---

[1] The total return is also referred to as the *horizon return*.

[2] An investor can choose multiple reinvestment rates for cash flows from the bond over the investment horizon.

Treasury spot rate curve) and the term structure of credit spreads. Moreover, for bonds with embedded options, the price will depend on the option-adjusted spread (OAS). So, to determine the horizon price in the total return analysis it is necessary to use at the horizon date an assumed Treasury spot rate curve, term structure of credit spreads, and OAS. Obviously, the assumed values reflect changes in interest rates and spreads from the beginning to the end of the investment horizon. We shall refer to these rates as the *structure of rates at the horizon date.*

However, in the illustrations to follow, we will assume a single yield to price a security at the horizon date to simplify the analysis. This yield would reflect the Treasury rate plus a spread and we will refer to it as the *horizon yield.*

Step 3: Add the values computed in Steps 1 and 2. Reduce this value by any borrowing cost to obtain the total future dollars that will be received from the investment given the assumed reinvestment rate and projected structure of rates at the horizon date (or horizon yield in our illustrations to follow).

Step 4: Compute the *semiannual total return* using the following formula:

$$\left(\frac{\text{total future dollars}}{\text{full price of bond}}\right)^{1/h} - 1$$

where the full price is the price plus accrued interest and h is the *number of semiannual periods in the investment horizon.*

Step 5: For semiannual-pay bonds, double the interest rate found in Step 4. The resulting interest rate is the total return expressed on a *bond-equivalent basis.* Instead, the total return can be expressed on an *effective rate basis* by using the following formula:

$$(1 + \text{semiannual total return})^2 - 1$$

A graphical depiction of the total return calculation is presented in Exhibit 1.

Exhibit 1: Graphical Depiction of Total Return Calculation

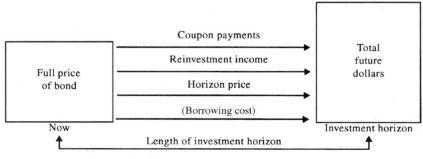

Total return is the interest rate that will make the full price of the bond grow to the total future dollars

The decision as to whether to calculate the total return on a bond-equivalent basis or an effective rate basis depends on the situation. If the total return is being compared to a benchmark index that is calculated on a bond-equivalent basis, then the total return should be calculated in that way. However, if the bond is being used to satisfy liabilities that are calculated on an effective rate basis, then the total return should be calculated in that way.

To illustrate the computation of the total return, suppose that an investor with a 1-year investment horizon is considering the purchase of a 20-year 6% corporate bond. The issue is selling for $86.4365 for a yield of 7.3%. The issue will be purchased for cash (i.e., no funds will be borrowed). Assume that the yield curve is flat (i.e., the yield for all maturities is the same) and the yield for the on-the-run 20-year Treasury issue is 6.5%. This means that the yield spread over the on-the-Treasury issue for this corporate bond is 80 basis points. The investor expects that:

1. he or she can reinvest the coupon payments (there will be two of them over the 1-year investment horizon) at 6%.
2. the Treasury yield curve will shift down by 25 basis points and remains flat at the end of 1 year, so that the yield for the 19-year Treasury issue is 6.25% (6.5% minus 25 basis points)
3. the yield spread to the 19-year Treasury issue is unchanged at 80 basis points so the horizon yield is 7.05% (6.25% plus 80 basis points)

The calculations are as shown below.

Step 1: Compute the total coupon payments plus the reinvestment income assuming an annual reinvestment rate of 6% or 3% every six months. The semiannual coupon payments are $3. The future value of an annuity can be used or because the investment horizon is only one year, it can be computed as follows:

First coupon payment reinvested for six months = $3 (1.03)   = $3.09
Second coupon payment not reinvested since at horizon date = $3.00
Total   = $6.09

Step 2: The horizon price at the end of the 1-year investment horizon is determined as follows. The horizon yield is 7.05% by assumption. The 6% coupon 20-year corporate bond now has 19 years to maturity. The price of this bond when discounted at a flat 7.05% yield (the yield curve is assumed to be flat) is $89.0992.

Step 3: Adding the amounts in Steps 2 and 3 gives the total future dollars of $95.1892.

Step 4: Compute the following (*h* is 2 in our illustration):

$$\left(\frac{\$95.1892}{\$86.4365}\right)^{1/2} - 1 = 4.94\%$$

Step 5: The total return on a bond-equivalent basis and on an effective rate basis are shown below:

$$2 \times 4.94\% = 9.88\% \qquad \text{(BEY)}$$

$$(1.0494)^2 - 1 = 10.13\% \quad \text{(effective rate basis)}$$

OAS-TOTAL RETURN

In Chapter 8, the option-adjusted spread (OAS) was described. The OAS can be incorporated into a total return analysis to determine the horizon price. This requires a valuation model. At the end of the investment horizon, it is necessary to specify how the OAS is expected to change. The horizon price can then be "backed out" of a valuation model. This technique can be extended to the total return framework by making assumptions about the required variables at the horizon date.

Assumptions about the OAS value at the end of the investment horizon reflect the expectations of the portfolio manager. It is common to assume that the OAS at the horizon date will be the same as the OAS at the time of purchase. A total return calculated using this assumption is sometimes referred to as a *constant-OAS total* return. Alternatively, active total return managers will make bets on how the OAS will change — either widening or tightening. The total return framework can be used to assess how sensitive the performance of a bond with an embedded option is to changes in the OAS.

TOTAL RETURN TO MATURITY

In our discussion and illustration, we focused on the total return over some investment horizon shorter than the maturity date. It is useful to calculate a total return to the maturity date to see the relative importance of each source of return. The calculation of the semiannual total return to maturity is calculated as follows:

$$\left(\frac{\text{total future dollars}}{\text{full price of bond}}\right)^{1/m} - 1$$

where *m* is the number of semiannual periods to maturity.

To illustrate this, consider a 4% 25-year bond selling for $50.594 per $100 par value. The yield to maturity for this bond is 9%. The total coupon payments per

$100 par value is $100 ($4 per year times 25 years). The capital gain at the maturity date is $49.406 ($100 − $50.594). To calculate the reinvestment income, a reinvestment rate must be assumed. If a 6% reinvestment rate (3% semiannually) is assumed, it can be demonstrated that the reinvestment income is $125.5937.

The total future dollars is $325.5937 which is the sum of the total coupon payments ($100), the reinvestment income ($125.5937), and the maturity value ($100). The semiannual total return to maturity is found as follows:

$$\left(\frac{\$325.5937}{\$50.594}\right)^{1/50} - 1 = 0.0379 = 3.79\%$$

The bond-equivalent yield is 7.59% and the total return on an effective rate basis is 7.73%.

Thus, if an investor purchases this bond, holds it to maturity, and can reinvest the coupon payments at a 6% yield, the total return to maturity would be 7.59% on a bond-equivalent basis. This is less than the 9% yield to maturity.

The relative importance of each source of return for this bond is summarized below. From the relative contributions, it can be seen how critical the reinvestment rate is.

Sources of Return	Dollars	Percent
Total coupon	100.0000	36.36
Reinvestment income	125.5937	45.67
Capital gain or loss	49.406	17.97
Total	274.9997	100.00

Let's calculate another total return for a bond held to maturity with two added twists. First, what happens if a bond is purchased between coupon payment dates such that remaining number of periods until maturity is not a whole number (e.g., 15.25)? Second, what if the assumed reinvestment rate for the total return calculation is the bond's yield to maturity? To illustrate this calculation, consider a 6% coupon, medium-term note issued by General Mills Inc. that matures on January 22, 2011. Exhibit 2 presents the Bloomberg Security Description (DES) screen for this issue. This note pays coupon interest on January 22 and July 22.

We will assume this bond is purchased with a settlement date of October 13, 2000 and is held to maturity. Exhibit 3 presents the Bloomberg Yield Analysis (YA) screen for this security. We will calculate the total return to maturity using information presented on this screen. Since the settlement date is between coupon payment dates, we use the security's full price in our calculation. Assuming a $1 million par value position, the full price is $899,961.38 (the flat price plus 81 days accrued interest) which is located under the heading "PAYMENT INVOICE" on the left-hand side of the screen and is labeled "TOTAL."

The total futures dollars generated is located under "INCOME" which is also located on the left-hand side of the screen. The redemption value at maturity is $1,000,000. There are 21 coupon payments remaining so the total coupon interest over the bond's life is $630,000 (21 × $30,000). The reinvestment income assuming a reinvestment rate of 7.611% (the yield to maturity) is $308,830.80.[3] Summing these three components gives us the total future dollars of $1,938,830.80 and this is labeled "TOTAL."

The only input that remains is the number of periods until maturity. Since the settlement date is between coupon payment dates, the number of periods until maturity is not a whole number. The settlement date is October 13, 2000 and the next coupon payment date is January 22, 2001. Since corporate securities use a 30/360 day count convention as discussed in Chapter 3, a semiannual coupon period is assumed to have 180 days and there are 99 days from the settlement date until the next coupon date. Accordingly, the fraction of a coupon period remaining is 0.55 (99/180). As of January 22, 2001, there are 10 years remaining to maturity on January 22, 2011. Accordingly, if the bond is purchased with a settlement date of October 13, 2000 and held to maturity, there are 20.55 semiannual coupon periods remaining until maturity.

Exhibit 2: Bloomberg Security Description Screen for a General Mills Inc. Medium-Term Note

DES   DG36 Corp   **DES**

SECURITY DESCRIPTION   Page 1/ 2
GEN MILLS INC   GIS 6 01/22/11   88.64614/88.64614 (7.61/7.61) BFV @17:24

ISSUER INFORMATION	IDENTIFIERS		1) Additional Sec Info
Name GENERAL MILLS INC	CUSIP 37033LFF8		2) Call Schedule
Type Food-Misc/Diversified	ISIN US37033LFF85		3) Identifiers
Market of Issue MEDIUM TERM NOTE	BB number EC0868637		4) Ratings
SECURITY INFORMATION	RATINGS		5) Prospectus
Country US Currency USD	Moody's A2 *⊣		6) Involved Parties
Collateral Type NOTES	S&P A-		7) Custom Notes
Calc Typ(1)STREET CONVENTION	Composite A3		8) Issuer Information
Maturity 1/22/2011 Series MTNE	ISSUE SIZE		9) ALLQ
CALLABLE CALL 1/22/01@ 100.00	Amt Issued		10) Pricing Sources
Coupon 6 FIXED	USD 25,000.00 (M)		11) MTN Drawdown
S/A 30/360	Amt Outstanding		12) Prospectus Request
Announcement Dt 1/ 6/99	USD 25,000.00 (M)		13) Related Securities
Int. Accrual Dt 1/22/99	Min Piece/Increment		14) Issuer Web Page
1st Settle Date 1/22/99	1,000.00/ 1,000.00		
1st Coupon Date 7/22/99	Par Amount 1,000.00		
Iss Pr	BOOK RUNNER/EXCHANGE		
	SSB		65) Old DES
HAVE PROSPECTUS DTC			66) Send as Attachment
SERIES E.			

Copyright 2000 BLOOMBERG L.P. Frankfurt:69-920410 Hong Kong:2-977-6000 London:207-330-7500 New York:212-318-2000
Princeton:609-279-3000   Singapore:65-212-1000   Sydney:2-9777-8686   Tokyo:3-3201-8900   Sao Paulo:11-3048-4500
                                                                          I464-169-0 10-Oct-00 17:24:35

Bloomberg
PROFESSIONAL

Source: Bloomberg

---

[3] Bloomberg allows the user to input any reinvestment rate of their choosing to calculate the reinvestment income.

Exhibit 3: Bloomberg Yield Analysis Screen for a General Mills Inc. Medium-Term Note

```
YA                                                    DG36 Corp   YA
Bond Matures on a SATURDAY
                          YIELD ANALYSIS               CUSIP:37033LFF
GEN MILLS INC    GIS 6 01/22/11    88.64614/88.64614 (7.61/7.61) BFV @17:25
PRICE        88.646138         SETTLEMENT DATE 10/13/2000
current yield  6.768        [W] ORST    CASHFLOW ANALYSIS
YIELD              MATURITY  1/22/2011   TO 1/22/11  WORKOUT   1000M FACE
CALCULATIONS       1/22/2011 @100.000   PAYMENT INVOICE
 STREET CONVENTION          7.611   7.611
 U.S. GOVT EQUIVALENT       7.611   7.611 PRINCIPAL              886461.38
 TRUE YIELD                 7.607   7.607 81 DAYS ACCRUED INT     13500.00
 EQUIVALENT 1/YR COMPOUND   7.756   7.756 TOTAL                  899961.38
 JAPANESE YIELD (SIMPLE)    8.014   8.014        I N C O M E
 PROCEEDS/MMKT(ACT/360)                   REDEMPTION VALUE      1000000.00
                                          COUPON PAYMENT         630000.00
 A F T E R   T A X :                      INTEREST @  7.611%      308830.8
 INCOME 39.60% CAPITAL 20.00%  4.868  4.868 TOTAL               1938830.80
                                                 R E T U R N
  SENSITIVITY ANALYSIS              GROSS PROFIT           1038869.42
 CNV  DURATION (YEARS)      7.526   7.526 RETURN      2 /YR COMP   7.611
      ADJ/MOD DURATION      7.250   7.250 FURTHER ANALYSIS
      RISK                  6.525   6.525 HIT 1 <GO> YIELD TO CALL
      CONVEXITY             0.675   0.675 HIT 2 <GO> PRICE TABLE
 PRICE VALUE OF A  0.01    0.06525 0.06525 HIT 3 <GO> TOTAL RETURN
 YIELD VALUE OF A  0  32   0.00479 0.00479 HIT 4 <GO> OPTION ADJUSTED SPREAD
Copyright 2000 BLOOMBERG L.P.  Frankfurt:69-920410  Hong Kong:2-977-6000  London:207-330-7500  New York:212-318-2000
Princeton:609-279-3000  Singapore:65-212-1000  Sydney:2-9777-8686  Tokyo:3-3201-8900  Sao Paulo:11-3048-4500
                                                          I464-169-0 10-Oct-00 17:25:14
```

Bloomberg
PROFESSIONAL

Source: Bloomberg

We now have all the inputs necessary to calculate the total return to maturity. The semiannual total return to maturity is found as follows:

$$\left(\frac{\$1,938,830.80}{\$899,961.38}\right)^{1/20.55} - 1 = 3.8054\%$$

The bond-equivalent yield is 7.611% which is the same as the yield to maturity. Thus, if the assumed reinvestment rate is the yield to maturity, the total return to maturity is equal to the yield to maturity.

After-Tax Total Return to Maturity

Thus far, we have ignored the impact of taxes on the total return of a bond if it is held to maturity. There are taxes on interest income and any capital gain. There may or may not be a preferential tax treatment for the capital gain. Incorporating tax consequences into the total return calculation is fairly straightforward.

Effect of Taxes on Total Dollar Contributions

Taxation of coupon income has three adverse effects. First it reduces the amount of the coupon income by the tax rate. That is, the after-tax semiannual coupon is equal to:

par value $\times$ (1 − tax rate on interest income) $\times$ (coupon rate/2)

The total coupon income over the life of the bond is also reduced.

For example, consider a 30-year bond with a coupon rate of 4.2%. Suppose that the tax rate on interest income is 35%. The pre-tax semiannual coupon is $2.1 per $100 par value. The after-tax semiannual coupon is:

$$\$100 \times (1 - 0.35) \times (0.042/2) = \$1.365$$

The total pre-tax coupon payments are $126 per $100 par value; the total after-tax coupon payments are $81.90.

The second adverse effect of taxation of the coupon income is that there are less dollars to reinvest each period. Consequently, the reinvestment income is reduced. The third adverse effect is that the interest earned on the interest income is reduced since it is taxed.

The total after-tax income from coupon interest and reinvestment income is equal to:

coupon rate$/2 \times$ (1 − tax rate) $\times$ par value

$$\times \frac{[1 + (\text{reinvestment rate}/2) \times (1 - \text{tax rate})]^m - 1}{(\text{reinvestment rate}/2) \times (1 - \text{tax rate})}$$

where m is the number of semiannual periods to maturity.

For example, consider once again the 4.2% 30-year bond. If the reinvestment rate is assumed to be 6% and the tax rate is 35%, then the total after-tax income from coupon interest and reinvestment income is:

$$0.042/2 \times (1 - 0.35) \times \$100 \times \frac{[1 + (0.06/2) \times (1 - 0.35)]^{60} - 1}{(0.06/2) \times (1 - 0.35)}$$

$$= \$153.0139$$

Since the total after-tax coupon payments is $81.90, this means that the after-tax reinvestment income is $71.1139 ($153.0139 − $81.90).

The effect of taxes on coupon income and reinvestment income for a 4.2% 30-year bond selling at par is shown below:

Source	Taxes not considered	35% tax rate
Total coupon payments	$126.0000	$81.9000
Interest on interest	216.4132	71.1139
Total	$342.4132	$153.0139

Notice that while the total coupon payments are reduced proportionately by the tax rate, the reinvestment income is reduced more than proportionately. That is, the total coupon payments after consideration of a 35% tax rate is reduced by 35%. This is not so for the reinvestment income. Reinvestment income after taxes declines by 67%.

To calculate the total after-tax return to maturity for a bond, the effect of taxes on the capital gain must be considered. To illustrate how to incorporate the tax treatment of the capital gain, suppose that a 30-year 4.2% coupon bond is purchased at $75 per $100 of par and that the $25 gain is taxed at a preferential tax treatment of 20%. Then at the maturity date, the amount after the 20% capital gains tax rate will be $20. The total return to maturity for this bond assuming a reinvestment rate of 6% and that coupon income is taxed at 35% is as follows:

Source	Taxes not considered		Taxes considered	
	Dollars	Percent	Dollars	Percent
Total coupon payments	126.0000	34.3	81.9000	47.3
Reinvestment income	216.4132	58.9	71.1139	41.1
Capital gain	25.0000	6.8	20.0000	11.6
Total	342.4132	100.0	173.0139	100.0

Notice that the relative importance of each source has changed once taxes are considered.

Calculation of After-Tax Total Return to Maturity

Given the total future dollars at maturity after accounting for taxes, the *after-tax total return to maturity* (on a semiannual basis) can be calculated as follows:

$$\left(\frac{\text{total future dollars after taxes at maturity}}{\text{full price of bond}}\right)^{1/m} - 1$$

where m is the number of semiannual periods to maturity. The semiannual rate can then be annualized on a bond-equivalent basis or on an effective rate basis.

For the 4.2% 30-year bond selling at $75, based on a 35% tax rate on coupon income, 20% capital gains tax rate, and 6% reinvestment rate the total future dollars after taxes are $253.0139, consisting of

$$\begin{aligned}
\text{total coupon payments} &= \$81.9000 \\
\text{reinvestment income} &= 71.1139 \\
\text{maturity value} &= 100.0000
\end{aligned}$$

The semiannual total after-tax return to maturity is:

$$\left(\frac{\$253.0139}{\$75}\right)^{1/60} - 1 = 0.020473 = 2.0473\%$$

The bond-equivalent after-tax total return to maturity is 4.09%. On an effective rate basis, the after-tax total return to maturity is 4.14%.

The *after-tax yield to maturity* for this bond is the interest rate that will make the present value of the after-tax cash flow equal to the proceeds invested. For our hypothetical bond it is 4.1%. This yield assumes that the after-tax cash flow can be reinvested at 4.1%.

The after-tax total return to maturity is a more appropriate measure for comparing the potential return from holding a taxable bond and the same maturity municipal bond to the maturity date. For a municipal bond, the coupon payments will not be taxed; however, the capital gain will be.

TOTAL RETURN FOR A MORTGAGE-BACKED SECURITY

In calculating total return of mortgage-backed securities, the total future dollars will depend on (1) the projected principal repayment (scheduled plus projected prepayments) and (2) the interest earned on reinvestment of the projected interest payments and the projected principal payments. To obtain the total future dollars, a prepayment rate over the investment horizon must be assumed.

For a monthly-pay mortgage-backed security, the monthly total return is then found using the formula:

$$\text{monthly total return} = \left(\frac{\text{total future dollars}}{\text{full price}}\right)^{\frac{1}{\text{number of months in horizon}}} - 1$$

The monthly total return can be annualized on a bond-equivalent yield basis as follows:

$$\text{bond-equivalent annual return} = 2[(1 + \text{monthly total return})^6 - 1]$$

or, by computing the effective annual return as follows:

$$\text{effective annual return} = (1 + \text{monthly total return})^{12} - 1$$

To illustrate the calculation of total return for a mortgage-backed security, suppose a portfolio manager is considering investing in a passthrough with a 9% passthrough (coupon) rate, 360 months remaining to maturity, and an original mortgage balance of \$100,000. The price of this passthrough is \$94,521. The cash flow yield assuming 100% PSA is 10.21%. The portfolio manager has a 6-month investment horizon and believes the following:

1. for the next six months the prepayment rate will be 100% PSA,
2. the projected cash flow can be reinvested at 0.5% per month,
3. the passthrough will sell to yield 7.62% at the end of the investment horizon, and[4]
4. the projected PSA prepayment rate at the end of the investment horizon is 185% PSA.

Based on the first assumption, the projected interest, scheduled principal, and prepayments (PIPP) for the first six months is:

---

[4] In this illustration we will use the cash flow yield methodology to determine the price at the horizon date.

End of month	Projected PIPP
1	$816
2	832
3	849
4	865
5	881
6	897

The projected PIPP plus interest from reinvesting the cash flow at 0.5% per month is shown below:

End of month	Projected PIPP	Projected PIPP plus reinvestment income
1	$816	$837
2	832	849
3	849	862
4	865	874
5	881	885
6	897	897
	Total	$5,204

At the end of the investment horizon, this passthrough would have a remaining mortgage balance of $99,181 and remaining maturity of 355 months. Assuming an horizon yield of 7.62% and a prepayment rate of 185% PSA, the projected price of this passthrough would be $106,210.

The total future dollars is then:

projected PIPP plus reinvestment income	=	$ 5,204
projected price at horizon	=	106,210
total future dollars	=	$111,414

The total monthly return is:

$$\left(\frac{\$111,414}{\$94,521}\right)^{1/6} - 1 = 0.02778$$

On a bond-equivalent basis, the total return is:

$$2[(1.02778)^6 - 1] = 0.3574 = 35.74\%$$

On an effective rate basis, the total return is:

$$(1.02778)^{12} - 1 = 0.3893 = 38.93\%$$

PORTFOLIO TOTAL RETURN

The appropriate measure for assessing the potential performance of a portfolio is its total return. This is determined by first calculating the total future dollars of each bond in the portfolio under a given scenario considering horizon yields, reinvestment rates, spreads, and, if applicable, prepayment rates. The sum of all the total future dollars for each bond in the portfolio is then calculated. The portfolio total return is then found as explained earlier for a given bond: it is the interest rate that will make the market value of the portfolio today grow to the portfolio's total future dollars.

As explained below, by using scenario analysis a portfolio manager, an investment (or asset/ liability) committee, or a board can assess the potential performance of the portfolio or the surplus of a financial institution. Corrective action can be taken to rebalance a portfolio if a scenario that is expected to occur will be detrimental to the performance of the portfolio or financial institution. The portfolio yield measures often calculated provide no such warning.

TOTAL RETURN ANALYSIS FOR MULTIPLE SCENARIOS

The obvious problem with total return as we have presented it thus far is that it is based on one set of underlying assumptions regarding the factors that affect return over some investment horizon. To test the sensitivity of the total return to the underlying assumptions, a technique called *scenario analysis* is used. This technique involves evaluating the total return under different scenarios defined by the manager. Regulators also require certain institutions to perform scenario analysis based on assumptions specified by regulations.

Scenario analysis is referred to by some broker/dealers, vendors of analytical systems, and regulators as "simulation." As we will see later, they are not the same techniques. Simulation is a more powerful tool that takes into consideration the dynamics of interactions among the factors.

As an illustration of scenario analysis for a single security, FHLMC (Freddie Mac) 1407-PF was analyzed on 8/31/98 using the analytics of Capital Management Sciences. The tranche was a busted PAC trading at 99.697. The OAS was 75 basis points and the average life was 0.67 years.

Exhibit 4 shows the total return based on the assumptions shown in the exhibit. Note the assumption regarding the reinvestment rate (4.618%). The investment horizon is three months. The assumed change in yield is shown in the first column and the corresponding 3-month total return is reported in the second column. The price at the investment horizon is shown in the third column. Notice that the price is based on the PSA assumption shown in the fourth column. The base case (i.e., zero yield change) is 500 PSA. Prepayments are assumed to be faster when rates decline and slower when rates increase. The bottom of Exhibit 4 shows a graph of the total return.

Exhibit 5 shows the results of a total return analysis for a scenario in which the Treasury rates decrease and the spread on mortgages and CMOs widens. Specifically, the top panel of the exhibit shows the Treasury yield curve at the beginning of the horizon and the assumed curve at the end of the horizon, three months later. The spread on the collateral and the spread on the PAC tranche are assumed to increase by 15 basis points at the end of the horizon. The 3-month total return shown in the exhibit is 0.79%. The lower panel of the exhibit shows the composition of the total return for the assumed scenario. The major source of return is the interest income (0.96). The total return was reduced by rolling down the yield curve ("yield curve roll") which resulted in a reduction of 22 basis points.

Exhibit 4: Total Return for a FHLMC 1407 PF (Busted PAC): Pricing Date 8/31/98

Horizon:	3 months	Issuer:	FHLMC 1407-PF
Reinv. Rate	4.618	CUSIP:	312912Z3
		Coupon:	6.250%
		Maturity:	10/15/16
		Yield:	6.369%

Yield Change	Return (%)	Price($)	PSA Speed (%) Lifetime	PSA Speed (%) 12 Month	CPR
−300	1.44	99.801	650	969	39.00
−250	1.46	99.764	650	969	39.00
−200	1.47	99.721	650	969	39.00
−150	1.49	99.672	647	965	38.82
−100	1.50	99.642	644	960	38.64
−50	1.51	99.641	597	890	35.83
0	1.45	99.596	500	729	30.00
50	1.28	99.429	355	472	21.30
100	0.97	99.115	223	240	13.38
150	0.52	98.657	160	147	9.57
200	−0.03	98.112	141	137	8.46
250	−0.60	97.538	131	130	7.87
300	−1.18	96.954	122	117	7.32

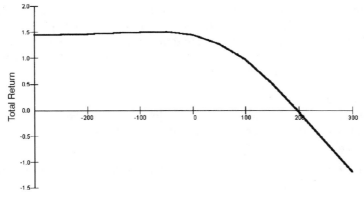

Interest Rate Changes (BP)

Source: Illustration provided by Capital Management Sciences.

Exhibit 5: Scenario Analysis for FHLMC 1407-PF Assuming a Downward Shift in the Yield Curve and an Increase in Spread

Scenario assumptions:
  3-month investment horizon
  4.618% reinvestment rate

Treasury yield curve shift:

Maturity	Initial yield	Horizon Yield
6 months	4.595%	4.095%
1 year	4.595	4.102
2 years	5.532	4.052
3 years	5.539	4.073
5 years	4.555	4.116
7 years	4.570	4.158
10 years	4.578	4.207
20 years	5.279	5.043
30 years	5.246	5.146

Change in spread of agency collateral to Treasuries: 15 basis points
Change in spread of PACs: 15 basis points

Total return analysis: 3-month return = 0.79%

Composition of return:

Income	0.96%
Price change due to:	
Change in parallel rates	−0.03%
Change in slope	0.08%
Yield curve roll	−0.21%
Change in mortgage spreads	−0.01%

Source: Illustration provided by Capital Management Sciences, Inc.

Using Scenario Analysis to Evaluate Potential Trades

Scenario analysis can be used to assess potential trades. For each scenario, one or more trades can be assessed relative to each other or some other benchmark (such as a funding cost or a market index). We will look at two actual trade recommendations and see how total return analysis is used to evaluate them. The first is the potential to enhance return by capitalizing on a view that a maturity sector of the yield curve is cheap. This trade is referred to as a "butterfly trade." The second trade seeks to enhance return by creating a "barbell" position in the MBS market.

Butterfly Trade

There are several types of trades that are employed by practitioners to capitalize on perceived cheapness in a maturity sector of the yield curve. One such trade is the *butterfly trade*. This trade involves three securities which we refer to as follows:

short maturity issue: the issue with the shortest maturity from among the three issues

long maturity issue: the issue with the longest maturity from among the three issues *intermediate maturity issue*: the issue between the shortest maturity issue and longest maturity issue

The "body" or center of the butterfly is the intermediate maturity issue. The wings of the butterfly in this trade are the long maturity issue and the short maturity issue.

The trade is structured so that the interest rate risk exposure to small parallel shifts in the level of rates is neutralized by creating a position so that the change in the market value of the center of the butterfly is equal to the change in the total market value of the wings. In Chapter 11 we will see that "duration" is a measure of the percentage price change of a security to a small parallel shift in interest rates and "dollar duration" is a measure of the change in the market value of the position to a small parallel shift in interest rates. Consequently, this butterfly trade is called a *duration and cash neutral trade*. Since there is no cash in this trade, the investor is fully invested in the bond market. The duration and cash neutral trade has a different dollar duration in each wing.

With this background, let's look at a trade recommended by Douglas Johnston and Andrew Sparks of Lehman Brothers. In April 1998, their view was that the 2-year sector of the yield curve was cheap relative to the intermediate term sector of the yield curve (i.e., the 5-year sector).[5] The reason for their recommendation is beyond the scope of this chapter but is based on the concept of "convexity" discussed in Chapter 11. Their suggested trade was to buy the U.S. Treasury 6.875% of 3/3/00. This is the short maturity issue in the butterfly trade. It is one of the wings of the butterfly and is purchased because it is believed to be undervalued relative to the 5-year sector. The intermediate maturity issue is the U.S. Treasury 5.75% of 10/31/02. This security is shorted. The proceeds from the short sale are used to purchase the issues in the two wings of the butterfly. Johnston and Sparks suggest several possible candidates for the long maturity issue. These are listed in the first column of Exhibit 6. There are Treasury issues, Treasury coupon strip (identified by TINT), and a Treasury principal strip (identified by PRIN).

The top panel of Exhibit 6 shows the 3-month total return for each candidate for the long maturity issue assuming no change in rates three months from the date of the analysis, a ±50 basis point parallel shift in rates, and ±100 basis point parallel shift in rates. In the second panel, the outcome is shown assuming different twists in the yield curve.[6] The information in these two panels can be used to (1) assess the outcome of the trade under these parallel shift scenarios and yield curve twist scenarios and (2) select the best long maturity issue. It is clear that the trade is adversely affected by a steepening of the yield curve and favorably impacted by a flattening of the yield curve.[7]

---

[5] *Global Relative Value*, Lehman Brothers, Fixed Income Research, April 6, 1998, GOV-1 and GOV-2.

[6] For the yield curve shift scenarios there was a 25 basis point shift in the curve with one end held constant and yield shifts interpolated by duration. For example, the Bull Flat scenario would be the short-end (i.e., 3-month) remaining constant with the 30-year rallying 25 basis points. The yields in-between are interpolated via duration (not maturity).

[7] For more information about the performance of yield curve strategies when the yield curve changes shape, see Steven V. Mann and Pradipkumar Ramanlal, "The Relative Performance of Yield Curve Strategies," *Journal of Portfolio Management*, Summer 1997, pp. 64-70.

Exhibit 6: Three-Month Total Returns for the Butterfly Trade

Buy 6.875% of 3/31/00 (short maturity issue)
Sell 5.75% of 10/31/02 (intermediate maturity issue)

Panel (a) Parallel Yield Change

Buy (long maturity issue)	Parallel Yield Change (bp)				
	−100	−50	0	50	100
6.5% of 8/15/05	19.5	12.0	10.0	12.8	20.4
10.625% of 8/15/15	41.6	13.2	6.8	19.2	48.8
12% of 8/15/03-08	47.2	26.4	14.0	8.4	10.0
8.125% of 8/15/21	53.2	12.4	2.8	20.0	61.2
6.625% of 2/15/27	67.6	13.2	−1.2	18.4	67.2
TINT of 2/15/03	2.0	1.6	1.6	2.0	2.4
TINT of 8/15/10	44.8	19.2	10.8	17.6	38.8
PRIN of 8/15/21	80.4	17.2	−2.4	15.6	65.6

Panel (b) Yield Curve Twists

Buy (long maturity issue)	Yield Twists			
	Bull Flat	Bull Steep	Bear Steep	Bear Flat
6.5% of 8/15/05	32.8	−8.0	−12.0	28.0
10.625% of 8/15/15	67.2	−56.0	−52.4	68.8
12% of 8/15/03-08	64.0	−25.2	−39.2	53.2
8.125% of 8/15/21	78.0	−80.0	−70.4	84.4
6.625% of 2/15/27	88.4	−101.2	−87.2	98.0
TINT of 2/15/03	2.4	3.2	0.8	0.0
TINT of 8/15/10	69.2	−44.0	−46.0	65.2
PRIN of 8/15/21	95.2	−110.0	−96.4	104.4

TINT = strip created from coupon
PRIN = strip created from principal
Adapted from Figure 1, *Global Relative Value*, Lehman Brothers, Fixed Income Research, April 6, 1998, GOV-2.

PAC Barbell versus Collateral Trade

In our second trade we will look at a proposed trade involving PACs versus collateral (i.e., passthroughs). This trade was recommended in December 1998. Typically, the OAS on PACs is positively sloped. That is, the OAS for short PACs trade tighter to the collateral than intermediate PACs, and intermediate PACs trade tighter than long PACs. In December 1998, the shape of the OAS for PACs became U-shaped such that short PACs offered a higher OAS than intermediate PACs.[8]

To benefit from this suspected anomaly in the OASs, a manager could create a "PAC barbell" as a substitute for collateral. A PAC barbell involves buying a combination of short and long PACs. The PaineWebber Mortgage Group assessed this strategy using scenario analysis. Exhibit 7 shows the analysis for a barbell created from 71% FHR 2105 PA and 29% from FHR 2105 PE. The comparison is to a

---

[8] The reasons for this anomaly are explained in "PAC Barbells: The Way to Go," *PaineWebber Mortgage Strategist* (December 15, 1998), pp. 9-12.

6% coupon FNMA passthrough. The OAS for the portfolio is 70 basis points, which is 12 basis points greater than the collateral (OAS of 58 basis points).

The bottom panel of Exhibit 7 shows the total return for different scenarios. It is only in the scenario where rates are unchanged that the collateral outperformed the PAC barbell and the underperformance is slight (only 2 basis points). Moreover, the analysis underestimates the relative performance of the PAC barbell because it does not allow for the OAS to tighten for the short PAC.[9]

Scenario Analysis to Measure Risk Exposure

Now we will look at how scenario analysis can be used to measure risk exposure. In order to demonstrate this, we will use a portfolio of Freddie Mac fixed-rate CMOs. Exhibit 8 provides the characteristics of the portfolio.[10] To determine the portfolio's exposure to changes in interest rates, scenario analysis can be performed and then the total return under each scenario can be assessed. These scenarios consist of various upward and downward shifts in the yield curve. The horizon assumed in the analysis was six months, the reinvestment rate was 4.62%, and a proprietary prepayment model (the Andrew Davidson Prepayment Model) was used to generate the cash flows for the CMOs under each of the yield curve scenarios. The results of the scenario analysis were then analyzed to determine where the portfolio was exposed to yield curve shocks. Once a portfolio manager determines where there is exposure, a series of scenarios can be run to find a hedging position that stabilizes total return across all the scenarios.

Exhibit 7: Analysis of PAC Barbell versus 6.0% Collateral

	Face	Proceeds	%	Price	OAS
FHR 2105 PA	23,082	23,446	71	101:03	70
FHR 2105 PE	10,000	9,762	29	97:04+	70
Barbell	—	33,208	100	—	70
30 yr FNMA 6.0%	10,000	9,892	100	98:22+	59

Total Rate-of-Return Analysis

	−200	−150	−100	−50	Unch	50	100	150	200	Steep	Flat
FHR 2105 PA	3.74	4.08	5.24	6.67	6.19	5.36	4.40	3.40	2.38	6.62	5.72
FHR 2105 PE	24.31	20.51	15.70	10.95	6.49	1.99	−2.47	−6.87	−11.13	6.21	6.71
Barbell	10.00	9.04	8.37	7.94	6.28	4.37	2.41	0.44	−1.50	6.50	6.01
30 yr FNMA 6.0%	7.34	7.34	7.68	7.75	6.29	4.19	1.77	−0.68	−3.13	6.57	5.99
Difference	2.66	1.70	0.69	0.18	−0.02	0.18	0.64	1.12	1.63	−0.07	0.03

Source: Table 3 in "PAC Barbells: The Way to Go," *PaineWebber Mortgage Strategist* (December 15, 1998), p.11.

[9] In Chapter 11, we looked at a measure of interest rate exposure called duration. We discovered in that chapter that by just looking at the duration measure, a manager would have been misled about the potential performance of the PAC barbell and the collateral because the duration of the PAC barbell was less than that of the collateral. (4.53 versus 4.10). Based solely on duration, this would suggest that the collateral would outperform the PAC barbell if rates decline. As can be seen in the bottom panel of Exhibit 7, this is not the case.

[10] This illustration was provided by Jeffrey Foley using Wall Street Analytics, Inc.'s Portfolio Management Workstation.

Exhibit 8: Illustration of Scenario Analysis for Risk Assessment

Portfolio

Freddie Mac Fixed Rate CMOs

Wtd Ave Coupon:	5.67%
Wtd Ave Life:	1.9 years
Ave Price:	99-13
Ppy Assumption:	Andrew Davidson Prepayment Model
Return Horizon:	6 months
Reinvestment Rate:	4.62%

Total Return Profile (6-Month Horizon)

Shift (bp)	Portfolio
−200	7.07
−150	7.18
−100	7.26
0	5.62
+100	2.67
+150	1.07
+200	−0.58

Source: Wall Street Analytics, Inc.'s Portfolio Management Workstation

Exhibit 8 shows the total return of the portfolio for seven scenarios. The analysis begins with a base case (0 shift) and then the curve was shifted up 100 basis points (bps), up 150 bps, up 200 bps, down 100 bps, down 150 bps, and down 200 bps. The total return for the Freddie Mac fixed-rate CMOs is listed in the second panel of the exhibit under the column labeled "Portfolio." Notice that under the base case (0 shift), the total return is 5.62%. The total return increases significantly in the −100 bps scenario. The total return remains above 7.0% in the −150 bps and −200 bps scenarios (the slight decrease from the −100 bps scenario is due to significantly increased prepayments). The portfolio begins performing very poorly in the upward shift scenarios — 2.67% at +100 bps, 1.07% at +150 bps, and −0.58% at +200 bps.

The results of the scenario analysis indicate that the portfolio does well in decreasing yield curve environments, but is adversely affected by increasing yield curve environments. The next step is to devise a hedging position that enhances the portfolio's performance in the increasing yield curve environments without diminishing the performance in the decreasing yield curve environments. This involves running scenario analysis to determine how the portfolio's exposure to interest rates is affected by adding certain hedging instruments to the portfolio.

Scenario Analysis to Measure Performance versus a Bond Index

A manager may make several bets. The only way to assess these bets is to examine how the portfolio will perform relative to the benchmark index under various scenarios in terms of total return.

Exhibit 9: Portfolio Holding versus the Lehman Aggregate Bond Index (9/29/95)

Issuing Sector	Current Portfolio (9/29/95)		Lehman Aggregate Bond Index (% Held)
	Market Value ($)	Percent Held	
Cash	100	1.7	0.0
Government	1,401	23.7	48.1
Agency	521	8.8	6.0
Passthrough	568	9.6	28.3
CMO	996	16.8	0.0
ABS	504	8.5	1.2
Corporate	1,823	30.8	16.4
Industrials	457	7.7	5.7
Electric/GA	611	10.3	2.1
Telephones	97	1.6	1.1
Finance	658	11.1	4.5
International	0	0.0	3.0
Totals	5,912	100.0	100.0

Exhibit 10: Current Yield Curve (9/29/95) and Five Yield Curve Scenarios one Year Later (9/29/96)

Current Yield Curve		Yield Curve Scenarios				
		+100bps	−50bps	Flatten	No Change	Steepen
6 month	5.55%	100	−50	100	0	0
1 year	5.66	100	−50	98	0	5
2 year	5.90	100	−50	96	0	10
3 year	5.94	100	−50	93	0	15
5 year	6.09	100	−50	88	0	20
7 year	6.12	100	−50	83	0	30
10 year	6.17	100	−50	75	0	50
20 year	6.56	100	−50	50	0	75
30 year	6.46	100	−50	25	0	100
Long BAA vs. Long Treasury		0	0	−25	0	−30
8% Mtgs. vs. 10-year Treasury		0	0	25	0	30
Probability (%)		15	15	30	20	20

To illustrate how this is done, consider the hypothetical portfolio shown in Exhibit 9. The exhibit shows the market value of each issuing sector held. Also shown is the percentage distribution of the portfolio and the corresponding percentage distribution for the Lehman Aggregate Bond Index at the time of the analysis (9/29/95). The *Compare System* of Capital Management Sciences permits the assessment of the relative returns under various scenarios. Exhibit 10 shows the Treasury yield curve as of the date of the analysis. The last five columns show the following scenarios examined for the portfolio and the index: (1) 100 basis point parallel increase in the yield curve, (2) 50 basis point parallel decrease in the yield curve, (3) a flattening of the yield curve, (4) no change in the yield curve, and (5) a steepening of the yield curve. Also shown in Exhibit 10 are assumptions as to how the corporate spreads and mortgage spreads change for each yield curve scenario. The assumed spread change between triple B and long-term Treasuries represents the corporate spread change. The assumed spread change between 8% mortgages and 10-year Treasuries represents the mortgage spread change. The probability of each yield curve scenario occurring is shown.

Exhibit 11 shows the 1-year return (i.e., total return) for each scenario for the portfolio and the index. The return is shown for each factor that affects the return. This consists of coupon income and price change due to (1) change in parallel rates, (2) change in the slope of the yield curve, (3) rolling down the yield curve, (4) change in corporate spreads, and (5) change in mortgage spreads. The last panel of Exhibit 11 indicates that in all but the flattening yield curve scenario will the portfolio underperform the index. Even in this case, the portfolio only outperforms by one basis point.

Based on the probabilities of each yield curve scenario, the expected return (i.e., probability-weighted return) for the portfolio and the index can be calculated. The expected return for the portfolio is 4.97% versus 5.22% for the index. Therefore, the expected return difference is −25 basis points. The analysis strongly suggests that if the manager expects to outperform the index and the scenarios analyzed are those that are likely to occur, then this is not likely to happen with the current portfolio. A manager should then rebalance the portfolio so that the expected return difference is positive.

Exhibit 11: 1-Year Total Return for Current Portfolio and Lehman Aggregate Bond Index for Five Yield Curve Scenarios

	Yield Curve Scenarios				
Portfolio Return	+100bps	−50bps	Flatten	No Change	Steepen
Income	6.56	6.41	6.49	6.47	6.56
Price change due to:					
Change in parallel rates	-4.60	2.41	-1.17	0.00	-4.60
Change in slope	0.00	0.00	-1.73	0.00	2.01
Yield curve roll	0.13	0.13	0.12	0.13	0.14
Change in corporate spreads	0.00	0.00	0.31	0.00	0.37
Change in mortgage spreads	0.00	0.00	-0.20	0.00	-0.24
Total return	2.08	8.95	3.83	6.59	4.24
Index Return:					
Income	6.77	6.71	6.74	6.73	6.77
Price change due to:					
Change in parallel rates	-4.58	2.29	-1.15	0.00	-4.58
Change in slope	0.00	0.00	-1.93	0.00	2.35
Yield curve roll	0.21	0.21	0.20	0.21	0.22
Change in corporate spreads	0.00	0.00	0.20	0.00	0.24
Change in mortgage spreads	0.00	0.00	-0.25	0.00	-0.30
Total return	2.40	9.21	3.82	6.94	4.71
Return Difference:					
Income	-0.21	-0.30	-0.25	-0.27	-0.21
Price change due to:					
Change in parallel rates	-0.03	0.12	-0.02	0.00	-0.03
Change in slope	0.00	0.00	0.21	0.00	-0.34
Yield curve roll	-0.08	-0.08	-0.08	-0.08	-0.08
Change in corporate spreads	0.00	0.00	0.11	0.00	0.13
Change in mortgage spreads	0.00	0.00	0.05	0.00	0.06
Total return	-0.32	-0.27	0.01	-0.35	-0.47

Expected Portfolio Return: 4.97%
Expected Index Return: 5.22%
Expected Return Difference: -0.25%

Source: Analysis based on Capital Management Sciences *Compare System*.
Copyright 1995. Capital Management Sciences.

Chapter 11

Measuring Interest Rate Risk

A general principle of valuation is the present value of an expected future cash flow changes in the opposite direction from changes in the interest rate used to discount the cash flows. We observed this principle at work when we discussed the price/yield relationship for option-free bonds in Chapter 4. This inverse relationship lies at the heart of the major risk faced by fixed-income investors — *interest rate risk*. Interest rate risk involves the possibility that the value of a bond position or a bond portfolio's value will decline due to an adverse interest rate movement. Specifically, a long bond position's value will decline if interest rates rise, resulting in a loss. Conversely, for a short bond position, a loss will be realized if interest rates fall. To effectively control interest rate risk, a portfolio manager must be able to quantify the portfolio's interest rate risk exposure. The purpose of this chapter is to understand the dimensions of interest rate risk and explain how it is measured.

We will discuss two approaches for assessing the interest rate risk exposure of a bond or a portfolio. The first approach is the *full valuation approach* that involves selecting possible interest rate scenarios for how interest rates and yield spreads may change and revaluing the bond position. The second approach entails the computation of measures that approximate how a bond's price or the portfolio's value will change when interest rates change. The most commonly used measures are *duration* and *convexity*. We will discuss duration/convexity measures for option-free bonds, bonds with embedded options, and bond portfolios. In addition, we will present other widely used interest rate risk measures — price value of a basis point and yield value of a price change.

THE FULL VALUATION APPROACH

The most obvious way to measure the interest rate risk exposure of a bond position or a portfolio is to re-value it when interest rates change. The analysis is performed for a given scenario with respect to interest rate changes. For example, a manager may want to measure the interest rate exposure to a 50 basis point, 100 basis point, and 200 basis point instantaneous change in interest rates. This approach requires the re-valuation of a bond or bond portfolio for a given interest rate change scenario and is referred to as the *full valuation approach*. It is sometimes referred to as *scenario analysis* because it involves assessing the exposure to interest rate change scenarios.

Exhibit 1: Bloomberg Yield Analysis Screen for a Principal Strip

```
YA                                            DG36 Govt  YA
Enter all values and hit <GO>.
                    YIELD  ANALYSIS          CUSIP    912B03CH4
STRIP PRINC        SP 05/15/30      18.2645/ 18.2645 ( 5.83 /83) BFV  @17:04
PRICE 18.264499               SETTLEMENT DATE 10/11/2000
    YIELD               MATURITY    CASHFLOW ANALYSIS
    CALCULATIONS        5/15/2030  To  5/15/2030WORKOUT   1000M FACE
STREET CONVENTION            5.828      PAYMENT  INVOICE
TREASURY CONVENTION          5.828  PRINCIPAL[RND(Y/N)N]     182644.99
TRUE YIELD                   5.820  149 DAYS ACCRUED INT         0.00
EQUIVALENT  1/YEAR COMPOUND  5.913  TOTAL                   182644.99
JAPANESE YIELD (SIMPLE)     15.122           INCOME
PROCEEDS/MMKT EQUIVALENT            REDEMPTION VALUE        1000000.00
                                    COUPON PAYMENT
REPO EQUIVALENT                     INTEREST @ 5.828%
EFFECTIVE  @ 5.828 RATE(%)    5.828  TOTAL                   1000000.00
TAXED: INC 39.60% CG 28.00%   4.473           RETURN
*NO ISSUE PRICE. ASSUME 100.  NON OID BOND WITH MKT DISCOUNT*  GROSS PROFIT           817355.01
    SENSITIVITY ANALYSIS           RETURN  (SIMPLE INT)       5.828
 NV DURATION(YEARS)          29.595
 ADJ/MOD DURATION            28.757     FURTHER ANALYSIS
 RISK                         5.252  HIT 1 <GO> COST OF CARRY
 CONVEXITY                    8.409  HIT 2 <GO> PRICE/YIELD TABLE
 DOLLAR VALUE OF A   0.01     0.05252  HIT 3 <GO> TOTAL RETURN
 YIELD VALUE OF A    0 32    0.00595
Copyright 2000 BLOOMBERG L.P.  Frankfurt:69-920410  Hong Kong:2-977-6000  London:207-330-7500  New York:212-318-2000
Princeton:609-279-3000  Singapore:65-212-1000  Sydney:2-9777-8686  Tokyo:3-3201-8900  Sao Paulo:11-3048-4500
                                                        I464-169-0 10-Oct-00 17:04:22
```

Bloomberg

Source: Bloomberg Financial Markets

To illustrate this approach, suppose that a manager has a $50 million par value position in a U.S. Treasury principal strip (i.e., zero-coupon) that matures on May 15, 2030. Exhibit 1 presents Bloomberg's Yield Analysis (YA) screen for this security. With a settlement date of October 11, 2000, the price is 18.264499 for a yield (i.e., yield to maturity) of 5.828%. The market value of the position is $9,132,249.50 (18.264499% × $50,000,000). Since the manager has a long position in this issue, she is concerned with a rise in yield since this will decrease the position's market value. To assess the portfolio's exposure to a rise in market yields, the manager decides to examine how the bond's value will change if yields change *instantaneously* for the following four scenarios: (1) 50 basis point increase, (2) 100 basis point increase, (3) 150 basis point increase, and (4) 200 basis point increase. In other words, the manager wants to assess the consequences to the portfolio's value if the bond's yield increases from its current level at 5.828% to (1) 6.328%, (2) 6.828%, (3) 7.328%, and (4) 7.828%. Because this zero-coupon bond is option-free, valuation is straightforward. The bond's price per $100 of par value and the market value of the $50 million par position is shown in Exhibit 2. Also presented are the change in the market value and the percentage change.

In the case of a portfolio, each included bond is valued and the portfolio's total value is computed for a given scenario. For example, suppose that a manager has a portfolio that consists of the following two Treasury securities: (1)

a 6% coupon Treasury note that matures on September 30, 2002 and (2) a 6.25% coupon Treasury bond that matures on May 15, 2030. Exhibits 3 and 4 present Bloomberg's Yield Analysis (YA) screens for these two securities. For the 2-year note, $10 million of par value is owned and with a settlement date of October 11, 2000 the note's full price is 100.290674 for a yield of 5.939%. For the 30-year bond, $20 million of par value is owned and with a settlement date of October 11, 2000 the full price is 108.603405 for a yield of 5.817%. Suppose that the manager wants to assess the portfolio's interest rate risk for a 50, 100, 150, and 200 basis point increases in interest rates, assuming both the 2-year yield and the 30-year yield change by the same number of basis points. Exhibit 5 shows the exposure. Panel A of the exhibit shows the market value of the 2-year note for the four scenarios. Panel B does the same for the 30-year bond. Panel C shows the total market value of the portfolio and the percentage change in the market value for the four outcomes.

In the illustration in Exhibit 5, it is assumed that both the 2-year note and the 30-year bond yields changed by the same number of basis points. The full valuation approach can also handle scenarios where the yield curve does not change in a parallel fashion. Exhibit 6 illustrates this for our portfolio that includes the 2-year notes and 30-year bonds. The scenario analyzed is a yield curve shift combined with shifts in the level of yields. In the illustration in Exhibit 6, the following yield changes are assumed for the 2-year and 30-year Treasury yields:

Scenario	Change in the 2-year rate (bp)	Change in the 30-year rate (bp)
1	40	20
2	80	40
3	120	60
4	160	80

The last panel in Exhibit 6 shows how the portfolio's market value changes for each scenario.

Exhibit 2: Illustration of Full Valuation Approach to Assess the Interest Rate Risk of a Bond Position for Four Scenarios

Current bond position: Principal STRIP that matures 5/15/30
Price: 18.264499
Yield to maturity: 5.828%
Par value owned: $50 million
Market value of position: $9,132,249.50

Scenario	Yield change (bp)	New yield (%)	New price	New market value ($)	Percentage change in market value (%)
1	50	6.328	15.8221	7,911,050	−13.372
2	100	6.828	13.7103	6,855,150	−24.935
3	150	7.328	11.8844	5,942,200	−34.932
4	200	7.828	10.3053	5,152,650	−43.577

Exhibit 3: Bloomberg Yield Analysis Screen for a 2-Year Treasury Note

```
YA                                                   DG36 Govt  YA
Enter all values and hit <GO>.
                     YIELD  ANALYSIS           CUSIP    9128276L1
US TREASURY N/B    T 6 09/30/02   100-3  /100-3+  ( 5.95 /94) BGN @16:45
PRICE 100-3+                      SETTLEMENT DATE 10/11/2000
    YIELD              MATURITY   CASHFLOW ANALYSIS
    CALCULATIONS       9/30/2002  To  9/30/2002WORKOUT , 1000M FACE
STREET CONVENTION         5.939       PAYMENT  INVOICE
TREASURY CONVENTION       5.938   PRINCIPAL[RND(Y/N)N]     1001093.75
TRUE YIELD                5.938    11 DAYS ACCRUED INT        1813.19
EQUIVALENT 1/YEAR COMPOUND 6.027  TOTAL                    1002906.94
JAPANESE YIELD (SIMPLE)   5.937          INCOME
PROCEEDS/MMKT EQUIVALENT  6.130   REDEMPTION VALUE         1000000.00
                                  COUPON PAYMENT            120000.00
REPO EQUIVALENT           5.917   INTEREST @ 5.939 %          5451.69
EFFECTIVE @ 5.939 RATE(%) 5.939   TOTAL                    1125451.69
TAXED: INC 39.60% CG 28.00% 3.587        RETURN
 ISSUE PRICE = 99.995. BOND PURCHASED WITH PREMIUM.  GROSS PROFIT       122544.75
SENSITIVITY  ANALYSIS             RETURN                     5.939
CNV DURATION(YEARS)       1.804
ADJ/MOD DURATION          1.830   FURTHER  ANALYSIS
RISK                      1.835   HIT 1 <GO> COST OF CARRY
CONVEXITY                 0.043   HIT 2 <GO> PRICE/YIELD TABLE
DOLLAR VALUE OF A  0.01   0.01835 HIT 3 <GO> TOTAL RETURN
YIELD VALUE OF A   0 3/2   0.01703
Copyright 2000 BLOOMBERG L.P.  Frankfurt:69-920410  Hong Kong:2-977-6000  London:207-330-7500  New York:212-318-2000
Princeton:609-279-3000    Singapore:65-212-1000   Sydney:2-9777-8686   Tokyo:3-3201-8900   Sao Paulo:11-3048-4500
                                                                   1464-169-0 10-Oct-00 16:50:30
```

Source: Bloomberg Financial Markets

Exhibit 4: Bloomberg Yield Analysis Screen for a 30-Year Treasury Bond

```
YA                                                   DG36 Govt  YA
Enter all values and hit <GO>.
                     YIELD  ANALYSIS           CUSIP    912810FM5
US TREASURY N/B    T 6 1/4 05/15/30  106-1+ /106-2+  ( 5.82 /82) BGN @17:00
PRICE 106-2+                      SETTLEMENT DATE 10/11/2000
    YIELD              MATURITY   CASHFLOW ANALYSIS
    CALCULATIONS       5/15/2030  To  5/15/2030WORKOUT , 1000M FACE
STREET CONVENTION         5.817       PAYMENT  INVOICE
TREASURY CONVENTION       5.816   PRINCIPAL[RND(Y/N)N]     1060781.25
TRUE YIELD                5.816   149 DAYS ACCRUED INT       25305.71
EQUIVALENT 1/YEAR COMPOUND 5.901  TOTAL                    1086086.96
JAPANESE YIELD (SIMPLE)   5.698          INCOME
PROCEEDS/MMKT EQUIVALENT          REDEMPTION VALUE         1000000.00
                                  COUPON PAYMENT           1875000.00
REPO EQUIVALENT           5.630   INTEREST @ 5.817 %       3051683.04
EFFECTIVE @ 5.817 RATE(%) 5.817   TOTAL                    5926683.04
TAXED: INC 39.60% CG 28.00% 3.543        RETURN
 ISSUE PRICE = 107.860. BOND PURCHASED WITH PREMIUM.  GROSS PROFIT    4840596.08
SENSITIVITY  ANALYSIS             RETURN (SIMPLE INT)        5.817
CNV DURATION(YEARS)      13.925
ADJ/MOD DURATION         13.531   FURTHER  ANALYSIS
RISK                     14.696   HIT 1 <GO> COST OF CARRY
CONVEXITY                 2.878   HIT 2 <GO> PRICE/YIELD TABLE
DOLLAR VALUE OF A  0.01   0.14696 HIT 3 <GO> TOTAL RETURN
YIELD VALUE OF A   0 3/2   0.00213
Copyright 2000 BLOOMBERG L.P.  Frankfurt:69-920410  Hong Kong:2-977-6000  London:207-330-7500  New York:212-318-2000
Princeton:609-279-3000    Singapore:65-212-1000   Sydney:2-9777-8686   Tokyo:3-3201-8900   Sao Paulo:11-3048-4500
                                                                   1464-169-0 10-Oct-00 17:01:24
```

Source: Bloomberg Financial Markets

Exhibit 5: Illustration of Full Valuation Approach to Assess the Interest Rate Risk of a Bond Portfolio for Four Scenarios Assuming a Parallel Shift in the Yield Curve
Two bond portfolio (both bonds are option-free)

Panel A

Bond 1: 6% coupon Treasury note maturing September 30, 2002
Full Price: 100.290674
Yield to maturity: 5.939%
Market value: $10,029,067.40
Par value: $10,000,000

Scenario	Yield change (bp)	New yield (%)	New price	New market value ($)	Percentage change in market value (%)
1	50	6.439	99.3785	9,937,850	−0.910
2	100	6.939	98.4770	9,847,700	−1.810
3	150	7.439	97.5861	9,758,610	−2.700
4	200	7.939	96.7055	9,670,550	−3.575

Panel B

Bond 2: 6.25% coupon Treasury bond maturing May 15, 2030
Full Price: 108.603405
Yield to maturity: 5.817%
Market value: $21,720,680.96
Par value: $20,000,000

Scenario	Yield change (bp)	New yield (%)	New price	New market value ($)	Percentage change in market value (%)
1	50	6.317	101.6308	20,326,160	−6.420
2	100	6.817	95.3490	19,069,800	−12.204
3	150	7.317	89.6779	17,935,580	−17.426
4	200	7.817	84.5475	16,909,500	−22.150

Panel C

Portfolio Market Value: $31,749,748.36

Scenario	Yield change (bp)	Market value of Bond 1 ($)	Market value of Bond 2 ($)	Market value of Portfolio ($)	Percentage change in market value (%)
1	50	9,937,850	20,326,160	30,264,010	−4.680
2	100	9,847,700	19,069,800	28,917,500	−8.921
3	150	9,758,610	17,935,580	27,694,190	−12.774
4	200	9,670,550	16,909,500	26,580,050	−16.283

A common question that often arises when using the full valuation approach is which scenarios should be evaluated to assess interest rate risk exposure. For some regulated entities, there are specified scenarios established by regulators. For example, it is common for regulators of depository institutions to require entities to determine the impact on the value of their bond portfolio for a

100, 200, and 300 basis point instantaneous change in interest rates (up and down). (Regulators tend to refer to this as "simulating" interest rate scenarios rather than scenario analysis.) Risk managers and highly leveraged investors such as hedge funds tend to look at extreme shocks to assess exposure to interest rate changes. This practice is referred to as *stress testing*.

Exhibit 6: Illustration of Full Valuation Approach to Assess the Interest Rate Risk of a Bond Portfolio for Four Scenarios Assuming a Nonparallel Shift in the Yield Curve
Two bond portfolio (both bonds are option-free)

Panel A

Bond 1: 6% coupon Treasury note maturing September 30, 2002
Full Price: 100.290674
Yield to maturity: 5.939%
Market value: $10,029,067.37
Par value: $10,000,000

Scenario	Yield change (bp)	New yield (%)	New price	New market value ($)	Percentage change in market value (%)
1	40	6.339	99.5601	9,956,008	−0.728
2	60	6.739	98.8363	9,883,635	−1.450
3	80	7.139	98.1194	9,811,940	−2.165
4	120	7.539	97.4092	9,740,916	−2.873

Panel B

Bond 2: 6.25% coupon Treasury bond maturing May 15, 2030
Full Price: 108.6034
Yield to maturity: 5.817%
Market value: $21,720,680.96
Par value: $20,000,000

Scenario	Yield change (bp)	New yield (%)	New price	New market value ($)	Percentage change in market value (%)
1	20	6.017	105.7259	21,145,180	−2.6496
2	40	6.217	102.9673	20,593,460	−5.1896
3	60	6.417	100.3219	20,064,380	−7.6255
4	80	6.617	97.7842	19,556,840	−9.9621

Panel C

Portfolio Market Value: $31,749,748.36

Scenario	Market Value of			Percentage change in the market value (%)
	Bond 1 ($)	Bond 2 ($)	Portfolio ($)	
1	9,937,880	20,639,060	30,576,940	−3.694
2	9,986,500	20,087,340	29,952,840	−5.660
3	9,793,810	19,558,260	29,352,070	−7.552
4	9,722,780	19,050,720	28,773,500	−9.374

Of course, in assessing how changes in the yield curve can affect the exposure of a portfolio, there are an infinite number of scenarios that can be evaluated. The state-of-the-art technology involves using a complex statistical procedure[1] to determine a likely set of yield curve shift scenarios from historical data.

In summary, we can use the full valuation approach to assess the exposure of a bond or portfolio to interest rate shocks, assuming – and this cannot be stressed enough – that the manager has a good valuation model to estimate what the price of the bond will be in each interest rate scenario. Moreover, we recommend use of the full valuation approach for assessing the position of a single bond or a portfolio of a few bonds. For a portfolio with a large number of bonds and/or the bonds containing embedded options, the full valuation process may be too time consuming. In its stead, managers want a single measure that they can employ to estimate how a portfolio or even a single bond will change if interest rates change in a parallel fashion rather than having to revalue an entire portfolio to obtain that answer. Duration is such a measure and we will discuss it as well as a supplementary measure called convexity later in the chapter. We describe the basic price volatility characteristics of bonds in the next section. It should come as no surprise that there are limitations of using one or two measures to describe the interest rate exposure of a position or portfolio. Nevertheless, these measures provide us with some important intuition about assessing interest rate risk.

PRICE VOLATILITY CHARACTERISTICS OF BONDS

There are four characteristics of a bond that affect its price volatility: (1) term to maturity, (2) coupon rate, (3) the level of yields, and (4) the presence of embedded options. In this section, we will examine each of these price volatility characteristics.

Price Volatility Characteristics of Option-Free Bonds

Let's begin by focusing on option-free bonds (i.e., bonds that do not have embedded options). A fundamental characteristic of an option-free bond is that the price of the bond changes in the opposite direction from a change in the bond's required yield. Exhibit 7 illustrates this property for four hypothetical bonds assuming a par value of $100.

When the price/yield relationship for any hypothetical option-free bond is graphed, it exhibits the basic shape shown in Exhibit 8. Notice that as the required yield decreases, the price of an option-free bond increases. Conversely, as the required yield decreases, the price of an option-free bond increases. In other words, the price/yield relationship is negatively sloped. In addition, the price/yield relationship is not linear (i.e., not a straight line) for reasons mentioned in Chapter 4. The shape of the price/yield relationship for any option-free bond is referred to as *convex*. The price/yield relationship is for an instantaneous change in the required yield.

---

[1] The procedure used is principal component analysis.

Exhibit 7: Price/Yield Relationship for Four Hypothetical Option-Free Bonds

Yield (%)	Price ($)			
	7%, 10-year	7%, 30-year	9%, 10-year	9%, 30-year
5.00	115.5892	130.9087	131.1783	161.8173
6.00	107.4387	113.8378	122.3162	141.5133
6.50	103.6348	106.5634	118.1742	132.8171
6.90	100.7138	101.2599	114.9908	126.4579
6.99	100.0711	100.1248	114.2899	125.0947
7.00	100.0000	100.0000	114.2124	124.9447
7.01	99.9290	99.8754	114.1349	124.7950
7.10	99.2926	98.7652	113.4409	123.4608
7.50	96.5259	94.0655	110.4222	117.8034
8.00	93.2048	88.6883	106.7952	111.3117
9.00	86.9921	79.3620	100.0000	100.0000

Exhibit 8: Price/Yield Relationship for a Hypothetical Option-Free Bond

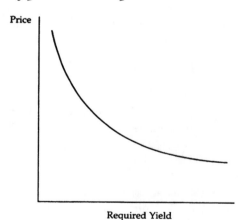

Exhibit 9 shows the price/yield for the U.S. Treasury principal strip that is shown in Exhibit 1. Recall, using a settlement date of October 11, 2000, the yield is 5.828%. To construct the graph, the principal strip was repriced using increments and decrements of 10 basis points from 7.828% to 3.828%. Exhibit 10 shows the two price/yield relationships for the 6% coupon, 2-year Treasury note and 6.25% coupon, 30-year Treasury bond shown in Exhibits 3 and 4, respectively. Note the Treasury bond's price/yield relationship is more steeply sloped and more curved than the price/yield relationship for the 2-year Treasury note. The reasons for these differences will be discussed shortly.

Exhibit 9: Price/Yield Relationship for a
Treasury Principal Strip*

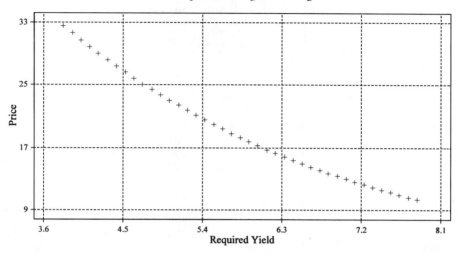

* Priced with a settlement date of 10/11/00.

Exhibit 10: Price/Yield Relationships for a 6% 2-Year
Treasury Note and a 6.25% 30-Year Treasury Bond*

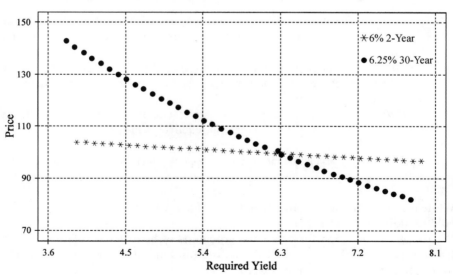

* Both bonds are priced with a settlement date of 10/11/00.

Exhibit 11: Instantaneous Percentage Price Change for Four Hypothetical Bonds
(Initial Yield for all four bonds is 7%)

Yield (%)	Price ($)			
	7%, 10-year	7%, 30-year	9%, 10-year	9%, 30-year
5.00	15.5892	30.9087	14.8547	29.5111
6.00	7.4387	13.8378	7.0954	13.2607
6.50	3.6368	6.5634	3.4688	6.3007
6.90	0.7138	1.2599	0.6815	1.2111
6.99	0.0711	0.1248	0.0679	0.1201
7.00	0.0000	0.0000	0.0000	0.0000
7.01	−0.0710	−0.1246	−0.0679	−0.1200
7.10	−0.0707	−1.2350	−0.6750	−1.1880
7.50	−3.4740	−5.9350	−3.3190	−5.7160
8.00	−6.7950	−11.3120	−6.4940	−10.9110
9.00	−13.0080	−20.6380	−12.4440	−19.9650

The price sensitivity of a bond to changes in the required yield can be measured in terms of the dollar price change or the percentage price change. Exhibit 11 uses the four hypothetical bonds in Exhibit 7 to show the percentage change in each bond's price for various changes in yield, assuming that the initial yield for all four bonds is 7%. An examination of Exhibit 11 reveals the following properties concerning the price volatility of an option-free bond:

Property 1: Although the price moves in the opposite direction from the change in required yield, the percentage price change is not the same for all bonds.

Property 2: For small changes in the required yield, the percentage price change for a given bond is roughly the same, whether the required yield increases or decreases.

Property 3: For large changes in required yield, the percentage price change is not the same for an increase in required yield as it is for a decrease in required yield.

Property 4: For a given large change in basis points in the required yield, the percentage price increase is greater than the percentage price decrease.

While the properties are expressed in terms of percentage price change, they also hold for dollar price changes.

An explanation for these two properties of bond price volatility lies in the convex shape of the price/yield relationship. Exhibit 12 illustrates this. The following notation is used in the exhibit

Y = initial yield
Y_1 = lower yield

Y_2 = higher yield
P = initial price
P_1 = price at lower yield Y_1
P_2 = price at higher yield Y_2

What was done in the exhibit was to change the initial yield (Y) up and down by the same number of basis points. That is, in Exhibit 12, the yield is decreased from Y to Y_1 and increased from Y to Y_2 such that the magnitude of the change is the same:

$$Y - Y_1 = Y_2 - Y$$

Also, the amount of the change in yield is a large number of basis points.

The vertical distance from the horizontal axis (the yield) to the intercept on the graph shows the price. The change in the initial price (P) when the yield declines from Y to Y_1 is equal to the difference between the new price (P_1) and the initial price. That is,

change in price when yield decreases = $P_1 - P$

The change in the initial price (P) when the yield increases from Y to Y_2 is equal to the difference between the new price (P_2) and the initial price. That is,

change in price when yield increases = $P - P_2$

Exhibit 12: Graphical Illustration of Properties 3 and 4 for an Option-Free Bond

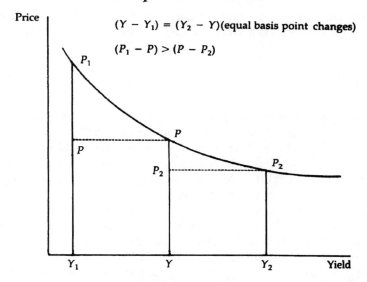

Exhibit 13: Impact of Convexity on Property 4: Less Convex Bond

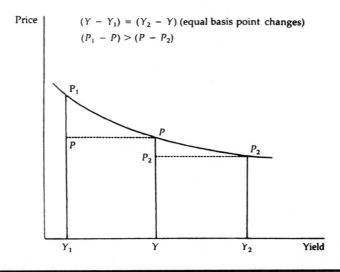

As can be seen in the exhibit, the change in price when yield decreases is not equal to the change in price when yield increases by the same number of basis points. That is,

$$P_1 - P \neq P - P_2$$

This is what Property 3 states. Moreover, a comparison of the price change shows that the change in price when yield decreases is greater than the change in price when yield increases. That is,

$$P_1 - P > P - P_2$$

This is Property 4.

The implication of Property 4 is that if an investor is long a bond, the price appreciation that will be realized if the required yield decreases is greater than the capital loss that will be realized if the required yield increases by the same number of basis points. For an investor who is short a bond, the reverse is true: the potential capital loss is greater than the potential capital gain if the yield changes by a given number of basis points.

To see how the convexity of the price/yield relationship impacts Property 4, look at Exhibits 13 and 14. Exhibit 13 shows a less convex price/yield relationship than Exhibit 12. That is, the price/yield relationship in Exhibit 13 is less bowed than the price/yield relationship in Exhibit 12. Because of the difference in the convexities, look at what happens when the yield increases and decreases by the same number of basis points and the yield change is a large number of basis points. We use the same notation in Exhibits 13 and 14 as in Exhibit 12. Notice that while the price gain when the required yield decreases is greater than the price decline when the required yield increases, the gain is not much greater than the loss. In contrast, Exhibit 14 has much greater convexity than the bonds in Exhibits 12 and 13 and the price gain is significantly greater than the loss for the bonds depicted in Exhibits 12 and 13.

Price Volatility Characteristics of Bonds with Embedded Options

Now let's turn to the price volatility characteristics of bonds with embedded options. As explained in previous chapters, the price of a bond with an embedded option is comprised of two components. The first is the value of the same bond if it had no embedded option. That is, the price if the bond is option free. The second component is the value of the embedded option.

The two most common types of embedded options are call (or prepay) options and put options. As interest rates in the market decline, the issuer may call or prepay the debt obligation prior to the scheduled principal repayment date. The other type of option is a put option. This option gives the investor the right to require the issuer to purchase the bond at a specified price. Below we will examine the price/yield relationship for bonds with both types of embedded options (calls and puts) and implications for price volatility.

Exhibit 14: Impact of Convexity on Property 4: Highly Convex Bond

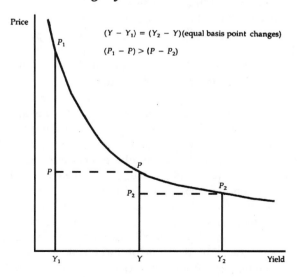

Exhibit 15: Price/Yield Relationship for a Callable Bond and an Option-Free Bond

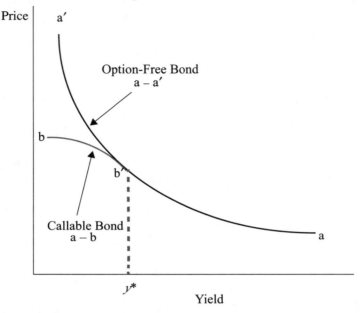

Bonds with Call and Prepay Options

In the discussion below, we will refer to a bond that may be called or is prepayable as a callable bond. Exhibit 15 shows the price/yield relationship for an option-free bond and a callable bond. The convex curve given by *a-a′* is the price/yield relationship for an option-free bond. The unusual shaped curve denoted by *a-b* in the exhibit is the price/yield relationship for the callable bond.

The reason for the price/yield relationship for a callable bond is as follows. When the prevailing market yield for comparable bonds is higher than the coupon rate on the callable bond, it is unlikely that the issuer will call the issue. For example, if the coupon rate on a bond is 7% and the prevailing market yield on comparable bonds is 12%, it is highly unlikely that the issuer will call a 7% coupon bond so that it can issue a 12% coupon bond. Since the bond is unlikely to be called, the callable bond will have a similar price/yield relationship as an otherwise comparable option-free bond. Consequently, the callable bond is going to be valued as if it is an option-free bond. However, since there is still some value to the call option, the bond won't trade exactly like an option-free bond.

As yields in the market decline, the concern is that the issuer will call the bond. The issuer won't necessarily exercise the call option as soon as the market yield drops below the coupon rate. Yet, the value of the embedded call option increases as yields approach the coupon rate from higher yield levels. For example, if the coupon rate on a bond is 7% and the market yield declines to 7.5%, the issuer will most likely not call the issue. However, market yields are at a level at which the investor is concerned that the issue may eventually be called if market yields decline further. Cast in terms of the value of the embedded call option, that option becomes more valuable to the issuer and therefore it reduces the price relative to an otherwise comparable option-free bond.[2] In Exhibit 15, the value of the embedded call option at a given yield can be measured by the difference between the price of an option-free bond (the price shown on the curve *a-d*) and the price on the curve *a-b*. Notice that at low yield levels (below *y** on the horizontal axis), the value of the embedded call option is high.

Let's look at the difference in the price volatility properties relative to an option-free bond given the price/yield relationship for a callable bond shown in Exhibit 15. Exhibit 16 blows up the portion of the price/yield relationship for the callable bond where the two curves in Exhibit 15 depart (segment b-b' in Exhibit 15). We know from our discussion of the price/yield relationship that for a large change in yield of a given number of basis points, the price of an option-free bond increases by more than it decreases (Property 4 above). Is that what happens for a callable bond in the region of the price/yield relationship shown in Exhibit 16? No, it is not. In fact, as can be seen in the exhibit, the opposite is true! That is, for a given large change in yield, the price appreciation is less than the price decline.

Exhibit 16: Negative Convexity Region of the Price/Yield Relationship for a Callable Bond

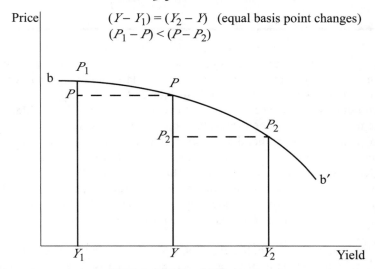

$$(Y - Y_1) = (Y_2 - Y) \quad \text{(equal basis point changes)}$$
$$(P_1 - P) < (P - P_2)$$

[2] For readers who are already familiar with option theory, this characteristic can be restated as follows: When the coupon rate for the issue is below the market yield, the embedded call option is said to be "out-of-the-money." When the coupon rate for the issue is above the market yield, the embedded call option is said to be "in-the-the money."

Exhibit 17: Negative and Positive Convexity Exhibited by a Callable Bond

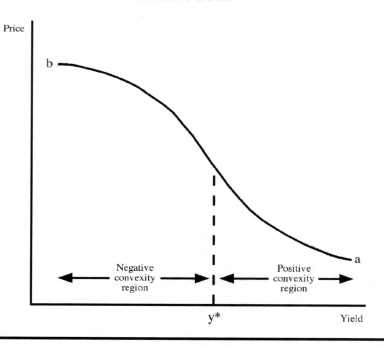

The price volatility characteristic of a callable bond is important to understand. The characteristic of a callable bond — that its price appreciation is less than its price decline when rates change by a large number of basis points — is referred to as *negative convexity*.[3] But notice from Exhibit 15 that callable bonds do not exhibit this characteristic at every yield level. When yields are high (relative to the issue's coupon rate), the bond exhibits the same price/yield relationship as an option-free bond and therefore at high yield levels it also has the characteristic that the gain is greater than the loss. Because market participants have referred to the shape of the price/yield relationship shown in Exhibit 16 as negative convexity, market participants refer to the relationship for an option-free bond as *positive convexity*. Consequently, a callable bond exhibits negative convexity at low yield levels and positive convexity at high yield levels. This is depicted in Exhibit 17.

As can be seen from the exhibits, when a bond exhibits negative convexity, the bond compresses in price as rates decline. That is, at a certain yield level there is very little price appreciation when rates decline. When a bond enters this region, the bond is said to exhibit "price compression."

---

[3] Mathematicians refer to this shape as being "concave."

Exhibit 18: Price/Yield Relationship for a Putable Bond and an Option-Free Bond

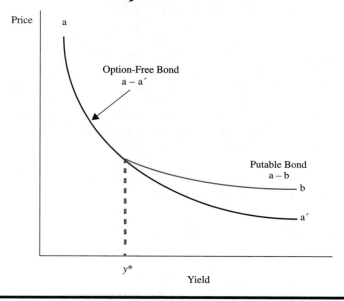

Bonds with Embedded Put Options

Putable bonds may be redeemed by the bondholder on the dates and at the put price specified in the indenture. Typically, the put price is par value. The advantage to the investor is that if yields rise such that the bond's value falls below the put price, the investor will exercise the put option. If the put price is par value, this means that if market yields rise above the coupon rate, the bond's value will fall below par and the investor will then exercise the put option.

The value of a putable bond is equal to the value of an option-free bond plus the value of the put option. Thus, the difference between the value of a putable bond and the value of an otherwise comparable option-free bond is the value of the embedded put option. This can be seen in Exhibit 18 which shows the price/yield relationship for a putable bond (the curve *a-b*) and an option-free bond (the curve *a-a′*).

At low yield levels (low relative to the issue's coupon rate), the price of the putable bond is basically the same as the price of the option-free bond because the value of the put option is small. As rates rise, the price of the putable bond declines, but the price decline is less than that for an option-free bond. The divergence in the price of the putable bond and an otherwise comparable option-free bond at a given yield level is the value of the put option. When yields rise to a level where the bond's price would fall below the put price, the price at these levels is the put price.

DURATION

Given the background about a bond's price volatility characteristics, we can now turn our attention to an alternate approach to full valuation: the duration/convexity approach. Simply put, *duration* is a measure of the approximate sensitivity of a bond's value to rate changes. More specifically, *duration is the approximate percentage change in value for a 100 basis point change in rates.* We will see in this section that duration is the first approximation (i.e., linear) of the percentage price change. To improve the estimate obtained using duration, a measure called "convexity" can be used. Hence, using duration and convexity together to estimate a bond's percentage price change resulting from interest rate changes is called the *duration/convexity approach.*

Calculating Duration

The duration of a bond is estimated as follows:

$$\frac{\text{price if yields decline} - \text{price if yields rise}}{2(\text{initial price})(\text{change in yield in decimal})}$$

If we let

Δy = change in yield in decimal
V_0 = initial price
V_- = price if yields decline by Δy
V_+ = price if yields increase by Δy

then duration can be expressed as

$$\text{duration} = \frac{V_- - V_+}{2(V_0)(\Delta y)} \tag{1}$$

For example, consider the 6.25% coupon, 30-year Treasury discussed earlier (Exhibit 4) that matures on May 15, 2030 and on a settlement date of October 11, 2000 is priced to yield 5.817% with a full price of 108.6034 since it is between coupon payment dates. Let's change (i.e., shock) the yield down and up by 20 basis points and determine what the new prices will be in the numerator of equation (1). If yield were decreased by 20 basis points from 5.817% to 5.617%, the bond's full price would increase to 111.6060. If the yield increases by 20 basis points, the full price would decrease to 105.7259. Thus,

Δy = 0.002
V_0 = 108.6034
V_- = 111.6060
V_+ = 105.7259

Then,

$$\text{duration} = \frac{111.6060 - 105.7259}{2 \times (108.6034) \times (0.002)} = 13.536$$

Note that our calculation for duration of 13.536 agrees (within rounding error) with Bloomberg's calculation in Exhibit 4. Bloomberg's duration measures are located in a box titled "SENSITIVITY ANALYSIS" in the lower left-hand corner of the screen. The duration measure we just calculated is labeled "ADJ/MOD DURATION" which stands for adjusted/modified duration.

Duration is interpreted as the approximate percentage change in price for a 100 basis point change in rates. Consequently, a duration of 13.536 means that the approximate change in price for this bond is 13.536% for a 100 basis point change in rates. A common question raised about this interpretation is the consistency between the yield change that is used to compute duration using equation (1) and the interpretation of duration. For example, recall that in computing the duration of the 30-year Treasury bond, we used a 20 basis point yield change to obtain the two prices to use in the numerator of equation (1). Yet, we interpret the duration computed as the approximate percentage price change for a 100 basis point change in yield. The reason is that regardless of the yield change used to estimate duration in equation (1), the interpretation is unchanged. If we used a 30 basis point change in yield to compute the prices used in the numerator of equation (1), the resulting duration measure is interpreted as the approximate percentage price change for a 100 basis point change in yield. Shortly, we will use different changes in yield to illustrate the sensitivity of the computed duration using equation (1).

Approximating the Percentage Price Change Using Duration

In order to approximate the percentage price change for a given change in yield and a given duration, we employ the following formula:

$$\text{approximate percentage price change} = - \text{duration} \times \Delta y \times 100 \qquad (2)$$

The reason for the negative sign on the right-hand side of equation (2) is due to the inverse relationship between price change and yield change.

For example, consider the 6.25% coupon, 30-year U.S. Treasury bond trading at a full price of 108.6034 whose duration we just showed is 13.536. The approximate percentage price change for a 10 basis point increase in yield (i.e., $\Delta y = +0.001$) is:

$$\text{approximate percentage price change} = -13.536 \times (+0.001) \times 100 = -1.3536\%$$

How good is this approximation? The actual percentage price change is -1.339% ($= 107.1494 - 108.6034)/108.6034$). Duration, in this case, did an excellent job of estimating the percentage price change. We would come to the same conclusion if we used duration to estimate the percentage price change if the yield declined by 10 basis points (i.e., $\Delta y = +0.001$). In this case, the approximate percentage price change would be +1.3536% (i.e., the direction of the estimated price change is the reverse but the magnitude of the change is the same.)

In terms of estimating the new price, let's see how duration performed. The initial full price is 108.6034. For a 10 basis point increase in yield, duration estimates that the price will decline by −1.3536%. Thus, the full price will decline to 107.1333 (found by multiplying 108.6034 by one minus 0.013536). The actual price if the yield increases by 10 basis points is 107.1494. Thus, the price estimated using duration is very close to the actual price. For a 10 basis point decrease in yield, the actual full price is 110.0887 and the estimated price using duration is 110.0735 (a price increase of 1.3536%).

Now let us examine how well duration does in estimating the percentage price change when the yield increases by 200 basis points instead of 10 basis points. In this case, Δy is equal to +0.02. Substituting into equation (2) we have

$$\text{approximate percentage price change} = -13.536 \times (+0.02) \times 100$$
$$= -27.072$$

How good is this estimate? The actual percentage price change when the yield increases by 200 basis points (5.817% to 7.817%) is −22.15%. Thus, the estimate is not as accurate as when we used duration to approximate the percentage price change for a change in yield of only 10 basis points. If we use duration to approximate the percentage price change when the yield decreases by 200 basis points, the approximate percentage price change in this scenario is +27.072. The actual percentage price change is +33.93%.

As before, let's examine the use of duration in terms of estimating the new price. Since the initial full price is 108.6034 and a 200 basis point increase in yield will decrease the price by −27.072%, the estimated new price using duration is 79.20 (found by multiplying 100.2907 by one minus 0.27072). The actual full price if the yield rises by 200 basis points (5.939% to 7.939%) is 84.5475. Consequently, the estimate is not as accurate as the estimate for a 10 basis point change in yield. The estimated new price using duration for a 200 basis point decrease in yield is 138.01 compared to the actual price of 145.4489. Once again, the estimation of the price using duration is not as accurate as for a 10 basis point change. Notice that whether the yield is increased or decreased by 200 basis points, duration underestimates what the new price will be. We will discover why shortly. Exhibit 19 summarizes what we found in our application to approximate the 30-year U.S. Treasury bond's percentage price change.

This result should come as no surprise to careful readers of the last section on price volatility characteristics of bonds. Specifically equation (2) is somewhat at odds with the properties of the price/yield relationship.

Exhibit 19: Application of Duration to Approximate the Percentage Price Change

Yield change (bp)	Initial price	New price — Based on duration	New price — Actual	Percent price change — Based on duration	Percent price change — Actual	Comment
+10	108.6034	107.1333	107.1494	−1.3536	−1.3390	estimated price close to new price
−10	108.6034	110.0735	110.0887	+1.3536	+1.3676	estimated price close to new price
+200	108.6034	79.2000	84.5475	−27.0720	−22.1500	underestimates new price
−200	108.6034	138.0100	145.4489	+27.0720	+33.9300	underestimates new price

Exhibit 20: Price/Yield Relationship for an Option-Free Bond with a Tangent Line

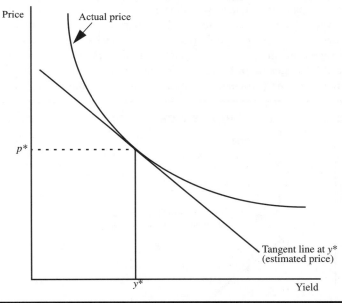

Graphical Depiction of Using Duration to Estimate Price Changes

Earlier we used the graph of the price/yield relationship to demonstrate the price volatility properties of bonds. We can use graphs to illustrate what we observed in our examples about how duration estimates the percentage price change, as well as some other noteworthy points.

The shape of the price/yield relationship for an option-free bond is convex. Exhibit 20 shows this relationship. In the exhibit a tangent line is drawn to the price/yield relationship at yield y^*. (For those unfamiliar with the concept of a tangent line, it is a straight line that just touches a curve at one point within a relevant (local) range. In Exhibit 20, the tangent line touches the curve at the point where the yield is equal to y^* and the price is equal to p^*.) The tangent line is used to *estimate* the new price if the yield changes. If we draw a vertical line from any yield (on the horizontal axis), as in Exhibit 20, the distance between the horizontal axis and the tangent line represents the price approximated by using duration starting with the initial yield y^*.

Now how is the tangent line, used to approximate what the new price will be if yields change, related to duration? The tangent line tells us the approximate new price of a bond if the yield changes. Given (1) the initial price and (2) the new price of a bond if the yield changes using the tangent line, the approximate percentage price change can be computed for a given change in yield. But this is precisely what duration (using equation (2)) gives us: the approximate percentage change for a given change in yield. Thus, using the tangent line one obtains the same approximate percentage price change as using equation (2).

This helps us understand why duration did an effective job of estimating the percentage price change, or equivalently the new price, when the yield changes by a small number of basis points. Look at Exhibit 21. Notice that for a small change in yield, the tangent line does not depart much from the price/yield relationship. Hence, when the yield changes up or down by 10 basis points, the tangent line does a good job of estimating the new price, as we found in our earlier numerical illustration.

Exhibit 21: Estimating the New Price Using a Tangent Line

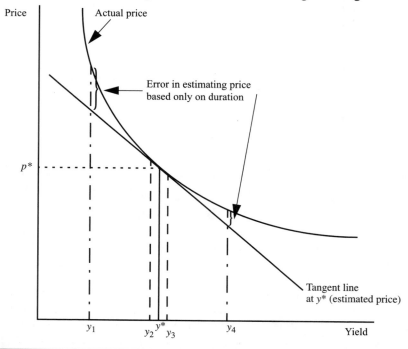

Exhibit 22: Estimating the New Price for a Large Yield Change for Bonds with Different Convexities

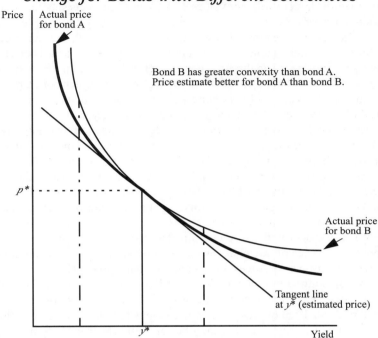

Exhibit 21 also shows what happens to the estimate using the tangent line when the yield changes by a large number of basis points. Notice that the error in the estimate gets larger the further one moves from the initial yield. The estimate is less accurate the more convex the bond. This is illustrated in Exhibit 22.

Also note that regardless of the magnitude of the yield change, the tangent line always underestimates what the new price will be for an option-free bond because the tangent line is below the price/yield relationship. This explains why we found in our illustration that when using duration we underestimated what the actual price will be.

Rate Shocks and Duration Estimate

In calculating duration using equation (1), it is necessary to shock interest rates (yields) up and down by the same number of basis points to obtain the values for V_- and V_+. In our illustration, 20 basis points was arbitrarily selected. But how large should the shock be? That is, how many basis points should be used to shock the rate? Looking at equation (1) it is relatively easy to discern why the size of the interest rate shock should not matter too much. Specifically, the choice of Δy has two effects on equation (1). In the numerator, the choice of Δy affects the spread between V_- and V_+ in that the larger the interest rate shock, the larger the spread between the two prices. In the denominator, the choice of Δy appears directly and the denominator is larger for larger values of Δy. The two effects should largely neutralize each other, unless the price/yield relationship is highly convex (i.e., curved).

In Exhibit 23, the duration estimate for our three U.S. Treasury securities from Exhibits 1, 3, and 4 using equation (1) for rate shocks of 1 basis point to 100 basis points is reported.[4] The duration estimates for the 2-year note are unaffected by the size of the shock. The duration estimates for the 30-year bond are affected only slightly even though a 30-year bond will have higher positive convexity (i.e., a price/yield relationship that is more curved) than a 2-year note. Lastly, if the duration estimates are ever going to be affected by the size of the interest rate shock, this should be evident when this exercise is performed on a 30-year principal strip from Exhibit 1, which has very large positive convexity (i.e., a price/yield relationship that is very curved). However, even in this case, the duration estimates are affected only marginally. It would appear that the size of the interest rate shock is unimportant for approximating the duration of *option-free bonds* using equation (1).

When we deal with more complicated securities, small rate shocks that do not reflect the types of rate changes that may occur in the market do not permit the determination of how prices can change because expected cash flows may change when dealing with bonds with embedded options. In comparison, if large rate shocks are used, we encounter the asymmetry caused by convexity. Moreover, large rate shocks may cause dramatic changes in the expected cash flows for bonds with embedded options that may be far different from how the expected cash flows will change for smaller rate shocks.

There is another potential problem with using small rate shocks for complicated securities. The prices that are inserted into the duration formula as given by equation (1) are derived from a valuation model. These valuation models and their underlying assumptions are discussed in Chapters 6 and 8. The duration measure depends crucially on a valuation model. If the rate shock is small and the valuation model used to obtain the prices for equation (1) is poor, dividing poor price estimates by a small shock in rates in the denominator will have a significant affect on the duration estimate.

Exhibit 23: Duration Estimates for Different Rate Shocks

Assumptions: All of these bonds are priced with a settlement date of 10/11/00. The initial yields for the note, bond and principal strip are 5.939%, 5.817%, and 5.828% respectively.

Bond	1 bp	10 bps	20 bps	50 bps	100 bps
2-year, 6% coupon U.S. Treasury note maturing 9/30/02	1.83	1.83	1.83	1.83	1.83
30-year, 6.25% coupon U.S. Treasury bond maturing 5/15/30	13.53	13.53	13.54	13.56	13.65
30-year U.S. Treasury principal strip maturing 5/15/30	28.74	28.76	28.78	28.86	29.18

---

[4] Note that our calculations match the Bloomberg calculations in Exhibits 1, 3, and 4.

What is done in practice by dealers and vendors of analytical systems? Each system developer uses rate shocks that they have found to be realistic based on historical rate changes.

Modified Duration versus Effective Duration

One form of duration that is cited by practitioners is *modified duration*. Modified duration is the approximate percentage change in a bond's price for a 100 basis point change in yield *assuming that the bond's expected cash flows do not change when the yield changes*. What this means is that in calculating the values of V_- and V_+ in equation (1), the same cash flows used to calculate V_0 are used. Therefore, the change in the bond's price when the yield is changed is due solely to discounting cash flows at the new yield level.

The assumption that the cash flows will not change when the yield is changed makes sense for option-free bonds such as noncallable Treasury securities. This is because the payments made by the U.S. Department of the Treasury to holders of its obligations do not change when interest rates change. However, the same cannot be said for bonds with embedded options (i.e., callable and putable bonds and mortgage-backed securities). For these securities, a change in yield may significantly alter the expected cash flows.

Earlier in the chapter, we presented the price/yield relationship for callable and prepayable bonds. Failure to recognize how changes in yield can alter the expected cash flows will produce two values used in the numerator of equation (1) that are not good estimates of how the price will actually change. The duration is then not a good number to use to estimate how the price will change.

When we discussed valuation models for bonds with embedded options, we learned how these models (lattice models and Monte Carlo simulation) take into account how changes in yield will affect the expected cash flows. Thus, when V_- and V_+ are the values produced from these valuation models, the resulting duration takes into account both the discounting at different interest rates and how the expected cash flows may change. When duration is calculated in this manner, it is referred to as *effective duration* or *option-adjusted duration* or *OAS duration*. Below we explain how effective duration is calculated based on the lattice model and the Monte Carlo model.

Calculating the Effective Duration Using the Lattice Model

In Chapter 6, we explained how the lattice model is used to value bonds with embedded options. In our illustrations we used one form of the lattice model, the binomial model. The procedure for calculating the values to be substituted into the duration formula [equation (1)] using the binomial model is described below.

V_+ is determined as follows:

Step 1: Calculate the option-adjusted spread (OAS) for the issue.

Step 2: Shift the on-the-run yield curve up by a small number of basis points.

Step 3: Construct a binomial interest rate tree based on the new yield curve in Step 2.

Step 4: To each of the short rates in the binomial interest rate tree, add the OAS to obtain an "adjusted tree."

Step 5: Use the adjusted tree found in Step 4 to determine the value of the bond, which is V_+.

To determine the value of V_-, the same five steps are followed except that in Step 2, the on-the-run yield curve is shifted down by a small number of basis points.

Notice that in the calculation of V_+ and V_- the yield for each maturity is changed by the same number of basis points. This assumption is called the *parallel yield curve shift assumption.*

To illustrate how V_+ and V_- are determined in order to calculate effective duration, we will use the same on-the-run yield curve that we used in Chapter 6 assuming a volatility of 10%. The 4-year callable bond with a coupon rate of 6.5% and callable at par selling at 102.218 will be used in this illustration. We showed that the OAS for this issue is 35 basis points.

Exhibit 24a shows the adjusted tree by shifting the yield curve up by an arbitrarily small number of basis points, 25 basis points, and then adding 35 basis points (the OAS) to each 1-year rate. The adjusted tree is then used to value the bond. The resulting value, V_+, is 101.621. Exhibit 24b shows the adjusted tree by shifting the yield curve down by 25 basis points and then adding 35 basis points to each 1-year rate. The resulting value, V_-, is 102.765.

The results are summarized below:

$$\Delta y = 0.0025 \quad V_+ = 101.621 \quad V_- = 102.765 \quad V_0 = 102.218$$

Therefore,

$$\text{effective duration} = \frac{102.765 - 101.621}{2(102.218)0.0025} = 2.24$$

This procedure is the one used by Bloomberg to calculate effective duration.

As an illustration of the difference between modified and effective duration, let's consider a callable bond issued by the Bank of New York. Bloomberg's Security Description screen (DES) for this issue is presented in Exhibit 25. Note that this bond matures on August 15, 2010 but is callable at par beginning on February 15, 2001. Bloomberg's Yield & Spread Analysis (YAS) screen shown in Exhibit 26 gives the modified duration and effective duration (OAS duration is the term used by Bloomberg) for this callable bond in the upper right-hand portion of the screen in the section labeled "RISK & HEDGE RATIOS." Based on a settlement date of October 13, 2000, the modified duration is 6.62 (shown in the first column under "Mod Dur") and OAS duration is 4.08 (shown in the second column under "Mod Dur").

Exhibit 24: Calculating Effective Duration and Convexity Using the Binomial Model

a. Determination of V₊ *

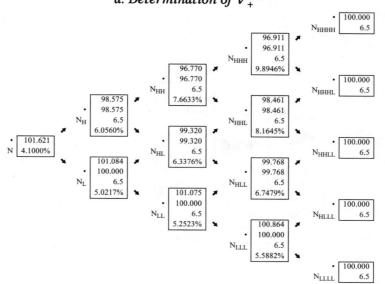

* +25 basis point shift in on-the-run yield curve.

b. Determination of V₋ *

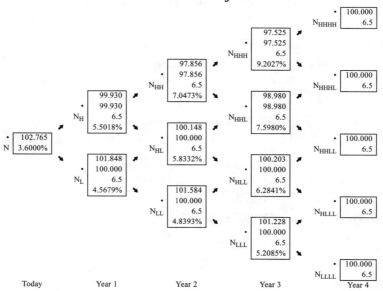

* −25 basis point shift in on-the-run yield curve.

Exhibit 25: Bloomberg Security Description Screen for a Bank of New York Medium-Term Note

```
DES                                                          DG36 Corp   DES

SECURITY DESCRIPTION                                 Page 1/ 2
BANK OF NY CO      BK 7.54 08/15/10    97.23628/97.23628  (7.95/7.95) BFV  @17:43
ISSUER INFORMATION                  | IDENTIFIERS              | 1) Additional Sec Info
Name BANK OF NEW YORK CO INC        | CUSIP        06406JAC9   | 2) Call Schedule
Type Money Center Banks             | ISIN       US06406JAC99  | 3) Identifiers
Market of Issue MEDIUM TERM NOTE    | BB number    MM1086857   | 4) Ratings
SECURITY INFORMATION                | RATINGS                  | 5) Prospectus
Country US        Currency USD      | Moody's       A1         | 6) Involved Parties
Collateral Type SUB NOTES           | S&P           A          | 7) Custom Notes
Calc Typ(   1)STREET CONVENTION     | Composite     A2         | 8) Issuer Information
Maturity  8/15/2010  Series MTN     | ISSUE SIZE               | 9) ALLQ
CALLABLE   CALL   2/15/01@ 100.00   | Amt Issued               | 10) Pricing Sources
Coupon  7.54        FIXED           | USD  50,000.00    (M)    | 11) MTN Drawdown
MONTHLY          30/360             | Amt Outstanding          | 12) Related Securities
Announcement Dt   8/18/95           | USD  50,000.00    (M)    | 13) Issuer Web Page
Int. Accrual Dt   8/22/95           | Min Piece/Increment      |
1st Settle Date   8/22/95           |   1,000.00/  1,000.00    |
1st Coupon Date   9/15/95           | Par Amount    1,000.00   |
Iss Pr 100.0000                     | BOOK RUNNER/EXCHANGE     |
                                    | ML                       | 65) Old DES
USER SHOULD VERIFY INFORMATION      |                          | 66) Send as Attachment
UNSEC'D. SHORT 1ST CPN.

Copyright 2000 BLOOMBERG L.P.   Frankfurt:69-920410  Hong Kong:2-977-6000  London:207-330-7500  New York:212-318-2000
Princeton:609-279-3000    Singapore:65-212-1000    Sydney:2-9777-8686    Tokyo:3-3201-8900    Sao Paulo:11-3048-4500
                                                                            I464-169-0 10-Oct-00 17:43:06
Bloomberg PROFESSIONAL
```

Source: Bloomberg Financial Markets

Exhibit 26: Bloomberg Yield and Spread Analysis Screen for a Bank of New York Medium-Term Note

```
YAS                                                          DG36 Corp   YAS
Enter #<GO> for Detailed Analysis. Enter 99<GO> for Menu of Related Functions.
YIELD & SPREAD ANALYSIS                               CUSIP06406JAC  PCS BFV
BANK OF NY CO      BK 7.54 08/15/10    97.23628/97.23628  (7.95/7.95) BFV  @17:43
  SETTLE 10/13/00    FACE AMT          1000 M  or PROCEEDS            978,227.20
1) YA              YIELDS                   | RISK &   BK 7.54 08/15/10
PRICE 97.236276                             | HEDGE      workout        HEDGE BOND
YIELD       8.078 Wst                       | RATIOS   8/15/10    OAS      OAS
 SPRD      224.88 bp      yld-decimals 3    |  Mod Dur  6.62     4.08     3.82
          versus                            |  Risk     6.475    3.994    4.063
5yr  T 6 ¾  05/15/05           <HEDGE BOND  | Convexity 0.58    -1.94     0.18
    PRICE 103-21                            |  Workout HEDGE Amount:1,591 M
    YIELD       5.830 %        sd: 10/11/00 |      OAS HEDGE Amount:983 M
   Yields are: Semi-Annual
2) OAS             SPREADS           3) ASW | 4) FPA        FINANCING
OAS:  182.3 CRV# CMT        VOL 12.0 Opt 3.01 |  Repo% 6.400  (360/365)360   Days  1
OAS:   57.4 CRV# I52                        | Int Income      209.44      Carry P&L
ASSET SWAP:  (A/A)    99.9  | TED:   -87.8  |  Fin Cost      -173.91          35.54
ISPRD 108.0 CRV# I52    US $ SWAP 30/360    |   Amortiz    -8822.92<->     -8787.38
 Yield Curve:I25    US TREASURY ACTIVES     | Forwrd Prc    97.232722
+ 228 v  9.8yr ( 5.795 %) INTERPOLATED      |  Prc Drop     0.003554
+ 212 v 2yr   ( 5.96) T 6 09/30/02          |  Drop (bp)      -13.57
+ 225 v 5yr   ( 5.83) T 6 ¾  05/15/05       | Accrued Interest  /100    0.586444
+ 228 v 10yr  ( 5.80) T 5 ¾  08/15/10       |  Number Of Days Accrued   28
+ 225 v 30yr  ( 5.83) T 6 ¼  05/15/30       |
Copyright 2000 BLOOMBERG L.P.   Frankfurt:69-920410  Hong Kong:2-977-6000  London:207-330-7500  New York:212-318-2000
Princeton:609-279-3000    Singapore:65-212-1000    Sydney:2-9777-8686    Tokyo:3-3201-8900    Sao Paulo:11-3048-4500
                                                                            I464-169-0 10-Oct-00 17:43:30
Bloomberg PROFESSIONAL
```

Source: Bloomberg Financial Markets

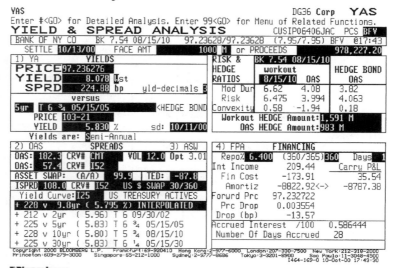

Calculating the Effective Duration Using the Monte Carlo Model

The same procedure is used to calculate the effective duration for a security valued using the Monte Carlo model. The short-term rates are used to value the cash flow on each interest rate path. To obtain the two values to substitute into the duration formula, the OAS is calculated first. The short-term rates are then shifted up a small number of basis points, obtaining new refinancing rates and cash flows. V_+ is then calculated by discounting the cash flow on an interest rate path using the new short-term rates plus the OAS. V_- is then calculated in the same manner by shifting the short-term rates down by a small number of basis points. Again, since all rates are shifted by the same number of basis points, the resulting duration assumes a parallel shift in the yield curve.

Macaulay Duration and Modified Duration

It is worth comparing the relationship between modified duration to another duration measure. Modified duration can also be written as:[5]

$$\frac{1}{(1+\text{yield}/k)}\left[\frac{1 \times \text{PVCF}_1 + 2 \times \text{PVCF}_2 + ... + n \times \text{PVCF}_n}{k \times \text{Price}}\right] \quad (3)$$

where

$\quad k \quad$ = number of periods, or payments, per year (e.g., $k = 2$ for semiannual-pay bonds and $k = 12$ for monthly-pay bonds)

$\quad n \quad$ = number of periods until maturity (i.e., number of years to maturity times k)

$\quad$ yield $\quad$ = yield to maturity of the bond

$\quad \text{PVCF}_t$ = present value of the cash flow in period t discounted at the yield to maturity where $t = 1, 2, ..., n$

The expression in the brackets of the modified duration formula given by equation (3) is a measure formulated in 1938 by Frederick Macaulay.[6] This measure is popularly referred to as *Macaulay duration*. Thus, modified duration is commonly expressed as:

$$\text{Modified duration} = \frac{\text{Macaulay duration}}{(1 + \text{yield}/k)}$$

Bloomberg reports Macaulay duration on its YA (yield analysis) screen in the Sensitivity Analysis box in the lower left-hand corner of Exhibits 1, 3, and 4. Macaulay duration is labeled "CNV DURATION (YEARS)" where the CNV stands for "conventional."

The general formulation for duration as given by equation (1) provides a short-cut procedure for determining a bond's modified duration. Because it is eas-

---

[5] More specifically, this is the formula for the modified duration of a bond on a coupon anniversary date.

[6] Frederick Macaulay, *Some Theoretical Problems Suggested by the Movement of Interest Rates, Bond Yields, and Stock Prices in the U.S. Since 1856* (New York: National Bureau of Economic Research, 1938).

ier to calculate the modified duration using the short-cut procedure, most vendors of analytical software will use equation (1) rather than equation (3) to reduce computation time.

However, it must be clearly understood that modified duration is a flawed measure of a bond's price sensitivity to interest rate changes for a bond with an embedded option and therefore so is Macaulay duration. The use of the formula for duration given by equation (3) *misleads* the user because it masks the fact that changes in the expected cash flows must be recognized for bonds with embedded options. Although equation (3) will give the same estimate of percent price change for an option-free bond as equation (1), equation (1) is still better because it acknowledges that cash flows and thus value can change due to yield changes.

Portfolio Duration

A portfolio's duration can be obtained by calculating the weighted average of the duration of the bonds in the portfolio. The weight is the proportion of the portfolio that a security comprises. Mathematically, a portfolio's duration can be calculated as follows:

$$w_1 D_1 + w_2 D_2 + w_3 D_3 + \ldots + w_K D_K$$

where

w_i = market value of bond i/market value of the portfolio
D_i = duration of bond i
K = number of bonds in the portfolio

To illustrate the calculation, consider the following 3-bond portfolio in which all three bonds are U.S. Treasuries from Exhibits 1, 3, and 4. Exhibit 27 presents the full price per $100 of par value for each bond, its yield, the par amount owned, the market value, and its duration.

In this illustration, the 2-year note and the 30-year bond are priced with a settlement date between coupon payments dates so the market prices reported are full prices. The market value for the portfolio is $9,723,961. Since each bond is option-free, modified duration can be used.

Exhibit 27: Summary of a 3-Treasury Bond Portfolio

Bond	Full Price ($)	Yield (%)	Par amount owned ($)	Market Value ($)	Duration
2-year, 6% coupon U.S. Treasury note maturing 9/30/02	100.2907	5.939	5,000,000	5,014,535	1.83
30-year, 6.25% coupon U.S. Treasury bond maturing 5/15/30	108.6034	5.817	4,000,000	4,344,136	13.53
30-year U.S. Treasury principal strip maturing 5/15/30	18.2645	5.828	2,000,000	365,290	28.76

In this illustration, K is equal to 3 and:

$w_1 = \$5,014,535/\$9,723,961 = 0.516$ $D_1 = 1.83$
$w_2 = \$4,344,136/\$9,723,961 = 0.447$ $D_2 = 13.53$
$w_3 = \$365,290/\$9,723,961 = 0.037$ $D_3 = 28.76$

The portfolio's duration is:

$$0.516(1.83) + 0.447(13.53) + 0.037(28.76) = 8.056$$

A portfolio duration of 8.056 means that for a 100 basis point change in the yield for each of the three bonds, the portfolio's market value will change by approximately 8.056%. It is paramount to keep in mind that it is assumed that the yield for each of the three bonds must change by 100 basis points. This is a critical assumption and its importance cannot be overemphasized. Portfolio managers will find it necessary to be able to measure a portfolio's exposure to shifts in the yield curve. We will examine one popular method for doing this later in the chapter when we discuss *key rate duration*.

An alternative procedure for calculating a portfolio's duration is to calculate the dollar price change for a given number of basis points for each security in the portfolio and then add up all the changes in market value. Dividing the total of the changes in market value by the portfolio's initial market value produces a percentage change in market value that can be adjusted to obtain the portfolio's duration.

For example, consider the 3-bond portfolio given in Exhibit 27. Suppose that we calculate the dollar change in market value for each bond in the portfolio based on its respective duration for a 50 basis point change in yield. We would then have:

Bond	Market Value ($)	Duration	Change in value for 50 bp yield change ($)
2-year, 6% coupon U.S. Treasury note maturing 9/30/02	5,014,535	1.83	45,882
30-year, 6.25% coupon U.S. Treasury bond maturing 5/15/30	4,344,136	13.53	293,881
30-year U.S. Treasury principal strip maturing 5/15/30	365,290	28.76	52,529
Total			392,292

Thus, a 50 basis point change in all rates changes the market value of the 3-bond portfolio by $392,292. Since the market value of the portfolio is $9,723,961, a 50 basis point change produced a change in value of 4.034% ($393,292 divided by $9,723,961). Since duration is the approximate percentage change for a 100 basis point change in rates, this means that the portfolio duration is 8.068 (found by doubling 4.034). This is virtually the same value for the portfolio's duration as found earlier.

Contribution to Portfolio Duration

Some portfolio managers view their exposure to a particular issue or to a sector in terms of the percentage of that issue or sector in the portfolio. A better measure of exposure of an individual issue or sector to changes in interest rates is in terms of its *contribution to the portfolio duration*. Contribution to portfolio duration is computed by multiplying the percentage that the individual issues comprises of the portfolio by the duration of the individual issue or sector. Specifically,

contribution to portfolio duration

$$= \frac{\text{market value of issue or sector}}{\text{market value of portfolio}} \times \text{duration of issue or sector}$$

This exposure can also be cast in terms of dollar exposure. To accomplish this, the dollar duration of the issue or sector is used instead of the duration of the issue or sector.

A portfolio manager who desires to determine the contribution to a portfolio of a sector relative to the contribution of the same sector in a broad-based market index can compute the difference between these two contributions.

OTHER DURATION MEASURES

Numerous duration measures are routinely employed by fixed-income practitioners that relate to both fixed-rate and floating-rate securities. Furthermore, there are more sophisticated duration measures that allow for nonparallel yield curve shifts. We discuss these measures in this section.

Spread Duration for Fixed-Rate Bonds

As we have seen, duration is a measure of the change in a bond's value when interest rates change. The interest rate that is assumed to shift is the Treasury rate which serves as the benchmark interest rate. However, for non-Treasury instruments, the yield is equal to the Treasury yield plus a spread to the Treasury yield curve. This is why non-Treasury securities are often called "spread products." Of course, the price of a bond exposed to credit risk can change even though Treasury yields are unchanged because the spread required by the market changes. A measure of how a non-Treasury security's price will change if the spread sought by the market changes is called *spread duration.*

The problem is, what spread is assumed to change? There are three measures that are commonly used for fixed-rate bonds: nominal spread, zero-volatility spread, and option-adjusted spread. Each of these spread measures were defined earlier in the book.

The nominal spread is the traditional spread measure. The nominal spread is simply the difference between the yield on a non-Treasury issue and the yield on a comparable maturity Treasury. When the spread is taken to be the nominal spread, spread duration indicates the approximate percentage change in price for a 100 basis point change in the nominal spread holding the Treasury yield constant.

The zero-volatility or static spread is the spread that when added to the Treasury spot rate curve will make the present value of the cash flows equal to the bond's price plus accrued interest. When spread is defined in this way, spread duration is the approximate percentage change in price for a 100 basis point change in the zero-volatility spread holding the Treasury spot rate curve constant.

Finally, the option-adjusted spread (OAS) is the constant spread that, when added to all the rates on the interest rate tree, will make the theoretical value equal to the market price. Spread duration based on OAS can be interpreted as the approximate percentage change in price of a non-Treasury for a 100 basis point change in the OAS, holding the Treasury rate constant.

A sensible question arises: how do you know whether a spread duration for a fixed-rate bond is a spread based on the nominal spread, zero-volatility spread or the OAS? The simple answer is you do not know! You must ask the broker/dealer or vendor of the analytical system. To add further to the confusion surrounding spread duration, consider the term "OAS duration" that is referred to by some market participants. What does it mean? On the one hand, it could mean simply the spread duration that we just described. On the other hand, many market participants use the term "OAS duration" interchangeably with the term "effective duration." Once again, the only way to know what OAS is measuring is to ask the broker/dealer or vendor.

Spread Duration for Floaters

Two measures have been developed to estimate the sensitivity of a floater to each component of the coupon reset formula: the index (i.e., reference rate) and the spread (i.e., quoted margin). *Index duration* is a measure of the price sensitivity of a floater to changes in the reference rate holding the spread constant. *Spread duration* measures a floater's price sensitivity to a change in the spread assuming that the reference rate is unchanged.

Key Rate Durations

Duration measures the sensitivity of a bond's price to a given change in yield. The traditional formulation is derived under the assumption that the reference yield curve is flat and moves in parallel shifts. Simply put, all bond yields are the same regardless of when the cash flows are delivered across time and changes in yields are perfectly correlated. Several recent attempts have been made to address this inadequacy and develop interest rate risk measures that allow for more realistic changes in the yield curve's shape.[7]

One approach to measuring the sensitivity of a bond to changes in the shape of the yield curve is to change the yield for a particular maturity of the yield curve and determine the sensitivity of a security or portfolio to this change holding all other yields constant. The sensitivity of the bond's value to a particular change in yield is called *rate duration*. There is a rate duration for every point on the yield curve. Consequently, there is not one rate duration but a vector of rate durations representing each maturity on the yield curve. The total change in value

---

[7] For a discussion, see Steven V. Mann and Pradipkumar Ramanlal, "Duration and Convexity Measures When the Yield Curve Changes Shape," *Journal of Financial Engineering* (March 1998), pp. 35-58.

if all rates move by the same number of basis points is simply the duration of a security or portfolio to a parallel shift in rates.

The most popular version of this approach was developed by Thomas Ho in 1992.[8] This approach examines how changes in Treasury yields at different points on the spot curve affect the value of a bond portfolio. Ho's methodology has three basic steps. The first step is to select several key maturities or "key rates" of the spot rate curve. Ho's approach focuses on 11 key maturities on the spot rate curve. These rate durations are called *key rate durations*. The specific maturities on the spot rate curve for which a key rate duration is measured are 3 months, 1 year, 2 years, 3 years, 5 years, 7 years, 10 years, 15 years, 20 years, 25 years, and 30 years. However, in order to illustrate Ho's methodology, we will select only three key rates: 1 year, 10 years, and 30 years.

The next step is to specify how other rates on the spot curve change in response to key rate changes. Ho's rule is that a key rate's effect on neighboring rates declines linearly and reaches zero at the adjacent key rates. For example, suppose the 10-year key rate increases by 40 basis points. All spot rates between 10 years and 30 years will increase but the amount each changes will be different and the magnitude of the change diminishes linearly. Specifically, there are 40 semiannual periods between 10 and 30 years. Each spot rate starting with 10.5 years increases by 1 basis point less than the spot rate to its immediate left (i.e., 39 basis points) and so forth. The 30-year rate which is the adjacent key rate is assumed to be unchanged. Thus, only one key rate changes at a time. Spot rates between 1 year and 10 years change in an analogous manner such that all rates change but by differing amounts. Changes in the 1-year key rate affect spot rates between 1 and 10 years while spot rates 10 years and beyond are assumed to be unaffected by changes in the 1-year spot rate. In a similar vein, changes in the 30-year key rate affect all spot rates between 30 years and 10 years while spot rates shorter than 10 years are assumed to be unaffected by the change in the 30-year rate. This process is illustrated in Exhibit 28. Note that if we add the three rate changes together we obtain a parallel yield curve shift of 40 basis points.

The third and final step is to calculate the percentage change in the bond's portfolio value when each key rate and neighboring spot rates are changed. There will be as many key rate durations as there are preselected key rates. Let's illustrate this process by calculating the key rate duration for a coupon bond. Our hypothetical 6% coupon bond has a maturity value of $100 and matures in 5 years. The bond delivers coupon payments semiannually. Valuation is accomplished by discounting each cash flow using the appropriate spot rate. The bond's current value is $107.32 and the process is illustrated in Exhibit 29. The initial hypothetical (and short) spot curve is contained in column (3).[9] The present values of each of the bond's cash flows is presented in the last column.

---

[8] Thomas S. Y. Ho, "Key Rate Durations: Measures of Interest Rate Risk," *The Journal of Fixed Income* (September 1992), pp. 29-44.

[9] The spot rates are annual rates and are reported as bond-equivalent yields. When present values are computed, we use the appropriate semiannual rates which are taken to be one half the annual rate.

Exhibit 28: Graph of How Spot Rates Change when Key Rates Change

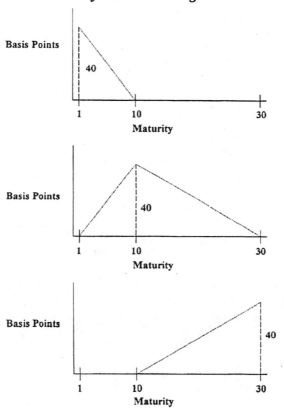

Exhibit 29: Valuation of 5-Year 6% Coupon Bond Using Spot Rates

Years	Period	Spot Rate (in percent)	Cash Flow (in dollars)	Present Value (in dollars)
0.5	1	3.00	3	2.96
1.0	2	3.25	3	2.90
1.5	3	3.50	3	2.85
2.0	4	3.75	3	2.79
2.5	5	4.00	3	2.72
3.0	6	4.10	3	2.66
3.5	7	4.20	3	2.59
4.0	8	4.30	3	2.53
4.5	9	4.35	3	2.47
5.0	10	4.40	103	82.86
			Total	107.32

Exhibit 30: Graph of the Initial Spot Curve and the Spot Curve After the 0.5-Year Key Rate Shift

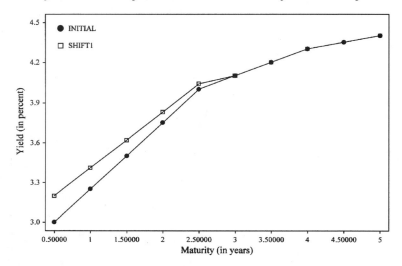

Exhibit 31: Valuation of the 5-Year 6% Coupon Bond After 0.5 Year Key Rate and Neighboring Spot Rates Change

Years	Period	Spot Rate (in percent)	Cash Flow (in dollars)	Present Value (in dollars)
0.5	1	3.20	3	2.95
1.0	2	3.41	3	2.90
1.5	3	3.62	3	2.84
2.0	4	3.83	3	2.78
2.5	5	4.04	3	2.71
3.0	6	4.10	3	2.66
3.5	7	4.20	3	2.59
4.0	8	4.30	3	2.53
4.5	9	4.35	3	2.47
5.0	10	4.40	103	82.86
			Total	107.30

To compute the key rate duration of the 5-year bond, we must select some key rates. We assume the key rates are 0.5, 3, and 5 years. To compute the 0.5-year key rate duration, we shift the 0.5-year rate upwards by 20 basis points and adjust the neighboring spot rates between 0.5 and 3 years as described earlier. (The choice of 20 basis points is arbitrary.) Exhibit 30 is a graph of the initial spot curve and the spot curve after the 0.5-year key rate and neighboring rates are shifted. The next step is to compute the bond's new value as a result of the shift. This calculation is shown in Exhibit 31. The bond's value subsequent to the shift is $107.30. To estimate the 0.5-year key rate duration, we divide the percentage change in the bond's price as a result of the shift in the spot curve by the change in the 0.5-year key rate. Accordingly, we employ the following formula:

$$\text{key rate duration} = -\frac{P_0 - P_1}{P_0 \Delta y}$$

where

P_1 = the bond's value after the shift in the spot curve
P_0 = the bond's value using the initial spot curve
Δy = shift in the key rate (in decimal)

Substituting in numbers from our illustration presented above, we can compute the 0.5-year key rate duration as follows:

$$0.5\text{-year key rate duration} = \frac{107.32 - 107.30}{107.32(0.002)}$$
$$= 0.0932$$

To compute the 3-year key rate duration, we repeat this process. We shift the 3-year rate by 20 basis points and adjust the neighboring spot rates as described earlier. Exhibit 32 shows a graph of the initial spot curve and the spot curve after the 3-year key rate and neighboring rates are shifted. Note that in this case the only two spot rates that do not change are the 0.5-year and the 5-year key rates. Then, we compute the bond's new value as a result of the shift. The bond's post-shift value is $107.25 and the calculation appears in Exhibit 33. Accordingly, the 3-year key rate duration is computed as follows:

$$3\text{-year key rate duration} = \frac{107.32 - 107.25}{107.32(0.002)}$$
$$= 0.3261$$

The final step is to compute the 5-year key duration. We shift the 5 year rate by 20 basis points and adjust the neighboring spot rates. Exhibit 34 presents a graph of the initial spot curve and the spot curve after the 5-year key rate and neighboring rates are shifted. The bond's post-shift value is $106.48 and the calculation appears in Exhibit 35. Accordingly, the 5 year key rate duration is computed as follows:

$$5\text{-year key rate duration} = \frac{107.32 - 106.48}{107.32(0.002)}$$
$$= 3.9135$$

What information can be gleaned from these key rate durations? Each key rate duration by itself means relatively little. However, the distribution of the bond's key rate durations helps us assess its exposure to yield curve risk. Intuitively, the sum of the key rate durations is approximately equal to a bond's duration.[10] As a result, it is useful to think of a set of key rate durations as a decomposition of duration into sensitivities to various portions of the yield curve. In our illustration, it is not surprising that the lion's share of the yield curve risk exposure of the coupon bond in our illustration is due to the bond's terminal cash flow, so the 5-year key rate duration is the largest of the three. Simply put, the 5-years bond's value is more sensitive to movements in longer spot rates and less sensitive to movements in shorter spot rates.

Exhibit 32: Graph of the Initial Spot Curve and the Spot Curve After the 3-Year Key Rate Shift

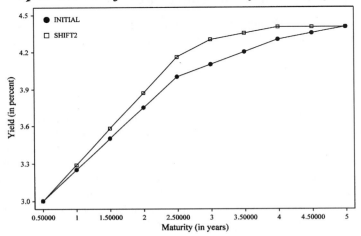

Exhibit 33: Valuation of the 5-Year 6% Coupon Bond After 3-Year Key Rate and Neighboring Spot Rates Change

Years	Period	Spot Rate (in percent)	Cash Flow (in dollars)	Present Value (in dollars)
0.5	1	3.00	3	2.96
1.0	2	3.29	3	2.90
1.5	3	3.58	3	2.84
2.0	4	3.87	3	2.78
2.5	5	4.16	3	2.71
3.0	6	4.30	3	2.64
3.5	7	4.35	3	2.58
4.0	8	4.40	3	2.52
4.5	9	4.40	3	2.47
5.0	10	4.40	103	82.86
			Total	107.25

[10] The reason it is only approximate is because modified duration assumes a flat yield curve whereas key rate duration takes the spot curve as given.

Exhibit 34: Graph of the Initial Spot Curve and the Spot Curve After the 5-Year Key Rate Shift

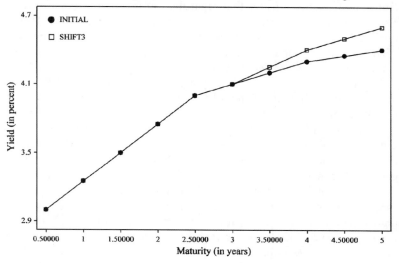

Exhibit 35: Valuation of the 5-Year 6% Coupon Bond After 5-Year Key Rate and Neighboring Spot Rates Change

Years	Period	Spot Rate (in percent)	Cash Flow (in dollars)	Present Value (in dollars)
0.5	1	3.00	3	2.96
1.0	2	3.25	3	2.90
1.5	3	3.50	3	2.85
2.0	4	3.75	3	2.79
2.5	5	4.00	3	2.72
3.0	6	4.10	3	2.66
3.5	7	4.25	3	2.59
4.0	8	4.40	3	2.52
4.5	9	4.50	3	2.46
5.0	10	4.60	103	82.05
			Total	106.48

Key rate durations are most useful when comparing two (or more) bond portfolios that have approximately the same duration. If the spot curve is flat and experiences a parallel shift, these two bond portfolios can be expected to experience approximately the same percentage change in value. However, the performance of the two portfolios will generally not be the same for a nonparallel shift in the spot curve. The key rate duration profile of each portfolio will give the portfolio manager some clues about the relative performance of the two portfolios when the yield curve changes shape and slope.

CONVEXITY

The duration measure indicates that regardless of whether interest rates increase or decrease, the approximate percentage price change is the same. However, as we noted earlier, this is not consistent with Property 3 of a bond's price volatility. Specifically, while for small changes in yield the percentage price change will be the same for an increase or decrease in yield, for large changes in yield this is not true. This suggests that duration is only a good approximation of the percentage price change for small changes in yield.

We demonstrated this property earlier using a 6.25% 30-year Treasury bond priced to yield 5.817% with a duration of 13.53. For a 10 basis point change in yield, the estimate was accurate for both an increase and decrease in yield. However, for a 200 basis point change in yield the approximate percentage price change was off considerably.

The reason for this result is that duration is in fact a first (linear) approximation for a small change in yield.[11] The approximation can be improved by using a second approximation. This approximation is referred to as "convexity." *The use of this term in the industry is unfortunate since the term convexity is also used to describe the shape or curvature of the price/yield relationship.* The *convexity measure* of a security can be used to approximate the change in price that is not explained by duration.

Convexity Measure

The convexity measure of a bond is approximated using the following formula:

$$\text{Convexity measure} = \frac{V_+ + V_- - 2V_0}{2V_0(\Delta y)^2} \tag{4}$$

where the notation is the same as used earlier for duration as given by equation (4).

For the 6.25%, 30-year Treasury bond priced to yield 5.817% with a settlement date of October 11, 2000, we know that for a 20 basis point change in yield ($\Delta y = 0.002$):

$$V_0 = 108.6034, \ V_- = 111.6060, \text{ and } V_+ = 105.7259$$

Note once again because the settlement date is not a coupon payment date (see Exhibit 4) that we use full prices in the calculation. Substituting these values into the convexity measure given by equation (4):

$$\text{Convexity measure} = \frac{105.7259 + 111.6060 - 2(108.6034)}{2(108.6037)(0.002)^2} = 143.99$$

---

[11] The reason it is a linear approximation can be seen in Exhibit 21 where the tangent line is used to estimate the new price. That is, a straight line is being used to approximate a non-linear (i.e., convex) relationship.

We'll see how to use this convexity measure shortly. Before doing so, there are three points that should be noted. First, there is no simple interpretation of the convexity measure as there is for duration. Second, it is more common for market participants to refer to the value computed in equation (4) as the "convexity of a bond" rather than the "convexity measure of a bond." Finally, the convexity measure reported by dealers and vendors will differ for an option-free bond. The reason is that the value obtained from equation (4) is often scaled for the reason explained after we demonstrate how to use the convexity measure.

Convexity Adjustment to Percentage Price Change

Given the convexity measure, the approximate percentage price change adjustment due to the bond's convexity (i.e., the percentage price change not explained by duration) is:

Convexity adjustment to percentage price change
$$= \text{Convexity measure} \times (\Delta y)^2 \times 100 \qquad (5)$$

For example, for the 6.25% 30-year Treasury bond, the convexity adjustment to the percentage price change based on duration if the yield increases from 5.817% to 7.817% is

$143.99 \times (0.02)^2 \times 100 = 5.76\%$

If the yield decreases from 5.817% to 3.817%, the convexity adjustment to the approximate percentage price change based on duration would also be 5.76%.

The approximate percentage price change based on duration and the convexity adjustment is found by summing the two estimates. So, for example, if yields change from 5.817% to 7.817%, the estimated percentage price change would be:

Estimated change using duration alone	=	−27.06
Convexity adjustment	=	+5.76
Total estimated percentage price change	=	−21.30

The actual percentage price change is −22.15.

For a decrease of 200 basis points, from 5.817% to 3.817%, the approximate percentage price change would be as follows:

Estimated change using duration alone	=	+27.06
Convexity adjustment	=	+5.76
Total estimated percentage price change	=	+32.82%

The actual percentage price change is +33.93%. Thus, duration combined with the convexity adjustment does a much better job of estimating the sensitivity of a bond's price to large changes in yield.

Notice that when the convexity measure is positive, we have the situation described earlier that the gain is greater than the loss for a given large change in rates. That is, the bond exhibits positive convexity. We can see this in the example above. However, if the convexity measure is negative, we have the situation where the loss will be greater than the gain. For example, suppose that a callable bond has an effective duration of 4 and a convexity measure of −30. This means that the approximate percentage price change for a 200 basis point change is 8%. The convexity adjustment for a 200 basis point change in rates is then

$$-30 \times (0.02)^2 \times 100 = -1.2$$

The convexity adjustment is −1.2% and therefore the bond exhibits the negative convexity property illustrated in Exhibit 17. The approximate percentage price change after adjusting for convexity is:

Estimated change using duration	= −8.0%
Convexity adjustment	= −1.2%
Total estimated percentage price change	= −9.2%

For a decrease of 200 basis points, the approximate percentage price change would be as follows:

Estimated change using duration	= +8.0%
Convexity adjustment	= −1.2%
Total estimated percentage price change	= +6.8%

Notice that the loss is greater than the gain – a property called *negative convexity* that we discussed earlier and illustrated in Exhibit 17.

Scaling the Convexity Measure

The convexity measure as given by equation (4) means nothing in isolation. It is the substitution of the computed convexity measure into equation (5) that provides the estimated adjustment for convexity that is meaningful. Therefore, it is possible to scale the convexity measure in any way as long as the same convexity adjustment is obtained.

For example, in some books the convexity measure is defined as follows:

$$\text{Convexity measure} = \frac{V_+ + V_- - 2V_0}{V_0(\Delta y)^2} \tag{6}$$

Equation (6) differs from equation (4) since it does not include 2 in the denominator. Thus, the convexity measure computed using equation (6) will be double the convexity measure using equation (4). So, for our earlier illustration, since the convexity measure using equation (4) is 143.99, the convexity measure using equation (6) would be 287.98.

Which is correct, 143.99 or 287.98? The answer is both. The reason is that the corresponding equation for computing the convexity adjustment would not be given by equation (5) if the convexity measure is obtained from equation (6). Instead, the corresponding convexity adjustment formula would be:

Convexity adjustment to percentage price change
$$= (\text{Convexity measure}/2) \times (\Delta y)^2 \times 100 \tag{7}$$

Equation (7) differs from equation (5) in that the convexity measure is divided by 2. Thus, the convexity adjustment will be the same whether one uses equation (4) to get the convexity measure and equation (5) to get the convexity adjustment or one uses equation (6) to compute the convexity measure and equation (7) to determine the convexity adjustment.

Some dealers and vendors scale convexity in a different way. One can also compute the convexity measure as follows:

$$\text{Convexity measure} = \frac{V_+ + V_- - 2V_0}{2V_0(\Delta y)^2(100)} \tag{8}$$

Equation (8) differs from equation (4) by the inclusion of 100 in the denominator. In our illustration, the convexity measure would be 1.4399 rather than 143.99 using equation (4). The convexity adjustment formula corresponding to the convexity measure given by equation (8) is then

Convexity adjustment to percentage price change
$$= \text{Convexity measure} \times (\Delta y)^2 \times 10{,}000 \tag{9}$$

Similarly, one can express the convexity measure as shown in equation (10):

$$\text{Convexity measure} = \frac{V_+ + V_- - 2V_0}{V_0(\Delta y)^2(100)} \tag{10}$$

For the 30-year Treasury bond we have been using in our illustrations, the convexity measure is 2.8798. The corresponding convexity adjustment is:

Convexity adjustment to percentage price change
$$= (\text{Convexity measure}/2) \times (\Delta y)^2 \times 10{,}000 \tag{11}$$

Consequently, the convexity measures (or just simply "convexity" as it is referred to by some market participants) that could be reported for this option-free bond are 143.99, 287.98, 1.4399, or 2.8798. All of these values are correct, but they mean nothing in isolation. To use them to obtain the convexity adjustment to the price change estimated by duration requires knowing how they are computed so that the correct convexity adjustment formula is used. *It is the convexity adjustment that is important – not the convexity measure in isolation.*

It is also important to understand this when comparing the convexity measures reported by dealers and vendors. For example, if one dealer shows a manager Bond A with a duration of 4 and a convexity measure of 50, and a second dealer shows the manager Bond B with a duration of 4 and a convexity measure of 80, which bond has the greater percentage price change response to changes in interest rates? Since the duration of the two bonds is identical, the bond with the larger convexity measure will change more when rates decline. However, not knowing how the two dealers computed the convexity measure means that the manager does not know which bond will have the greater convexity adjustment. If the first dealer used equation (4) while the second dealer used equation (6), then the convexity measures must be adjusted in terms of either equation. For example, the convexity measure of 80 computed using equation (6) is equal to a convexity measure of 40 based on equation (4).

Let's return to Exhibit 4 which is the Bloomberg Yield Analysis screen for the 30-year Treasury bond in our illustration. Bloomberg's convexity measure is displayed in the Sensitivity Analysis box in the lower left-hand corner of the screen. Specifically, the convexity measure reported is 2.878 which is the same number we calculated using equation (10). This means that equation (11) should be employed to obtain the convexity adjustment when using the convexity measure reported by Bloomberg.

Modified Convexity and Effective Convexity

The prices used in equation (4) to calculate convexity can be obtained by either assuming that when the yield changes the expected cash flows either do not change or they do change. In the former case, the resulting convexity is referred to as *modified convexity*. (Actually, in the industry, convexity is not qualified by the adjective "modified.") In contrast, *effective convexity* assumes that the cash flows do change when yields change. This is the same distinction made for duration.

As with duration, there is little difference between modified convexity and effective convexity for option-free bonds. However, for bonds with embedded options there can be quite a difference between the calculated modified convexity and effective convexity measures. In fact, for all option-free bonds, either convexity measure will have a positive value. For bonds with embedded options, the calculated effective convexity measure can be negative when the calculated modified convexity measure is positive.

PRICE VALUE OF A BASIS POINT

Some managers use another measure of the price volatility of a bond to quantify interest rate risk – the *price value of a basis point* (PVBP). This measure, also called the *dollar value of an 01* (DV01), is the absolute value of the change in the price of a bond for a 1 basis point change in yield. That is,

PVBP = | initial price – price if yield is changed by 1 basis point |

Exhibit 36: Bloomberg Yield Analysis Screen for a
10-Year Treasury Note

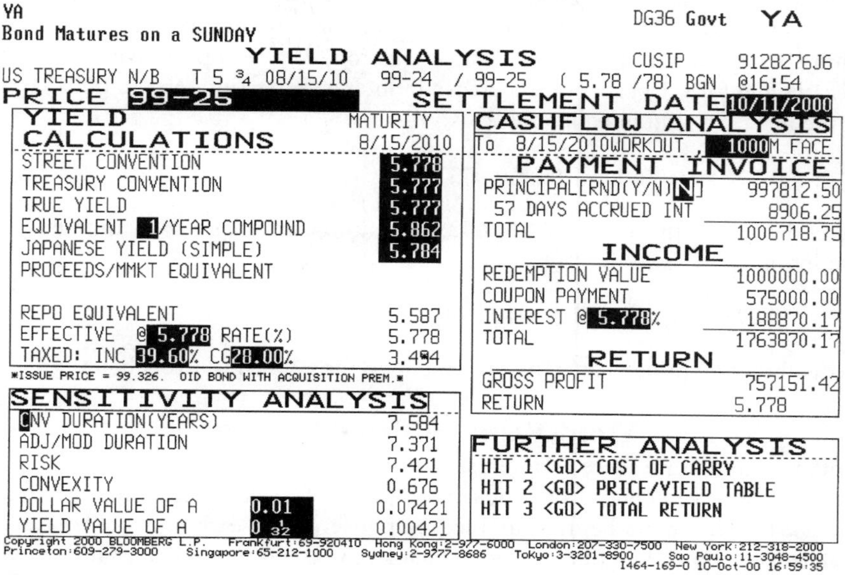

```
YA                                                    DG36 Govt   YA
Bond Matures on a SUNDAY
                        YIELD  ANALYSIS           CUSIP      9128276J6
US TREASURY N/B   T 5 ¾ 08/15/10   99-24 / 99-25   ( 5.78 /78) BGN  @16:54
PRICE  99-25                    SETTLEMENT  DATE 10/11/2000
YIELD                    MATURITY   CASHFLOW  ANALYSIS
CALCULATIONS             8/15/2010  To  8/15/2010WORKOUT ,  1000M FACE
STREET CONVENTION            5.778       PAYMENT  INVOICE
TREASURY CONVENTION          5.777   PRINCIPAL[RND(Y/N) N ]    997812.50
TRUE YIELD                   5.777    57 DAYS ACCRUED INT        8906.25
EQUIVALENT  1 /YEAR COMPOUND 5.862   TOTAL                    1006718.75
JAPANESE YIELD (SIMPLE)      5.784          INCOME
PROCEEDS/MMKT EQUIVALENT              REDEMPTION VALUE         1000000.00
                                     COUPON PAYMENT            575000.00
REPO EQUIVALENT              5.587   INTEREST @ 5.778 %        188870.17
EFFECTIVE  @ 5.778 RATE(%)   5.778   TOTAL                    1763870.17
TAXED: INC 39.60% CG 28.00%  3.494          RETURN
*ISSUE PRICE = 99.326.  OID BOND WITH ACQUISITION PREM.*   GROSS PROFIT        757151.42
SENSITIVITY  ANALYSIS                RETURN                     5.778
 C NV DURATION(YEARS)        7.584
ADJ/MOD DURATION             7.371   FURTHER  ANALYSIS
RISK                         7.421   HIT 1 <GO> COST OF CARRY
CONVEXITY                    0.676   HIT 2 <GO> PRICE/YIELD TABLE
DOLLAR VALUE OF A   0.01     0.07421 HIT 3 <GO> TOTAL RETURN
YIELD VALUE OF A    0 3/2    0.00421
Copyright 2000 BLOOMBERG L.P.   Frankfurt:69-920410  Hong Kong:2-977-6000  London:207-330-7500  New York:212-318-2000
Princeton:609-279-3000   Singapore:65-212-1000   Sydney:2-9777-8686   Tokyo:3-3201-8900   Sao Paulo:11-3048-4500
                                                                      1464-169-0 10-Oct-00 16:59:35
```

Bloomberg
PROFESSIONAL

Source: Bloomberg Financial Markets

Does it make a difference if the yield is increased or decreased by 1 basis point? It does not because of Property 2 — the change will be about the same for a small change in basis points.

To illustrate the computation, let's examine a 5.75% coupon, 10-year U.S. Treasury note that matures on August 15, 2010. Bloomberg's YA (Yield Analysis) Screen is presented in Exhibit 36. If the bond is priced to yield 5.778% on a settlement date of October 11, 2000, we can compute the PVBP by using the prices for either the yield at 5.768 or 5.788. The bond's initial full price at 5.778% is 100.6739. If the yield is decreased by 1 basis point to 5.768%, the PVBP is 0.0742 (|100.7481 − 100.6739|). If the yield is increased by 1 basis point to 5.788%, the PVBP is 0.0742 (|100.5997 − 100.6739|). Note that our PVBP calculation agrees with Bloomberg's calculation labeled "DOLLAR VALUE OF A 0.01" that is presented in the Sensitivity Analysis box located in the lower left-hand corner of the screen.

The PVBP is related to duration. In fact, PVBP is simply a special case of a measure called *dollar duration*. Dollar duration is the approximate dollar price change for a 100 basis point change in yield. We know that a bond's duration is the approximate percentage price change for a 100 basis point change in interest rates. We also know how to compute the approximate percentage price change for any number of basis points given a bond's duration using equation (2). Given the initial price and the approximate percentage price change for 1 basis point, we can compute the change in price for a 1 basis point change in rates.

For example, consider the 5.75% coupon, 10-year Treasury note. From Exhibit 36, the duration is 7.371. Using equation (2), the approximate percentage price change for a 1 basis point increase in interest rates (i.e., $\Delta y = 0.0001$) ignoring the negative sign in equation (2) is:

$$7.371 \times (0.0001) \times 100 = 0.07371\%$$

Given the initial full price of 100.6739, the dollar price change estimated using duration is

$$0.07371\% \times 100.6739 = \$0.0742$$

This is the same price change as shown above for a PVBP for this bond.[12]

Yield Value of Price Change

Another common measure of interest rate risk is called the *yield value of a price change*. The price change is the tick (e.g., $\frac{1}{32}$ for Treasuries or $\frac{1}{8}$ for corporates) for the particular bond being examined. Suppose we are examining a Treasury so a tick is $\frac{1}{32}$. The yield value of a price change for a Treasury is the change in yield for a $\frac{1}{32}$ change in price. The yield value of a price change is determined by calculating the difference between the yield to maturity at the current price and the yield to maturity if the bond price's was increased/decreased by $\frac{1}{32}$. In other words, how much does the current yield to maturity have to change to either increase or decrease the current price by $\frac{1}{32}$ (i.e., 1 tick)? The smaller the yield value of a price change, the greater the dollar price volatility.

To illustrate, let's return to the 5.75% coupon, 10-year Treasury note in Exhibit 36. On a settlement date of October 11, 2000, the bond is yielding 5.778% with a full price of 100.673878. The yield value of a $\frac{1}{32}$, reported by Bloomberg in the Sensitivity Analysis box in the lower left-hand corner of the screen, is 0.00421. This number tells us how the yield must fall/rise to increase/decrease the bond's price by one tick (i.e., $\frac{1}{32}$). If we reprice the bond at 5.77379% − 5.778% = 0.00421%, the full price is 100.705126. The difference between these two prices is 0.03125 (100.705126 − 100.673878) which is the dollar value of $\frac{1}{32}$ when par is $100.

THE IMPORTANCE OF YIELD VOLATILITY

What we have not considered thus far is the volatility of interest rates. For example, as we explained earlier, all other factors equal, the higher the coupon rate, the

---

[12] Bloomberg's "Risk" measure is simply the PVBP × 100. For bonds that are trading close to par, Risk should be close to modified duration.

lower the price volatility of a bond to changes in interest rates. In addition, the higher the level of yields, the lower the price volatility of a bond to changes in interest rates. This is illustrated in Exhibit 37, which shows the price/yield relationship for an option-free bond. When the yield level is high (Y_H in the exhibit) a change in interest rates does not produce a large change in the initial price (P_H in the exhibit). However, when the yield level is low (Y_L in the exhibit) a change in interest rates of the same number of basis points as shown when the yield is high does produce a large change in the initial price (P_L in the exhibit).

   This can also be cast in terms of duration properties: the higher the coupon, the lower the duration; and the higher the yield level the lower the duration. Given these two properties, a 10-year non-investment grade bond has a lower duration than a current coupon 10-year Treasury note since the former has a higher coupon rate and trades at a higher yield level. Does this mean that a 10-year non-investment grade bond has less interest rate risk than a current coupon 10-year Treasury note? Consider also that a 10-year Swiss government bond has a lower coupon rate than a current coupon 10-year U.S. Treasury note and trades at a lower yield level. Therefore, a 10-year Swiss government bond will have a higher duration than a current coupon 10-year Treasury note. Does this mean that a 10-year Swiss government bond has greater interest rate risk than a current coupon 10-year U.S. Treasury note? The missing link is the relative volatility of rates which we shall refer to as *yield volatility* or *interest rate volatility*.

Exhibit 37: The Effect of Yield Level on Price Volatility

$$(Y_H' - Y_H) = (Y_H - Y_H'') = (Y_L' - Y_L) = (Y_L - Y_L'')$$
$$(P_H - P_H') < (P_L - P_L') \text{ and}$$
$$(P_H - P_H'') < (P_L - P_L'')$$

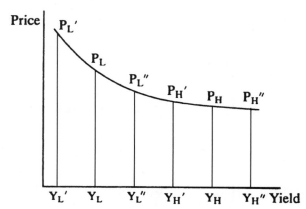

The greater the expected yield volatility, the greater the interest rate risk for a given duration and current value of a position. In the case of non-investment grade bonds, while their durations are less than current coupon Treasuries of the same maturity, the yield volatility is greater than that of current coupon Treasuries. For the 10-year Swiss government bond, while the duration is greater than for a current coupon 10-year U.S. Treasury note, the yield volatility is considerably less than that of 10-year U.S. Treasury notes.

Consequently, to measure the exposure of a portfolio or position to rate changes, it is necessary to measure yield volatility. This requires an understanding of the fundamental principles of probability distributions. The measure of yield volatility is the standard deviation of yield changes. In Chapter 13, we show how to estimate yield volatility. As we will see, depending on the underlying assumptions, there could be a wide range for the yield volatility estimate.

A framework that ties together the price sensitivity of a bond position to rate changes and yield volatility is the *value-at-risk (VaR) framework*.

Chapter 12

Analysis of Interest Rate Swaps

An interest rate swap contract provides a vehicle for market participants to transform the nature of cash flows and the interest rate exposure of a portfolio or balance sheet. In this chapter we explain how to analyze interest rate swaps. We will describe a generic interest rate swap, the parties to a swap, the risk and return of a swap, and the economic interpretation of a swap. Then we look at how to compute the floating-rate payments and calculate the present value of these payments. Next we will see how to calculate the fixed-rate payments given the swap rate. Before we look at how to calculate the value of a swap, we will see how to calculate the swap rate. Given the swap rate, we will then see how the value of swap is determined after the inception of a swap. Since an interest rate swap can be used to control the interest rate risk of a portfolio or a balance, we will explain how to estimate a swap's dollar duration. Swap markets help investors assess the relative value of a complicated security in two basic ways. First, the cash flows of a floater can be converted into a synthetic fixed-rate security using swaps. Once transformed into a fixed-rate security, its yield can then be compared to the yields on other comparable fixed-rate instruments. Second, the cash flows of a complicated security can be converted into a synthetic fixed-rate security using a combination of swaps and options. We will see how this is done in the final section of this chapter.

DESCRIPTION OF AN INTEREST RATE SWAP

In an *interest rate swap*, two parties (called *counterparties*) agree to exchange periodic interest payments. The dollar amount of the interest payments exchanged is based on some predetermined dollar principal, which is called the *notional amount*. The dollar amount each counterparty pays to the other is the agreed-upon periodic interest rate times the notional amount. The only dollars that are exchanged between the parties are the interest payments, not the notional amount. Accordingly, the notional principal serves only as a scale factor to translate an interest rate into a cash flow. In the most common type of swap, one party agrees to pay the other party fixed interest payments at designated dates for the life of the contract. This party is referred to as the *fixed-rate payer*. The other party, who agrees to make interest rate payments that float with some reference rate, is referred to as the *floating-rate payer*.

The reference rates that have been used for the floating rate in an interest rate swap are various money market rates: Treasury bill rate, the London interbank offered rate, commercial paper rate, bankers acceptances rate, certificates of deposit rate, the federal funds rate, and the prime rate. The most common is the London interbank offered rate (LIBOR). LIBOR is the rate at which prime banks offer to pay on Eurodollar deposits available to other prime banks for a given maturity. There is not just one rate but a rate for different maturities. For example, there is a 1-month LIBOR, 3-month LIBOR, and 6-month LIBOR.

To illustrate an interest rate swap, suppose that for the next five years party X agrees to pay party Y 10% per year, while party Y agrees to pay party X 6-month LIBOR (the reference rate). Party X is a fixed-rate payer/floating-rate receiver, while party Y is a floating-rate payer/fixed-rate receiver. Assume that the notional amount is $50 million, and that payments are exchanged every six months for the next five years. This means that every six months, party X (the fixed-rate payer/floating-rate receiver) will pay party Y $2.5 million (10% times $50 million divided by 2). The amount that party Y (the floating-rate payer/fixed-rate receiver) will pay party X will be 6-month LIBOR times $50 million divided by 2. If 6-month LIBOR is 7%, party Y will pay party X $1.75 million (7% times $50 million divided by 2). Note that we divide by two because one-half year's interest is being paid.

Interest rate swaps are over-the-counter instruments. This means that they are not traded on an exchange. An institutional investor wishing to enter into a swap transaction can do so through either a securities firm or a commercial bank that transacts in swaps.[1] These entities can do one of the following. First, they can arrange or broker a swap between two parties that want to enter into an interest rate swap. In this case, the securities firm or commercial bank is acting in a brokerage capacity.

The second way in which a securities firm or commercial bank can get an institutional investor into a swap position is by taking the other side of the swap. This means that the securities firm or the commercial bank is a dealer rather than a broker in the transaction. Acting as a dealer, the securities firm or the commercial bank must hedge its swap position in the same way that it hedges its position in other securities. Also it means that the swap dealer is the counterparty to the transaction.

The risks that the two parties take on when they enter into a swap is that the other party will fail to fulfill its obligations as set forth in the swap agreement. That is, each party faces default risk. The default risk in a swap agreement is called *counterparty risk*. In any agreement between two parties that must perform according to the terms of a contract, counterparty risk is the risk that the other party will default. With futures and exchange-traded options the counterparty risk is the risk that the clearinghouse establishes to guarantee performance of the contracts will default. Market participants view this risk as small. In contrast, counterparty risk in a swap can be significant.

Because of counterparty risk, not all securities firms and commercial banks can be swap dealers. Several securities firms have established subsidiaries

---

[1] Don't get confused here about the role of commercial banks. A bank can use a swap in its asset/liability management. Or, a bank can transact (buy and sell) swaps to clients to generate fee income. It is in the latter sense that we are discussing the role of a commercial bank in the swap market here.

that are separately capitalized so that they have a high credit rating which permit them to enter into swap transactions as a dealer.

Thus, it is imperative to keep in mind that any party who enters into a swap is subject to counterparty risk.

INTERPRETING A SWAP POSITION

There are two ways that a swap position can be interpreted: (1) a package of forward/futures contracts and (2) a package of cash flows from buying and selling cash market instruments.

Package of Forward Contracts

Consider the hypothetical interest rate swap used earlier to illustrate a swap. Let's look at party X's position. Party X has agreed to pay 10% and receive 6-month LIBOR. More specifically, assuming a $50 million notional amount, X has agreed to buy a commodity called "6-month LIBOR" for $2.5 million. This is effectively a 6-month forward contract where X agrees to pay $2.5 million in exchange for delivery of 6-month LIBOR. The fixed-rate payer is effectively long a 6-month forward contract on 6-month LIBOR. The floating-rate payer is effectively short a 6-month forward contract on 6-month LIBOR. There is therefore an implicit forward contract corresponding to each exchange date.

Consequently, interest rate swaps can be viewed as a package of more basic interest rate derivative instruments — forwards. The pricing of an interest rate swap will then depend on the price of a package of forward contracts with the same settlement dates in which the underlying for the forward contract is the same reference rate.

While an interest rate swap may be nothing more than a package of forward contracts, it is not a redundant contract for several reasons. First, maturities for forward or futures contracts do not extend out as far as those of an interest rate swap; an interest rate swap with a term of 15 years or longer can be obtained. Second, an interest rate swap is a more transactionally efficient instrument. By this we mean that in one transaction an entity can effectively establish a payoff equivalent to a package of forward contracts. The forward contracts would each have to be negotiated separately. Third, the interest rate swap market has grown in liquidity since its establishment in 1981; interest rate swaps now provide more liquidity than forward contracts, particularly long-dated (i.e., long-term) forward contracts.

Package of Cash Market Instruments

To understand why a swap can also be interpreted as a package of cash market instruments, consider an investor who enters into the transaction below:

- buy $50 million par value of a 5-year floating-rate bond that pays 6-month LIBOR every six months

• finance the purchase by borrowing $50 million for five years at a 10% annual interest rate paid every six months.

The cash flows for this transaction are set forth in Exhibit 1. The second column of the exhibit shows the cash flows from purchasing the 5-year floating-rate bond. There is a $50 million cash outlay and then ten cash inflows. The amount of the cash inflows is uncertain because they depend on future levels of 6-month LIBOR. The next column shows the cash flows from borrowing $50 million on a fixed-rate basis. The last column shows the net cash flows from the entire transaction. As the last column indicates, there is no initial cash flow (no cash inflow or cash outlay). In all ten 6-month periods, the net position results in a cash inflow of LIBOR and a cash outlay of $2.5 million. This net position, however, is identical to the position of a fixed-rate payer/floating-rate receiver.

It can be seen from the net cash flow in Exhibit 1 that a fixed-rate payer has a cash market position that is equivalent to a long position in a floating-rate bond and a short position in a fixed-rate bond — the short position being the equivalent of borrowing by issuing a fixed-rate bond.

What about the position of a floating-rate payer? It can be easily demonstrated that the position of a floating-rate payer is equivalent to purchasing a fixed-rate bond and financing that purchase at a floating-rate, where the floating rate is the reference rate for the swap. That is, the position of a floating-rate payer is equivalent to a long position in a fixed-rate bond and a short position in a floating-rate bond.

Exhibit 1: Cash Flows for the Purchase of a 5-Year Floating-Rate Bond Financed by Borrowing on a Fixed-Rate Basis

Transaction:
• Purchase for $50 million a 5-year floating-rate bond:
  floating rate = LIBOR, semiannual pay
• Borrow $50 million for five years:
  fixed rate = 10%, semiannual payments

Six Month Period	Cash Flow (In Millions of Dollars) From:		
	Floating-rate Bond[*]	Borrowing Cost	Net
0	−$50	+$50.0	$0
1	+ (LIBOR$_1$/2) × 50	−2.5	+ (LIBOR$_1$/2) × 50 − 2.5
2	+ (LIBOR$_2$/2) × 50	−2.5	+ (LIBOR$_2$/2) × 50 − 2.5
3	+ (LIBOR$_3$/2) × 50	−2.5	+ (LIBOR$_3$/2) × 50 − 2.5
4	+ (LIBOR$_4$/2) × 50	−2.5	+ (LIBOR$_4$/2) × 50 − 2.5
5	+ (LIBOR$_5$/2) × 50	−2.5	+ (LIBOR$_5$/2) × 50 − 2.5
6	+ (LIBOR$_6$/2) × 50	−2.5	+ (LIBOR$_6$/2) × 50 − 2.5
7	+ (LIBOR$_7$/2) × 50	−2.5	+ (LIBOR$_7$/2) × 50 − 2.5
8	+ (LIBOR$_8$/2) × 50	−2.5	+ (LIBOR$_8$/2) × 50 − 2.5
9	+ (LIBOR$_9$/2) × 50	−2.5	+ (LIBOR$_9$/2) × 50 − 2.5
10	+ (LIBOR$_{10}$/2) × 50 + 50	−52.5	+ (LIBOR$_{10}$/2) × 50 − 2.5

[*] The subscript for LIBOR indicates the 6-month LIBOR as per the terms of the floating-rate bond at time t.

Exhibit 2: Describing the Counterparties to a Swap

Fixed-rate Payer	Floating-rate Payer
• pays fixed rate in the swap	• pays floating rate in the swap
• receives floating in the swap	• receives fixed in the swap
• is short the bond market	• is long the bond market
• has bought a swap	• has sold a swap
• is long a swap	• is short a swap
• has established the price sensitivities of a longer-term liability and a floating-rate asset	• has established the price sensitivities of a longer-term asset and a floating-rate liability

Source: Robert F. Kopprasch, John Macfarlane, Daniel R. Ross, and Janet Showers, "The Interest Rate Swap Market: Yield Mathematics, Terminology, and Conventions," Chapter 58 in Frank J. Fabozzi and Irving M. Pollack (eds.), *The Handbook of Fixed Income Securities* (Homewood, IL: Dow Jones-Irwin, 1987).

TERMINOLOGY, CONVENTIONS, AND MARKET QUOTES

Here we review some of the terminology used in the swaps market and explain how swaps are quoted. The date that the counterparties commit to the swap is called the *trade date*. The date that the swap begins accruing interest is called the *effective date*, while the date that the swap stops accruing interest is called the *maturity date*. How often the floating-rate is changed is called the *reset frequency*.

While our illustrations assume that the timing of the cash flows for both the fixed-rate payer and floating-rate payer will be the same, this is rarely the case in a swap. An agreement may call for the fixed-rate payer to make payments annually but the floating-rate payer to make payments more frequently (semiannually or quarterly). Also, the way in which interest accrues on each leg of the transaction differs, because there are several day count conventions in the fixed-income markets as discussed in Chapter 3.

Normally, the fixed interest payments are paid on the basis of a 30/360 day count; floating-rate payments are paid on the basis of an actual/360 day count. Accordingly, the fixed interest payments will differ slightly owing to the differences in the lengths of successive coupon periods. The floating payments will differ owing to day counts as well as movements in the reference rate.

The terminology used to describe the position of a party in the swap markets combines cash market jargon and futures market jargon, given that a swap position can be interpreted as a position in a package of cash market instruments or a package of futures/forward positions. As we have said, the counterparty to an interest rate swap is either a fixed-rate payer or floating-rate payer. Exhibit 2 describes these positions in several ways.

The first two expressions in Exhibit 2 to describe the position of a fixed-rate payer and floating-rate payer are self-explanatory. To understand why the fixed-rate payer is viewed as short the bond market, and the floating-rate payer is viewed as long the bond market, consider what happens when interest rates change. Those who borrow on a fixed-rate basis will benefit if interest rates rise because they have locked in a lower interest rate. But those who have a short bond position will also benefit if interest rates rise. Thus, a fixed-rate payer can be said to be short the bond market. A floating-rate payer benefits if interest rates fall. A long position in a bond also benefits if interest rates fall, so terminology describing a floating-rate payer as long the bond market is not surprising. From our discussion of the interpretation of a swap as a package of cash market instruments, describing a swap in terms of the sensitivities of long and short cash positions follows naturally.

The convention that has evolved for quoting swaps levels is that a swap dealer sets the floating rate equal to the reference rate and then quotes the fixed rate that will apply. To illustrate this convention, consider the following 10-year swap terms available from a dealer:

- *Floating-rate payer:*
  Pay floating rate of 3-month LIBOR quarterly.
  Receive fixed rate of 8.75% semiannually.
- *Fixed-rate payer:*
  Pay fixed rate of 8.85% semiannually
  Receive floating rate of 3-month LIBOR quarterly.

The offer price that the dealer would quote the fixed-rate payer would be to pay 8.85% and receive LIBOR "flat." (The word flat means with no spread.) The bid price that the dealer would quote the floating-rate payer would be to pay LIBOR flat and receive 8.75%. The bid-offer spread is 10 basis points.

In order to solidify our intuition, it is useful to think of the swap market as a market where two counterparties trade the floating reference rate in a series of exchanges for a fixed price. In effect, the swap market is a market to buy and sell LIBOR. So, buying a swap (pay fixed/receive floating) can be thought of as buying LIBOR on each reset date for the fixed rate agreed to on the trade date. Conversely, selling a swap (receive fixed/pay floating) is effectively selling LIBOR on each reset date for a fixed rate agreed to on the trade date. In this framework, a dealer's bid-offer spread can be easily interpreted. Using the numbers presented above, the bid price of 8.75% is the price the dealer will pay to the counterparty to receive 3-month LIBOR. In other words, buy LIBOR at the bid. Similarly, the offer price of 8.85% is the price the dealer receives from the counterparty in exchange for 3-month LIBOR. In other words, sell LIBOR at the offer.

The fixed rate is some spread above the Treasury yield curve with the same term to maturity as the swap. In our illustration, suppose that the 10-year Treasury yield is 8.35%. Then the offer price that the dealer would quote to the fixed-rate payer is the 10-year Treasury rate plus 50 basis points versus receiving LIBOR flat. For the floating-rate payer, the bid price quoted would be LIBOR flat versus the 10-year Treasury rate plus 40 basis points. The dealer would quote such a swap as 40-50, meaning that the dealer is willing to enter into a swap to receive LIBOR and pay a fixed rate equal to the 10-year Treasury rate plus 40 basis points; and it would be willing to enter into a swap to pay LIBOR and receive a fixed rate equal to the 10-year Treasury rate plus 50 basis points. The difference between the Treasury rate paid and received is the bid-offer spread.[2]

VALUING INTEREST RATE SWAPS

In an interest rate swap, the counterparties agree to exchange periodic interest payments. The dollar amount of the interest payments exchanged is based on the notional principal. In the most common type of swap, there is a fixed-rate payer and a fixed-rate receiver. The convention for quoting swap rates is that a swap dealer sets the floating rate equal to the reference rate and then quotes the fixed rate that will apply.

Computing the Payments for a Swap

In the previous section we described in general terms the payments by the fixed-rate payer and fixed-rate receiver but we did not give any details. That is, we explained that if the swap rate is 6% and the notional amount is $100 million, then the fixed-rate payment will be $6 million for the year and the payment is then adjusted based on the frequency of settlement. So, if settlement is semian-nual, the payment is $3 million. If it is quarterly, it is $1.5 million. Similarly, the floating-rate payment would be found by multiplying the reference rate by the notional amount and then scaled based on the frequency of settlement.

It was useful to show the basic features of an interest rate swap using quick calculations for the payments such as described above and then explaining how the parties to a swap either benefit or hurt when interest rates changes. How-ever, we will show how to value a swap in this section. To value a swap it is neces-sary to determine the present value of the fixed-rate payments and the present value of the floating-rate payments. The difference between these two present val-ues is the value of a swap. As will be explained below, whether the value is posi-tive (i.e., an asset) or negative (i.e., a liability) will depend on the party.

At the inception of the swap, the terms of the swap will be such that the present value of the floating-rate payments is equal to the present value of the fixed-rate payments. That is, the value of the swap is equal to zero at its incep-tion. This is the fundamental principle in determining the swap rate (i.e., the fixed rate that the fixed-rate payer will make).

Here is a roadmap of the presentation. First we will look at how to com-pute the floating-rate payments. We will see how the future values of the refer-

---

[2] A question that commonly arises is why is the fixed rate of a swap quoted as a fixed spread above a Trea-sury rate when Treasury rates are not used directly in swap valuation? Because of the timing difference between the quote and settlement, quoting the fixed-rate side as a spread above a Treasury rate allows the swap dealer to hedge against changing interest rates.

ence rate are determined to obtain the floating rate for the period. From the future values of the reference rate we will then see how to compute the floating-rate payments taking into account the number of days in the payment period. Next we will see how to calculate the fixed-rate payments given the swap rate. Before we look at how to calculate the value of a swap, we will see how to calculate the swap rate. This will require an explanation of how the present value of any cash flow in an interest rate swap is computed. Given the floating-rate payments and the present value of the floating-rate payments, the swap rate can be determined by using the principle that the swap rate is the fixed rate that will make the present value of the fixed-rate payments equal to the present value of the floating-rate payments. Finally, we will see how the value of swap is determined after the inception of a swap.

Calculating the Floating-Rate Payments

For the first floating-rate payment, the amount is known. For all subsequent payments, the floating-rate payment depends on the value of the reference rate when the floating rate is determined. To illustrate the issues associated with calculating the floating-rate payment, we will assume that

- a swap starts today, January 1 of year 1(swap settlement date)
- the floating-rate payments are made quarterly based on "actual/360"
- the reference rate is 3-month LIBOR
- the notional amount of the swap is $100 million
- the term of the swap is three years

The quarterly floating-rate payments are based on an "actual/360" day count convention. Recall that this convention means that 360 days are assumed in a year and that in computing the interest for the quarter the actual number of days in the quarter are used. The floating-rate payment is set at the beginning of the quarter but paid at the end of the quarter — that is, the floating-rate payments are made in arrears.

Suppose that today 3-month LIBOR is 4.05%. Let's look at what the fixed-rate payer will receive on March 31 of year 1 — the date when the first quarterly swap payment is made. There is no uncertainty about what the floating-rate payment will be. In general, the floating-rate payment is determined as follows:

$$\text{notional amount} \times (3\text{-month LIBOR}) \times \frac{\text{no. of days in period}}{360}$$

In our illustration, assuming a non-Leap year, the number of days from January 1 of year 1 to March 31 of year 1 (the first quarter) is 90. If 3-month LIBOR is 4.05%, then the fixed-rate payer will receive a floating-rate payment on March 31 of year 1 equal to:

$$\$100,000,000 \times 0.0405 \times \frac{90}{360} = \$1,012,500$$

Now the difficulty is in determining the floating-rate payment after the first quarterly payment. That is, for the 3-year swap there will be 12 quarterly floating-rate payments. So, while the first quarterly payment is known, the next 11 are not. However, there is a way to hedge the next 11 floating-rate payments by using a futures contract. Specifically, the futures contract used to hedge the future floating-rate payments in a swap whose reference rate is 3-month LIBOR is the Eurodollar CD futures contract. We will digress to discuss this contract.

The Eurodollar CD Futures Contract

As explained earlier in the chapter, a swap position can be interpreted as a package of forward/futures contracts or a package of cash flows from buying and selling cash market instruments. It is the former interpretation that will be used as the basis for valuing a swap. In the case of a LIBOR-based swap, the appropriate futures contract is the Eurodollar CD futures contract. For this reason, we will describe this important contract.

Eurodollar certificates of deposit (CDs) are denominated in dollars but represent the liabilities of banks outside the United States. The contracts are traded on both the International Monetary Market of the Chicago Mercantile Exchange and the London International Financial Futures Exchange. The rate paid on Eurodollar CDs is the London interbank offered rate (LIBOR).

The 3-month Eurodollar CD is the underlying instrument for the Eurodollar CD futures contract. The contract is for $1 million of face value and is traded on an index price basis. The index price basis in which the contract is quoted is equal to 100 minus the annualized LIBOR futures rate. For example, a Eurodollar CD futures price of 94.00 means a 3-month LIBOR futures rate of 6% (100 minus 6%).

The Eurodollar CD futures contract is a cash settlement contract. That is, the parties settle in cash for the value of a Eurodollar CD based on LIBOR at the settlement date. The 3-month Eurodollar CD futures contracts trade with delivery months of March, June, September, and December, up to ten years in the future. In addition, the four nearest serial contract months are listed. For example, on January 5, 2001, there were 44 listed Eurodollar CD futures contracts listed. For the year 2001, the contract delivery months included January, February, March, April, May, June, September, and December. For the years 2002-2010, the delivery months were March, June, September, and December.

The Eurodollar CD futures contract allows the buyer of the contract to lock in the rate on 3-month LIBOR today for a future 3-month period. For example, suppose that on February 1, 2000 an investor purchases a Eurodollar CD futures contract that settles in March 2000. Suppose that the LIBOR futures rate for this contract is 5%. This means that the investor has agreed to effectively invest in a 3-month Eurodollar CD that pays a rate of 5%. Specifically, the investor has locked in a rate for a 3-month investment of 5% beginning March 2000. If the investor on February 1, 2000 purchased a contract that settles in September 2001 and the LIBOR futures rate is 5.4%, the investor has locked in the rate on a 3-month investment beginning September 2001.

From the perspective of the seller of a Eurodollar CD futures contract, the seller is agreeing to lend funds for three months at some future date at the LIBOR futures rate. For example, suppose on February 1, 2000 a bank sells a Eurodollar CD futures contract that settles in March 2000 and the LIBOR futures rate is 5%. The bank locks in a borrowing rate of 5% for three months beginning in March 2000. If the settlement date is September 2001 and the LIBOR futures rate is 5.4%, the bank is locking in a borrowing rate of 5.4% for the 3-month period beginning September 2001.

The key point here is that the Eurodollar CD futures contract allows a participant in the financial market to lock in a 3-month rate on an investment or a 3-month borrowing rate. The 3-month rate begins in the month that the contract settles.

Determining Future Floating-Rate Payments

Now let's return to our objective of determining the future floating-rate payments. These payments can be locked in over the life of the swap using the Eurodollar CD futures contract. We will show how these floating-rate payments are computed using this contract.

We will begin with the next quarterly payment — from April 1 of year 1 to June 30 of year 1. This quarter has 91 days. The floating-rate payment will be determined by 3-month LIBOR on April 1 of year 1 and paid on June 30 of year 1. Where might the fixed-rate payer look to today (January 1 of year 1) to project what 3-month LIBOR will be on April 1 of year 1? One possibility is the Eurodollar CD futures market. There is a 3-month Eurodollar CD futures contract for settlement on June 30 of year 1. That futures contract will have the market's expectation of what 3-month LIBOR on April 1 of year 1 is. For example, if the futures price for the 3-month Eurodollar CD futures contract that settles on June 30 of year 1 is 95.85, then as explained above, the 3-month Eurodollar futures rate is 4.15%. We will refer to that rate for 3-month LIBOR as the "forward rate." Therefore, if the fixed-rate payer bought 100 of these 3-month Eurodollar CD futures contract on January 1 of year 1 (the inception of the swap) that settles on June 30 of year 1, then the payment that will be locked in for the quarter (April 1 to June 30 of year 1) is

$$\$100,000,000 \times 0.0415 \times \frac{91}{360} = \$1,049,028$$

(Note that each futures contract is for $1 million and hence 100 contracts have a notional amount of $100 million.) Similarly, the Eurodollar CD futures contract can be used to lock in a floating-rate payment for each of the next 10 quarters.[3] Once again, it is important to emphasize that the reference rate at the beginning of period t determines the floating-rate that will be paid for the period. However, the floating-rate payment is not made until the end of period t.

---

[3] The Chicago Mercantile Exchange offers pre-packaged series of Eurodollar CD futures contracts that expire on consecutive dates called *bundles*. Specifically, a bundle is the simultaneous sale or purchase of one of each of a consecutive series of Eurodollar CD futures contracts. So, rather than construct the same positions with individual contracts, a series of contracts can be sold or purchased in a single transaction.

Exhibit 3: Floating-Rate Payments Based on Initial LIBOR and Eurodollar CD Futures

(1)	(2)	(3)	(4)	(5)	(6)	(7)	(8)
Quarter starts	Quarter ends	Number of days in quarter	Current 3-month LIBOR	Eurodollar CD futures price	Forward rate	Period = End of quarter	Floating-rate payment at end of quarter
Jan 1 year 1	Mar 31 year 1	90	4.05%	—		1	1,012,500
Apr 1 year 1	June 30 year 1	91		95.85	4.15%	2	1,049,028
July 1 year 1	Sept 30 year 1	92		95.45	4.55%	3	1,162,778
Oct 1 year 1	Dec 31 year 1	92		95.28	4.72%	4	1,206,222
Jan 1 year 2	Mar 31 year 2	90		95.10	4.90%	5	1,225,000
Apr 1 year 2	June 30 year 2	91		94.97	5.03%	6	1,271,472
July 1 year 2	Sept 30 year 2	92		94.85	5.15%	7	1,316,111
Oct 1 year 2	Dec 31 year 2	92		94.75	5.25%	8	1,341,667
Jan 1 year 3	Mar 31 year 3	90		94.60	5.40%	9	1,350,000
Apr 1 year 3	June 30 year 3	91		94.50	5.50%	10	1,390,278
July 1 year 3	Sept 30 year 3	92		94.35	5.65%	11	1,443,889
Oct 1 year 3	Dec 31 year 3	92		94.24	5.76%	12	1,472,000

Exhibit 3 shows this for the 3-year swap. Shown in Column (1) is when the quarter begins and in Column (2) when the quarter ends. The payment will be received at the end of the first quarter (March 31 of year 1) and is $1,012,500. That is the known floating-rate payment as explained earlier. It is the only payment that is known. The information used to compute the first payment is in Column (4) which shows the current 3-month LIBOR (4.05%). The payment is shown in the last column, Column (8).

Notice that Column (7) numbers the quarters from 1 through 12. Look at the heading for Column (7). It identifies each quarter in terms of the end of the quarter. This is important because we will eventually be discounting the payments (cash flows). We must take care to understand when each payment is to be exchanged in order to properly discount. So, for the first payment of $1,012,500 it is going to be received at the end of quarter 1. When we refer to the time period for any payment, the reference is to the end of quarter. So, the fifth payment of $1,225,000 would be identified as the payment for period 5, where period 5 means that it will be exchanged at the end of the fifth quarter.

Calculating the Fixed-Rate Payments

The swap will specify the frequency of settlement for the fixed-rate payments. The frequency need not be the same as the floating-rate payments. For example, in the 3-year swap we have been using to illustrate the calculation of the floating-rate payments, the frequency is quarterly. The frequency of the fixed-rate payments could be semiannual rather than quarterly.

In our illustration we will assume that the frequency of settlement is quarterly for the fixed-rate payments, the same as with the floating-rate payments. The day count convention is the same as for the floating-rate payment, "actual/360". The equation for determining the dollar amount of the fixed-rate payment for the period is:

$$\text{notional amount} \times (\text{swap rate}) \times \frac{\text{no. of days in period}}{360}$$

It is the same equation as for determining the floating-rate payment except that the swap rate is used instead of the reference rate (3-month LIBOR in our illustration).

For example, suppose that the swap rate is 4.98% and the quarter has 90 days. Then the fixed-rate payment for the quarter is:

$$\$100,000,000 \times 0.0498 \times \frac{90}{360} = \$1,245,000$$

If there are 92 days in a quarter, the fixed-rate payment for the quarter is:

$$\$100,000,000 \times 0.0498 \times \frac{92}{360} = \$1,272,667$$

Note that the rate is fixed for each quarter but the dollar amount of the payment depends on the number of days in the period.

Exhibit 4 shows the fixed-rate payments based on different assumed values for the swap rate. The first three columns of the exhibit show the same information as in Exhibit 3 — the beginning and end of the quarter and the number of days in the quarter. Column (4) simply uses the notation for the period. That is, period 1 means the end of the first quarter, period 2 means the end of the second quarter, and so on. The other columns of the exhibit show the payments for each assumed swap rate.

Exhibit 4: Fixed-Rate Payments for Several Assumed Swap Rates

(1)	(2)	(3)	(4)	(5)	(6)	(7)	(8)	(9)
		Number	Period =	Fixed-rate payment if				
Quarter	Quarter	of days in	End of	swap rate is assumed to be				
starts	ends	quarter	quarter	4.9800%	4.9873%	4.9874%	4.9875%	4.9880%
Jan 1 year 1	Mar 31 year 1	90	1	1,245,000	1,246,825	1,246,850	1,246,875	1,247,000
Apr 1 year 1	June 30 year 1	91	2	1,258,833	1,260,679	1,260,704	1,260,729	1,260,856
July 1 year 1	Sept 30 year 1	92	3	1,272,667	1,274,532	1,274,558	1,274,583	1,274,711
Oct 1 year 1	Dec 31 year 1	92	4	1,272,667	1,274,532	1,274,558	1,274,583	1,274,711
Jan 1 year 2	Mar 31 year 2	90	5	1,245,000	1,246,825	1,246,850	1,246,875	1,247,000
Apr 1 year 2	June 30 year 2	91	6	1,258,833	1,260,679	1,260,704	1,260,729	1,260,856
July 1 year 2	Sept 30 year 2	92	7	1,272,667	1,274,532	1,274,558	1,274,583	1,274,711
Oct 1 year 2	Dec 31 year 2	92	8	1,272,667	1,274,532	1,274,558	1,274,583	1,274,711
Jan 1 year 3	Mar 31 year 3	90	9	1,245,000	1,246,825	1,246,850	1,246,875	1,247,000
Apr 1 year 3	June 30 year 3	91	10	1,258,833	1,260,679	1,260,704	1,260,729	1,260,856
July 1 year 3	Sept 30 year 3	92	11	1,272,667	1,274,532	1,274,558	1,274,583	1,274,711
Oct 1 year 3	Dec 31 year 3	92	12	1,272,667	1,274,532	1,274,558	1,274,583	1,274,711

Calculation of the Swap Rate

Now that we know how to calculate the payments for the fixed-rate and floating-rate sides of a swap where the reference rate is 3-month LIBOR given (1) the current value for 3-month LIBOR, (2) the expected 3-month LIBOR from the Eurodollar CD futures contract, and (3) the assumed swap rate, we can demonstrate how to compute the swap rate.

At the initiation of an interest rate swap, the counterparties are agreeing to exchange future payments and no upfront payments by either party are made. This means that the swap terms must be such that the present value of the payments to be made by the counterparties must be at least equal to the present value of the payments that will be received. In fact, to eliminate arbitrage opportunities, the present value of the payments made by a party will be equal to the present value of the payments received by that same party. *The equivalence (or no arbitrage) of the present value of the payments is the key principle in calculating the swap rate.*

Since we will have to calculate the present value of the payments, let's show how this is done.

Calculating the Present Value of the Floating-Rate Payments

As explained earlier, we must be careful about how we compute the present value of payments. In particular, we must carefully specify (1) the timing of the payment and (2) the interest rates that should be used to discount the payments. We have already addressed the first issue. In constructing the exhibit for the payments, we indicated that the payments are at the end of the quarter. So, we denoted the time periods with respect to the end of the quarter.

Now let's turn to the interest rates that should be used for discounting. In Chapter 4, we emphasized two things. First, every cash flow should be discounted at its own discount rate using a spot rate. So, if we discounted a cash flow of $1 using the spot rate for period t, the present value would be:

$$\text{present value of \$1 to be received in period } t = \frac{\$1}{(1 + \text{spot rate for period } t)^t}$$

The second thing we emphasized is that forward rates are derived from spot rates so that if we discounted a cash flow using forward rates rather than a spot rate, we would come up with the same value. That is, the present value of $1 to be received in period t can be rewritten as:

$$\text{present value of \$1 to be received in period } t =$$

$$\frac{\$1}{(1 + \text{forward rate for period 1})(1 + \text{forward rate for period 2})\cdots(1 + \text{forward rate for period } t)}$$

We will refer to the present value of $1 to be received in period t as the *forward discount factor*. In our calculations involving swaps, we will compute the forward discount factor for a period using the forward rates. These are the same forward rates that are used to compute the floating-rate payments — those obtained from the Eurodollar CD futures contract. We must make just one more adjustment. We must adjust the forward rates used in the formula for the number of days in the period (i.e., the quarter in our illustrations) in the same way that we made this adjustment to obtain the payments. Specifically, the forward rate for a period, which we will refer to as the period forward rate, is computed using the following equation:

$$\text{period forward rate} = \text{annual forward rate} \times \left(\frac{\text{days in period}}{360}\right)$$

For example, look at Exhibit 3. The annual forward rate for period 4 is 4.72%. The period forward rate for period 4 is:

$$\text{period forward rate} = 4.72\% \times \left(\frac{92}{360}\right) = 1.2062\%$$

Column (5) in Exhibit 5 shows the annual forward rate for all 12 periods (reproduced from Exhibit 3) and Column (6) shows the period forward rate for all 12 periods. Note that the period forward rate for period 1 is 4.05%, the known rate for 3-month LIBOR.

Also shown in Exhibit 5 is the forward discount factor for all 12 periods. These values are shown in the last column. Let's show how the forward discount factor is computed for periods 1, 2, and 3. For period 1, the forward discount factor is:

$$\text{forward discount factor} = \frac{\$1}{(1.010125)} = 0.98997649$$

For period 2,

$$\text{forward discount factor} = \frac{\$1}{(1.010125)(1.010490)} = 0.97969917$$

Exhibit 5: Calculating the Forward Discount Factor

(1)	(2)	(3)	(4)	(5)	(6)	(7)
Quarter starts	Quarter ends	Number of days in quarter	Period = End of quarter	Forward rate	Period forward rate	Forward discount factor
Jan 1 year 1	Mar 31 year 1	90	1	4.05%	1.0125%	0.98997649
Apr 1 year 1	June 30 year 1	91	2	4.15%	1.0490%	0.97969917
July 1 year 1	Sept 30 year 1	92	3	4.55%	1.1628%	0.96843839
Oct 1 year 1	Dec 31 year 1	92	4	4.72%	1.2062%	0.95689609
Jan 1 year 2	Mar 31 year 2	90	5	4.90%	1.2250%	0.94531597
Apr 1 year 2	June 30 year 2	91	6	5.03%	1.2715%	0.93344745
July 1 year 2	Sept 30 year 2	92	7	5.15%	1.3161%	0.92132183
Oct 1 year 2	Dec 31 year 2	92	8	5.25%	1.3417%	0.90912441
Jan 1 year 3	Mar 31 year 3	90	9	5.40%	1.3500%	0.89701471
Apr 1 year 3	June 30 year 3	91	10	5.50%	1.3903%	0.88471472
July 1 year 3	Sept 30 year 3	92	11	5.65%	1.4439%	0.87212224
Oct 1 year 3	Dec 31 year 3	92	12	5.76%	1.4720%	0.85947083

Exhibit 6: Present Value of the Floating-Rate Payments

(1)	(2)	(3)	(4)	(5)	(6)
Quarter starts	Quarter ends	Period = End of quarter	Forward discount factor	Floating-rate payment at end of quarter	PV of floating-rate payment
Jan 1 year 1	Mar 31 year 1	1	0.98997649	1,012,500	1,002,351
Apr 1 year 1	June 30 year 1	2	0.97969917	1,049,028	1,027,732
July 1 year 1	Sept 30 year 1	3	0.96843839	1,162,778	1,126,079
Oct 1 year 1	Dec 31 year 1	4	0.95689609	1,206,222	1,154,229
Jan 1 year 2	Mar 31 year 2	5	0.94531597	1,225,000	1,158,012
Apr 1 year 2	June 30 year 2	6	0.93344745	1,271,472	1,186,852
July 1 year 2	Sept 30 year 2	7	0.92132183	1,316,111	1,212,562
Oct 1 year 2	Dec 31 year 2	8	0.90912441	1,341,667	1,219,742
Jan 1 year 3	Mar 31 year 3	9	0.89701471	1,350,000	1,210,970
Apr 1 year 3	June 30 year 3	10	0.88471472	1,390,278	1,229,999
July 1 year 3	Sept 30 year 3	11	0.87212224	1,443,889	1,259,248
Oct 1 year 3	Dec 31 year 3	12	0.85947083	1,472,000	1,265,141
				Total	14,052,917

For period 3.

$$\text{forward discount factor} = \frac{\$1}{(1.010125)(1.010490)(1.011628)}$$

$$= 0.96843839$$

Given the floating-rate payment for a period and the forward discount factor for the period, the present value of the payment can be computed. For example, from Exhibit 3 we see that the floating-rate payment for period 4 is $1,206,222. From Exhibit 5, the forward discount factor for period 4 is 0.95689609. Therefore, the present value of the payment is:

present value of period 4 payment = $1,206,222 × 0.95689609 = $1,154,229

Exhibit 6 shows the present value for each payment. The total present value of the 12 floating-rate payments is $14,052,917. Thus, the present value of the payments that the fixed-rate payer will receive is $14,052,917 and the present value of the payments that the fixed-rate receiver will make is $14,052,917.

Determination of the Swap Rate

The fixed-rate payer will require that the present value of the fixed-rate payments that must be made based on the swap rate not exceed the $14,052,917 payments to be received from the floating-rate payments. The fixed-rate receiver will require that the present value of the fixed-rate payments to be received is at least as great as the $14,052,917 that must be paid. This means that both parties will require a present value for the fixed-rate payments to be $14,052,917. If that is the case, the present value of the fixed-rate payments is equal to the present value of the floating-rate payments and therefore the value of the swap is zero for both parties at the inception of the swap. The interest rates that should be used to compute the present value of the fixed-rate payments are the same interest rates as those used to discount the floating-rate payments.

To show how to compute the swap rate, we begin with the basic relationship for no arbitrage to exist:

$$\text{PV of floating-rate payments} = \text{PV of fixed-rate payments}$$

We know the value for the left-hand side of the equation.

If we let

$$SR = \text{swap rate}$$

and

$$\text{Days}_t = \text{number of days in the payment period } t$$

then the fixed-rate payment for period t is equal to:

$$\text{notional amount} \times SR \times \frac{\text{Days}_t}{360}$$

The present value of the fixed-rate payment for period t is found by multiplying the previous expression by the forward discount factor. If we let FDF_t denote the forward discount factor for period t, then the present value of the fixed-rate payment for period t is equal to:

$$\text{notional amount} \times SR \times \frac{\text{Days}_t}{360} \times \text{FDF}_t$$

We can now sum up the present value of the fixed-rate payment for each period to get the present value of the floating-rate payments. Using the Greek symbol sigma, Σ, to denote summation and letting N be the number of periods in the swap, then the present value of the fixed-rate payments can be expressed as:

$$\sum_{t=1}^{N} \text{notional amount} \times SR \times \frac{\text{Days}_t}{360} \times \text{FDF}_t$$

This can also be expressed as

$$SR \sum_{t=1}^{N} \text{notional amount} \times \frac{\text{Days}_t}{360} \times \text{FDF}_t$$

The condition for no arbitrage is that the present value of the fixed-rate payments as given by the expression above is equal to the present value of the floating-rate payments. That is,

$$SR \sum_{t=1}^{N} \text{notional amount} \times \frac{\text{Days}_t}{360} \times \text{FDF}_t = PV \text{ of floating-rate payments}$$

Solving for the swap rate

$$SR = \frac{PV \text{ of floating-rate payments}}{\sum_{t=1}^{N} \text{notional amount} \times \dfrac{\text{Days}_t}{360} \times \text{FDF}_t}$$

All of the values to compute the swap rate are known.

Let's apply the formula to determine the swap rate for our 3-year swap. Exhibit 7 shows the calculation of the denominator of the formula. The forward discount factor for each period shown in Column (5) is obtained from Column (4) of Exhibit 6. The sum of the last column in Exhibit 7 shows that the denominator of the swap rate formula is $281,764,282. We know from Exhibit 6 that the present value of the floating-rate payments is $14,052,917. Therefore, the swap rate is

$$SR = \frac{\$14,052,917}{\$281,764,282} = 0.049875 = 4.9875\%$$

Given the swap rate, the *swap spread* can be determined. For example, since this is a 3-year swap, the convention is to use the 3-year on-the-run Treasury rate as the benchmark. If the yield on that issue is 4.5875%, the swap spread is 40 basis points (4.9875% − 4.5875%).

Exhibit 7: Calculating the Denominator for the Swap Rate Formula

(1)	(2)	(3)	(4)	(5)	(6)	(7)
Quarter starts	Quarter ends	Number of days in quarter	Period = End of quarter	Forward discount factor	Days/360	Forward discount factor × Days/360 × notional
Jan 1 year 1	Mar 31 year 1	90	1	0.98997649	0.25000000	24,749,412
Apr 1 year 1	June 30 year 1	91	2	0.97969917	0.25277778	24,764,618
July 1 year 1	Sept 30 year 1	92	3	0.96843839	0.25555556	24,748,981
Oct 1 year 1	Dec 31 year 1	92	4	0.95689609	0.25555556	24,454,011
Jan 1 year 2	Mar 31 year 2	90	5	0.94531597	0.25000000	23,632,899
Apr 1 year 2	June 30 year 2	91	6	0.93344745	0.25277778	23,595,477
July 1 year 2	Sept 30 year 2	92	7	0.92132183	0.25555556	23,544,891
Oct 1 year 2	Dec 31 year 2	92	8	0.90912441	0.25555556	23,233,179
Jan 1 year 3	Mar 31 year 3	90	9	0.89701471	0.25000000	22,425,368
Apr 1 year 3	June 30 year 3	91	10	0.88471472	0.25277778	22,363,622
July 1 year 3	Sept 30 year 3	92	11	0.87212224	0.25555556	22,287,568
Oct 1 year 3	Dec 31 year 3	92	12	0.85947083	0.25555556	21,964,255
					Total	281,764,282

Exhibit 8: Rates and Floating-Rate Payments
One Year Later if Rates Increase

(1)	(2)	(3)	(4)	(5)	(6)	(7)	(8)
Quarter starts	Quarter ends	Number of days in quarter	Current 3-month LIBOR	Eurodollar futures price	Forward rate	Period = End of quarter	Floating-rate payments at end of quarter
Jan 1 year 2	Mar 31 year 2	90	5.25%			1	1,312,500
Apr 1 year 2	June 30 year 2	91		94.27	5.73%	2	1,448,417
July 1 year 2	Sept 30 year 2	92		94.22	5.78%	3	1,477,111
Oct 1 year 2	Dec 31 year 2	92		94.00	6.00%	4	1,533,333
Jan 1 year 3	Mar 31 year 3	90		93.85	6.15%	5	1,537,500
Apr 1 year 3	June 30 year 3	91		93.75	6.25%	6	1,579,861
July 1 year 3	Sept 30 year 3	92		93.54	6.46%	7	1,650,889
Oct 1 year 3	Dec 31 year 3	92		93.25	6.75%	8	1,725,000

The calculation of the swap rate for all swaps follows the same principle: equating the present value of the fixed-rate payments to that of the floating-rate payments.

Valuing a Swap

Once the swap transaction is completed, changes in market interest rates will change the payments of the floating-rate side of the swap. The value of an interest rate swap is the difference between the present value of the payments of the two sides of the swap. The 3-month LIBOR forward rates from the current Eurodollar CD futures contracts are used to (1) calculate the floating-rate payments and (2) determine the discount factors at which to calculate the present value of the payments.

To illustrate this, consider the 3-year swap used to demonstrate how to calculate the swap rate. Suppose that one year later, interest rates change as shown in Columns (4) and (6) in Exhibit 8. In Column (4) shows the current 3-month LIBOR. In Column (5) are the Eurodollar CD futures price for each period. These rates are used to compute the forward rates in Column (6). Note that the interest rates have increased one year later since the rates in Exhibit 8 are greater than those in Exhibit 3. As in Exhibit 3, the current 3-month LIBOR and the forward rates are used to compute the floating-rate payments. These payments are shown in Column (8) of Exhibit 8.

In Exhibit 9, the forward discount factor is computed for each period. The calculation is the same as in Exhibit 5 to obtain the forward discount factor for each period. The forward discount factor for each period is shown in the last column of Exhibit 9.

In Exhibit 10 the forward discount factor (from Exhibit 9) and the floating-rate payments (from Exhibit 8) are shown. The fixed-rate payments need not be recomputed. They are the payments shown in Column (8) of Exhibit 4. This is the fixed-rate payments for the swap rate of 4.9875% and is reproduced in Exhibit 10. Now the two payment streams must be discounted using the new forward discount factors. As shown at the bottom of Exhibit 10, the two present values are as follows:

Present value of floating-rate payments $11,459,495
Present value of fixed-rate payments $9,473,390

The two present values are not equal and therefore for one party the value of the swap increased and for the other party the value of the swap decreased. Let's look at which party gained and which party lost.

Exhibit 9: Period Forward Rates and Forward Discount Factors One Year Later if Rates Increase

(1)	(2)	(3)	(4)	(5)	(6)	(7)
Quarter starts	Quarter ends	Number of days in quarter	Period = End of quarter	Forward rate	Period forward rate	Forward discount factor
Jan 1 year 2	Mar 31 year 2	90	1	5.25%	1.3125%	0.98704503
Apr 1 year 2	June 30 year 2	91	2	5.73%	1.4484%	0.97295263
July 1 year 2	Sept 30 year 2	92	3	5.78%	1.4771%	0.95879023
Oct 1 year 2	Dec 31 year 2	92	4	6.00%	1.5333%	0.94431080
Jan 1 year 3	Mar 31 year 3	90	5	6.15%	1.5375%	0.93001186
Apr 1 year 3	June 30 year 3	91	6	6.25%	1.5799%	0.91554749
July 1 year 3	Sept 30 year 3	92	7	6.46%	1.6509%	0.90067829
Oct 1 year 3	Dec 31 year 3	92	8	6.75%	1.7250%	0.88540505

Exhibit 10: Valuing the Swap One Year Later if Rates Increase

(1)	(2)	(3)	(4)	(5)	(6)	(7)
Quarter starts	Quarter ends	Forward discount factor	Floating cash flow at end of quarter	PV of floating cash flow	Fixed cash flow at end of quarter	PV of fixed cash flow
Jan 1 year 2	Mar 31 year 2	0.98704503	1,312,500	1,295,497	1,246,875	1,230,722
Apr 1 year 2	June 30 year 2	0.97295263	1,448,417	1,409,241	1,260,729	1,226,630
July 1 year 2	Sept 30 year 2	0.95879023	1,477,111	1,416,240	1,274,583	1,222,058
Oct 1 year 2	Dec 31 year 2	0.94431080	1,533,333	1,447,943	1,274,583	1,203,603
Jan 1 year 3	Mar 31 year 3	0.93001186	1,537,500	1,429,893	1,246,875	1,159,609
Apr 1 year 3	June 30 year 3	0.91554749	1,579,861	1,446,438	1,260,729	1,154,257
July 1 year 3	Sept 30 year 3	0.90067829	1,650,889	1,486,920	1,274,583	1,147,990
Oct 1 year 3	Dec 31 year 3	0.88540505	1,725,000	1,527,324	1,274,583	1,128,523
			Total	11,459,495		9,473,390

Summary	Fixed-rate payer	Fixed-rate receiver
PV of payments received	11,459,495	9,473,390
PV of payments made	9,473,390	11,459,495
Value of swap	1,986,105	-1,986,105

The fixed-rate payer will receive the floating-rate payments. And these payments have a present value of $11,459,495. The present value of the payments that must be made by the fixed-rate payer is $9,473,390. Thus, the swap has a positive value for the fixed-rate payer equal to the difference in the two present values of $1,986,105. This is the value of the swap to the fixed-rate payer. Notice, consistent with what we said in the previous chapter, when interest rates increase (as they did in the illustration analyzed), the fixed-rate payer benefits because the value of the swap increases.

In contrast, the fixed-rate receiver must make payments with a present value of $11,459,495 but will only receive fixed-rate payments with a present value equal to $9,473,390. Thus, the value of the swap for the fixed-rate receiver is −$1,986,105. Again, as explained earlier, the fixed-rate receiver is adversely affected by a rise in interest rates because it results in a decline in the value of a swap.

The same valuation principle applies to more complicated swaps. For example, there are swaps whose notional amount changes in a predetermined way over the life of the swap. These include amortizing swaps, accreting swaps, and roller coaster swaps. Once the payments are specified, the present value is calculated as described above by simply adjusting the payment amounts by the changing notional amounts — the methodology does *not* change.

PRIMARY DETERMINANTS OF SWAP SPREADS

As we have seen, interest rate swaps are valued using no-arbitrage relationships relative to instruments (funding or investment vehicles) that produce the same cash flows under the same circumstances. Earlier we provided two interpretations of a swap: (1) a package of futures/forward contracts and (2) a package of cash market instruments. The swap spread is defined as the difference between the swap's fixed rate and the rate on a Treasury whose maturity matches the swap's tenor.

Exhibit 11 displays interest rate swap rates (in percent) and swap spreads (in basis points) for various maturities out to 30 years on January 10, 2001. Recall, the bid price is the fixed rate that the broker/dealer is willing to pay in order to receive a floating rate. Conversely, the ask price is the fixed rate the broker/dealer wants to receive in order to pay a floating rate. Current swap rates and spreads for a number of countries can be obtained on Bloomberg with the function IRSB. Bloomberg collects the spread information throughout the trading day and an average is calculated using the spreads from three market makers. The actual swap rates can be obtained simply by adding the swap spreads to the on-the-run U.S. Treasury yield curve. Exhibit 12 is a time series plot obtained from Bloomberg for daily values of the 5-year swap spread (in basis points) for the period March 13, 2000 to January 10, 2001. This plot can be obtained using the function USSP5 Index GP.

Exhibit 11: Swap Rates and Spreads for Various Maturities

Press 98<GO> to make a copy, 99<GO> to clear news alerts.   Curncy **IRSB**

17:14   **US SWAP RATES**   Page 1 / 2
94<GO> View News.

SECURITY	Bid	Ask	CHANGE	SECURITY	Bid	Ask	CHANGE
US Semi 30/360				US Spreads 30/360			
3)2 YR	5.4350	5.4750	+.1290	23)2YR	65.00	70.00	-3.00
4)3 YR	5.5240	5.5640	+.1290	24)3YR	72.00	77.00	--
5)4 YR	5.6090	5.6490	+.1370	25)4YR	79.33	83.85	+2.22
6)5 YR	5.6810	5.7210	+.1340	26)5YR	85.01	89.37	+3.77
7)6 YR	5.7460	5.7860	+.1400	27)6YR	85.96	90.33	+4.03
8)7 YR	5.8080	5.8480	+.1400	28)7YR	86.61	90.98	+3.68
9)8 YR	5.8560	5.8960	+.1450	29)8YR	85.86	90.24	+3.94
10)9 YR	5.9010	5.9410	+.1480	30)9YR	84.80	89.20	+3.90
11)10 YR	5.9530	5.9930	+.1550	31)10YR	84.45	88.85	+4.26
12)15 YR	6.0980	6.1380	+.1600	32)15YR	99.15	103.55	+5.36
13)20 YR	6.1710	6.2110	+.1430	33)20YR	106.45	110.45	+3.66
14)30 YR	6.1700	6.2100	+.1250	34)30YR	67.05	71.25	+5.58
Change on Day				Change on Day			
IYC4 I52<GO>				IYC4 I48<GO>			
Change on Month				Change on Month			
IYC6 I52<GO>				IYC6 I48<GO>			

Page for ANN Rates

Source: Bloomberg Financial Markets

The swap spread is determined by the same factors that drive the spread over Treasuries on instruments that replicate a swap's cash flows i.e., produce a similar return or funding profile. As discussed below, the swap spread's key determinant for swaps with tenors (i.e., maturities) of five years or less is the cost of hedging in the Eurodollar CD futures market.[4] Although listed contracts exist with delivery dates out to 10 years, the liquidity of the Eurodollar CD futures market diminishes considerably after about five years. For longer tenor swaps, the swap spread is largely driven by credit spreads in the corporate bond market.[5] Specifically, longer-dated swaps are priced relative to rates paid by investment-grade credits in traditional fixed- and floating-rate markets.

[4] Naturally, this presupposes the reference rate used for the floating-rate cash flows is LIBOR. Furthermore, part of swap spread is attributable simply to the fact that LIBOR for a given maturity is higher than the rate on a comparable-maturity U.S. Treasury.

[5] The default risk component of a swap spread will be smaller than for a comparable bond credit spread. The reasons are straightforward. First, since only net interest payments are exchanged rather than both principal and coupon interest payments, the total cash flow at risk is lower. Second, the probability of default depends jointly on the probability of the counterparty defaulting and whether or not the swap has a positive value. See John C. Hull, *Introduction to Futures and Options Markets, Third Edition* (Upper Saddle River, NJ: Prentice Hall, 1998).

Exhibit 12: Time Series of the 5-Year Swap Spread

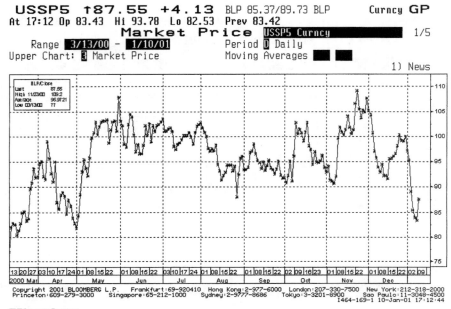

Source: Bloomberg Financial Markets

Given that a swap is a package of futures/forward contracts, the shorter-term swap spreads respond directly to fluctuations in Eurodollar CD futures prices. As noted, there is a liquid market for Eurodollar CD futures contracts with maturities every three months for approximately five years. A market participant can create a synthetic fixed-rate security or a fixed-rate funding vehicle by taking a position in a bundle of Eurodollar CD futures contracts (i.e., a position in every 3-month Eurodollar CD futures contract up to the desired maturity date).

For example, consider a financial institution that has fixed-rate assets and floating-rate liabilities. Both the assets and liabilities have a maturity of three years. The interest rate on the liabilities resets every three months based on 3-month LIBOR. This financial institution can hedge this mismatched asset/liability position by buying a 3-year bundle of Eurodollar CD futures contracts. By doing so, the financial institution is receiving LIBOR over the 3-year period and paying a fixed dollar amount (i.e., the futures price). The financial institution is now hedged because the assets are fixed rate and the bundle of long Eurodollar CD futures synthetically creates a fixed-rate funding arrangement. From the fixed dollar amount over the three years, an effective fixed rate that the financial institution pays can be computed. Alternatively, the financial institution can synthetically create a fixed-rate funding arrangement by entering into a 3-year swap in which it pays fixed and receives 3-

month LIBOR. Other things equal, the financial institution will use the vehicle that delivers the lowest cost of hedging the mismatched position. That is, the financial institution will compare the synthetic fixed rate (expressed as a percentage over U.S. Treasuries) to the 3-year swap spread. The difference between the synthetic spread and the swap spread should be within a few basis points under normal circumstances.

For swaps with tenors greater than five years, we cannot rely on the Eurodollar CD futures due to diminishing liquidity of such contracts. Instead, longer-dated swaps are priced using rates available for investment-grade corporate borrowers in fixed-rate and floating-rate debt markets. Since a swap can be interpreted as a package of long and short positions in a fixed-rate bond and a floating-rate bond, it is the credit spreads in those two market sectors that will be the primary determinant of the swap spread. Empirically, the swap curve lies above the U.S. Treasury yield curve and below the on-the-run yield curve for AA-rated banks.[6] Swap fixed rates are lower than AA-rated bond yields because their lower credit due to netting and offsetting of swap positions.

In addition, there are a number of other technical factors that influence the level of swap spreads.[7] While the impact of some these factors is ephemeral, their influence can be considerable in the short run. Included among these factors are: (1) the level and shape of the Treasury yield curve; (2) the relative supply of fixed- and floating-rate payers in the interest rate swap market; (3) the technical factors that affect swap dealers; and (4) the level of asset-based swap activity.

The level, slope, and curvature of the U.S. Treasury yield is an important influence of swap spreads at various maturities. The reason is that embedded in the yield curve are the market's expectations of the direction of future interest rates. While these expectations are sometimes challenging to extract, the decision to borrow at a fixed-rate or a floating-rate will be based, in part, on these expectations. The relative supply of fixed- and floating-rate payers in the interest rate swap market should also be influenced by these expectations. For example, many corporate issuers — financial institutions and federal agencies in particular — swap their newly issued fixed-rate debt into floating using the swap market. Consequently, swap spreads will be affected by the corporate debt issuance calendar. In addition, swap spreads, like credit spreads, also tend to increase with the swap's tenor or maturity. To see this, we examined a time series of weekly observations of swap spreads (in basis points) for the sample period January 8, 1999 to December 29, 2000.[8] We computed the following summary statistics for each tenor: mean, standard deviation, minimum, and maximum. These results are presented in Exhibit 13. It is apparent from the exhibit that swap spreads, on average, increase monotonically with the swap's tenor.

---

[6] For a discussion of this point, see Andrew R. Young, *A Morgan Stanley Guide to Fixed Income Analysis* (New York: Morgan Stanley, 1997).

[7] See Ellen L. Evans and Gioia Parente Bales, "What Drives Interest Rate Swap Spreads," Chapter 13 in Carl R. Beidleman (ed.), *Interest Rate Swaps* (Burr Ridge, IL: Irwin Professional Publishing, 1991).

[8] These data are obtained with permission from The *Yield Book*® Salomon Analytics Inc. These spreads are calculated but are representative of spreads obtained from actual market prices.

Exhibit 13: Summary Statistics for Swap Spreads by Tenor

Tenor (years)	Mean	Std. Dev.	Min.	Max.
2	61.37	12.44	40.30	86.40
3	70.56	11.49	49.20	92.80
4	76.36	12.63	53.10	98.10
5	81.37	14.65	54.90	105.60
7	89.78	16.01	60.70	116.60
10	99.04	19.59	65.30	133.80
30	102.07	27.54	61.00	158.50

Source: The *Yield Book*® Salomon Analytics Inc.

Swap spreads are also affected by the hedging costs faced by swap dealers. Dealers hedge the interest rate risk of long (short) swap positions by taking a long (short) position in a Treasury security with the same maturity as the swap's tenor and borrowing funds (lending funds) in the repo market. As a result, the spread between LIBOR and the appropriate repo rate will be a critical determinant of the hedging costs. For example, with the burgeoning U.S. government budget surpluses starting in the late 1990s, the supply of Treasury securities has diminished. One impact of the decreased supply is an increase in the spread between the yields of on-the-run and off-the-run Treasuries. As this spread widens, investors must pay up for the relatively more liquid on-the-run issues. This chain reaction continues and results in on-the-run Treasuries going "on special" in repo markets. When on-the-run Treasuries go "on special," it is correspondingly more expensive to use these Treasuries as a hedge. This increase in hedging costs results in wider swap spreads.[9]

Another influence on the level of swap spreads is the volume of asset-based swap transactions. An asset-based swap transaction involves the creation of a synthetic security via the purchase of an existing security and the simultaneous execution of a swap. For example, after the Russian debt default and ruble devaluation in August 1998, risk-averse investors sold corporate bonds and fled to the relative safety of U.S. Treasuries. Credit spreads widened considerably and liquidity diminished. A contrary-minded floating-rate investor like a financial institution could have taken advantage of these circumstances by buying newly issued investment grade corporate bonds with relatively attractive coupon rates and simultaneously taking a long position in an interest rate swap (pay fixed/receive floating). Because of the higher credit spreads, the coupon rate that the financial institution receives is higher than the fixed-rate paid in the swap. Accordingly, the financial institution ends up with a synthetic floating-rate asset with a sizeable spread above LIBOR.

By similar reasoning, investors can use swaps to create a synthetic fixed-rate security. For example, during the mid-1980s, many banks issued perpetual

[9] Traders often use the repo market to obtain specific securities to cover short positions. If a security is in short supply relative to demand, the repo rate on a specific security used as collateral in repo transaction will be below the general (i.e., generic) collateral repo rate. When a particular security's repo rate falls markedly, that security is said to be "on special." Investors who own these securities are able to lend them out as collateral and borrow at bargain basement rates.

floating-rate notes in the Eurobond market. A perpetual floating-rate note is a security that delivers floating-rate cash flows forever. The coupon is reset and paid usually every three months with a coupon formula equal to the reference rate (e.g., 3-month LIBOR) plus a spread. When the perpetual floating-rate note market collapsed in late 1986, the contagion spread into other sectors of the floaters market.[10] Many floaters cheapened considerably. As before, contrary-minded fixed-rate investors could exploit this situation through the purchase of a relatively cheap (from the investor's perspective) floater while simultaneously taking a short position in an interest rate swap (pay floating/receive fixed) thereby creating a synthetic fixed-rate investment. The investor makes floating-rate payments (say based on LIBOR) to their counterparty and receives fixed-rate payments equal to the Treasury yield plus the swap spread. Accordingly, the fixed rate on this synthetic security is equal to the sum of the following: (1) the Treasury bond yield that matches the swap's tenor; (2) the swap spread; and (3) the floater's index spread.

DOLLAR DURATION OF A SWAP

Effectively, a position in an interest rate swap is a leveraged position. This agrees with both of our economic interpretations of an interest rate swap explained earlier this chapter. In the case of a package of futures/forward contracts, we know that futures/forwards are leveraged instruments. In the case of a package of cash instruments, it is a leveraged position involving either buying a fixed-rate bond and financing it on a floating-rate basis (i.e., fixed-rate receiver position) or buying a floating-rate bond on a fixed-rate basis (i.e., fixed-rate payer position). So, we would expect that the dollar duration of a swap is a multiple of the bond that effectively underlies the swap.

To see how to calculate the dollar duration, let's work with the second economic interpretation of a swap explained earlier — a package of cash flows from buying and selling cash market instruments. From the perspective of the fixed-rate receiver, the position can be viewed as follows:

long a fixed-rate bond + short a floating-rate bond

The fixed-rate bond is a bond with a coupon rate equal to the swap rate, a maturity equal to the term of the swap, and a par value equal to the notional amount of the swap.

This means that the dollar duration of an interest rate swap from the perspective of a fixed-rate receiver is just the difference between the dollar duration of the two bond positions that comprise the swap. That is,

dollar duration of a swap for a fixed-rate receiver
= dollar duration of a fixed-rate bond − dollar duration of a floating-rate bond

---

[10] Suresh E. Krishman, "Asset-Based Interest Rate Swaps," Chapter 8 in *Interest Rate Swaps*.

Most of the interest rate sensitivity of a swap will result from the dollar duration of the fixed-rate bond since, as explained in Chapter 11, the dollar duration of the floating-rate bond will be small. The dollar duration of a floating-rate bond is smaller the closer the swap is to its reset date. If the dollar duration of the floating-rate bond is close to zero then:

dollar duration of a swap for a fixed-rate receiver
= dollar duration of a fixed-rate bond

Thus, adding an interest rate swap to a portfolio in which the manager pays a floating-rate and receives a fixed-rate increases the dollar duration of the portfolio by roughly the dollar duration of the underlying fixed-rate bond. This is true because the swap position effectively involves buying a fixed-rate bond on a leveraged basis.

We can use the cash market instrument economic interpretation to compute the dollar duration of a swap for the fixed-rate payer. The dollar duration is:

dollar duration of a swap for a fixed-rate payer
= dollar duration of a floating-rate bond − dollar duration of a fixed-rate bond

Again, assuming that the dollar duration of the floater is small, we have

dollar duration of a swap for a fixed-rate payer
= −dollar duration of a fixed-rate bond

Consequently, a manager who adds a swap to a portfolio involving paying fixed and receiving floating decreases the dollar duration of the portfolio by an amount roughly equal to the dollar duration of the fixed-rate bond.

The dollar duration of a portfolio that includes a swap is:

dollar duration of assets − dollar duration of liabilities
+ dollar duration of a swap position

RELATIVE VALUE ANALYSIS USING THE SWAP MARKET

As discussed in Chapter 9, investors employ a variety of approaches to evaluate floaters. Every approach has some merit as well as some attending limitations. The purpose of this section is to describe how swap markets are used as a tool to gauge the relative value of floaters. Simply put, the swap market is used to convert a floater into a fixed-rate bond (effectively swapping out the implied LIBOR financing).

The coupon on this hypothetical fixed-rate security with the same maturity and coupon frequency as the floater is called the *fixed-equivalent coupon*.[11] Once computed, a floater's fixed-equivalent coupon rate can then be compared to the yields on instruments in liquid fixed-rate markets.

---

[11] The fixed rate is also referred to as *yield-to-forward LIBOR*.

Exhibit 14: Description of Enron Corp. Floater

```
S E C U R I T Y   D E S C R I P T I O N
ENRON CORP           ENE Float 03/00   N O T   P R I C E D
```

ISSUER INFORMATION	IDENTIFIERS		1) Additional Sec Info
Name ENRON CORP	ISIN	US293561BV79	2) Floating Rates
Type Pipelines	CUSIP	293561BV7	3) Identifiers
Market of Issue US DOMESTIC	BB number	EC0486471	4) Ratings
SECURITY INFORMATION	RATINGS		5) Prospectus
Country USA Currency USD	Moody's	Baa2	6) Sec. Specific News
Collateral Type NOTES	S&P	BBB+	7) Involved Parties
Calc Typ (21)FLOAT RATE NOTE	FI	BBB+	8) Custom Notes
Maturity 3/30/2000 Series	ISSUE SIZE		9) Issuer Information
NORMAL	Amt Issued		10) Pricing Sources
Coupon5.45 FLOATING QUARTLY	USD 250,000.00 (M)		
QUARTL US LIB +45 ACT/360	Amt Outstanding		
Announcement Dt 9/24/98	USD 250,000.00 (M)		
Int. Accrual Dt 9/30/98	Min Piece/Increment		
1st Settle Date 9/30/98	1,000.00/ 1,000.00		
1st Coupon Date 12/30/98	Par Amount 1,000.00		
Iss Pr 100	LEAD MANAGER/EXCHANGE		
	ML,SSB		65) Old DES
HAVE PROSPECTUS			66) Send as Attachment

```
CPN RATE=3MO US$LIBOR +45BP. UNSEC'D.
```

Source: Bloomberg Financial Markets

We will illustrate the calculation of a fixed-equivalent coupon with a floating-rate note issued by Enron Corp. (ticker symbol "ENE 03/00") that matures March 30, 2000. The Security Description screen (DES) from Bloomberg is presented in Exhibit 14. This issue contains no embedded options (e.g., caps, floors, call feature, etc.). As can be seen from the description screen, this floater delivers cash flows quarterly and has a coupon formula equal to 3-month LIBOR plus 45 basis points. The day count convention is ACT/360.

Floater valuation analysis is carried out using Bloomberg's *YAF function*. The YAF screen is displayed in Exhibit 15. Recall that a floater's value can be decomposed into three parts: (1) the value of a pure floater whose coupon formula is equal to the floater's reference rate flat; (2) the value of any quoted margin (the amount added/subtracted to the reference rate in the coupon formula); and (3) the value of any embedded options. Let's partition the Enron floater's market price of 99.99 into these first two components parts since this floater does not contain an embedded cap and/or floor.[12]

The *QM Value* is the quoted margin value. It represents the present value of any payments paid (received) attributable to the quoted margin above (below) the floater's reference rate.[13] In our example, the quoted margin is 45 basis points so the cash flows attributable to the quoted margins are 45 basis points multiplied by 100 (i.e., the floater's maturity value) divided by 4 to reflect the quarterly pay-

---

[12] Although there is no current market price available for this floater as indicated by the words "NOT PRICED" at the top center of the screen, we will use the Bloomberg default price for a floater of 99.99 in our analysis.

[13] If the quoted margin is negative, the QM value will be negative.

ments. The discount rates for these cash flows are the swap curve's implied zero rates derived from Bloomberg's dealer-contributed swap curves.[14] The QM value for this floater is 0.4445 (per $100 of par value).

The value of a pure floater is determined by subtracting the QM value from the market price. In our example, the pure floater value is 99.54554 (99.99 − 0.4445). The pure floater can then be used to determine the fixed-equivalent coupon (*Fixed Equiv.* in the center of the screen). The fixed-equivalent coupon is simply the coupon rate (annualized) that would be required of a hypothetical fixed-rate bond (with the same maturity and coupon frequency) that would generate the same present value as the pure floater given the projected cash flows. For the Enron floater, the fixed-equivalent coupon rate is 5.5693%. Once again, the discount rates are derived from the dealer-contributed swap curves.

Now that the basic concept is in place, let's illustrate the fixed-equivalent coupon calculation with a floater that contains an embedded option. Consider a floater issued by the Economic Development Corp (ticker symbol "EDC 02/3") that matures February 5, 2003. The *Security Description* screen from Bloomberg is presented in Exhibit 16. This floater delivers cash flows semiannually with a coupon formula of 6-month LIBOR minus 25 basis points. Moreover, the floater has an embedded collar such that the minimum coupon rate is 5% and the maximum coupon rate is 8% regardless of the level of the underlying reference rate. The day count convention is ACT/360.

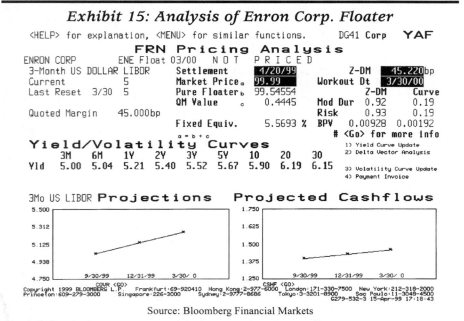

Exhibit 15: Analysis of Enron Corp. Floater

Source: Bloomberg Financial Markets

[14] The swap curve can be accessed under yield curve update at the center-right edge of the screen.

Exhibit 16: Description of Economic Development Corp. Floater

```
65                                                    DG41 Corp    O D E 5
<Page> For More Information On This Security.
                    S E C U R I T Y   D I S P L A Y          PAGE    1/ 4
EXPORT DEV CORP   EDC Float 02/03    N O T   P R I C E D
```

SECURITY INFORMATION	SERIES: **EMTN**	**ISSUER INFORMATION** NAME **EXPORT DEVELOPMENT CORP**	
CPN FREQ	**SEMI-AN**	SEASONED	TYPE **GOVT AGENCY**
CPN TYPE	**FLOATING**	**IDENTIFICATION #'s**	**REDEMPTION INFO**
MTY/REFUND TYP **NORMAL**	ISIN **XS0041640672**	MATURITY DT 2/ 5/03	
CALC TYP (**21**)**FLOAT RATE NOTE**	MLNUM **FCCP9**	REFUNDING DT	
DAY COUNT(**2**) **ACT/360**		NEXT CALL DT	
MARKET ISS **EURO MTN**	COMMON **004164067**	WORKOUT DT 2/ 5/03	
COUNTRY/CURR **CAN /USD**		RISK FACTOR	
COLLATERAL TYP **DEBENTURES**	**ISSUANCE INFO**		
AMT ISSUED 100,000(M)	ANNOUNCE DT 1/ 5/93	**RATINGS**	
AMT OUTSTAND 100,000(M)	1ST SETTLE DT 2/ 5/93	MOODY **Aa2**	
MIN PC/INC 1,000/ 1,000	1ST CPN DT 8/ 5/93	S & P **AA+**	
PAR AMT 1,000.00	INT ACCRUE DT 2/ 5/93	COMP **AA2**	
LEADMGR/UWRTR **ML INTL**	PRICE @ ISSUE **100**	CBRS **NR**	
EXCHANGE UNKNOWN		DOMINION NR	

```
NOTES  NO PROSPECTUS
CPN RATE=6MO $LIBOR -25BP. SR, UNSEC'D. SEASONED EFF 3/17/93.

Copyright 1999 BLOOMBERG L.P.   Frankfurt:69-920410  Hong Kong:2-977-6000  London:171-330-7500  New York:212-318-2000
Princeton:609-279-3000    Singapore:226-3000    Sydney:2-9777-8686    Tokyo:3-3201-8900    Sao Paulo:11-3048-4500
                                                                      G279-532-3 29-Apr-99 17:19:07
```

Source: Bloomberg Financial Markets

As before, floater valuation analysis in Bloomberg is accomplished using the YAF function. The YAF screen is displayed in Exhibit 17. The floater value is partitioned into its three components parts. The value of the pure LIBOR floater is 100.1187 while the QM value is −0.9121. Note the QM value is negative because the quoted margin is negative (i.e., minus 25 basis points). The collar premium represents the value of the embedded collar. An investor's position in a collared floater can be described as a combination of three positions, namely: (1) a long position in a pure floater plus/minus the quoted margin; (2) a short position in a call option with an exercise price equal to the cap rate; and (3) a long position in a put option with an exercise price equal to the floor rate. Accordingly, the collar premium represents the net value of these two options positions. In our illustration, the collar premium is 0.7834 (per $100 of par value).

Bloomberg's YAF function values caps, floor, and collars using a modified Black-Scholes model. The volatility assumptions used in the calculation are derived from Bloomberg's dealer-contributed volatility curves. This Volatility Curve Update screen is accessed from the YAF function located in center-right part of the screen. The *Volatility Curve Update* screen is presented in Exhibit 18.

The pure floater value for this security is determined by adding the QM value to the market price and then subtracting the collar premium. In our example, the pure floater value of 100.1187 is determined as follows: 99.99 (market price) + 0.9121 (QM value) − 0.7834 (collar premium). Once the pure floater value is determined, the fixed-equivalent coupon can be computed in the same manner as above. For the Economic Development Corporation floater, the fixed-equivalent coupon is 5.0266%.

Exhibit 17: Analysis of Export Development Corp. Floater

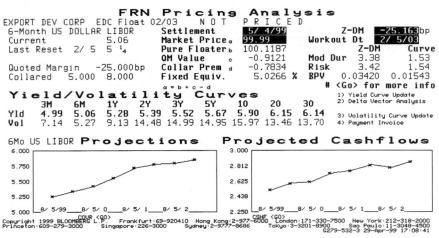

```
<HELP> for explanation, <MENU> for similar functions.      DG41 Corp   YAF
                    F R N   P r i c i n g   A n a l y s i s
EXPORT DEV CORP   EDC Float 02/03    N O T   P R I C E D
  6-Month US DOLLAR LIBOR     Settlement      5/ 4/99        Z-DM   -25.163bp
  Current             5.06    Market Price a  99.99       Workout Dt   2/ 5/03
  Last Reset  2/ 5   5 ¼      Pure Floater b  100.1187               Z-DM   Curve
                              QM Value      c  -0.9121     Mod Dur   3.38    1.53
  Quoted Margin   -25.000bp   Collar Prem  d  -0.7834     Risk      3.42    1.54
  Collared   5.000  8.000     Fixed Equiv.    5.0266 %    BPV     0.03420  0.01543
                              a = b + c - d              #  <Go> for more info
  Y i e l d / V o l a t i l i t y   C u r v e s         1) Yield Curve Update
       3M    6M    1Y    2Y    3Y    5Y    10    20    30  2) Delta Vector Analysis
  Yld  4.99  5.06  5.28  5.39  5.52  5.67  5.90  6.15  6.14
  Vol  7.14  5.27  9.13 14.48 14.99 14.95 15.97 13.46 13.70  3) Volatility Curve Update
                                                           4) Payment Invoice
  6Mo US LIBOR  P r o j e c t i o n s      P r o j e c t e d   C a s h f l o w s
  6.000                              3.000
  5.750                              2.812
  5.500                              2.625
  5.250                              2.438
  5.000  8/ 5/99  8/ 5/ 0  8/ 5/ 1  8/ 5/ 2   2.250  8/ 5/99  8/ 5/ 0  8/ 5/ 1  8/ 5/ 2
                     CCUR <GO>                        CSHF <GO>
Copyright 1999 BLOOMBERG L.P.   Frankfurt:69-920410  Hong Kong:2-977-6000  London:171-330-7500  New York:212-318-2000
Princeton:609-279-3000    Singapore:226-3000    Sydney:2-9777-8686    Tokyo:3-3201-8900    Sao Paulo:11-3048-4500
                                                                  G279-532-3 29-Apr-99 17:08:41
```

Source: Bloomberg Financial Markets

Exhibit 18: Bloomberg's Volatility Curve Update

```
<HELP> for explanation.                                    DG41 Corp   Y A F
        V O L A T I L I T Y   C U R V E   U P D A T E   S C R E E N
```

Mty/Term	VOL	Mty/Term	VOL	Mty/Term	VOL
8/ 3/99	7.16				
11/ 3/99	5.25				
5/ 6/00	9.17				
5/ 5/01	14.50				
5/ 4/02	15.00				
5/ 4/03	14.21				
5/ 4/04	14.95				
5/ 4/05	15.43				
5/ 6/06	15.22				
5/ 5/07	15.63				
5/ 4/08	15.79				
5/ 4/09	15.97				
5/ 4/14	14.78				
5/ 4/19	13.46				
5/ 5/29	13.70				
		Legend			
Shift all	Vol Curve#: 23				
Volatilities	Type: Swap 90-Day			**X3**	to return to
0.00%	ccy: US Date: 4/29/99				calculator

```
Copyright 1999 BLOOMBERG L.P.   Frankfurt:69-920410  Hong Kong:2-977-6000  London:171-330-7500  New York:212-318-2000
Princeton:609-279-3000    Singapore:226-3000    Sydney:2-9777-8686    Tokyo:3-3201-8900    Sao Paulo:11-3048-4500
                                                                  G279-532-3 29-Apr-99 17:10:52
```

Source: Bloomberg Financial Markets

Chapter 13

Estimating Yield Volatility

A n important input required in a valuation model is the expected interest rate volatility. We have seen how in the binomial model this parameter is required to generate the binomial interest rate tree. In the Monte Carlo model, we have seen how this parameter is required to generate the interest rate paths. In statistical analysis, the standard deviation is a measure of the variation of a random variable around its mean or expected value. Consequently, market participants use the standard deviation as a measure of volatility. In this chapter we will look at how the standard deviation of interest rates is estimated and methods for forecasting interest rate volatility.

HISTORICAL VOLATILITY

The variance of a random variable using historical data is calculated using the following formula:

$$\text{Variance} = \sum_{t=1}^{T} \frac{(X_t - \bar{X})^2}{T-1} \tag{1}$$

and then

$$\text{Standard deviation} = \sqrt{\text{Variance}}$$

where

X_t = observation t on variable X
$\bar{X}$ = the sample mean for variable X
T = the number of observations in the sample

Our focus is on yield volatility. More specifically, we are interested in the percentage change in daily yields. So, X_t will denote the percentage change in yield from day t and the prior day, $t-1$. If we let y_t denote the yield on day t and y_{t-1} denote the yield on day $t-1$, then X_t which is the natural logarithm of percentage change in yield between two days, can be expressed as:

$$X_t = 100[\text{Ln}(y_t/y_{t-1})]$$

For example, on 1/3/01 the 2-year Constant Maturity Treasury (CMT) yield was 4.92% and on 1/4/01 it was 4.77%.[1] Therefore, the natural logarithm of X for 10/19/95 was:

$$X = 100[Ln(4.77/4.92)] = -3.09622$$

To illustrate how to calculate a daily standard deviation from historical data, consider the data in Exhibit 1 which show the yield on a 2-year CMT from 12/12/00 to 1/19/01 in the third column. From the 26 observations, 25 days of percentage yield changes are calculated in the fourth column. The fifth column shows the square of the deviations of the observations from the mean. The bottom of Exhibit 1 shows the calculation of the daily mean for the 25 observations, the variance, and the standard deviation. The daily standard deviation is 1.9226%.

The daily standard deviation will vary depending on the 25 days selected. For example, the daily yields from 12/31/99 to 2/7/00 were used to generate 25 daily percentage yield changes. The computed daily standard deviation was 0.8752%.

The selection of the number of observations can have a significant effect on the calculated daily standard deviation. This can be seen in Exhibit 2 which shows the daily standard deviation for a 30-year CMT yield, 10-year CMT yield, 2-year CMT yield, and 6-month LIBOR for 265 days, 60 days, 25 days, and 10 days ending 1/19/01.

Annualizing the Standard Deviation

The daily standard deviation can be annualized by multiplying it by the square root of the number of days in a year.[2] That is,

Daily standard deviation $\times \sqrt{\text{Number of days in a year}}$

Market practice varies with respect to the number of days in the year that should be used in the annualizing formula above. Typically, either 250 days, 260 days, or 365 days are used.

Thus, in calculating an annual standard deviation, the investor must decide on:

1. the number of daily observations to use
2. the number of days in the year to use to annualize the daily standard deviation.

---

[1] At the end of each trading day, primary U.S. Treasury securities dealers report closing prices of the most actively traded bills, notes and bonds to the Federal Reserve Bank of New York. CMT indexes are computed from yields on these securities. For example, the 1-year CMT yield is the average yield of the actively traded securities with a constant maturity of one year. The Federal Reserve publishes this index in its weekly statistical release H.15.

[2] For any probability distribution, it is important to assess whether the value of a random variable in one period is affected by the value that the random variable took on in a prior period. Casting this in terms of yield changes, it is important to know whether the yield today is affected by the yield in a prior period. The term *serial correlation* is used to describe the correlation between the yield in different periods. Annualizing the daily yield by multiplying the daily standard deviation by the square root of the number of days in a year assumes that serial correlation is not significant.

Exhibit 1: Calculation of the Daily Standard Deviation Based on 25 Daily Observations for the 2-Year Constant Maturity Treasury (December 12, 2000 to January 19, 2001)

t	Date	y_t	$X_t = 100[Ln(y_t/y_{t-1})]$	$(X_t - \bar{X})^2$
0	12-Dec-00	5.540		
1	13-Dec-00	5.450	−1.63789	1.04584
2	14-Dec-00	5.430	−0.36765	0.06138
3	15-Dec-00	5.380	−0.92508	0.09590
4	18-Dec-00	5.330	−0.93371	0.10132
5	19-Dec-00	5.350	0.37453	0.97997
6	20-Dec-00	5.240	−2.07751	2.13776
7	21-Dec-00	5.140	−1.92684	1.71988
8	22-Dec-00	5.100	−0.78125	0.02751
9	26-Dec-00	5.100	0.00000	0.37872
10	27-Dec-00	5.100	0.00000	0.37872
11	28-Dec-00	5.180	1.55645	4.71694
12	29-Dec-00	5.110	−1.36057	0.55527
13	02-Jan-01	4.870	−4.81055	17.59926
14	03-Jan-01	4.920	1.02146	2.67931
15	04-Jan-01	4.770	−3.09622	6.15448
16	05-Jan-01	4.560	−4.50237	15.10852
17	08-Jan-01	4.540	−0.43956	0.03092
18	09-Jan-01	4.640	2.17874	7.80719
19	10-Jan-01	4.760	2.55333	10.04085
20	11-Jan-01	4.770	0.20986	0.68106
21	12-Jan-01	4.900	2.68889	10.91833
22	16-Jan-01	4.890	−0.20429	0.16901
23	17-Jan-01	4.840	−1.02776	0.17004
24	18-Jan-01	4.720	−2.51059	3.59175
25	19-Jan-01	4.750	0.63358	1.55996
	Total		−15.385	88.70952

Sample mean $= \bar{X} = \dfrac{-15.385}{25} = -0.6154$

Variance $= \dfrac{88.70952}{25 - 1} = 3.69623\%$

Std $= \sqrt{3.69623} = 1.9226\%$

Source for yields: Federal Reserve Statistical Release H.15

Exhibit 2 shows the difference in the annual standard deviation for the daily standard deviation based on the different number of observations and using 250 days, 260 days, and 365 days to annualize. Exhibit 3 compares the 25-day annual standard deviation for two different time periods for a 30-year CMT yield, 10-year CMT yield, 2-year CMT yield, and 6-month LIBOR.

Exhibit 2: Comparison of Daily and Annual Volatility for a Different Number of Observations (Ending Date January 19, 2001) for Various Constant Maturity Treasuries and 6-Month LIBOR

Number of observations	Daily standard deviations (%)	Annualized standard deviation (%)		
		250 days	260 days	365 days
30-Year Constant Maturity Treasury				
265	0.7914	12.5131	12.7609	15.1197
60	0.8090	12.7914	13.0447	15.4559
25	1.0291	16.2715	16.5937	19.6609
10	1.0636	16.8170	17.1500	20.3201
10-Year Constant Maturity Treasury				
265	0.9616	15.2042	15.5053	18.3713
60	1.2418	19.6346	20.0234	23.7246
25	1.7213	27.2161	27.7551	32.8854
10	1.4587	23.0641	23.5208	27.8684
2-Year Constant Maturity Treasury				
265	0.9286	14.6824	14.9732	17.7409
60	1.3708	21.6743	22.1035	26.1891
25	1.9226	30.3990	31.0010	36.7312
10	2.2801	36.0516	36.7655	43.5613
6-month LIBOR				
265	0.6406	10.1288	10.3294	12.2387
60	1.0377	16.4075	16.7324	19.8252
25	1.5168	23.9827	24.4577	28.9784
10	1.3370	21.1398	21.5584	25.5434

Source for yields: Federal Reserve Statistical Release H.15

Exhibit 3: Comparison of Daily Standard Deviations Calculated for Two 25-Day Periods

Dates		Daily standard deviation (%)	Annualized standard deviation (%)		
From	To		250 days	260 days	365 days
30-Year Constant Maturity Treasury					
12/31/99	2/7/00	1.1504	18.1894	18.5496	21.9784
12/12/00	1/19/01	1.0291	16.2715	16.5937	19.6609
10-Year Constant Maturity Treasury					
12/31/99	2/7/00	1.0744	16.9878	17.3242	20.5264
12/12/00	1/19/01	1.7213	27.2161	27.7551	32.8854
2-Year Constant Maturity Treasury					
12/31/99	2/7/00	0.8752	13.8381	14.1122	16.7207
12/12/00	1/19/01	1.9226	30.3990	31.0010	36.7312
6-month LIBOR					
12/31/99	2/7/00	0.5061	8.0021	8.1606	9.6690
12/12/00	1/19/01	1.5168	23.9827	24.4577	28.9784

Source for yields: Federal Reserve Statistical Release H.15

Interpreting the Standard Deviation

What does it mean if the annual standard deviation for the 2-year CMT yield is 12%. It means that if the prevailing yield is 8%, then the annual standard deviation is 96 basis points (12% times 8%).

Assuming that the yield volatility is approximately normally distributed, we can use this probability distribution to construct an interval or range for what the future yield will be. For example, we know that for a normal distribution there is a 68.3% probability that the yield will be between one standard deviation below and above the expected value. The expected value is the prevailing yield. If the annual standard deviation is 96 basis points and prevailing yield is 8%, then there is a 68.3% probability that the yield next year will be between 7.04% (8% minus 96 basis points) and 8.96% (8% plus 96 basis points). For three standard deviations below and above the prevailing yield, there is a 99.7% probability that the yield next year will be in this interval. Using the numbers above, three standard deviations is 288 basis points (3 times 96 basis points). The interval is then 5.12% (8% minus 288 basis points) and 10.88% (8% plus 288 basis points).

The interval or range constructed is called a *confidence interval.* Our first interval of 7.04%-8.96% is a 68.3% confidence interval. Our second interval of 5.12%-10.88% is a 99.7% confidence interval. A confidence interval with any probability can be constructed using a normal probability distribution table.

HISTORICAL VERSUS IMPLIED VOLATILITY

Market participants estimate yield volatility in one of two ways. The first way is by estimating historical yield volatility. This is the method that we have thus far described in this chapter. The resulting volatility is called *historical volatility.* The second way is to estimate yield volatility based on the observed prices of interest rate options or caps. Yield volatility calculated using this approach is called *implied volatility.*

The implied volatility is based on some option pricing model. One of the inputs to any option pricing model in which the underlying is a Treasury security or Treasury futures contract is expected yield volatility. If the observed price of an option is assumed to be the fair price and the option pricing model is assumed to be the model that would generate that fair price, then the implied yield volatility is the yield volatility that when used as an input into the option pricing model would produce the observed option price.

There are several problems with using implied volatility. First, it is assumed the option pricing model is correct. Second, option pricing models typically assume that volatility is constant over the life of the option. Therefore, interpreting an implied volatility becomes difficult.

Exhibit 4: 10-Day Moving Daily Average for a 2-Year Constant Maturity Treasury

10-Trading Days Ending	Daily Average (%)
03-Jan-01	−0.8004
04-Jan-01	−1.1475
05-Jan-01	−1.3900
08-Jan-01	−1.2413
09-Jan-01	−0.9453
10-Jan-01	−0.6899
11-Jan-01	−0.6689
12-Jan-01	−0.5557
16-Jan-01	−0.4401
17-Jan-01	−0.0618
18-Jan-01	−0.4150
19-Jan-01	−0.0420

Source: Federal Reserve Statistical Release H.15

FORECASTING YIELD VOLATILITY[3]

As can be seen, the yield volatility as measured by the standard deviation can vary based on the time period selected and the number of observations. Now we turn to the issue of forecasting yield volatility. There are several methods. Before describing these methods, let's address the question of what mean should be used in the calculation of the forecasted standard deviation.

Suppose at the end of 1/3/01 an investor is interested in a forecast for volatility using the 10 most recent days of trading and updating that forecast at the end of each trading day. What mean value should be used?

The investor can calculate a 10-day moving average of the daily percentage yield change. Exhibit 1 shows the daily percentage change in yield for a 2-year CMT from 12/12/00 to 1/19/01. To calculate a moving average of the daily percentage yield change on 1/3/01, the trader would use the 10 trading days from 12/19/00 to 1/3/01. At the end of 1/4/01, the trader will calculate the 10-day average by using the percentage yield change on 12/20/00 and would exclude the percentage yield change on 12/19/00. That is, the trader will use the 10 trading days from 12/20/00 to 1/4/01.

Exhibit 4 shows the 10-day moving average calculated from 1/3/01 to 1/19/01. The considerable variation over this period was due, in large part, to a Federal Reserve 50 basis point interest rate cut on the afternoon of 1/3/01. The 10-day moving average ranges from −0.0420% to −1.3900%. For the period from 1/14/00 to 2/1/00, the moving average ranged from 0.0307% to 0.3155%.

---

[3] For a more extensive and rigorous discussion of forecasting yield volatility, see Frank J. Fabozzi and Wai Lee, "Forecasting Yield Volatility," in Frank J. Fabozzi (ed.), *Perspectives on Interest Rate Risk Management for Money Managers and Traders* (New Hope, PA: Frank J. Fabozzi Associates, 1997).

Exhibit 5: Moving Daily Standard Deviation Based on 10-Days of Observations Assuming a Mean of Zero and Equal Weighting

10-Trading Days Ending	Daily Standard Deviation (%)
03-Jan-01	1.1088
04-Jan-01	1.0933
05-Jan-01	1.0749
08-Jan-01	1.0586
09-Jan-01	1.0461
10-Jan-01	1.0370
11-Jan-01	1.0281
12-Jan-01	1.0206
16-Jan-01	1.0147
17-Jan-01	1.0139
18-Jan-01	1.0084
19-Jan-01	1.0079

Source for yields: Federal Reserve Statistical Release H.15

Rather than using a moving average, it is more appropriate to use an expectation of the average. It has been argued that it would be more appropriate to use a mean value of zero.[4] In that case, the variance as given by equation (1) simplifies to:

$$\text{Variance} = \sum_{t=1}^{T} \frac{X_t^2}{T-1} \qquad (2)$$

Now let's look at the various methods for forecasting daily volatility.

Equally-Weighted Average Method

The daily standard deviation given by equation (2) assigns an equal weight to all observations. So, if an investor is calculating volatility based on the most recent 10 days of trading, each day is given a weight of 10%. For example, suppose that an investor is interested in the daily volatility of a 2-year CMT yield and decides to use the 10 most recent trading days. Exhibit 5 reports the 10-day volatility for various days using the data in Exhibit 1 and the formula for variance given by equation (2). For the period 1/3/01 to 1/19/01, the 10-day volatility ranged from 1.0079% to 1.1088%.

Weighted Average Method

To give greater importance to more recent information, observations further in the past should be given less weight. This can be done by revising the variance as given by equation (2) as follows:

---

[4] Jacques Longerstacey and Peter Zangari, *Five Questions about RiskMetrics™,* JP Morgan Research Publication, 1995.

$$\text{Variance} = \sum_{t=1}^{T} \frac{W_t X_t^2}{T-1} \tag{3}$$

where W_t is the weight assigned to observation t such that the sum of the weights is equal to 1 (i.e., $\Sigma\ W_t = 1$) and the further the observation from today, the lower the weight.

The weights should be assigned so that the forecasted volatility reacts faster to a recent major market movement and declines gradually as we move away from any major market movement. One approach is to use an *exponential moving average*.[5] The formula for the weight W_t in an exponential moving average is:

$$W_t = (1 - \beta)\beta^t$$

where β is a value between 0 and 1. The observations are arrayed so that the closest observation is $t = 1$, the second closest is $t = 2$, etc.

For example, if β is 0.90, then the weight for the closest observation ($t = 1$) is:

$$W_1 = (1 - 0.90)\,(0.90)^1 = 0.09$$

For $t = 5$ and β equal to 0.90, the weight is:

$$W_5 = (1 - 0.90)\,(0.90)^5 = 0.05905$$

The parameter β is measuring how quickly the information contained in past observations is "decaying" and hence is referred to as the "decay factor." The smaller the β, the faster the decay. What decay factor to use depends on how fast the mean value for the random variable X changes over time. A random variable whose mean value changes slowly over time will have a decay factor close to 1. A discussion of how the decay factor should be selected is beyond the scope of this book.[6]

ARCH Method and Variants

A times series characteristic of financial assets suggests that a period of high volatility is followed by a period of high volatility. Furthermore, a period of relative stability in returns appears to be followed by a period that can be characterized in the same way. This suggests that volatility today may depend upon recent prior volatility. This can be modeled and used to forecast volatility.

The statistical model used to estimate this time series property of volatility is called an *auto*regressive *c*onditional *h*eteroscedasticity or ARCH model.[7] The term "conditional" means that the value of the variance depends on or is con-

---

[5] This approach is suggested by JP Morgan *RiskMetrics™*.

[6] A technical description is provided in *RiskMetrics™—Technical Document*, pp. 77-79.

[7] See Robert F. Engle, "Autoregressive Conditional Heteroskedasticity with Estimates of Variance of U.K. Inflation," *Econometrica* 50 (1982), pp. 987-1008.

ditional on the value of the random variable. The term heteroscedasticity means that the variance is not equal for all values of the random variable.

The simplest ARCH model is

$$\sigma_t^2 = a + b(X_{t-1} - \overline{X})^2 \tag{4}$$

where

$$\sigma_t^2 \quad = \text{ variance on day } t$$
$$X_{t-1} - \overline{X} = \text{ deviation from the mean on day } t-1$$

and a and b are parameters.

The parameters a and b must be estimated statistically. The statistical technique of regression analysis is used to estimate the parameters.

Equation (4) states that the estimate of the variance on day t depends on how much the observation on day $t-1$ deviates from the mean. Thus, the variance on day t is "conditional" on the deviation from day $t-1$. The reason for squaring the deviation is that it is the magnitude, not the direction of the deviation, that is important for forecasting volatility.[8] By using the deviation on day $t-1$, recent information (as measured by the deviation) is being considered when forecasting volatility.

The ARCH model can be generalized in two ways. First, information for days prior to $t-1$ can be included into the model by using the squared deviations for several prior days. For example, suppose that four prior days are used. Then equation (4) can be generalized to:

$$\sigma_t^2 = a + b_1(X_{t-1} - \overline{X})^2 + b_2(X_{t-2} - \overline{X})^2$$
$$+ b_3(X_{t-3} - \overline{X})^2 + b_4(X_{t-4} - \overline{X})^2 \tag{5}$$

where a, b_1, b_2, b_3, and b_4 are parameters to be estimated statistically.

A second way to generalize the ARCH model is to include not only squared deviations from prior days as a random variable that the variance is conditional on but also the estimated variance for prior days. For example, the following equation generalizes equation (4) for the case where the variance at time t is conditional on the deviation squared at time $t-1$ and the variance at time $t-1$:

$$\sigma_t^2 = a + b(X_{t-1} - \overline{X})^2 + c\sigma_{t-1}^2 \tag{6}$$

where a, b, and c are parameters to be estimated statistically.

---

[8] The variance for the unconditional variance (i.e., a variance that does not depend on the prior day's deviation) is

$$\sigma_t^2 = a/(1-b)$$

Suppose that the variance at time t is assumed to be conditional on four prior periods of squared deviations and three prior variances, then equation (4) can be generalized as follows:

$$\sigma_t^2 = a + b_1(X_{t-1} - \overline{X})^2 + b_2(X_{t-2} - \overline{X})^2 + b_3(X_{t-3} - \overline{X})^2$$

$$+ b_4(X_{t-4} - \overline{X})^2 + c_1\sigma_{t-1}^2 + c_2\sigma_{t-2}^2 + c_3\sigma_{t-3}^2 \qquad (7)$$

where the parameters to be estimated are a, the b_i's ($i = 1, 2, 3, 4$), and c_j's ($j = 1, 2, 3$).

Equations (5), (6), and (7) are referred to as *generalized* ARCH or GARCH models. GARCH models are conventionally denoted as follows: GARCH(i,j) where i indicates the number of prior squared deviations included in the model and j the number of prior variances in the model. Equations (5), (6), and (7) would be denoted GARCH(4,0), GARCH(1,1), and GARCH(4,3), respectively.

There have been further extensions of ARCH models but these extensions are beyond the scope of this chapter.[9]

---

[9] For an overview of these extensions as well as the GARCH models, see Robert F Engle, "Statistical Models for Financial Volatility," *Financial Analysts Journal* (January-February 1993), pp. 72-78.

Index

NUMERICS

30/360 day count rule, 60
30/360 day count, 58
30/360, 54

A

Absolute prepayment speed (ABS),
    175
Accretion (amortization) of the dis-
    count (premium), 219
Accrual tranche, 164
Accrued interest, 53, 63, 78
Actual number of days between two
    dates, 54
Actual/360 day count convention, 56
Actual/360 day count, 58
Actual/360, 54
Actual/Actual day count, 58
Actual/Actual, 54
Adjustable-rate mortgages, 142
Adjustable-rate securities, 203
Adjusted price, 220
Adjusted simple margin, 203, 220
Adjusted total margin, 203, 221
Adjusted/modified duration, 269
After-tax reinvestment income, 236
After-tax total return to maturity,
    235, 237
After-tax yield to maturity, 237
Agency CMO, 160, 197
Agency discount notes, 109
Agency passthrough securities, 197
Alternative mortgage designs, 142
Amortization, 142
Amortization schedule, 143
Amortization table, 174
Amortizing assets, 174
Amortizing securities, 99, 209
Analysis of prepayments, 175
Andrew Davidson Prepayment
    Model, 245
Annuity, 10, 68
Appropriate interest rate, 66
Arbitrage profit, 33, 84, 85, 87
Arbitrage-free valuation approach
    28, 81
Arbitrage-free value, 33, 82
Arbitrage-free value for a security,
    120
ARCH model, 336
Asset-backed securities, 122, 141
Asset-based swap transaction, 322
Auto loans, 141
Autoregressive conditional het-
    eroscedasticity, 336
Average life, 159

B

Bales, Gioia Parente, 321
Balloon mortgages, 142

Bank discount basis, 109
Bankers acceptances rate, 299
Barbell, 242
Beidleman, Carl R., 321
Benchmark interest rates, 138
Benchmark spot rate curve, 88
Benchmark zero-coupon rate curve,
    88
Bid/ask prices, 29
Bid-offer spread, 304
Binomial interest rate tree, 123
    constructing the binomial inter-
        est rate tree, 127
    determining the value at a node,
        126
Binomial lattice model, 121
Binomial model, 121, 275
Black box, 122
Bloomberg, 28
Bloomberg screen, 30
    fair market curves, function
        FMC, 88
    function C15, 51
    function FMCS, 89
    function STR4, 34
    function IYC1, 33
    PFN function, 153
    PX1 governments, 28, 110
    security description (DES), 59
    YAF function, 325
    yield & spread analysis, function
        YAS, 114, 276
    yield analysis (YA), 56, 252
Bloomberg's "Risk" measure, 296
Bloomberg's DCX (Days Between
    Dates), 54, 56, 60, 61
Bond price
    pull to par value, 73, 75
    relative to its par value, 72
Bond-equivalent basis, 45
Bond-equivalent yield (BEY), 29,
    38, 42, 97
Bond-equivalent yield convention,
    98
Bonds with embedded options, 275
    with call and prepay options, 264
    with embedded put options, 267
    with multiple or interrelated
        embedded options, 136
Bootstrapping, 32
Bundles, 308
Business cycle, 67
Butterfly trade, 242
Buy-and-hold alternative, 48
Buy-and-hold strategy, 41, 43

C

Call option, 118, 263
Call rule, 121, 133
Callable bonds, 114, 120, 264
Callable, 275

Campbell, John Y., 51
Canadian government bonds, 58
Cap rate for floater, 168
Cap, 167, 208
Capital gain, 91
Capital loss, 91
Capital Management Sciences, 240
Capped floater, 218
Caps and floors, 204
Cash flow yield, 95, 105, 179
Cash flow, 65, 146
CD equivalent yield, 110
Certificates of deposit rate, 299
Chicago Mercantile Exchange, 307,
    308
Clean price, 79
Closed-end home equity loans, 174,
    195
Collar, 209
Collateral tranche interest, 168
Collateral trade, 244
Collateral, 141
Collateralized mortgage obligations
    (CMOs), 141, 160, 181
    creating agency CMOs, 160
    creation of a nonagency CMO,
        171
    creation of a PAC tranche, 171
    PAC structures, 171
    simple CMO structure, 189
Commercial paper rate, 299
Commercial paper, 109
Committee on Uniform Security
    Identification Procedures, 86
Companion tranches, 169
Comparison of traditional approach
    and arbitrage-free approach, 82
Compensation the market expects,
    66
Compounded continuously, 24
Compounding and discounting in
    continuous time, 23
Compounding frequency, 8
Computing any forward rate, 47
Computing the accrued interest and
    the clean price, 79
Computing the full price, 77
Computing the yield on any invest-
    ment, 18
Concave, 266
Conditional default rate (CDR), 177
Conditional prepayment rate, 149
Confidence interval, 333
Constant Maturity Treasury (CMT),
    330
Constant Maturity Treasury rate,
    203, 206
Constant-OAS total return, 232
Consumer and business loans and
    receivables, 141
Contribution to portfolio duration,
    281, 282

Convertible bonds, 66
Convex, 6, 72, 271
Convexity adjustment to percentage price change, 291, 293
Convexity measure, 290, 291, 292
  scaling the convexity measure, 292
Convexity of a bond, 291
Convexity, 251, 290
Corporates, 122
Cost of hedging, 319, 321
Counterparties, 16, 299
Counterparty risk, 300
Coupon interest payments, 67
Coupon payments, 91
Coupon rate, 257
Coupon strips, 33, 34
Coupon structures, 204
Credit card receivables, 141
Credit enhancement, 172
Credit rating, 88
Credit risk, 137, 138, 172
Credit spreads, 88, 322
Cumulative default rate, 177
Currencies, 5
Current yield, 95
Curved shape, 6
Cushion bond, 266
CUSIP, 86

D

Data, 28
Dattatreya, Ravi E., 214
Day count basis, 53
Day count conventions, 53, 54
Days between settlement date and next coupon payment date, 77
Days in the accrued interest period, 63
Days in the coupon period, 63, 77
Dealers, 275
Decay factor, 336
Default rate, 177
Default risk component of a swap spread, 319
Default-free theoretical spot rate curve, 40
Deleveraged floater, 206
Derivative instruments, 203
Determining a bond's value 67
Determining the call option value, 134
Differences between 30/360 and actual/actual, 61
Differential risk annuity payment, 215
Differential risk annuity, 212
Dirty price, 78
Discount factor, 4
Discount margin, 203, 222, 223
Discount rate, 4, 6, 66
Discount, 70
Discounted margin, 18
Discounting cash flows with multiple interest rates, 16

Discounting the expected cash flows, 67
Discounting, 4
Dollar duration, 295
  floating-rate bond, 324
  portfolio, 324
  of a swap for a fixed-rate payer, 324
  of a swap, 323
Dollar return, 91, 229
Dollar value of an 01 (DV01), 294
Drift term, 186
Drop-lock bonds, 209
Dual-indexed floater, 206
Duration and cash neutral trade, 243
Duration, 251, 268
  approximating the percentage price change using duration, 269
  calculating, 268
  calculating effective duration using the lattice model, 275
  calculating effective duration using the Monte Carlo model, 279
  of option-free bonds, 274
  graphical depiction to estimate price changes, 271
Duration/convexity approach, 268
Dutch auction procedure, 207
Dym, Steven I., 214

E

Early redemption features, 204, 210
Effective annual yield, 22, 23
Effective convexity, 294
Effective date, 303
Effective duration, 275
Effective margin, 220
Embedded options, 1, 114, 257, 263
End-of-Month rule, 59
Engle, Robert F., 336
Equally-weighted average method, 335
Euler, 25
Eurodollar CD futures contract, 17, 213, 307
Eurodollar certificates of deposit (CDs), 307
Eurodollar deposits, 300
Eurodollar futures rate, 308
Evans, Ellen L., 321
Exchangeable bonds, 66
Expected cash flow, 67
Expected final maturity for tranches, 165
Expected future cash flows, 65
Expected interest rate volatility, 114
Expected return, 248
Expected value, 333
Exponential growth, 25
Exponential moving average, 336
Extendible reset bonds, 207
External credit enhancements, 172

F

Fabozzi, Frank J., 123, 160, 182, 186, 189, 196, 218, 303, 334
Fannie Mae, 59
Federal funds rate, 300
Federal Home Loan Mortgage Corporation (Freddie Mac), 152
Federal National Mortgage Association (Fannie Mae), 152
Federal Open Market Committee, 51
Financial engineers, 203
First loss tranche, 172
Fixed rate, level-payment, fully amortized mortgages, 142
Fixed-equivalent coupon, 324
Fixed-rate payer, 299
Fixed-rate payer/floating-rate receiver, 300
Floating-rate investor, 322
Floating-rate payer, 299
Floating-rate payer/fixed-rate receiver, 17, 300
Floating-rate securities, 66, 203
  basic features, 203
  embedded options, 226
  non-callable floating-rate note, 211
  non-interest rate indexes, 208
  price of risky floater, 216
  with a changing quoted margin, 207
Floating-rate tranche, 165
Floor, 209
Foley, Jeffrey, 245
Forecasting daily volatility, 335
Forecasting yield volatility, 334
Forward discount factor, 311, 312
Forward rates, 27, 40, 213, 308
  as the market's expectation of future rates, 50
French government bonds, 33
Full price, 78
Full valuation approach, 251
Fundamental rule for valuation, 126
Funded investors, 139
Future value
  of a single cash flow with more frequent compounding, 7
  of an ordinary annuity of $1 per year, 11
  of an ordinary annuity when payments occur more than once per year, 11
  of an ordinary annuity, 10

G

GARCH models, 338
Gauthier, Laurent, 196
General (i.e., generic) collateral repo rate, 322
General principles of fixed-income security valuation, 65
Generalized ARCH, 338

Generic on-the-run yield curve for issuers, 139
Geometric average, 46
German government bonds, 33
Government National Mortgage Association (Ginnie Mae), 152
Gregorian date, 54
Gross weighted average coupon (GWAC), 175
Growing equity mortgages, 142

H

Hayre, Lakhbir S., 186
Hedging costs, 322
Heteroscedasticity, 337
Historical volatility, 329, 333
History of prepayments, 181
Ho, Thomas S.Y., 216, 284
Home equity loans, 141, 174
Horizon price, 229
Horizon yield, 230
Horowitz, David S., 182, 189
Hull, John C., 319

I

Illmanen, Antti, 51
Impact of changing discount rates, 76
Implicit forward rates, 41, 46
Implied LIBOR forward rates, 213
Implied spot rates, 32
Implied volatility, 197, 333
Incentive to refinance, 182
Index duration, 283
Indexed amortizing notes, 209
Inflation-linked (or inflation-indexed) bonds, 208
Interest rate model, 121
Interest rate options or caps, 333
Interest rate risk exposure, 255
Interest rate risk, 101, 180, 251
Interest rate shocks, 257
Interest rate swaps, 1, 16, 65, 299, 322
  calculating the fixed-rate payments, 309
  calculating the floating-rate payments, 306
  calculating the present value of the floating-rate payments, 311
  calculation of the swap rate, 311
  computing the payments for a swap, 305
  describing a swap, 304
  determination of the swap rate, 313
  determining future floating-rate payments, 308
  determining the swap rate, 305
  interpreting a swap position, 301
    as a package of cash market instruments, 301
    as a package of forward contracts, 301

key determinant for swaps with tenors (i.e., maturities) of five years or less, 319
level of asset-based swap activity, 321
longer tenor swaps, 319
longer-dated swaps, 319
relative supply of fixed- and floating-rate payers, 321
relative value analysis using the swap market, 324
term of the swap, 306
Interest rate volatility, 297
Interest strips, 86
Interest-only mortgage strips, 174
Interim cash flows, 91
Internal credit enhancements, 172
Internal rate of return, 18
International Monetary Market, 307
In-the-the money, 265
Inverse floater, 166, 167, 204
  coupon formula, 205
Inverse floating-rate tranche, 165
Investment horizon, 229
Involuntary prepayment, 147, 176, 177
IO class, 174
Issuers of nonagency mortgage-backed securities, 153
Italian government strips, 33
Iterative process, 128
Iwanowski, Raymond J., 216, 225

J

Johnston, Douglas, 243
JP Morgan RiskMetrics, 336
Julian date, 54

K

Kalotay, Andrew J., 123
Kaufold, Howard, 211
Key rate duration, 281, 283, 284, 287
Kopprasch, Robert F., 303
Kreisler, Michele, 51
Krigin, Dragomir, 53
Krishman, Suresh E., 323

L

Lattice model, 120, 218, 275
Lauterbach, Kenneth, 186
Lee, Wai, 334
Level and shape of the Treasury yield curve, 321
Level I PAC tranche, 171
Level II PAC tranche, 171
Level III PAC tranche, 171
Level of benchmark interest rates, 66
Level of subordination, 173
Level of swap spreads, 322
Level of the interest rate, 6
Level of yields, 257
Leveraged inverse floater, 205
Leveraged position, 323

LIBOR yield curve, 226
LIBOR, 139
LIBOR-based funding costs, 226
Liquidation proceeds, 177
Liquidation, 176
Liquidity risk, 137, 138
Lo, Andrew W., 51
Loan-level analysis, 175
Lockout period, 147
Lognormal random walk, 124
London interbank offered rate, 299
London International Financial Futures Exchange, 307
Longerstacey, Jacques, 335
Loss of severity, 177
Lump sum, 68

M

Macaulay duration, 279
Macaulay, Frederick, 279
Macfarlane, John, 303
Macirowski, Thomas, 211
MacKinlay, Craig, 51
Mann, Steven V., 218, 244, 283
Manufactured housing ABS, 197
Manufactured housing loans, 141
Margin measures, 218
Market sector, 88
Market's consensus of future interest rates, 40
Market's risk aversion, 67
Maturity date, 303
Mayle, Jan, 53, 58
Mean reversion, 186
Medium-term notes, 203
Minimum interest rate, 66
Minimum principal payment, 169
Mismatched floaters, 204
Modeling defaults for the collateral, 175
Modified convexity, 294
Modified duration, 275, 279, 280
  versus effective duration, 275
Money market equivalent yield, 110
Money market rates, 299
Monte Carlo simulation valuation model, 122, 179, 185, 275
  distribution of path present values, 187
Monthly loss, 177
Mortgage loan, 141, 142
  calculating the monthly mortgage balance, scheduled principal repayment, and interest, 145
  cash flow of a fixed-rate, level-payment, fully amortized mortgage, 142
  monthly mortgage payment, 142
  mortgage balance at the end of month, 146
  penalty period, 147
Mortgage passthrough securities, 120, 141, 174
  cash flow, 148

formulas for computing the projected monthly cash flow, 158
interest for month, 146
Monthly cash flow construction for a passthrough based on a PSA assumption, 154
projected interest net of servicing fee for month, 158
projected monthly interest net of the servicing fee, 159
projected monthly scheduled principal repayment, 159
projected principal prepayment for the month, 159
projected servicing fee, 158
Mortgage-backed securities, 120, 141, 275
cash flow, 141
Mortgage-related products, 160
Mortgagors, 147
Municipal bond structures with embedded options, 122

N

Natural logarithm, 25
Negative convexity, 265, 266, 292
Net coupon, 147
Net interest, 147
No-arbitrage condition, 48
Node, 123
Nominal spread, 114, 180, 282
Nonagency CMOs, 160, 172
Nonagency mortgage-backed securities, 175
Non-amortizing assets, 174
Non-amortizing versus amortizing, 116
Non-PAC tranches, 169
Non-senior tranches, 172
Notional amount, 299
Notional principal, 16

O

OAS duration, 275, 283
OAS versus the benchmark, 188
On special, 29
One-factor models, 121
One-month historical prepayment rate, 153
On-the-run Treasuries, 30
On-the-run Treasury coupon issues, 29
On-the-run Treasury par curve (function C18), 49
Option cost, 118, 119
Option price, 118
Option risk, 137, 138
Option-adjusted duration, 275
Option-adjusted spread (OAS), 114, 118, 180, 185, 196, 203, 226
Option-adjusted yield, 140
Option-free bond, 257, 264
Options, 203
Ordinary annuity, 10

Original mortgage balance, 143
Original principal, 1
Out-of-the-money, 265

P

PAC barbell, 245
Package of zero-coupon bonds, 27
PaineWebber Mortgage Group, 245
Par curve, 28, 30
Par rates, 27
Parallel shift scenarios, 243
Parallel yield curve shift assumption, 276
Passthrough coupon rate, 148
Path dependency, 181
Path-dependent, 181
Payment invoice, 96
Performing loan, 176
Period forward rate, 312
Periodic interest payments, 91
Periodic interest rate, 7, 12, 23
Perpetual annuity payment, 15
Perpetual annuity, 15
Perpetual issue, 209
Planned amortization class tranche, 169
PAC bond, 188
PAC I tranche, 171
PAC II tranche, 171
PAC II tranches, 192
PAC III tranche, 171
PO class, 174
Pool factor, 149
Pool-level analysis, 175
Portfolio duration, 280
Portfolio internal rate of return, 106
Portfolio total return, 239
Portfolio yield measures, 106
Positive convexity, 266, 292
Potential return, 91
PPC, 153
Premium, 71
Prepayment burnout, 201
Prepayment conventions and cash flow, 149
Prepayment option, 210
Prepayment penalty, 147
Prepayment protection, 171
Prepayment rate, 105
Prepayment risk, 147, 169, 171
Prepayment speed, 105
Prepayment, 147, 210
Prepayments, 148, 179, 183, 240
cash flow uncertainty, 147
Present value
of a package of cash flows with unequal interest rates, 16
of a perpetual annuity, 15
of a single cash flow using periodic interest rates, 8
of a single cash flow, 3
of an annuity, 12
of an ordinary annuity of $1 per period, 14

of an ordinary annuity when payments occur more than once per year, 14
of the fixed-rate payments, 305
of the floating-rate payments, 305
of the maturity value, 69
Present value/interest rate relationship, 6
Price change
attributable to an increase in the discount rate, 76
attributable to moving to maturity, 76
Price value of a basis point (PVBP), 251, 294
Price volatility characteristics
of bonds with embedded options, 263
of option-free bonds, 257, 260
Price/discount rate relationship, 71
Price/yield relationship for a callable bond, 264, 265
Prime banks, 300
Prime borrowers, 195
Prime rate, 300
Principal component analysis, 257
Principal floaters, 210
Principal only, 174
Principal pay down window, 164
Principal repayment features, 204
Principal repayments, 91
Principal strip, 33, 87
Principal-only mortgage strips, 174
Probability-weighted return, 248
Projecting prepayments, 175
Proprietary prepayment model, 245
Prospectus prepayment curve (PPC), 149, 153
Public Securities Association (PSA) prepayment benchmark, 150
Public Securities Association prepayment benchmark, 149
Pure expectations theory of interest rates, 50
Put options, 263
Put price, 210
Put provision, 210
Putable bond, 118, 135, 267, 275

Q

Quadratic formula, 113
Quoted margin value, 325
Quoted margin, 204, 212, 223
Quoting swaps, 304

R

Ramamurthy, Shrikant, 196
Ramanlal, Pradipkumar, 244, 283
Ramsey, Chuck, 160
Random paths of interest rates, 182
Range note, 206, 218
Ratchet bond, 206
Rate duration, 283

Rate shocks and duration estimate, 273
Rate shocks, 274
Real estate-backed asset-backed securities, 141
Reconstituting, 82
Reconstitution and arbitrage-free valuation, 86
Reconstitution, 33, 86
Redistributing the prepayment risk, 160
Reference benchmark, 28
Reference rate, 204, 211, 299
Refinancing opportunities, 196
Refunded-protected period, 104
Regulators of depository institutions, 255
Reinvestment income, 94, 236
Reinvestment rate, 229
Reinvestment risk, 101, 180
Relationship between spot rates and short-term forward rates, 45
Relationships between the price of a bond (relative to par), coupon rate, current yield, and yield to maturity, 98
Remarketing process, 207
Repayment of principal at maturity, 68
Repo financing, 29
Representative path method, 187
Representative paths, 187
Required margin, 211
Required yield, 66
Reset frequency, 303
Reset margin determined at issuer discretion, 207
Reverse mortgages, 142
Richard, Scott F., 182, 189
Riding the yield curve, 41, 44
Risk-averse investors, 322
Risks that the market perceives, 66
Risky floaters, 211
Rollover strategy, 41
Ross, Daniel R., 303

S

Sample mean, 329
Scenario analysis, 240, 242, 251
    to evaluate potential trade strategies, 242
    to measure performance versus a bond index, 247
    to measure risk exposure, 245
Scheduled amortization, 144
Scheduled principal repayment for month, 146
Scheduled principal repayment, 142, 144
Scheduled tranche, 171, 192
Seasoned loans, 201
Securities Industry Association Standard Securities Calculation Methods, 53
Securitized, 141

Semiannual yield to maturity, 97
Senior-subordinated structure, 171, 172
Sequential-pay CMOs, 160
Sequential-pay support tranches, 171
Sequential-pay tranches, 160
Serial correlation, 330
Servicing fee rate, 158
Servicing fee, 146
Servicing of a mortgage loan, 146
Servicing spread, 147
Settlement date, 77, 92
Shape of the price/yield relationship, 271
Shifting interest mechanism, 173
Short an option, 120
Short-term forward-rate curve, 45
Short-term money market rate, 203
Showers, Janet, 303
Simple margin, 219
Simulated prepayment rates, 182
Simulating interest rate scenarios, 256
Simulation, 182, 240
Single-monthly mortality rate (SMM), 149
Small Business Administration loans, 141
Smirlock, Michael, 211
Sources of return, 91
Spanish government strips, 33
Sparks, Andrew, 243
Special in repo markets, 322
Spot curve, 39
Spot rates, 27
Spread duration, 282, 283
    for fixed-rate bonds, 282
    for floaters, 283
Spread for life, 203, 219
Spread over the yield on the Treasury issue, 67
Spread products, 282
Standard deviation, 125, 329
    annualizing the standard deviation, 330
    daily standard deviation, 330
    interpretation, 333
Standard residential mortgage loan, 174
Static cash flow yield analysis, 179
Static spread, 115, 119
Stepped spread floaters, 207
Street convention, 98
Stress testing, 256
Stripped mortgage-backed securities, 141, 174
Stripped securities, 28
Stripping a bond, 28
Stripping and the arbitrage-free valuation, 84
Stripping, 82
STRIPS, 33
Structure of rates at the horizon date, 230

Structured note, 203, 206
Structuring the deal, 160
Student loans, 141
Subordinate interest, 173
Subordinated tranche, 172
Support tranche, 169, 171, 180, 192
Swap dealers, 322
Swap rate, 305, 306
Swap spread, 315, 319, 321, 322
    primary determinants of swap spreads, 318
Swaps curves, 116
Swaps, 203
Swiss government bond, 298
Synthetic fixed-rate security, 299, 322
Synthetic spread, 321

T

Tangent line, 272
Target federal funds, 51
Tax advantages associated with a strip, 34
Technical factors, 321
Term structure of credit spreads, 88
Term structure of default-free spot rate, 39
Term to maturity, 257
Theoretical spot rates, 28, 33
Ticks, 29
Tiered payment mortgages, 142
Time path of bond, 73
    of discount bond, 74
    of a par bond between coupon payment dates, 80
    of a premium bond, 73
Time value of money, 1
Times series characteristic of financial assets, 336
Total adjusted margin, 221
Total dollar return, 99
    dependence on reinvestment income, 101
Total future dollars, 99
Total return for a mortgage-backed security, 238
Total return to maturity, 232
Trade date, 303
Traditional approach to valuation, 81
Traditional yield measures, 95
Tranches, 160
Transaction costs, 85
Treasury bill rate, 299
Treasury buyback program, 51
Treasury Inflation Protected Securities (TIPs), 28, 66, 208
Treasury method, 78
Treasury spot rate curve, 82
Treasury spot rate, 28
    reason for using, 83
Treasury strips, 33, 84
Treasury yield curve, 27, 81
Trinomial lattice models, 121
True yield, 98

U

U.K. gilt strips, 33
U.S. Treasury bills, 109
Undated issue, 209
Unsecuritized mortgage loans, 171

V

Valuation model, 119
Valuation of bonds with embedded
    options, 117
    special considerations in valuing
        asset-backed securities, 195
Valuation of floaters with embedded
    options, 217
Valuation of non-Treasury securi-
    ties, 88
Valuation of option-free bonds, 65
Valuation using multiple interest
    rates, 67
Valuation using Treasury spot
    rates, 82
Valuation, 65
Value agency debentures, 122
Value of a call option, 117
Value of a callable bond, 117
Value of a financial asset, 67
Value of a pure floater, 326
Value of a put option, 118
Value of a putable bond, 118, 267
Value of an option-free bond, 117
Value of the embedded option, 263
Value-at-risk (VaR) framework, 298
Valuing a bond between coupon
    payments, 77
Valuing a bond when the discount
    rate and coupon rate are equal, 69
Valuing a bond when the discount
    rate is greater than the coupon
    rate, 70
Valuing a bond when the discount
    rate is less than the coupon rate, 71
Valuing a callable bond, 133
Valuing a risky floater, 211
Valuing a swap, 316
Valuing a zero-coupon bond, 76
Valuing an option-free bond with
    the tree, 132
Valuing bonds with embedded
    options, 65
Valuing interest rate swaps, 305
Variable-rate security, 203
Variance reduction, 187
Variance, 329
Vendors, 283, 293
Vendors of analytical systems, 116,
    275
Venkatesh, Raj E.S., 214
Venkatesh, Vijaya E., 214
Volatility, 125
    and the theoretical value, 136

W

Wall Street Analytics, Inc.'s Portfolio
    Management Workstation, 245

Weighted average coupon rate, 148
Weighted average life, 159
Weighted average maturity (WAM),
    148, 175
Weighted average method, 335
Weighted-average portfolio yield,
    107
When-issued bills, 28
When-issued notes, 28
Whole-loan CMOs, 172
Williams, George O., 123
Worley, Richard, 51

Y

Yawitz, Jess, 211
Yield 18
    calculation when there is only
        one cash flow, 21
Yield curve, 27, 67
    upward-sloping, 43
    roll, 241
    scenario, 248
    twist scenarios, 243
Yield curve notes, 205
Yield hog, 180
Yield measures for U.S. Treasury
    bills, 109
    with less than 182 days to matu-
        rity, 111
    with more than 182 days to matu-
        rity, 112
Yield on a bank discount basis, 109
Yield spread measures relative to a
    spot rate curve, 113
Yield to call, 18, 95, 102
Yield to custom, 103
Yield to maturity, 18, 95, 96
    limitations, 99
Yield to next call, 103
Yield to put, 95, 104
Yield to refunding, 104
Yield to worst, 95, 104
Yield value of a price change, 251,
    296
Yield volatility, 297
    historical versus implied volatil-
        ity 333
    importance of, 296
Yield-to-forward LIBOR, 324
Young, Andrew R., 321

Z

Z bond, 164
Zangari, Peter, 335
Zero-coupon bonds, 28
Zero-volatility spread, 115, 186, 196
Z-spread, 115
    divergence between Z-spread and
        nominal spread, 116
    relative to any benchmark, 116